Critical Thinking

Thinking critically about the arguments and messages we see every day—in words or in pictures—gives us the power to make up our own minds. Thinking critically about the way we express ourselves—in writing or in person—gives us the power to persuade.

In *Critical Thinking: An Appeal to Reason*, Peg Tittle empowers students with a solid grounding in the lifelong skills of considered analysis and argumentation—skills that should underpin every student's education.

Starting with the building blocks of a good argument rather than with the pitfalls to avoid, this comprehensive new textbook offers a full course in critical thinking. It includes chapters on the nature and structure of argument, the role of relevance, truth, and generalizations, and the subtleties of verbal and visual language. Throughout the text there are numerous sample arguments from books, journals, magazines, television, and the internet for students to analyze. With an interactive companion website and a comprehensive instructor's manual, *Critical Thinking* is the ideal textbook for a course in the fundamentals of sound reasoning.

Special features include:

- An emphasis on the constructive aspect of critical thinking—strengthening the arguments of others and constructing sound arguments of your own—rather than an exclusive focus on spotting faulty arguments
- A companion website with comprehensive pedagogical features, including an instructor's manual, extended answers, explanations, and analyses for the exercises and arguments in the book, and supplementary chapters on logic and ethics
- Dozens of images for critical analysis
- Annotated arguments that help students to read critically and actively
- Actual questions from standardized reasoning tests like the LSAT, GMAT, MCAT, and GRE.

Please visit the companion website for *Critical Thinking* at: www.routledge.com/textbooks/tittle

Peg Tittle has taught critical thinking and applied ethics at both the university and high school levels. She is the author of *What If . . . Collected Thought Experiments in Philosophy*, and the editor of *Should Parents be Licensed?* and *Ethical Issues in Business: Enquiries, Cases, and Readings*.

Critical
Thinking
An Appeal to Reason

Peg Tittle

Routledge
Taylor & Francis Group

NEW YORK AND LONDON

Acquring Editor: Andrew Beck
Senior Development Editor: Nicole Solano
Senior Editorial Assistant: Michael Andrews
Marketing Manager: Emilia Ayon
Senior Production Editor: Siân Findlay
Line Editor: Kristen LeFevre
Text Design: Karl Hunt at Keystroke
Proofreader: Sarah Pearsall

First published 2011
by Routledge
711 Third Avenue, New York, NY 10017

Simultaneously published in the UK
by Routledge
2 Park Square, Milton Park, Abingdon, Oxon OX14 4RN

Routledge is an imprint of the Taylor & Francis Group, an informa business

© 2011 Peg Tittle

Designed and typeset in Sabon and Frutiger
by Keystroke, Station Road, Codsall, Wolverhampton

Library of Congress Cataloging in Publication Data
Tittle, Peg, 1957-
    Critical thinking : an appeal to reason / Peg Tittle.
        p. cm.
    1. Critical thinking. I. Title.
    BC177.T536 2010
    160—dc22
    2010016540

ISBN 13: 978–0–415–99713–3 (hbk)
ISBN 13: 978–0–415–99714–0 (pbk)
ISBN 13: 978–0–203–84161–7 (ebk)

Contents

Thanks . . .

. . . to Andy Beck, Kate Ahl, Nicole Solano, Mike Andrews, and all the people at Routledge who made this happen!

. . . to the many reviewers for their comments

. . . to Brenda Piquette for research assistance and support

. . . to Scott Shortt, whose "thank you" sent years later provided well-timed encouragement

. . . and all the students who "motivated" me to make things really *really* clear

And special thanks to Taffi, who always let me know, ever so gently, when it was TIME TO PLAY!

Acknowledgements for Reasoning Test Questions

All actual LSAT questions printed within this work are used with the permission of Law School Admission Council, Inc., Box 2000, Newtown, PA 18940, the copyright owner. LSAC does not review or endorse specific test preparation materials or services, and inclusion of licensed LSAT questions within this work does not imply the review or endorsement of LSAC.

GMAT® questions, whether taken from the GMAT® mini-test or in any other form, are the property of the Graduate Management Admission Council® and are reprinted with their permission.

GRE® questions are the property of Educational Testing Service and are reprinted with permission.

chapter 1

critical thinking

Background picture © Corbis

Okay, the *point* is clear: buy Zoné jeans. But no *reason* is given. So as it stands, it's just a command. It's not an *argument*—a claim about something, supported by reasons (see Chapter 2). So, unless you tend to obey commands for no good reason, you won't buy Zoné jeans.

But let's "read" the visuals. There are some very cool people in the ad. So perhaps the ad is implying, "You should buy Zoné jeans *because* they'll make you look cool." Okay, so now we have an argument. It's a very simple argument, but it's an argument nonetheless: it's a claim ("You should buy Zoné jeans") with supporting reasoning ("because they'll make you look cool").

Let's take a closer look. Is the premise (the supporting reason) *true*? *Will* Zoné jeans make you look cool? Well, that depends on what, exactly, is meant by "cool." Let's accept the contemporary definition—whatever it may be. And let's assume that the ad portrays the contemporary definition, which means that we're assuming that Zoné jeans will indeed make you look cool. So the premise is indeed true.

Next, is the premise *relevant* to the conclusion? Yes: looking cool is by definition a matter of appearance, and jeans, as clothing, contribute to one's appearance. As such, buying—and wearing—the jeans is relevant to looking cool.

Suppose, however, there had been a photograph of the sun instead of a photograph of a bunch of cool people. Then the implied premise—whatever it might be—would be irrelevant. In that case, you wouldn't have a very good argument. No wait a minute. A picture of the sun *could* be relevant: what if Zoné jeans were stonewashed, but, unlike their competitors, Zoné used a process that did *not* damage the environment? And the sun was intended to suggest Zoné's environmental-friendliness? Admittedly, it's a bit of a stretch—which only goes to show the problems with arguments that aren't made clear.

Let's go on. Is the premise *sufficient*? That is, does it provide enough support for the conclusion? Well, is looking cool enough reason for buying Zoné jeans? Perhaps. If all you care about *is* looking cool, then yes, the reason is sufficient. So accept the argument and go buy yourself some Zoné jeans. However, if you also care about price, comfort, durability, and so on, then the reason given is insufficient for you to accept the conclusion.

Let's say that Zoné jeans *are* the right price. In that case, you have additional support for the conclusion—you've strengthened the argument. But let's say they're incredibly uncomfortable. In that case, you have something that weakens the argument.

Now let's consider counterarguments. Are there good reasons in support of the contradictory claim, "Do *not* buy Zoné jeans"? Perhaps the jeans are made by people who are paid less than a living wage. So if you buy them, your money is supporting, perhaps even encouraging, exploitation. Such an argument would consist of a premise that's true and relevant. Let's also assume that you care about economic justice. You may now have an argument that provides sufficient reason for *not* buying Zoné jeans. Especially if there are other jeans that make you look cool *and* that are not made with exploited labor.

Which argument is stronger, the one claiming you *should* buy Zoné jeans or the one claiming you should *not* buy Zoné jeans? That would depend on what's more important—looking cool or not contributing to economic injustice.

Welcome to Critical Thinking 101.

1.1 What is critical thinking?

Briefly put, **critical thinking** is *judicious reasoning about what to believe and, therefore, what to do.* (Note my assumption that what you do depends on what you believe—that is, that you act according to your beliefs.)

Judicious reasoning is *deliberate* and *thorough.* Being deliberate implies an intentional consideration of, a responsible attitude toward, ideas, values, and so forth. Being thorough requires, among other things, an appreciation of the breadth and depth of the issue in question, of the complexities of the issue.

As such, critical thinking is a *skill.* It's not something you can just memorize or look up. And it's a multi-dimensional skill—take a look at the list of skills involved, according to critical thinking guru Richard Paul. And, as a skill, it's something you get better at, gradually, with practice.

The elements of critical thought

Cognitive strategies—micro-skills:

- comparing and contrasting ideals with actual practice
- thinking precisely about thinking: using critical vocabulary
- noting significant similarities and differences
- examining or evaluating assumptions
- distinguishing relevant from irrelevant facts
- making plausible inferences, predictions, or interpretations
- giving reasons and evaluating evidence and alleged facts
- recognizing contradictions
- exploring implications and consequences.

Cognitive strategies—macro-skills:

- refining generalizations and avoiding oversimplifications
- comparing analogous situations: transferring insights to new contexts
- developing one's perspective: creating or exploring beliefs, arguments, or theories
- clarifying issues, conclusions, or beliefs
- developing criteria for evaluation: clarifying values and standards
- evaluating the credibility of sources of information

- questioning deeply: raising and pursuing root or significant questions
- analyzing or evaluating arguments, interpretations, beliefs, or theories
- generating or assessing solutions
- analyzing or evaluating actions or policies
- reading critically: clarifying or critiquing texts
- listening critically: the art of silent dialogue
- making interdisciplinary connections
- practicing Socratic discussion: clarifying and questioning beliefs, theories, or perspectives
- reasoning dialogically: comparing perspectives, interpretations, or theories
- reasoning dialectically: evaluating perspectives, interpretations, or theories.

(Richard W. Paul, *Developing Minds*, revised edition, vol. 1, 1991, p. 78. © Richard W. Paul)

While it is possible to think critically about something just for the fun of it (and I mean that quite sincerely), critical thinking is *judgmental*. It's thinking carefully about something in order to evaluate it and ultimately decide whether or not it's something you should accept. So critical thinking is a how-not-to-be-gullible kind of thing.

Now of course before you judge what someone has said, you have to understand what they've said. And that's a lot harder than you might think. Often, people aren't very clear or complete about the point they're making. They use words imprecisely or even incorrectly (see Chapter 5), and they leave out important stuff, most particularly how they got from here to there, or even where here is (see Chapters 2 and 3).

And of course often people aren't really making a point, they're just talking. And that's okay. As long as they don't think they're making a point, as opposed to expressing themselves or describing something. Consider, for example, a student who declares, "I need an extension on this assignment!" Until the student explains why an extension is needed, the statement is just an expression of need, or, more likely, of desire.

So how does one judge or evaluate an argument? Well, that depends on what kind of argument it is. We'll get into that. For now, let's just say there are deductive arguments and inductive arguments. For deductive arguments, if the supporting statements or premises are true, and if the structure is valid, following the rules of reasoning, then you've got a good argument. In fact, you've got a sound argument: the conclusion necessarily follows from true premises. For inductive arguments, if the supporting statements are true or at least acceptable, if they're relevant, and if they're sufficient or adequate, you've got a good argument. The conclusion probably follows from the premises; the higher the probability, the stronger the argument. So you'll accept or reject inductive

Critical thinking is the reasoned evaluation of opinions—our own and others'.

Jerome E. Bickenbach and Jacqueline M. Davies, *Good Reasons for Better Arguments*, 1996 arguments with more or less certainty. Keep in mind, however, that in many cases, certainty is a sign of shallow thinking! So sometimes you won't accept *or* reject the argument—you'll suspend judgment until you've got more evidence.

Critical thinking is "playing devil's advocate" as a matter of routine. The phrase "playing devil's advocate" is a very unfortunate one: it suggests that presenting or considering arguments for a claim you don't at the moment accept is somehow mischievous, even evil. On the contrary, presenting or considering arguments for a claim you don't currently accept is a good thing. It's something to be done quite seriously, not as a mere game. After all, how will you know what to accept if you don't consider all the possibilities?

And if you're presenting your views to others, articulating the counter-arguments is only fair. Also, if you're really after the best belief or explanation, and not just a debating victory, you'll present the counterarguments in case someone else sees something you don't that makes a counterargument stronger than you thought.

Warning: It is possible to become frustrated with this kind of thinking because very little is black-and-white. Many arguments are not simply either right or wrong, but nor are they all one shade of grey. And it is definitely possible to distinguish between the many shades of grey. It is possible to determine which argument is stronger. You might also find that there are far more questions than answers. Try not to be overwhelmed by the questions: you don't have to answer them all; merely asking them is something to be proud of.

The free man is he who does not fear to go to the end of his thought.

Léon Blum, Thoughts: Webster's Quotations, Facts and Phrases, 2008

1.2 What is critical thinking not?

First, critical thinking is not necessarily negative. As Peter H. Hennessy says, "A tendency to knock down new ideas reflexively is merely reactionary thinking, usually superficial and usually proof of a lazy or immature mind" (in "Critical Thinking in Schools," *Humanist in Canada*, Autumn 2004). Evaluation can be positive as well as negative. When you think "critical," don't think "criticize"; instead, think "criteria"—as in standards of reasoning. All three words, by the way, come from "criticus" and "kritikos," the Latin and Greek words for "able to make judgments."

Critical thinking is also not passive, not a matter of simply sitting and passing judgment (a process that's far from passive, by the way, since your neurons are a-buzzing). Why identify errors if not to correct them? Why identify weaknesses if not to strengthen them? Certainly, there may be fatal flaws, in which case you're best to reject the argument. But more often, there will be areas that "simply need a little work" before you can decide whether or not to accept the argument and its conclusion. Furthermore, you will not always be the passive recipient of an argument, defending yourself *from* others, defending yourself against manipulation by shoddy argument. You will also be active agents of argument, defending yourself *to* others, defending your own claims and arguments.

Thus, critical thinking is not solely destructive. Perhaps it often becomes destructive, and only destructive, because that's the easy part—it's easy to tear something down, to break it, to destroy it (be it something physical like a chair or something abstract like an argument). It's far more difficult to build something, to create it (be it a chair or an argument). And if you're truly after the best claim, you won't want to limit yourself to what simply happens to cross your path— you may often need to *construct* the argument you haven't yet come across, and it may well turn out to be the *best* one.

Nor is critical thinking necessarily adversarial. An antagonistic approach is for those who just want to win. For those who want more than that, for those who truly want to know what to believe and what to do, it's far more productive to take a co-operative approach: listen to every claim, every argument, and explore every claim and every argument, drawing on as many resources as you can—in order to arrive at the best claim, the best argument. Critical discussion seldom involves solely contradictory arguments, so "I'm right and you're wrong" will seldom apply. More often, "What I've said strengthens or weakens what you've said" describes the discussion.

Critical thinking is not necessarily cold, calculating, and unfeeling. Being rational does not preclude being passionate. On the contrary, I hope you get excited, I hope you care very deeply about your beliefs, your opinions, your ideas—especially when you have good grounds for them. And I hope you are, and remain, concerned, sympathetic, delighted, angry, and so on. But I hope your passion will be supported by, not a replacement for, reason.

In fact, good critical thinking takes emotion into account. But it does so as part of the reasoning toward, not as a direct motive for, a particular belief or action. Consider the following two arguments:

1. This child is afraid of the dark.
   Children who are afraid should be comforted.
   Therefore, this child should be comforted.

2. I'm afraid they'll hurt me if I don't co-operate.
   I should trust my fears; I believe they're well-founded.
   Therefore I should believe they'll hurt me if I don't co-operate.
   I don't want to be hurt by them.
   Therefore I should co-operate with them.

In both cases, you decide to do something *because* of fear, but—and this is the important bit—the fear is *thought about* and made part of a clear line of reasoning; it's not simply the unexamined, subconscious instigator of your belief or action. When you carefully consider emotion this way, you can then evaluate it, along with every other premise in your argument. And that leaves yourself open to more options than you'd have if you were just a slave to your emotions.

> Men are apt to mistake the strength of their feeling for the strength of their argument. The heated mind resents the chill touch and relentless scrutiny of logic.
>
> William Gladstone, *The Writings of William Ewart Gladstone,* 1880

For example, considering the first argument, you could reject the second premise: maybe children who are afraid should *not* be comforted (or at least not always, or at least not in this case).

Or, considering the second argument, you could also reject the second premise: maybe you should *not* trust your fears—maybe you have good reason (note that—"good *reason*") to think they're not well-founded (maybe you know that these particular people have made similar threats before and have never done what they have threatened to do—so your fear in this case is mistaken, based on an improbability).

Critical thinking is not intuitive. After all, what is intuition but a feeling, a hunch, some barely conscious disposition, quite likely the result of some early childhood conditioning (which, when moral issues are involved, we call "conscience")? We're hard-pressed to articulate why we feel the way we do when we attribute a feeling to "intuition"—and if we can't articulate the why, the reason, we certainly can't evaluate it. As Julian Baggini points out, intuition may be good for "sensing what other people are thinking, feeling, or about to do" (*Making Sense*, 2004), probably because we're unconsciously picking up on their body language, but it's not very good for deciding what to believe about the world at large. After all, intuition tells us that a heavy object always falls faster than a light one, but that's not, in fact, the case. (Try it. With inanimate objects.)

Lastly, critical thinking is not just using our "common sense." After all, "common sense" tells us the earth is flat. But even when "common sense" is correct—it may tell us, for example, that a thing can't be green and not-green at the same time—critical thinking goes well beyond just using such basic principles.

1.3 Why is critical thinking important?

Chances are, you think the earth is round. And chances are, you hold that opinion simply because other people hold that opinion; perhaps your parents told you the earth is round; perhaps your teachers told you the same thing; certainly, you're aware that the general consensus in our society is that the earth is round. Now answer these questions:

Are there gods?
Is abortion wrong?
Does capitalism meet our needs and wants?
Are men stronger than women?

Chances are, your answers to at least some of these questions are similarly based on "inherited" opinions. Chances are, if you're like most people, you can't provide any evidence or line of reasoning to support your answers. But shouldn't you be able to?

So for starters, critical thinking is important because people who engage in critical thinking tend to be able to provide evidence and reasoning for the opinions they hold. This may be particularly important for our judgmental opinions, our praise and condemnation. As Browne and Keeley put it, "Critical thinkers find it satisfying to know when to say 'no' to an idea or opinion and to know why that response is appropriate" (M. Neil Browne and Stuart M. Keeley, *Asking the Right Questions: A Guide to Critical Thinking*, 1997). Furthermore, critical thinking also enables people to provide reasons for their actions: most people would rather do things, especially important things, *for a reason*—and even better, for a *good* reason.

But not only reasons, and not only good reasons, but also *your own* reasons—that's what critical thinking leads to. So critical thinkers have more autonomy, independence, or freedom than people who just sort of go with the flow and accept whatever's given to them. As Richard Paul notes, "[M]ost people are not in charge of their ideas and thinking. Most of their ideas have come in to their minds without their having thought about it. They unconsciously pick up what the people around them think. They unconsciously pick up what is on television or in the movies. They unconsciously absorb ideas from the family they were raised in" (http://www.criticalthinking.org/resources/class-syllabus-fall-93.cfm). So *take charge of your own mind!* You'll be a better person for it. And you'll lead a better life: if *you're* in control—of your ideas and your actions—you'll be more apt to do what *you* want to do, live the life *you* want to live. If you think about stuff, if you take responsibility for what's in your own head, you'll live a conscious life, an examined life, a chosen life. Many a mid-life crisis is triggered by the realization that one has lived twenty years of *un*examined life, of just doing what was expected by parents, partners, supervisors, and kids. Don't wait until you're forty. Be precocious. Have your crisis now.

People who believe whatever they're told without examining the evidence and the reasons linking the evidence to the claims-in-question—that is, without examining the reasoning—are vulnerable to charlatans, crackpots, and bosses. They're especially vulnerable to calculating corporations who believe their mandate, their only mandate, is to maximize their income. Critical thinking is thus especially important as media conglomerates monopolize what we read, hear, and see. According to Free Press's website, updated in 2008, Disney owns ABC, Touchstone, and Miramax; Viacom owns MTV, CMT, and Paramount Pictures; CBS owns Simon & Schuster; Time-Warner owns AOL, HBO, Warner Bros., and Little, Brown and Company; GE owns NBC and Universal Pictures; and so on. Now since, for example, GE makes a lot of money selling weapons (at least back in 1986, when 11 percent of their revenues came from nuclear weapons; see http://multinationalmonitor.org/mm2001/01july-august/julyaug01interview mulvey.html), war is good for their business, so it's quite possible that NBC (remember they're owned by GE) intentionally shows movies that glorify war, portraying soldiers as heroes. And if you're not a critical thinker, you probably won't even notice that, let alone challenge it.

Not only do media conglomerates control what is said, they control what is *not* said: "the few men at the top of the giant media corporations control what the people are invited to think about—and more important, what they are not invited to think about" (Ronnie Dugger, *Free Inquiry*, 22.1, 2001). Roy Thomson, king of a newspaper empire, once quipped, "I buy newspapers to make money to buy newspapers to make more money. As far as editorial content, that's the stuff you separate the ads with" (quoted in Wallace Clement, *The Canadian Corporate Elite*, 1975). And those paying for the ads won't want anything negative about their products to be in that "stuff." In fact, their contracts with newspapers and magazines often stipulate that, which means you won't even know what you don't know. They thus control what you think, if only because they control what you think *about*. And since it's often in their interests that you *don't* think, they're probably also trying to control *whether* you think. (Read Neil Postman's work.)

And not only do they control what is said and what is not said, they control *how* it's said—call it spin, distortion, misinformation, or lies, but call it another reason to become a critical thinker! Critical thinking enables you to see the spin, recognize the distortion, and so on. Consider it self-defense against manipulation.

Critical thinking is also defense against one of the worst consequences of conglomerates: the loss of diversity. As corporations increase in size, merging and establishing interlocking directorates, diversity declines: diversity of product, diversity of service, and especially when corporations influence the media, diversity of opinion. And loss of diversity is the kiss of death not only for ecosystems, but also for cultures. It results in stagnation, the loss of the capacity to adapt, perhaps improve; without that capacity, organisms, systems, die.

A side-effect of all of this is that you will become a better citizen: not only will you see the problems in your society, but you will also, hopefully, see the solutions. Indeed, in this respect, one might consider it one's *duty* to be a critical thinker.

You'll also become a more interesting person to talk to. Of course, some people may also find you a more frustrating person to talk to, but hey, that's their problem. What's the point of discussing something if no one changes their mind? Just to hear each other talk? Hopefully, the purpose of at least *some* discussion, whether it happens conversationally or in print, is to come to some sort of agreement on, broadly speaking, how to make life better. Unfortunately, most discussion resembles ships passing in the night or moose butting their antlered heads. Surely we're better than inanimate objects and instinct-driven animals; surely we should be able to say "Here's where I stand, here's where you stand, here we disagree, because of this, and here we agree, because of this, and here we can move forward, separately our own ways, and here we can move forward together, and we have these possibilities about how to do that."

Being able to discuss in that way indicates that critical thinking is simply superior to other forms of behavior/response. It enables us to handle conflict—

Where all think alike, no one thinks very much.

Walter Lippmann,
The Stakes of Diplomacy,
1915

Two cheers for democracy; one because it admits variety and two because it permits criticism.

E.M. Forster, *Two Cheers for Democracy,* 1951

to decide between opinions and options—without evasion (the ships) or aggression (the moose). Just as someone skilled in forestry can distinguish between a spruce and a fir, between a sick tree and a healthy tree, someone skilled in critical thinking can distinguish between justified discrimination and unjustified discrimination, between credible evidence and incredible evidence. So we don't need to walk away from the problem. We can resolve the indecision or disagreement—and justify our resolution to anyone who asks.

Critical thinking is based on rational thought, and rational thought is superior to emotion, intuition, or faith as a basis for belief and action. Emotion can't always be trusted: I may really hate to do something, but I know, rationally, that it's the right thing to do; thus, the emotion, the hate, is an unreliable guide to, at least, morally right behavior. Intuition, as pointed out in the previous section, is likewise unreliable. And it is especially unconvincing to those without the same intuition—why should your hunch be more worthy than anyone else's hunch? As for faith, it stands, by definition, *without* rational justification, without evidence or proof. As such, faith is very limited in its appeal: *you* might accept something on faith "just because," but you'd be hard-pressed to convince someone else. Think about it: what could you possibly say but "Trust me, I'm right"?

Lastly, critical thinking skills can be applied not only to the "big issues" like social, political, and environmental issues, but also to your day-to-day decisions, especially the ones that have long-term consequences. Should you transfer to another college? Should you reconsider your career goal? Do you really want a career or will a job make you happy? Do you really want to be married? Do you really want to be a parent and look after one or more children? *What do you really want to do?* Identifying the problem, understanding what information is relevant (and what's not), figuring out what all the options are, assessing each one, and then choosing the best one—a course in critical thinking can help you do all that.

In particular, being able to think critically will be valuable when you have to think about new or unfamiliar questions, ideas, and situations. Critical thinkers have the tools for handling the unfamiliarity. As Mark Twain said, if all you have is a hammer, an awful lot of things are going to look like nails. But they're not all nails. And being a critical thinker means you have a full set of tools, instruments, techniques, capacities, for dealing with stuff (including the capacity to identify when, and what, other tools are required!). What answer you get depends a lot on what questions you ask (or don't ask), and the critical thinker has *lots* of questions.

When there is evidence, no one speaks of faith. We do not speak of faith that two and two are four or that the earth is round. We only speak of faith when we wish to substitute emotion for evidence.

Bertrand Russell, *Human Society in Ethics and Politics,* 1954

1.4 Why do we typically *not* think critically? (why do we need a *course* in critical thinking?)

For many reasons, thinking critically isn't something we generally do. Partly we can't—many critical thinking skills need to be learned. And partly we just don't—it's hard, it's not particularly encouraged, and it can be disturbing.

It's certainly harder than, say, watching television or reading a newspaper. And it's harder than other kinds of thinking, such as thinking about what you're going to do today. So we may simply be *unable* to do it. It's not something we can just do; it's certainly not something we were born able to do. We have to learn how to think critically, and then we have to practice in order to get good at it—like any skill. Like walking and talking. And while critical thinking is a *skill*, it's a skill that is dependent on *knowledge*—and often we just don't know enough to challenge the truth of what we hear or read.

It's hard enough to think through our own opinions. Yet when we engage in critical thinking, we often have to do other people's thinking too: we have to fill in the blanks, the gaps, in what they've said or written. As we noted in the first section of this chapter, this is because very few people articulate their thoughts clearly and completely—probably because very few people know their thoughts that well. Remember, if you can't say, "This is my opinion and these are my reasons . . .," you probably don't really know what you think.

Not only is it hard to *understand* the argument someone is making (or *whether* they're even making an argument), once we do understand the argument, it's hard to then *evaluate* it: it takes a lot of mental energy to weigh every premise, to check every connection, to make sure no errors of reasoning have occurred—in essence, to engage in critical thinking.

Evaluation is made even harder by the loss of diversity mentioned in the previous section. It's easier to evaluate an argument when you're already aware of a counterargument. For example, suppose you're aware of the argument that global warming is caused by the greenhouse gases produced by burning fossil fuels, and so on. Suppose you're also aware of the argument that global warming is part of a natural cycle. Knowledge of the second argument makes it easier to be critical of—to evaluate—the first argument. If you hadn't been aware of the natural cycle argument, you would have been more likely to have just accepted the greenhouse gases argument—you wouldn't have been aware of any challenges to it. Of course, you could come up with challenging counterarguments on your own. But that's hard too. It's hard to put all the pieces together. It's even harder when you don't have all the pieces and you have to imagine what evidence would support a certain claim. And keep in mind that you may have to imagine that evidence if it's not published in any of the mainstream media, or even in the alternative media. Which might be the case if no one's even researching the issue in question, either because no one else has thought of it or because no one has funded it.

So, suppose you're exposed only to arguments that lead to A. You'll develop an understandable predisposition to think that all arguments lead to A; you'll develop a predisposition to *accept* A. *Only* A. After all, you're not aware of any arguments that lead to B and C. And suppose you're unable to come up with them on your own. What then? To some extent, people do make choices about what they're exposed to, and that's good; it's exerting a certain amount of control over who you are, what you become, what you believe, what you do because of those beliefs. But usually that choice is a choice from among the readily available options. It's like choosing which juice to buy from the four kinds of orange juice at your local grocery store. What happens when you move to a bigger city and the grocery store there has not only orange juice but also orange-cranberry juice? Wow. Great! But what if it turns out you want cranberry-coconut juice? You won't even know this until it occurs to you—until you imagine that there could be such a thing as cranberry-coconut juice. So freedom of choice, whether regarding juice or opinions, depends to some extent on the limits of your own *imagination*—on whether you can imagine whatever it is you will choose to believe. So in addition to lack of skill and lack of knowledge, lack of imagination accounts for our inability to think critically.

If you *can* imagine whatever it is you will choose to believe, great. If not, then why not expand the range of options you're exposed to? Many books, newspapers, magazines, websites, television, radio, and so on often just increase the kinds of orange juice available to you because they're owned by the same conglomerate: they show the same ideas, or the same menu of ideas. But, as suggested above, what if what you really want isn't on that menu? How will you even know that's what you want? Read alternative-to-mainstream sources—expose yourself to a multitude of differing opinions, arguments, positions. For example, take a look at *Adbusters*, *Free Inquiry*, *The Skeptical Inquirer*, *This Magazine*, *Project Censored*, and so on. They'll show you the orange-cranberry juice and maybe even the cranberry-coconut juice. (You may still have to come up with cinnamon-walnut juice on your own.) Remember that the narrower the mainstream gets, and the stronger it gets, the harder it is to go against the current. The mainstream may be going where you want to go, but if you don't know where else you *could* go, how will you know for sure?

But realize what you're up against: for better or worse, we seem to take the path of least resistance. Perhaps we're hard-wired for laziness, or we're just too tired, or we're in a rush and don't take the time. The bottom line is that it's easier to think (to believe and to do) as others think than it is to think for ourselves. It always takes more energy to initiate than to follow. Most of us simply absorb the ideas we're exposed to—by parents, friends, society-in-general—and that's the end of it. And mixed in with that tendency to go with the flow, to conform (often a good thing, by the way, especially when you're choosing which side

Freedom of the mind requires not only, or even specially, the absence of legal constraints but the presence of alternative thoughts. The most successful tyranny is not the one that uses force to assure uniformity but the one that removes the awareness of other possibilities.

Alan Bloom, *The Closing of the American Mind*, 1987

13

of the road to drive on), is the matter of loyalty: people often feel like they're betraying their parents or friends if they don't agree with them.

Thinking critically is harder still because we are often intentionally misguided: people use language to obscure their arguments, discourage examination, and otherwise manipulate us into agreement (or at least silence). Consider the difference between "I need" and "I want": you're far less likely to challenge a need than a want, aren't you? So if someone says "I need to do this," you're more likely to comply than if they had said "I want to do this." If that had been the case, you may well have asked "Why?"

Outright lies, incomplete truths, and exaggerations similarly prevent or distract us from thinking critically about what we encounter. Unfortunately, such deception is becoming increasingly acceptable: "disinformation," "spin doctors," "PR," "advertising"—all are presented as perfectly legitimate.

Another explanation for our tendency not to think critically is the many ways in which critical thinking is discouraged. There was a time in the 1960s, when dissent was perfectly acceptable; it was even popular. Now dissenters are frequently dismissed as quarrelsome, even unpatriotic. And that's really too bad. Someone *did* speak up about the faulty O-rings before the space shuttle *Challenger* exploded in 1986, killing the entire crew. But that person's critical comment was ignored. Scratch the surface of any such disaster and you'll often find at least one person who said something critical but was ignored—perhaps even reprimanded.

Our culture seems to endorse the belief that we shouldn't be judgmental. Why? To some extent, it seems to be a manners thing: "If you can't say anything nice, don't say anything at all." But if it's rude to be critical, does that mean it's polite to be gullible?

And to some extent, a non-judgmental attitude stems from a post-modern belief that there is no such thing as absolute truth and, hence, that opinions can't be right or wrong. But surely *some* opinions *can* be right or wrong because *some* matters *are* subject to absolute truth. For example, water freezes when its temperature is at or below 32 degrees Fahrenheit. And if it's your opinion that it does not, well, you're simply wrong.

Lastly, a non-judgmental attitude stems from a kind of relativism that is often associated with tolerance: our opinions depend on how we were raised and what culture we live in—and who are we to say someone else is wrong? The first part is generally (but unfortunately) correct: most people do hold the opinions that are held by their community—be that family or culture. However, except for certain kinds of opinions, such as moral or aesthetic opinions, the *truth* of our opinions is *independent* of time and place. For example, whether or not the earth is flat doesn't depend on whether you live in North America or in Europe. The earth is more or less round all over the place. True, if you lived in the Middle Ages, you probably *believed* the earth was flat, but that doesn't make your belief *true*. Consequently, as to the second part of tolerance-via-relativism—the question of who are we to say someone else is wrong—well, we are those who critically examine the support

There are two threats to reason: the opinion that one knows the truth about the most important things, and the opinion that there is no truth about them.

Alan Bloom, *The Closing of the American Mind,* 1987

given or assumed by that someone else for the opinion in question. And if we find the support weak or downright mistaken, then why shouldn't we say so—especially if there are harmful consequences to holding the opinion in question?

And that brings us to the next point: a more direct expression of tolerance is the view that everyone's entitled to their own opinion. Of course, it's true that everyone is entitled to their opinion. But some opinions are better than others. You can express your opinion that Santa Claus exists until you're blue in the face, but until you present some *reasons* for your opinion, others are justified in ignoring you. And until you present *good* reasons, they're justified in not changing their mind (assuming they disagreed with you in the first place). Good opinions are like the tip of an iceberg—the weight of evidence and logic supports them. So know at the outset that opinions are not exempt from examination and evaluation—from judgment.

The view expressed by the phrase "everyone's entitled to their own opinion" is often understood not only as tolerant, but also as open-minded. It is good to be open-minded, to consider everything, including everyone's opinions. However, while you should *consider* everything, you can't *accept* everything—at least, not without being inconsistent. So you're going to have to be judgmental. And hopefully, your judgment will be based on critical examination. Being judgmental in this way is not a bad thing. After all, if you're not judgmental, you're gullible. Do you want to be someone who believes, who uncritically accepts, everything and anything that everyone and anyone says?

Another reason for our tendency *not* to engage in critical thinking is that we live in a decidedly anti-intellectual era. It's almost cool to be stupid. It's certainly not cool to be smart. (You might want to think critically about that: what, exactly, is cool about being stupid?) Much to our detriment, critical thinking is simply not encouraged in our society. You'd think, given its importance and its difficulty, that critical thinking would be taught at elementary and secondary schools. But, generally, it's not. Perhaps teachers and principals think it would make students more difficult to manage. They're right. Perhaps that's why critical thinking is not only not encouraged, it's *discouraged*. It's interesting to note that cults discourage critical thinking. So do large corporations who want loyal employees who don't question the company's goals.

So critical thinking is hard. And it's not particularly encouraged. In what way is it disturbing? Well, it involves the possibility of changing your mind, which unfortunately is often seen as a weakness. Changing your mind also implies you were wrong, and some people can't admit they've been wrong. What's the big deal about saying "I was wrong until I found out about x, y, and z"? Do you really expect yourself to know all of the relevant evidence on every single issue? Perhaps you could have suspended judgment until you had all the relevant evidence, but sometimes it's years before things come to light, either publicly or just in your own life. So again, it should be no big deal to say, "Based on what I knew then, the opinion I formed was justified, but now that I know this, I'm going to change my mind, change my opinion . . ." Of course, perhaps it's not new evidence that

The right to be heard does not automatically include the right to be taken seriously.

Hubert Humphrey, U.S. Vice President, in a speech made in 1965

Persecution is the first law of society because it is always easier to suppress criticism than to meet it.

Howard Mumford Jones, *Primer of Intellectual Freedom*, 1949

15

makes you change your mind, but awareness that you didn't think carefully or thoroughly before. Maybe you *had* all the relevant evidence, but your reasoning process was faulty. Still, why *not* just say, "I was careless about that back then—now I'm being careful and I've come to a different conclusion . . ."? Would you really rather stand by your past carelessness? Changing your mind is simply a matter of recognizing that one position is better than another. Remember: recognizing that your own position is *not* the better one does not mean you've lost some competition. Thinking is not a competition! Life is not a competition!

Admittedly, sometimes the new, clearly better, argument calls into question a whole set of opinions, our entire worldview. And it can certainly be hard to accept that we are wrong about so much! But hey, it happens.

Too, it's hard to change one's mind, because one's mind—what's in it as well as how it works—is very much a matter of habit and habits are hard to break.

And any kind of change involves newness, which is uncomfortable to some people. We like the familiar; we find the unfamiliar threatening instead of interesting or potentially better.

And, often, we simply believe what we want to believe. We believe whatever is in our best interests to believe. Perhaps it's something connected to some specific personal gain. Perhaps it's the majority view, which, for some reason, gives us a sense of security and/or a sense of belonging. In any case, our capacity to delude ourselves should not be underestimated.

On some issues, our emotions get in our way and prevent us from thinking rationally about the matter. Zachary Seech calls these "points of logical vulnerability." (*Open Minds and Everyday Reasoning,* 1993). We may find it difficult to weigh all the evidence fairly or to accept that a certain conclusion necessarily follows from the evidence. But as mentioned previously, you don't have to give up your emotional involvement; you just have to recognize that emotions are better considered as spotlights illuminating matters of importance than as tools for working through those matters.

And of course, there is one final problem with thinking critically that might account for why we tend not to do it: we then have to take responsibility for what we think. If we haven't thought about what we think and do, we can always plead ignorance, and tell ourselves that ignorance absolves us of any responsibility for what we think and do.

1.5 Template for critical analysis of arguments

The purpose of this text is to help you develop the skills that will enable you to critically analyze arguments. As with any complex set of skills, the learning process is usually improved if you consciously follow a series of steps. Once you've mastered the skills, the steps become unconscious. The following template articulates the basic steps you should take in order to critically analyze an argument.

You or your professor may want to modify the template as you work your way through the course—feel free to do so!

Template for critical analysis of arguments

1. What's the point (claim/opinion/conclusion)?

   - Look for subconclusions as well.

2. What are the reasons/what is the evidence?

   - Articulate all unstated premises.
   - Articulate connections.

3. What exactly is meant by . . .?

   - Define terms.
   - Clarify all imprecise language.
   - Eliminate or replace "loaded" language and other manipulations.

4. Assess the reasoning/evidence:

   - If deductive, check for truth/acceptability and validity.
   - If inductive, check for truth/acceptability, relevance, and sufficiency.

5. How could the argument be strengthened?

   - Provide additional reasons/evidence.
   - Anticipate objections—are there adequate responses?

6. How could the argument be weakened?

   - Consider and assess counterexamples, counterevidence, and counter-arguments.
   - Should the argument be modified or rejected because of the counter-arguments?

7. If you suspend judgment (rather than accepting or rejecting the argument), identify further information required.

This template will be presented at the beginning of each chapter to show you where you are in the process; the step that will be covered by that particular chapter will be emphasized in **bold**.

Review of terms

Define the following terms:

■ **critical thinking**

The following end-of-chapter exercises are intended to establish your starting point. You'll note that the instructions are intentionally vague—to see how you do without any leading questions. You will be asked to do the same five kinds of exercise at the end of each subsequent chapter in order to practice and strengthen your accumulating skills. Hopefully you will notice improvement in your critical abilities—whether in considering what you see, read, write, hear, or say—as you cover the material in the subsequent chapters!

Thinking critically about what you see

What is your considered reaction to this?

© Corbis

Thinking critically about what you hear

Listen to the audio clip under the Student Resources tab on the companion website at www.routledge.com/textbooks/tittle. Any response?

Thinking critically about what you read

Read and evaluate the following.

There's nothing wrong with downloading music from the internet. First, everyone does it, and second, it's not like you're taking something—after you download, the song's still there, it's not like taking someone's car. Some people say downloading music from the internet isn't fair because the musicians don't get paid when you download, but you're paying for the internet connection—why should you have to pay twice? *That's* not fair! And people say that if everyone does it, sales of CDs will decrease, and then since there'll be no money in making CDs, the record companies will stop making them. But everyone's not doing it, so CD sales won't decrease. And actually, a friend of mine told me that after their band put one of their songs on their website, sales of their CD increased! Lastly, downloading is legal; anything that's morally acceptable is legal; so downloading must be morally acceptable. People should stop worrying about this stuff and go after the *real* criminals!

Thinking critically about what you write

Write a few paragraphs arguing that this course will or will not be of benefit to you.

Thinking critically when you discuss

In a group of three or four, discuss something.

Reasoning test questions

Graduate school entrance tests (the LSAT for law school applicants, the MCAT for medical school applicants, the GMAT for graduate business programs, and the GRE for other graduate programs) usually have whole sections testing reasoning ability. Since these are typically multiple-choice questions (the reasoning section of the GRE is now an analytic writing test rather than a multiple-choice question test), students often assume they are easy questions. They are not. Especially since you've got only two or three minutes for each one. You'll get a chance at the end of each chapter to work through such reasoning test questions. Since we haven't yet begun to cover the skills required to successfully answer such questions, consider this, as per the previous end-of-chapter bits, a sort of pre-test, to establish your starting point.

1. Computers perform actions that are closer to thinking than anything nonhuman animals do. But computers do not have volitional powers, although some nonhuman animals do.

Which one of the following is most strongly supported by the information above?

(A) Having volitional powers need not involve thinking.
(B) Things that are not animals do not have volitional powers.
(C) Computers possess none of the attributes of living things.
(D) It is necessary to have volitional powers in order to think.
(E) Computers will never be able to think as human beings do.

(The Official LSAT Prep Test XXIII, Section 2, #7)

2. Which of the following best completes the passage below?

In a survey of job applicants, two-fifths admitted to being at least a little dishonest. However, the survey may underestimate the proportion of job applicants who are dishonest, because _____.

(A) some dishonest people taking the survey might have claimed on the survey to be honest
(B) some generally honest people taking the survey might have claimed on the survey to be dishonest
(C) some people who claimed on the survey to be at least a little dishonest may be very dishonest
(D) some people who claimed on the survey to be dishonest may have been answering honestly
(E) some people who are not job applicants are probably at least a little dishonest

(GMAT® Mini-Test #1)

chapter 2

the nature
of argument

Template for critical analysis of arguments

1. What's the point (claim/opinion/conclusion)?

   ■ Look for subconclusions as well.

2. What are the reasons/what is the evidence?

   ■ Articulate all unstated premises.
   ■ Articulate connections.

3. What exactly is meant by . . .?

   ■ Define terms.
   ■ Clarify all imprecise language.
   ■ Eliminate or replace "loaded" language and other manipulations.

4. Assess the reasoning/evidence:

   ■ If deductive, check for truth/acceptability and validity.
   ■ If inductive, check for truth/acceptability, relevance, and sufficiency.

5. How could the argument be strengthened?

   ■ Provide additional reasons/evidence.
   ■ Anticipate objections—are there adequate responses?

6. How could the argument be weakened?

   ■ Consider and assess counterexamples, counterevidence, and counter-arguments.
   ■ Should the argument be modified or rejected because of the counter-arguments?

7. If you suspend judgment (rather than accepting or rejecting the argument), identify further information required.

2.1 The nature of argument

As mentioned at the end of the introductory chapter, this text will focus on thinking critically about arguments. So, you will need to know what an argument is (see Section 2.2); you will also need to be able to recognize an argument, even when it's not neatly presented as such and especially when it involves unstated assumptions (see Section 2.3). You'll also need to know about circular arguments in order *not* to make them (see Section 2.4). It's also important to know about counterarguments (see Section 2.5; possible responses to arguments will be discussed in greater detail with the end-of-chapter exercise entitled "Thinking Critically When You Discuss"). Identifying the issue of contention is important, especially when two or more people are talking; it's quite possible they're talking about different issues and, therefore, making completely separate arguments rather than attending to a single argument (see Section 2.6). Speaking of two or more people talking, it's important to understand who has the burden of proof (see Section 2.7) and to understand the error of "an appeal to ignorance" (see Section 2.8). Lastly, it's important to distinguish between facts and opinions, and between knowledge and belief, so we'll dip into these matters as well (see Section 2.9; Chapter 6 will address these last matters in greater depth).

2.2 Recognizing an argument

Arguments can be conveyed in just one sentence or they can extend over an entire book. They can be easy to follow or difficult to follow. They can be trivial or important. They can be full of mistakes or perfect. But one thing is certain—an **argument** consists of two parts:

1   *a claim*—some statement of fact or opinion; the point of what's being said; this point is usually called the **conclusion**.
2   *support for the claim*—evidence or reasons related to the claim in such a way as to endorse it or make it acceptable; these supporting lines of reasoning are usually called **premises**.

In a nutshell:

> **argument: premises ⟶ conclusion**

Consider this example:

> Unlike high school, college is not mandatory. And you don't really want to be here. So you should just quit.

The premises are "College is not mandatory" and "You don't really want to be here." The conclusion is "You should quit." Do you see how the first two statements lead to the last statement? The premises lead to, or support, the conclusion. The sentences fit together in a "this, therefore that" structure.

Now consider this statement:

He's armed, and he's dangerous.

Compare it to this statement:

He's armed, so he's dangerous.

The first one merely presents two separate claims: "he's armed" and "he's dangerous." However, the second one is an argument because of the "so"—that *connects* the two claims in such a way as to make the first claim *the reason for* believing the second claim.

Note that the word "conclusion" is being used in perhaps a different way than you're used to: it is not meant as a summary, an overall review of what's been said; rather, the conclusion is the *logical consequence* of what's been said— so it's clearly something *further* to what's been said, not just a review of what's been said. When you're trying to identify the conclusion of an argument, it might help to pay attention to words that can indicate a conclusion: so, consequently, thus, therefore, it follows that, hence, shows that, proves that, accordingly, indicates that. But don't depend on those words being there, and don't depend on them indicating a conclusion (not everyone uses their words carefully).

As for "premises," what counts as support will depend on the nature of the claim. For example, historical claims require different support than literary claims. What would support a claim about what actually happened in the past? Letters written at the time by credible people attesting to the fact that such and such happened, financial records in accordance with the supposed event, and so on. Those who become historians learn what counts as evidence for historical claims. What would support a claim about what a particular poem means? The words in the poem, the images in the poem and how they're presented, perhaps letters written by the poet, and so on. Again, those studying to become literary scholars learn what counts as evidence for literary claims.

When you're trying to identify the premises of an argument, ask yourself "What are the reasons or the evidence given in support of the conclusion?" In the first example above, you might ask "Why does the speaker think you should quit?" It might also help to pay attention to words that can indicate a premise: because, since, given that, as shown by, as indicated by, due to. But, again, don't depend on those words being there, and don't depend on them indicating a premise.

Furthermore, premises themselves often require support, so strongly supported premises are better than weakly supported or unsupported premises, making the whole argument stronger.

2.2a Practice recognizing premises and conclusions

Each of the following is an argument. In each case, identify the premises and conclusions.

1. It's puzzling that Taffi (the canine I live with) doesn't play with toys more often, given that she has her own toybox. And it's overflowing. But then, she has me!

2. Hydrogen is the most common element in the universe. Since it's so abundant, cars powered by hydrogen fuel cells will eventually be so much cheaper than gasoline-powered cars.

3. We know he's a real man because he threw a refrigerator across the room during a fight.
   (Jason Cohen and Michael Krugman, writing tongue-in-cheek about a popular television show. From *Generation Ecch!*)

4. Compared to the rest of the world, our kids are simply not very smart. I mean, look, on proficiency tests conducted in 30 countries, our 15-year-olds scored 25th on the math proficiency test, 18th on reading proficiency, and 21st on science proficiency.
   (Statistics for 2003, from United States Department of Education)

5. The Soviet pledge not to be the first to use nuclear weapons goes to confirm that the USSR is against any nuclear aggression and that its military doctrine is, indeed, a defensive one in nature.
   (Information Centre of the World Peace Council, "Nuclear Weapons: No First Strike, No First Use," no date)

6. Studies have shown that children in single-parent families are far more likely to have psychological problems than children in two-parent families. They are also more likely to drop out of school, get pregnant, become a drug-user, and become criminal. All of which goes to show how important it is to have a father, a male figure in the family.

7. Burglars generally avoid the houses known to have guns in them. And people have a right to defend what's theirs. Consequently, we should legalize guns; that way, people can defend themselves against burglars.

8. That's not the way I wanted to finish my season," [Danica] Patrick said. "I was on my radio all day about him. He [Jacques Lazier] was all over the track [during the 2005 Toyota Indy 400] even when he was running by himself.

No wonder he jumps around from team to team. Needless to say, I'm pretty frustrated.

("Patrick physically confronts Lazier after crash," ESPN News Services, October 17, 2005, www.espn.com)

9. Tuition fees should be lowered due to the scarcity of jobs. Most students don't want to work while they're going to school anyway. And parents don't always give their kids enough money for tuition *and* all the other stuff they want. I mean, you can't expect students to study all the time, they want to party, have fun, see movies, listen to music. And all of that costs money.

10. Legalizing drugs will not eliminate crime. It will not even necessarily decrease crime because while it might decrease the mugging and burglaries committed in order to get money to get the drugs, it will *increase* crimes committed under the influence of such drugs, such as homicides, car accidents, child abuse, and sexual abuse.

This special relationship between premises and conclusions may be easier to see and keep in mind when arguments are put into what's called *standard form*:

> First premise.
> <u>Second premise.</u>
> Therefore, conclusion.

The examples given at the beginning of this section would, in standard form, be thus:

> College is not mandatory.
> <u>You don't really want to be here.</u>
> Therefore, you should quit.
>
> <u>He's armed.</u>
> Therefore, he's dangerous.

When you put an argument into standard form, always state the premises and the conclusion in complete sentences (and extraneous words can be omitted, such as "just" in the first example). Since premises and conclusions, as they are often presented, are only part of a sentence, you may have to do a bit of rewriting.

2.2b Practice using standard form

Write each of the arguments from the preceding exercise in standard form.

It's amazing how few arguments are out there. Most of the time, what seems to be an argument is just a bunch of claims more or less on the same topic; there is no relationship between the claims, let alone the specific "this supports that" relationship. Worse, what is presumed to be an argument is just a single claim, looking much like a command.

Consider this example of a non-argument:

© Corbis

The statement "Defend life" alone is not an argument. Why should we defend life? On what grounds should we defend life? There is no support given for the claim.

So, claims by themselves, without substantiation, are not arguments. Nor are commands. Consider "Just do it!" and "Just say no." Well, should we do it or not? Should we say yes or no? We're given no reasons, so how can we decide? Questions, likewise, aren't arguments. Nor are expressions of emotion.

2.2c Practice distinguishing arguments from non-arguments

Some of the following are arguments and some are not. For those that are arguments, identify the premises and conclusions, and present them in standard form. For those that are not arguments, explain why, and, if you can, suggest what would turn them into arguments.

27

1. Men expect to tell women things, not to be told things by them, or even to explore a subject together.

   (March Fasteau, *The Male Machine*, 1975)

2. But why wouldn't you apply for a job even if it's beneath you? What does that mean, anyway? I mean, what does it imply to say that such-and-such a job is beneath you?

3. People who are wealthy are so because of ability, so we should respect them.

4. "I think it's about time there was 'the pill' for men!"
   "Yeah, right." [laughing]

5. We hold these truths to be self-evident, that all men are created equal, that they are endowed by their Creator with certain unalienable Rights, that among these are Life, Liberty and the pursuit of Happiness.

   (Thomas Jefferson)

6. I am definitely against the death penalty. First of all, it's applied discriminately—more black-skinned people and low-income people get the death penalty. Second, there is always the possibility of wrongful conviction. Third, the death penalty doesn't act as a deterrent, because people who commit crimes punishable by death generally don't think ahead—or they aren't deterred by the death penalty.

7. Dave Mundy from Caistor Centre, Ontario, went over the falls in a barrel in 1985 and lived. Several summers ago Dave attempted to shoot Niagara Falls again, but his barrel got grounded at the brink of the falls and he had to be rescued with a crane. Dave is determined to try again and has stated that if he succeeds, for his next trick he'd really like to fly an airplane into a bus.

   (William Thomas, *Guys: Not Real Bright—And Damn Proud of It!*)

8. There should be a maximum wage just as there is a minimum wage. Surely there's a limit to how hard a person can work—no one works a hundred times harder than I do, so they don't deserve to be paid a hundred times what I get an hour.

9. Here are some stats on Beverly Blossom: founding member of Alwin Nikolais's company, choreographer, esteemed teacher; 79 years old, cushiony body, lived-in face. These facts do not explain why, when she draws herself up, she seems to fill the stage, or how, as she ripples her arms grandly or scatters rose petals to Beethoven's somber chords, she evokes Isadora Duncan. Make that an Isadora who's a wily, eccentric comedian and relishes shtick.

   (Deborah Jowitt, "Swimming in It," a dance review
   from *The Village Voice*, September 19, 2005)

10. Ironically, if some alien anthropologists of the future were to visit our post-apocalyptic planet and try to make sense of American and Iranian culture on the basis of film archives, they could easily reach some puzzling conclusions. Iranian films—the product of an authoritarian, theocratic society—celebrate life in its most humble details and display enormous respect for the individuals whose stories are being told and for the viewers who are watching, while the big, mainstream American films—the product of a democratic, individualistic society—routinely humiliate their subjects, seduce their viewers by the most primitive means, and are alarmingly casual about killing and death.

(Shirley Goldberg, "Iran's Remarkable National Cinema," *Humanist in Canada*, Autumn 2003)

To review, a claim, just a statement that this is so (or was so, or will be so, or should be so), is not an argument. You have to say *why* this is so, what makes you think this is so, what your reasons are for thinking this is so.

So an argument is *an appeal to reason*; by definition, it requires rational thought. If the person making the argument wants you to agree, he or she wants you to do so because you find the reasoning convincing. Thus, the following ways of making a case are *not* arguments; they all lack an appeal to reason.

An appeal to emotion: "Do as I say NOW!" "But I need an A to get into law school!" Such utterances may, like argument, be intended to persuade you to do something or to believe something. The first one is an attempt to intimidate; the second one is an attempt to elicit pity. But unlike argument, they are appeals to emotion, not to reason. People often use emotion *instead of* reason in order to persuade others: threats use anger; pleas make use of pity or sympathy; flattery and ridicule make use of pride and self-doubt; bribes make use of greed; reverence makes use of fear and insecurity; and so on.

An appeal to intuition: "I just intuitively know that this is right!" Okay, that's all very nice for you (see the comments about intuition in Section 1.2). But if you hope to convince someone else that this is right, you'll have to do better than that—you'll have to provide reasons. That is, unless you expect others to simply trust your intuition. Consider that the other person's intuition may tell them something different.

Perhaps what some people call intuition is unconscious reasoning: maybe they have reasons for thinking as they do, but they just haven't done the work required to acknowledge and articulate those reasons, to themselves or to others. In that case, appeals to intuition, gut feeling, a sixth sense—they're all just ways to avoid the hard work of using one's intellect. At the very least, intuition might be simply our apprehension of our physiological responses to emotion; we "sense" we're uncomfortable with something because we've unconsciously felt a slight increase in our heart rate or a slight sweat, so we say our intuition is telling us it's wrong. Such apprehension (increased heart rate, sweat, and so on) may be

The enemies of freedom do not argue; they shout and they shoot.

William Ralph Inge, *The End of an Age,* 1948

29

THE FAR SIDE® By GARY LARSON

**"And so I ask the jury—is that the face of a
mass murderer?"**

useful as a signal that something is significant enough to warrant our rational deliberation, but as such, it should be our *starting* point—that's where our work should begin, not end. Take the time to figure out *why* you're uncomfortable; maybe what's causing a slight sweat is actually a very good thing, it's just something you've never done before . . .

An appeal to instinct: "Just follow your instincts." That's fine if you're a wolf. Wolves don't have to make decisions about elective surgery and the distribution of scarce resources. Brute biochemical wiring, or whatever instinct is, is generally inferior to rational thought. Furthermore, I'm not sure human instinct actually guides our beliefs about various facts or opinions; more often, it just directs our behavior, our action, short-circuiting our cognition.

An appeal to faith: "I just believe that it is so; I have faith that it will be so." Faith, *by definition*, is belief in the *absence* of reason. It is, according to *The American*

Heritage Dictionary of the English Language, "belief that does not rest on logical proof or material evidence." It's therefore impossible to argue with someone who appeals solely to faith—because reasons are irrelevant. When someone has reasons or evidence for their belief, then it's no longer a matter of faith; then it's a matter of rational belief.

I do not feel obliged to believe that the same God who has endowed us with sense, reason, and intellect has intended us to forgo their use.

Galileo Galilei
(1564–1642)

> Of course, there is a crucial moral difference between those whose faith tells them to murder innocent people, and those whose faith tells them to respect life. But the difference is not something we can get from faith. The Islamic militant who believes he is doing the will of God when he flies a plane full of passengers into the World Trade Center is just as much a person of faith as the Christian who believes she is doing the will of God when she spends her days picketing a clinic that offers abortions. Faith cannot tell us who is right and who is wrong, because each will simply assert that his or her faith is the true one. In the absence of a willingness to offer reasons, evidence, or arguments for why it is better to do one thing rather than another, there is no progress to be made. If we try to dissuade people from becoming radical Islamic terrorists, not by persuading them to be more thoughtful and reflective about their religious beliefs, but by encouraging them to switch from one unquestioned religious faith to another, we are fighting with our hands tied behind our backs. Much better, therefore, to insist that there is an ethical obligation to base one's views about life on evidence and sound reasoning.
>
> (Peter Singer, *The President of Good and Evil: The Ethics of George W. Bush*, 2004)

An argument is also not, by the way, a quarrel; at least that's not the kind of argument we're talking about. Consequently, argument, the kind we *are* talking about, is not competition, and arguing is not a matter of winning or losing. In fact, the best argument is not an adversarial engagement at all, but a cooperative effort to discover the truth or the opinions most worth holding.

The aim of argument, or of discussion, should be not victory but progress.

Joseph Joubert, *Pensées*, 1842

Lastly, it might be valuable at this point to make a few comments about arguments and explanations. Sometimes an explanation is an argument, and sometimes it is not. When you're explaining how or why something occurred, and the facts of the matter are not in dispute, you're just giving an explanation—more specifically, a causal explanation. You might, for example, explain how you came to have a broken leg (you tripped on a banana peel; it was raining; you were running, backwards).

However, when you're proposing an explanation for something about which the contributing factors *are* in dispute, then you're making an argument. You might argue for an economic explanation for your unhappiness (you just got fired, so you have no income, so you're unhappy), while your friend might argue for a

31

psychological explanation for your unhappiness (you hated your job, so you subconsciously sabotaged it, all but forcing your supervisor to fire you, and now you feel guilty, and therefore unhappy, plus you're bored) because now you have nothing to do and that makes you unhappy too. Such causal explanations are often arguments because one is making a case for a particular cause, or set of causes, over another perhaps equally plausible cause, or set of causes.

2.2d More practice distinguishing arguments from non-arguments

Again, some of the following are arguments and some are not. For those that are arguments, identify the premises and conclusions, and present them in standard form. For those that are not arguments, explain why, and, if you can, suggest what would turn them into arguments.

1. Thou shalt not kill.

2. You are surely smart enough to see that no amount of recycling is going to save the world.

3. Inheritance should be illegal. After all, that's why there's so much inequality. So many kids get such a headstart, they have money, they didn't even earn, and money makes money, it's all unfair. You should have to earn what you get, no matter who your parents are.

4. The last forty years saw the fastest rise in human numbers in all previous history, from only 2.5 billion people in 1950 to 5.6 billion in 1994. This same period saw natural habitats shrinking and species dying at an accelerating rate. The ozone hole appeared, and the threat of global warming emerged.
   Worse is in store. Each year in the 1980s saw an extra 85 million people on earth. The second half of the 1990s will add an additional 94 million people per year. That is equivalent to a new United States every thirty-three months, another Britain every seven months, a Washington every six days. A whole earth of 1980 was added in just one decade, according to United Nations Population Division statistics. After 2000, annual additions will slow, but by 2050 the United Nations expects the human race to total just over 10 billion—an extra earth of 1980 on top of today's, according to U.N. projections.
   (Paul Harrison, "Sex and the Single Planet: Need, Greed, and Earthly Limits," *The Amicus Journal*, Winter 1994)

5. I just know this is wrong. Can't you feel it?

6. I don't have to think about it. I just do what comes naturally. You can call it irresponsible if you want, but that's the way we are.

7. I argue that a nation has a right to control the number of people who immigrate to it. If a nation faces massive overpopulation, or if certain regions of that nation face massive overpopulation, national sovereignty allows a government to restrict the number of people who can cross the border. One nation is not required to pay for another's lack of family planning, corruption, or failure to achieve an equitable distribution of wealth by absorbing millions of citizens from that other country.

(Edward Tabash, "What Population Stabilization Requires," *Free Inquiry*, August/September 2004)

8. I have faith that the good Lord will protect us! I believe Jesus is our Lord and Savior!

9. Some people are allergic to cats because cat saliva contains a protein that is foreign to the human immune system; it therefore stimulates the human immune system, which, in some people, results in sneezing, runny eyes, and so on.

(Thanks to Dr. Ron Smith)

10. "Because."
    "Because why?"
    "Just because!"

2.3 Identifying implied conclusions and unstated premises (assumptions)

Alas, most people do not articulate their arguments very well. Sometimes they don't actually get around to saying what their conclusion is. Sometimes they don't actually state all their premises. And sometimes they just don't connect the two. Let's deal with each of these in turn.

Conclusions are sometimes *implied* instead of being articulated outright. Perhaps the person making the argument thinks the conclusion is obvious. Perhaps she or he is just lazy. In any case, before you can assess the argument, you have to figure out where the given premises lead—you have to figure out what conclusion follows from the given premises.

Suppose the argument presented was this:

If schools are to teach kids values, just who will be the one to decide which values?

You'll recall from the previous section that a question isn't an argument. And that's generally the case. In this case, though, let's assume that the context, what

33

the speaker said before and after this bit, suggests that the point is something like "Schools have no business teaching values." That would be the implied conclusion. On the other hand, though, perhaps the speaker meant that schools should hire people who are qualified to teach values. So you see, it's always best to come right out and state your conclusion; otherwise, you risk being misunderstood.

2.3a Practice articulating implied conclusions

Assume each of the following is intended to make an argument, and articulate what the implied conclusion might be. Put the argument in standard form if that helps.

1. Women provide two-thirds of the world's work hours. Women produce 44 percent of the world's food supply. Women receive 10 percent of the world's income. Women own 1 percent of the world's property.
   (Marilyn French, *Beyond Power*, 1985)

2. Astrology is both descriptive in that it purports to describe a person's personality based on time of birth and predictive in that it purports to foretell what sort of day, week, month, or year a person is going to have. However, consider a hundred people who were born at exactly the same time: surely they do not all have the same personality—they have not had the same life experiences. Further, given their differing personalities and given their differing life experiences, surely they will not all have the same sort of day, week, month, or year.

3. Most chickens are not stunned before their throats are slit, in the United States. Their heads are passed through an electrically charged water bath that immobilizes them but doesn't render them unconscious. Then they have their throats cut and are dumped into a scalding tank of boiling water (to remove feathers), often while they are still conscious.
   ("Murder King: The Fast-Food Giant's Shameful Record," *Animal Times*, 2000)

4. Nancy Henley, psychologist and author of *Body Politics*, has written, "In a way so accepted and so subtle as to be unnoticed even by its practitioners and recipients, males in couples will often literally push a woman everywhere she is to go—the arm from behind, steering around corners, through doorways, into elevators, onto escalators ... crossing the street. It is not necessarily heavy and pushy or physical in an ugly way; it is light and gentle but firm, in the way of most confident equestrians with the best-trained horses." ... Steering and leading are prerogatives of those in command.
   (Susan Brownmiller, *Femininity*, 1984)

34

5. In 48 states, daycare for a four-year-old costs more than tuition at a four-year public college.

   (*Mother Jones*, November/December 2004)

6. Schools should serve national economic needs, and a lot of the courses taught in school today—history, geography, literature, phys-ed, music—we don't have jobs for that, the marketplace needs people to fill jobs in computers and telemarketing. We're also going to need a lot of people to work in nursing homes, because the baby boomers are getting old.

7. Pigs can fly. John is a pig.

8. Since 2002, the average price of *gasoline* in the United States has increased 35.2 percent. Since 2002, the average consumption of gasoline by Americans per capita has not changed.

   (U.S. Department of Energy/Harper's research,
   Harper's Index, January 2005)

9. By staying in this country, you're saying you agree with its laws. So if you don't like them, well . . .

10. The purpose of marriage is family. And homosexuals can't have kids!

Figuring out unstated premises is usually a little more difficult than figuring out the unstated conclusions. Sometimes this is because they're so obvious, they go without saying; which is exactly what the person making the argument probably thought! That's why they're often called *assumptions* or presuppositions or even presumptions, rather than unstated premises. They're even called hidden assumptions, but this suggests a sort of intentional deception on the part of the person making the argument, when it's more likely the person is either unaware of the premises s/he is using, or the assumption is so unquestionable, as to be taken for granted. Maybe they should be called unknown premises instead. Whatever you may want to call them, they're still unstated (not articulated in the argument as presented), and they're still premises (required to make the argument complete).

Reconsider the argument of the first example in this chapter:

Unlike high school, <u>college is not mandatory</u>①. And <u>you don't really want to be here</u>②. ⓢⓞ you should just quit.
<u>conclusion</u>   ③ *people shouldn't do what they don't want to do*

There was actually a hidden assumption in that argument, and it's required to make the second premise work: people should not do what they don't want to do.

> *Special note: Since critical thinking is a skill, it's important that you engage with the material if you are to develop the skill. You can't learn to ride a bicycle just by watching someone else ride one. So, in case you haven't already done so, pick up your pen—not your highlighter—and engage with the words on the page: underline things, circle things, draw arrows, enter into a "conversation" with the people who have made these arguments, make note of comments and questions that occur to you that strengthen or weaken the argument being made, and so on. A few examples in this chapter will be annotated to get you started!*

The full argument, in standard form, would be this:

1. You don't have to be at college. (University is not mandatory.)
2. You don't want to be at college.
3. <u>People should not do what they don't want to do.</u>
Therefore, so you should quit.

Once we identify this hidden assumption, we see a way in which we might object to the argument: there might be reasons other than desire (or legal compulsion) to stay at college. Perhaps the person in question has a moral obligation to go to college.

It's natural, by the way, and indeed useful, to make assumptions. We couldn't get through a day, let alone our life, without them. For example, when we see a building, we actually seldom see a building: usually we see one or two walls, and we *assume* there's a third and a fourth, and therefore a building. And that's generally a useful assumption.

And many of our assumptions—like the assumption about the building—are indeed warranted. (At least the ones we make on a daily basis regarding buildings are.) But sometimes our assumptions are *un*warranted. And that's why it's important to identify our assumptions: if we identify our assumptions, we can figure out if they're warranted or not. If it turns out that an assumption is *un*warranted, then the conclusion it was apparently supporting is also unwarranted. This is true, and important, whether you're talking about someone else's argument or your own. You can't evaluate what you can't identify. So, as it turns out, maybe "hidden premises" are best called "unexamined premises."

Also, if you don't state your premises, someone else will. Someone else will have to fill in your blanks for you. There are two problems with this. One, they may get it wrong—did you mean to imply X or Y? And if they get it wrong, your argument will be misunderstood. (And unless you're quick to realize that and correct things, you may find yourself defending something you didn't say!) Two, they simply may not bother. It's easier to just watch TV. So much for your argument.

Now as for identifying unstated premises, it will help if you keep in mind that the unstated premise often connects the stated premise with the conclusion. For example, suppose I said, "Abortion is killing, so abortion is wrong." The missing link would be "Killing is wrong."

1. Abortion is killing.
2. Killing is wrong.
Therefore, abortion is wrong.

And now that that unstated premise has been articulated, it can be evaluated (along with the stated premise): *Is* killing wrong? Always? What about killing in self-defense? What about killing one thing to save a million other things?

Here's another example to illustrate all this:

Selling our product at cost would mean we won't make any profit, so we should implement a mark-up in price.

Let's put it in standard form, with a place for an unstated premise:

1. Selling our product at cost would mean we won't make any profit.
2. Businesses should seek to max π
Therefore, we should implement a mark-up in price.

What's missing? *What has the speaker assumed?* That it's necessary, or at least important, or perhaps even good, to make a profit. The complete argument would be this:

1. Selling our product at cost would mean we won't make any profit.
2. We should make a profit.
Therefore, we should sell our product at more than cost.

Now that we have figured out the unstated premise, we can examine the argument—*all* of it. *Should* we make a profit? Is it necessary? Important? Good? On what grounds? We might offer this sub-argument as grounds:

1. Businesses should make a profit.
2. We are a business.
Therefore, we should make a profit.

But then we're back to the question, "*Should* businesses make a profit? On what grounds? What about not-for-profit businesses?"

Another thing to keep in mind is that often, but not always, the missing premise is a generalization. It's the generalizations that we so often take for granted, so that makes sense. In the previous example, it was the general statement that "Businesses—which includes us—should make a profit" that was missing. In the example before that, the missing premise was "Killing is wrong"—again, a generalization.

Lastly, it might be helpful to realize that most assumptions are either *reality assumptions* (assumptions about what is, about the way things are in the world) or *value assumptions* (assumptions about what's important or about what's right and wrong). Both of the preceding examples involved value assumptions: killing is wrong and businesses should make a profit. A reality assumption occurs in the following example:

1. Students who are late for class should enter quietly and apologize afterward to the professor with an explanation.
2. _____

Therefore, you should enter quietly and apologize afterward to the professor with an explanation.

The missing premise, the assumption that makes the argument work, is that "You are late for class." As an assumption about what is indeed the case, it's a reality assumption—which may or may not be correct.

2.3b Practice articulating unstated premises

Each of the following arguments contains an assumption, a missing premise. Figure out what it is. Ask yourself, "What is the person assuming to be true, but not saying?" or "What premise is required to make the argument work?" Use standard form if that helps.

1. Abuse and neglect in various forms will continue until we as a society value parenthood; until we regard parenting as a privilege, rather than as a by-product of sexual intercourse, a route to adult identity, or a route to social assistance.
   (Katherine Covell and R. Brian Howe, "A Policy of Parent Licensing," *Policy Options*, September 1998)

2. It's wrong to sell unsafe products because unsafe products can cause harm to people.

3. "Standard of living" is measured by the amount of annual consumption—the country that consumes the most has the highest standard of living. What an assumption is in there!
   (E.F. Schumacher, *Small is Beautiful: Economics as if People Mattered*, 1999 [1973])

38

4. The percentage of heterosexuals with AIDS is less than the percentage of homosexuals with AIDS, proving that heterosexual sex is less risky than homosexual sex.

[handwritten: VP = risky sex is contracting AIDS]

5. No, we absolutely cannot raise wages! If we do that, we'll go out of business!

6. There's nothing wrong with the ladies, God bless them, let them play. But what they're doing is eliminating much of the available time when young players can get on the course.

(Jack Nicklaus, golfer, 1978)

[handwritten: 1. women take up time 2. Golf courses should maximize time slot 3. women should play]

7. Prohibiting drugs will lead to an increase in crime, not a decrease, because first, when the price of illegal drugs is very high, poor addicts rob and burglarize. And second, the police will be so occupied with drug arrests, more crime will occur.

[handwritten: 1. High drug prices produce crime 2. when demand is high, profits is high 3. Poor addicts will... 4. Prohibiting will ↑ crime]

8. If there is no God, then everything is permitted.

(Dostoyevsky)

9. Obviously, however, the client cannot be expected to reveal to the lawyer all information that is potentially relevant, including that which may well be incriminating, unless the client can be assured that the lawyer will maintain all such information in the strictest confidence.

(Monroe Freedman, "Where the Bodies are Buried," in *Lawyers' Ethics in an Adversary System*, 1977)

[handwritten: client should protect own interests]

10. Military training prepares the mind and body for war. It thus perpetuates the desire for war. So nations that force military training on their young are more likely to engage in the war they have prepared for. I call it the "All dressed up and no place to go? Hell no, we'll find a place!" phenomenon.

[handwritten: 1. 2. Ppl desire what prep for c: military training → war desire vp: favors should be repaid]

11. When the time comes, of course I'm going to have to pay for my parents' long-term care. They paid for my food and shelter for, what, eighteen years?

12. This company is run by sales, not by R and D. So the priority is style, not safety.

13. "It's a cultural taboo in this country," said Jeffery M. Leving, a lawyer and fathers' rights advocate in Chicago. "It's very unmanly to request a DNA test to determine that your child is your biological child. It's emasculating and many men would not do it."

(Mireya Navarro. "Painless Paternity Tests, but the Truth May Hurt," *New York Times*, October 2, 2005)

14. Are there intelligent life forms out there in the universe? Well yeah. No one's visited us yet.

(Jass Richards)

[handwritten: intelligent life can/will communicate]

15. Refusing blood transfusions protects us from AIDS; that shows that we are right.

16. I keep telling Anne [Fornoro, his longtime public relations representative] I might have been an asshole, but I must have done something right, I got so many people still following me.

    (A.J. Foyt, in interview "A.J. Foyt" with Leo Levine in *Road and Track*, February 2005)

UP: fame = right

17. If the marriage is going to work out, the woman shouldn't be older than her husband, or more educated, or more highly paid.

UP: women want marriage to succeed

18. On June 6, the Public Health Council should say no to mandating mass medicating New Jersey's public water supplies with the corrosive metal fluoride. There are too many questions about the risks of adding fluoride to water, and it is not proven to reduce cavities significantly enough to warrant adding it to the entire water supply.

    The benefit of fluoride to teeth, if there is one, can be provided through fluoride in toothpaste, mouth rinses, topical application and supplements.

    No other public health problem has been addressed by adding a chemical substance to public drinking water, taking away the choice of every consumer whether to ingest fluoride.

    It's difficult to justify putting in drinking water a corrosive metal that is likely to leach lead from older pipes more readily and enhance the human body's ability to absorb lead. In addition, fluoride ingestion over the long term can lead to brittle bones, joint disease that mimics arthritis and hormone disruption.

    Let individuals, not the state, make the choice.

    (Jane Nogaki, Marlton, letter to the editor, *The Times*, May 27, 2005)

19. After September 11, 2001, some Americans began asking: "Why would anyone in the Middle East hate America?" The fact that such a question had to be asked reflects a profound ignorance of the U.S. government's role in that region.

    (Richard Sanders)

UP: Q = ignorance

20. Years ago it was, "I'm the parent, you have to listen and that's it." And we can't feel guilty about that because that is the way we were raised and socialized.

    (Fran Ianacone, "Got Kids? Then You Got Anger," *U.S.1*, June 8, 2005)

So far, we've covered unstated conclusions and unstated premises; the third element that can be missing is the connection between the two—typically a "therefore" or an "and" is missing. Essentially, what is missing is a clear identification of a claim *as* a premise or *as* a conclusion.

Example:

It used to be that parents let their children watch only so much TV. I know
that when I was a kid, I was allowed to watch only one hour a day. And that
was contingent upon finishing my homework, either before or after the TV.
I also see that children are getting more and more violent. I don't remember
any fights at my school when I was a kid. Now, my kids come home and it
seems there's been a fight at recess every other day.

implication — kids are watching more tv today than they used to

①

?

So?

②

There are two claims here:

Children are watching more and more television.
Children are becoming more and more violent.

But what is the connection? Is the speaker trying to say that watching television
increases kids' violence—presumably because TV programs show a lot of violence? In that case, the first claim is a premise and the second claim is a conclusion.
It's just as plausible to argue that the violent kids are drawn to watch more and
more TV (if one assumes that TV has become more and more violent). In that
case, the first claim is the conclusion and the second claim is the premise. See how
important it is to articulate the connections between your ideas?

2.3c Practice identifying missing connections

In three of the following arguments, connections are missing. Articulate what they
might be, using standard form.

1. *C* *P*
   Preserve our right to bear arms! Guns don't kill people—people do.

2. *P*
   I knew war as few living people today know it. The extreme destruction that
   war produces amongst our friends as well as amongst our enemies renders it
   useless as a way to solve international conflicts.
   C   (General Douglas MacArthur)

3. *C*
   The feminist classroom does little to prepare students to cope in the world of
   work and culture. It is an embarrassing scandal that, in the name of feminism,
   young women in our colleges and universities are taking courses in feminist
   classrooms that subject them to a lot of bad prose, psychobabble, and "new
   age" nonsense. What has real feminism to do with sitting around in circles
   and talking about our feelings on menstruation? To use a phrase much used
   by resenter feminists, the feminist classroom *shortchanges* women students. ← *C*
   It wastes their time and gives them bad intellectual habits. It isolates them,
   socially and academically. While male students are off studying such "vertical" subjects as engineering and biology, women in feminist classrooms

41

are sitting around being "safe" and "honoring" feelings. In this way, gender feminist pedagogy plays into old sexist stereotypes that extol women's capacity for intuition, emotion, and empathy while denigrating their capacity to think objectively and systematically in the way men can.

(Christina Hoff Sommers, *Who Stole Feminism?*, 1994)

C

4. Hey there's nothing wrong with pursuing your own self-interest. If you don't, who will? What's wrong with being happy, with trying to be happy, to have a good life? ρ

5. It is natural that the husband is head of the family. Man is superior to woman. Adam was made first, and then Eve.

To review this section, remember that since an argument consists of premises (statements of evidence or reasons) that lead to a conclusion, there are three things that can be missing: the premises, the conclusion(s), and/or the connection between the two.

2.3d More practice identifying implied arguments

Assume that each of the following is an implied argument—what could that argument be? Again, consider using standard form.

(: marketing ( ) philosophy

1. In response to someone raising a question about morality, "This is a marketing meeting, not a philosophy seminar."

c. We should create jobs in solar

2. It costs more than $115,000 to create a job in crude oil production. It costs only $20,000 to create a job in solar energy production. We have an unemployment problem. We have an energy problem.

c: women should not join

3. The purpose of an army is to win wars, not promote equality. History shows that human factors like group cohesion, far more than weapons, determine victory. Women [in combat] would erode group cohesion because they distract men, who by instinct or culture would seek to protect them, and because they cannot enter into the male bonding process by which the esprit of combat units is built up.

(*New York Times*, January 6, 1990)

4. I don't doubt that the country is as rich in <u>moral values</u> as it is in apple trees, but I'm never sure that I know what the phrase means, or how it has come to be associated with the Republican Party, the Santa Fe Trail, or the war in Iraq. How is it moral for the President of the United States to ask a young American soldier to do him the service of dying in Fallujah in order that he might secure for himself a second term in the White House? Why is

it moral to deny medical care to 40 million people who can't pay the loan-shark prices demanded by the insurance companies and to allow 12 million American families to go hungry in the winter? What is moral about an administration that never goes before a microphone to which it doesn't tell a lie?

(Lewis H. Lapham, "Notebook—True Blue,"
Harper's Magazine, January 2005)

5. Species X became extinct through exposure to plant Y. But plant Y flourished for millions of years before X became extinct.

∴ Species X brought about plant Y's extinction

6. The day may come when the rest of the animal creation may acquire those rights which never could have been withholden from them but by the hand of tyranny. The French have already discovered that the blackness of the skin is no reason why a human being should be abandoned without redress to the caprice of a tormentor. It may one day come to be recognized that the number of the legs, the villosity of the skin, or the termination of the *os sacrum* are reasons equally insufficient for abandoning a sensitive being to the same fate. What else is it that should trace the insuperable line? Is it the faculty of reason, or perhaps the faculty of discourse? But a full-grown horse or dog is beyond comparison a more rational, as well as a more conversable animal, than an infant of a day, or a week, or even a month, old. But suppose they were otherwise, what would it avail? The question is not, Can they reason? nor Can they talk? but, Can they suffer?

(Jeremy Bentham, *The Principles of Morals and Legislation*, 1789)

Animals should be treated with respect concerning suffering

7. Setting up shop in developing countries and providing jobs will help those countries.

moving industry to developing nations will improve both sides

8. Why do we never ask, "Can a *man* have a career and a family too?"

9. "Stay here!" (said while brandishing a missile launcher)

— stay still or I will shoot

10. "Oh," said the doctor to the woman seeking contraception, "so you want to have your cake and eat it too!"

2.4 Circular arguments (an error in reasoning)

If the premise is supposed to prove the conclusion, or at least provide evidence or reasoning in support of accepting the conclusion, the premise cannot *presume* the conclusion. You can't assume to be true what you're trying to prove to be true. If you do, you won't have proved *anything*!

This error in reasoning, or fallacy, is called a **circular argument** or circular reasoning—because the truth of your conclusion depends on the truth of your premise, which depends on the truth of your conclusion, which depends on the truth of your premise . . . you get the picture. We often make this mistake when we don't pay careful attention to our assumptions, since the circularity is often in the assumptions.

Consider the following:

Amsche: I know God exists because it says so in the Bible.
Noorst: But why do you accept the Bible as evidence?
Amsche: Because it is inspired by God!

Amsche's premise *depends* on the conclusion; it's supposed to *prove* the conclusion. Perhaps laying out the argument as follows will help:

The Bible is the inspired word of God. (This premise assumes God exists.)
The Bible says God exists.
Therefore, God exists.

So in essence Amsche is saying God exists, He inspired the Bible, so God exists. See the circularity? (God exists, so God exists.)

A better argument would be to establish that the Bible is sufficient evidence *without* recourse to God. Perhaps every other claim in the Bible is correct, so this claim, that there is a God, also in the *Bible*, is also likely to be correct. Perhaps you can establish the credentials of the people who wrote the Bible as authorities whose writing should be accepted. And so on.

Here's another example of circular reasoning:

Abortion is wrong because it's murder!

The argument is "Abortion is murder, so abortion is wrong!" but note that the speaker's premise implies that abortion is wrong (that's why it's called murder rather than self-defense, for example), which is what the speaker is trying to prove. The speaker has assumed, or presumed, what she or he is trying to prove.

If the speaker had argued instead that abortion is killing, and killing is wrong, so abortion is wrong, it would *not* have been a circular argument since we don't necessarily assume killing is wrong—there are many kinds of killing we condone.

> [Circular arguments] are like the proverbial three morons, each of whom tied his horse to another's horse, thinking that he had in this way secured his own horse. Naturally, all three horses wandered away because they were anchored to nothing but each other.
>
> S. Morris Engel, *With Good Reason*, 1999

The surprise quiz

Suppose a professor announces, "Some day this term, there will be a surprise quiz." And suppose a few students reason as follows. The quiz can't be given on the last day of the term because if it hadn't been given before then, it would have to be given on that last day—in which case they'd expect it and it wouldn't be a surprise. Nor can it be given on the second-to-last day because, again, if it hadn't been given before then, it would have to be given on that second-to-last day (since they just reasoned that the last day is out of the question)—in which case, again, they'd expect it and it wouldn't be a surprise. And so on for the third-to-last day, and the fourth-to-last day . . . They conclude that a surprise quiz can't be given.

Are they right? Is it impossible for the professor to give a surprise quiz?

The surprise quiz paradox has puzzled philosophers for some time and many "solutions" have been offered. One such solution draws attention to the circularity of the students' reasoning: concluding that the quiz could not be given on the last day requires as a premise that it not be given on the second-to-last day, but then concluding that it could not be given on the second-to-last day requires as a premise that it not be given on the last day. At that point, one presumes exactly what one is trying to prove (that it not be given on the last day). Is that a correct assessment, and hence solution, of the problem?

2.4a Practice identifying circular arguments

Which of the following "arguments" are simply circular arguments? Where applicable, re-craft the argument so it is error-free.

1. *Section 31 guy*: Bashir is a spy for the Dominion!!
   Cisco: You have no evidence of that!
   Section 31 guy: That's because they cover their tracks so well!
   Cisco: That's a circular argument and you know it!

   > (Inexact quote of exchange between Section 31 guy and Cisco from an episode of *Star Trek: The Next Generation*)

2. We should accept more students because then our tuition revenue would increase. And if we have more money, we could expand. And if we were bigger, we could accept more students.

3. Evil exists. So either God knows about it and can't do anything about it, in which case he's not all-powerful; or he knows about it and doesn't want to do anything about it, in which case he's not all-good; or he doesn't know about it, in which case he's not omniscient.

4. You have to be really intelligent to get into medical school, and since fewer black-skinned people are admitted into medical school than white-skinned people, blacks must be less intelligent than whites. That's why fewer blacks than whites are admitted into medical school.

45

P. π → benefits
P: businesses should max π
Sp: bus'l benefit from π

moral knowledge comes
from upbringing

5. Profit is good because it enables you to expand—to hire more people, open branches in new locations, and increase production and expansion. And those things are good because they increase profit.

6. If capitalists are required to share the wealth with the workers who produced it, they'll lose motivation to put their money at risk in productive enterprises. Many good things have come of taking such risk. And surely they're entitled to the entire return on their investment. True, they invest only the money, not the labor of how many workers, but the workers are paid a wage. Are they to be paid a wage *and* a share of the profit? Much of that profit is not earned by work, but by taking the risk.

7. There is such a thing as moral knowledge because moral knowledge is something that a good upbringing provides.

8. You can tell Stud is a real sleazeball—look at the people who hang around with him! They're sleazeballs! Because only sleazeballs hang around other sleazeballs!

9. We can conceive of God, something that is greater in all ways than anything else. A something that actually exists in reality is greater than something that exists only in our mind. Therefore, God actually exists.

(Anselm, *Proslogion*, 1078)

10. When a new "sports bar" opens in New York and it feature topless dancers, we understand that this seems natural to the bar's owner and its enthusiastic patrons. We sense a connection: there's something about male sports privilege that contributes to the sexual objectification and abuse of women. Given how pervasive and what cultural icons men's sports are, that's a scary thought.

(Mariah Burton Nelson, *The Stronger Women Get, The More Men Love Football: Sexism and the American Culture of Sports*, 1994)

2.4b More practice with circular arguments

Write three arguments that exhibit circular reasoning. Then rewrite your three arguments so they're error-free.

2.5 Counterarguments

The term **counterargument** is often loosely used to refer to any kind of objection to a given argument. More specifically, however, the term is used to refer to *an argument whose conclusion in some way counters that of another argument*. Suppose someone argues that criminal behavior is due to bad parenting. A counterargument might be that criminal behavior is due to poverty. In this case, the counterargument presents an alternative; more specifically, it presents an alternative explanation for a given phenomenon. It suggests that there is more to be said on the matter—and it is possible that both arguments are correct.

However, suppose the counterargument were that criminal behavior is *not* due to bad parenting. In this case, the counterargument explicitly challenges the original argument—it suggests that it is incorrect. Since the two conclusions are contradictory—"criminal behavior is due to bad parenting" and "criminal behavior is not due to bad parenting"—both can't be true.

2.5a Practice recognizing counterarguments

In which of the following pairs, is the second argument a counterargument to the first? Indicate whether the counterargument presents an alternative or a challenge.

1. (i) Sexual harassment is unwanted sexual attention that makes a person feel uncomfortable or causes problems in school or at work, or in social settings.

    (Princeton pamphlet)

    challenge

    (ii) Unwanted sexual attention is part of nature. To find wanted sexual attention, you have to give and receive a certain amount of unwanted sexual attention.
    (Katie Roiphe, *The Morning After: Sex, Fear, and Feminism*, 1993)

2. (i) The increase in children's allergies is due to their decreased fitness level. Kids don't go outside to play anymore!

    alternative

    (ii) The increase in children's allergies is due to the increase in air pollution. I wouldn't be surprised if all species were having more trouble breathing these days.

3. (i) It is necessary to take growth hormones if you want to win; every good athlete does it—that's why they're so good.

    alternative
    challenge

    (ii) It's possible to win without taking growth hormones; diet and training informed by sound biological principles will maximize your potential just as well.

4. (i) That's why gays are immoral: because they don't have kids.

    (ii) Many marriages are childless, some by choice, some not. Furthermore, heterosexuals don't divorce when they're past reproductive age.

    alternative

5. (i) Cigarettes should be taxed more heavily than other products because they are harmful to those who smoke.

    (ii) Taxing products that are harmful to the user reveals a very patronizing attitude on the part of the government; we're adults and if we want to engage in harmful behavior, that's up to us.

    challenge

47

2.5b Practice constructing counterarguments

Construct a counterargument to each of the following. First identify the conclusion of the given argument. Then come up with a counterconclusion—either a claim that presents an alternative or a claim that is an outright contradiction. Then see if you can construct an argument that would lead to that counterconclusion.

1. A house made of styrofoam? Sounds flimsy. But spray it with a new brick-like concoction called Grancrete, and it's virtually indestructible. Invented by scientists at Argonne National Laboratory near Chicago and builders at Casa Grande, a construction firm in Mechanicsville, Virginia, Gancrete is twice as strong as structural concrete and won't leak or crack. It's also affordable: When the first bags roll off the production line later this month, builders will be able to raise a home for $10 a square foot, compared with $150 for a standard U.S. home.

    Traditional concrete, composed of calcite, water and sand or stone, can take up to three weeks to harden. Grancrete dries in one day. Its main ingredients—magnesium oxide and potassium phosphate—form tighter bonds than those in the concrete mixture. Load the slurry into a handheld pump, spray it over a Styrofoam frame, and you've got a home in 24 hours flat.

    (Rena Marie Pacella, "Check This Out, Three Little Pigs!,"
    Popular Science, May 2005)

2. I no longer believe those who say that a poor politician could be a good President if he could only be appointed to the job. Without the qualities required of a successful candidate—without the ability to rally support, to understand the public, to express its aspirations—without the organizational talent, the personal charm, and the physical stamina required to survive the primaries, the convention, and the election—no man would make a great President, however wise in other ways he might be.

    (Theodore G. Sorensen, *Decision-Making in the
    White House: The Olive Branch or the Arrows*, 1963)

3. When doctors perform euthanasia, they're deciding who lives and who dies. Who are they to play God? Deciding who lives and who dies, that's up to God. Doctors should not perform euthanasia.

4. How about NOT going hunting in silly camouflage outfits and being photographed with blood dripping from the rifle hand? Really, guys, it doesn't prove strength or leadership ability. Try mentioning women's healthcare and pay equity, and having real conversations about how women in the United States are trying to combine family and career. Just a thought.

    (Elaine Lafferty, "Letter from the Editor: Going Forward with
    Grit and Wit in 2005," *Ms. Magazine*, Winter 2004/2005)

5. Why do women remain second-class citizens? Why is there a religion-fostered war against women's rights? Because the bible is a handbook for the sub-jugation of women. The bible establishes woman's inferior status, her "uncleanliness," her transgressions, and God-ordained master/servant relation-ship to man. Biblical women are possessions: fathers own them, sell them into bondage, even sacrifice them. The bible sanctions rape during wartime and in other contexts. Wives are subject to Mosaic-law sanctioned "bedchecks" as brides, and male jealousy fits and no-notice divorce as wives. The most typical biblical labels of women are "harlot" and "whore." They are described as having evil, even satanic powers of allurement. Contempt for women's bodies and reproductive capacity is a bedrock of the bible. The few role models offered are stereotyped, conventional and inadequate, with bible heroines admired for obedience and battle spirit. Jesus scorns his own mother, refusing to bless her, and issues dire warnings about the fate of pregnant and nursing women.

(Nontract no. 10, Freedom from Religion Foundation, 1993)

2.6 Identifying the issue of contention

In a perfect world, our conversations would go like this:

Smith: I think X because a, b, and c.
Jones: Yeah, I agree that X, but I think you're mistaken about c—it's not true. Even if it were, c doesn't lead to X. In fact, *d* leads to X.

Alas, in reality, our conversations go something like this:

Dilton: You know, I think this whole space thing is a waste of money.
Everest: Yeah, science always gets more funding than the arts.
Dilton: I mean, I know they're making discoveries, but are they really *important* discoveries?
Everest: We should fix the problems here on Earth first!
Dilton: Right!
Everest: But the space program has given us some neat things. Weren't microwave ovens the side-effect of some super-duper NASA research?
Dilton: Yeah, but if we just set out to invent microwave ovens, wouldn't that've been much more sufficient?
Everest: You know what? I'd like to know what we're going to say to the aliens when we *do* finally meet them.

Note that Dilton and Everest are talking about the same thing, more or less: the space program. But other than that, they're all over the place. Dilton starts reasonably enough with a claim that the space program is a waste of money. But

49

Everest's response doesn't address that claim at all: getting more money is a different issue than being a waste of money. Dilton's next comment returns to the initial claim, implying a reason to support that claim: the space program is a waste of money because the discoveries that are being made aren't important. Everest then makes an interesting point, but it's not clearly relevant: the issue is not whether space program funding should take precedence over Earth program funding, but whether space program funding is a waste of money. Then Dilton gets distracted by Everest's point, agreeing with it, and leaving the intial claim dangling. Everest goes off on a bit of a tangent then, claiming that the space program has been beneficial. That *could* be related to whether or not it's a waste of money, but Everest doesn't connect the two points. Dilton then returns to the initial claim, if we understand "efficient" to mean "less expensive"—but then Everest takes the discussion onto yet another tangent: what are we going to say to the aliens?

In order for a discussion to go anywhere, the people participating in the discussion have to be addressing the same point. So being able to identify that point, the specific issue of contention, is crucial. As you've seen with the discussion between Dilton and Everest, identifying the issue of contention often involves separating a number of issues.

It may help to know what sorts of things people may disagree about. They may disagree about . . .

- facts: the facts of the matter
- interpretation: what the facts of the matter indicate or imply
- definition: how the matter is best defined
- evaluation: how the matter should be judged morally, aesthetically, practically
- recommendation: what should be done with regard to the matter (this overlaps somewhat with interpretation and evaluation).

Then when you're trying to identify the issue of contention, it might help to use the word "whether": think to yourself, "The issue is *whether* or not blah-blah . . ." Another helpful strategy might be to ask, "What would resolve the disagreement?"—knowing what would resolve a disagreement might indicate what the disagreement is about in the first place.

Clearly articulating the issue—as opposed to getting the general idea—will go a long way toward enabling you to identify the premises and conclusions of the arguments.

2.6a Practice identifying the issue of contention

Identify the issue of contention in each of the following. In half of them, the speakers are not talking about the same issue, so in those cases, identify what issue each speaker is talking about.

1. *Tirreas*: It's a miracle!

   Shilby: No, it's not! It's just something we don't understand.

   Tirreas: Well, that's true enough. We surely don't understand God's ways!

   Shilby: But just because we don't understand something doesn't mean it's a miracle.

   Definition

2. *Dburn*: We should get rid of the legal aid system. Why should we, you and I, taxpayers, pay for someone else's divorce?

   Johanssen: But what about people who are evicted without notice? That's not fair! They should be able to go to court about that!

   Evaluation

3. *Turner*: This campus hate speech code is a crock. If it isn't illegal in the real world, it shouldn't be banned here on campus.

   Washington: Yeah, people should get a life. I mean, insults are a part of life. You just roll with it.

4. *Chang*: Given how uninterested men really are in women, I'm surprised so many women still want to get married.

   Santana: I find it puzzling too. Gloria Steinem once said that to men, families mean support and an audience, but to women, they just mean more work. So why is everyone so desperate—for more work?

   Chang: Men just want the sex, and the kids—the precious progeny, the knowledge that their genes live on. That's why they want to get married. But what's the big deal? Why is it so important that their genetic make-up continues? It's not like they're all Einsteins. It's ego. That's all. If they had to be the ones looking after those little gene-carriers, full-time, I bet they'd change their minds.

   Santana: Yeah, so why are so many women so eager? *They're* the ones gonna be looking after those kids 24/7.

   Interp

   whether marriage reveals men's values.

5. *Longspoon*: I can't do my research project on my tribe's politics! Insiders can't research themselves! They're not sufficiently objective, they're too involved.

   Charrier: But objectivity, detachment, neutrality—these things don't necessarily make for the best social research.

   Evaluation

   whether tribe's politics insider research is good.

6. *Jibler*: You know, we wouldn't have a problem with these mega-stores coming in and putting all the local small stores out of business if things weren't cheaper by the dozen.

   Chowski: What do you mean?

   Jibler: Well, it's bulk pricing that enables the huge stores to have such low prices—they buy so much of the stuff, they get a good price, and they pass that on to the customer.

   Chowski: So you're saying they shouldn't get bulk pricing?

51

Jibler: Well, why should something be cheaper just because you're buying two of it?

Chowski: I think you might be right. I mean, a sweater is a sweater is a sweater. It should cost X number of dollars because that's how much it cost—that's how much wool how many hours it takes to make it. It doesn't suddenly take less wool or less time if someone buys two of them, so why should they pay less per sweater?

[margin note: Interp whether Big Business profits (+) or (-)]

7. Pro-life: Abortion is wrong because it's ending a life!
   Pro-choice: It's my body, so it's my choice!

8. *Notharly*: I don't think doctors should tell prospective parents whether it's a boy or a girl. Sex selection only reinforces our sexist society. What can boys do that girls can't? And vice versa?

   Smythe: But a lot of parents want boys to carry on the family name or take over the family business. Anyway, just because the parents know, it doesn't mean they'll abort if it's not the sex they want.

   Notharly: Sure they will.

   Smythe: No, they won't. A lot of people are against abortion. And anyway, a lot has to do with how you raise the kids. A baby girl isn't necessarily going to grow up to be a passive, little wife.

   [margin note: Whether it's right to prefer sex for baby]

9. *Massi*: Grocery stores should be forced to label genetically modified foods. We have a right to know what we're buying.

   Shkov: Don't worry! GM foods are safe! GM is a good thing! We can make crops drought-resistant, and pest-resistant. Fruit and vegetables can stay ripe longer. W can make them contain higher levels of vitamins and minerals. That's all good!

   Massi: But it's my money.

   Shkov: You're probably just upset because of all those articles that say GM stuff will disturb the natural balance. But we do that all the time, whenever we plant crops.

   Massi: But GM seed doesn't replicate itself like normal seeds; farmers will be forced by huge mega-agribusinesses to pay their high prices for seed.

   [margin note: Facts]

10. *McDein*: Now that I know he's into drugs, I'm going to boycott all his movies.

    Roulin: But that doesn't make any sense. You may think using drugs is morally wrong, but so what? If he's a bad actor, *then* don't go see his movies.

    McDein: Well, he should at least apologize.

    Roulin: To who? For what? If you lie to me, should you have to apologize at work, to your boss, to your office-mates?

    McDein: No, because that's my personal life. And it's none of my boss' business. Or my office-mates' business.

Roulin: Exactly. What an actor does on his own time is his personal life. If he messes up a role, *then* you can insist on an apology.

McDein: But it's different. He's a public figure, a celebrity. It's like when a politician has an affair.

Roulin: Yeah . . . and that's her own business too. If she embezzles public monies, then okay, you have cause for complaint.

McDein: But they're role models!

Roulin: Says who? Did he ever say he was a role model? No! *You've* made him into one—he didn't agree to be some shining example of humanity. So he hasn't broken any promise.

2.7 The burden of proof

The **burden of proof**—the responsibility for providing proof, or more loosely, for providing supporting evidence of some kind, for some claim—is on the person making the claim. That means that if you say X is so, it's up to you to prove that X is so; you can't say "Well, X is so because no one has proved it isn't." In fact, that would be an appeal to ignorance, which is an error in reasoning (see next section).

A qualification to the general rule that the person making the claim has the burden of proof is that the person making the *positive* claim has the burden of proof. So if your claim is "X is *not* so," it's up to the person who insists that "X *is* so" to provide the evidence. This is because it's generally harder to prove something is *not* the case than it is to prove that it *is* the case. For example, to prove that "Swans are black" (a positive claim), one need present only one black swan. But to prove that "Swans are *not* black" (a negative claim), one would have to find and present every known swan, showing that every single one of them was not black. (Not necessarily white, mind you, just not black.)

Consider this excerpt from *E is for Evidence*, a novel by Sue Grafton:

"Facts, my ass. I never saw Lance Wood before in my life."
"Sure, but can you prove it?"
"Of course not! How would I do that?"

Indeed! How *could* she prove that she never saw him? The burden of proof is not on her, but on whoever says she did.

Also, it's a general rule that the more extraordinary the claim, the more extraordinary the proof must be. If you claim that it will most likely snow this winter, we will probably be satisfied with a few facts about temperature and moisture and snowfall during past winters. However, if you claim that this winter the snow will be multi-colored, we'll expect your supporting reasoning to be a little more extensive.

> What can be asserted without proof can be dismissed without proof.
>
> Christopher Hitchens, *Free Inquiry*, June/July 2004

2.7a Practice recognizing the correct placement of the burden of proof

In which of the following arguments is the burden of proof in the right place? For those in which the burden of proof is in the wrong place, indicate where it should be; that is, who needs to prove which claim?

1. Exercise can help keep your mind young, and I can prove it!

2. *Hebner*: I was abducted by aliens!
   Lattler: I don't believe you. Do you have any evidence?
   Hebner: Of course not—do you think the aliens would let me bring anything back with me? You'll just have to believe me.
   Lattler: No, I don't have to just believe you. You have to convince me—with proof!

3. You don't believe in God? Okay, prove it! Prove to me there's no God!

4. We should not have to prove that they have weapons of mass destruction; it is up to them to prove that they don't.

5. We just supply the demand, consumers are in control; if they don't want it, they should stop buying it. We can't prove it, of course, and we shouldn't have to. That's just the way it is. So you can't blame us for the proliferation of products you think are bad.

6. *Kowalski*: If we legalize marijuana for medicinal use, a lot of people will use it for non-medicinal uses.
   Bendetta: Can you provide evidence for that claim?
   Kowalski: Yes, I can—I've researched the history of similar substances that have both medicinal and non-medicinal uses, and in every case, legalizing the substance led to both kinds of use.

7. *Etheridge*: I tell you, air pollution triggers heart attacks! A recent study in *The New England Journal of Medicine* reported that people traveling in cars were less apt to have a heart attack than people traveling by bicycle.
   Smeal: It's probably the exercise that triggered the heart attack, not the air pollution!
   Etheridge: Prove it!
   Smeal: No, *you* prove it!

8. This will cure your baldness! Don't ask how I know! Try it for yourself and see!

9. A risk-assessment approach to environmental protection puts the burden of proof on those environmental and residential groups claiming that certain industry activity puts the environment at risk of degradation.

10. You're firing me because I haven't been "appropriately deferential"? Prove it!

2.8 The appeal to ignorance (an error in reasoning)

This error in reasoning occurs because of an incorrect understanding of who has the burden of proof. Suppose I claim there's a rare dinosaur-like sea creature who lives in the deepest part of the ocean's trenches. You'd rightly say to me, "Prove it!" If I want to make that claim, I have to provide proof. I can't just say, "Well, prove to me there isn't!" That would make the default position something like "Accept everything until you have reason not to." Imagine that for a moment, and you'll realize how crazy that would be: people could claim all sorts of ridiculous things, and we'd all be walking around accepting them because no one had proved them wrong yet. And that scenario doesn't begin to address the ridiculous things that are simply unprove-able. How could you prove, for example, that there *isn't* a rare dinosaur-like sea creature who lives in the deepest part of the ocean's trenches—especially if I told you it has never been seen and lives in places that are so deep that humans will never be able to explore them. The far more reasonable default position is "Don't accept a claim until you have good reason to accept it." And that's exactly the position that is established by putting the burden of proof on the person making the claim.

So, *just because a claim hasn't been proven to be false, it doesn't mean it's true.* Conversely, *just because a claim hasn't been proven to be true, it doesn't mean it's false.* For example, it may be the case that there is no proof that wearing a copper bracelet reduces the severity of arthritis, but that doesn't mean you should conclude that wearing a copper bracelet does *not* reduce the severity of arthritis; it may simply be that we haven't yet done enough research or the right kind of research on the matter. (The appeal to ignorance is, thus, an error of truth, and we'll come back to it in Chapter 6.) When there is insufficient proof one way or the other, you should suspend judgment.

We tend to make this error when we don't actually have any evidence or reasons for our belief. So if you catch yourself shifting the burden of proof to the other person—insisting they provide evidence *against* your claim—check yourself: are you doing that because you don't have any proof *for* your claim? If so, it's much better to abandon your claim—or get the evidence!

Always ask, who has burden of proof?

2.8a Practice recognizing an appeal to ignorance (an error in reasoning)

Which of the following contain an appeal to ignorance?

1. We have found no evidence suggesting there wasn't a Loch Ness monster, so we conclude the story has credibility.

2. Why do you say that television should not be allowed in the courts? Where is the evidence that if court trials are televised, they'll be less fair?

3. *Jefferson*: You say now that you like the guy, but you'll go out with him for a while, and eventually the novelty will wear off, and you'll get bored, and then you'll say "Oh, how could I ever have liked him?!"
   Pratt: You don't know that!

4. To repeat, just about every important long-run measure of human welfare shows improvement over the decades and centuries, in the United States as well as in the rest of the world. And there is no persuasive reason to believe that these trends will not continue indefinitely.

   (Julian L. Simon, "More People, Greater Wealth, More Resources, Healthier Environment," *Economic Affairs*, April 1994)

5. One only has obligations to the future if these obligations are based on reliable information. There is no reliable information at present as regards the distant future. Therefore one has no obligations to the distant future. We don't know whether future generations will even exist, let alone their wants and needs.

2.8b More practice with appeals to ignorance

Write three arguments that have an appeal to ignorance.

Then rewrite your three arguments so they're error-free.

2.9 Facts and opinions

As mentioned in the opening section of this chapter, a claim can be a fact or an opinion. It's important to know the difference between the two because they require different support and can be argued to different degrees of certainty.

A **fact** is *a statement about the world as it is*; it is a statement verifiable, at least in theory, by empirical observation, *objectively* (that is, using agreed upon methods that don't depend on any one person). What I mean by "at least in theory" is that you know *how* to verify it even though, for some reason, it's impossible. For example, we can in theory verify that all swans are white; we just need to find every single swan in the world and take a look. But in practice, well, would we be able to do that? No doubt, a swan or two will escape our attention. Support for a fact, thus, usually consists of empirical evidence, evidence available to our sensory perception—things we can see, hear, touch, smell, and taste. And facts can often, but not always, be accepted with complete certainty. You can say "true" and "false" about a fact (though if it were false, I guess we wouldn't call it a fact). It is a fact that my dog Taffi is brown and white. I can say I *know* this, and it can be verified, by anyone, using simple visual observation as the colors of her fur are plainly visible.

An **opinion** is *a statement about the world as one thinks it is or should be or could be*. Support for an opinion usually consists of reasons, but facts, or at least empirical evidence, may also be involved (either as part of those reasons or as

56

reasons in and of themselves for holding the opinion in question). Opinions are not "true" or "false"—they are acceptable to varying degrees, dependent upon their support. It is my opinion that Taffi doesn't much care what color she is. I think this, but don't know it, because I have never seen her show a preference for other dogs on the basis of their color; that's the reason for my opinion. (However, if I could somehow verify objectively whether she does or does not care about what color she is—if I could figure out how to do that, even in theory—then it would be a matter of fact.)

It is important to note that arguments can, and should, be made to support *both* facts and opinions. As mentioned in the opening chapter, just because something is a matter of opinion, it doesn't follow that all opinions are equally good, equally strong. *Some opinions are better than others*: those backed by argument, that is, those with support, are better than those without support, and those with strong support are better than those with weak support.

Consider an argument for the claim that Bobby Jo did not kill Jeremiah. Whether he did or did not is a fact; we may not know at the moment, but there is an absolute, objective, truth of the matter one way or another. Evidence in support of that claim might include the following:

- According to well-qualified and well-experienced coroners (two of them, investigating independent of each other), Jeremiah was killed somewhere between 10:00 a.m. and 4:00 p.m. on June 6, 2004.
- Bobby Jo was teaching a class on flower arranging between 11:00 a.m. and 12:00 p.m. Several students insist that he was indeed there, in person, teaching such a class. They saw him, spoke with him, and generally interacted to a degree sufficient to establish that it is extremely unlikely it was someone other than Bobby Jo.
- Bobby Jo's family members and neighbors saw him leave his house at 9:00 a.m. Two neighbors actually accompanied him for the full two hours it takes to get from his house to the school by train. Those two neighbors also teach at the school.
- From 12:00 p.m. until 5:00 p.m., Bobby Jo was at an insufferably long staff meeting. He left on two occasions for about ten minutes each time, both times returning with a cup of coffee. He was chairing the meeting.
- The meeting occurred at the school, which is in Florida. Jeremiah was killed at his home. In France.

Each of these pieces of evidence can be determined to be true objectively. That means that any skilled coroner would establish the time of death in France as between 10 and 4, anyone present could see Bobby Jo in Florida from 9 to 5, and so on. And together, they prove that Bobby Jo could not have killed Jeremiah.

Now consider an argument for the claim that Bach's music is great music. Aesthetics are a matter of opinion, rather than a matter of fact. Nevertheless, empirical evidence can be relevant. Support for the claim might include the following:

- Great music is that which has a consistent rhythm and more than ten harmonic changes.
- Bach's music has a consistent rhythm. There is not one piece composed by him that changes rhythm from beginning to end.
- Bach's music has more than ten harmonic changes. Analysis of every single piece he's written indicates that the minimum number of harmonic changes in any one piece is fourteen.

The second and third premises can be established objectively, by anyone; they are matters of fact (note, however, that I'm not sure they're correct). Given the first bit, that great music has a consistent rhythm and more than ten harmonic changes, the empirical evidence presented in the second and third bits makes the argument an excellent argument. Note, however, that the first bit is a matter of opinion. So part of the support for the opinion that Bach's music is great is another opinion. That's how it often goes. But you have to start somewhere. The strong arguments start with "givens" that are generally uncontested, even though they may not qualify as facts. So if it was generally accepted that great music is that which has a consistent rhythm and more than ten harmonic changes, then the claim that Bach's music is great music has to be accepted.

Or consider an argument for the claim that parents should be licensed. Morality (and if we're dealing with "should" issues, we're dealing with moral issues) is a matter of opinion, rather than a matter of fact. Nevertheless, again, empirical evidence can be relevant. Support for the claim might include the following:

- We license plumbers; surely our children are more important to us than our toilets.
- Incompetent parents have the potential to cause serious injury, and licensing parents could prevent incompetent people from becoming parents.
- We screen people before we allow them to adopt children, and rightly so. There is no significant difference between raising a child that is biologically related to you and raising one that is not, so we should screen people before we allow them to raise their own children as well.
- It is morally wrong to create a human being that will experience pain and suffering because of some genetic disease; licensing could prevent such genetic cruelty.
- Most child abuse occurs because the children were not really wanted by their parents; if people have to go through some licensing process before becoming parents, children will more likely be wanted children.

Some premises can be established as fact: we *do* license plumbers; we *do* screen adoptive parents. Others are matters of opinion, some of which are pretty uncontestable (our children are more important to us than our toilets), and some of which are perhaps more contestable (it is morally wrong to create a human being that will experience pain and suffering). To the extent that one finds the contestable premises acceptable, and the overall reasoning sufficient, one would accept the conclusion.

The difference between fact and opinion is loosely paralleled by the difference between knowledge and belief. We know—or can come to know—facts. We believe opinions—or more precisely, we believe they are worth endorsing, worth acting on.

Note that I said "loosely"—in some cases, belief can become knowledge. I may not know now whether Taffi is inside or outside (she is free to go in and out through her own door), but I believe she's inside, and I have good reasons for believing that (I'm inside, and she generally prefers to be where I am). If I want, I can go look for her, and, assuming I find her either inside or outside, I will then know where she is. So at first I may have an opinion about a factual matter, and then, if I obtain proof that my opinion is correct, I have knowledge about that factual matter. But, as I've said, only in some cases can belief become knowledge; my belief that she doesn't care what color she is isn't likely to become something I will ever know as a fact.

At least, that's the simplified version of facts and opinions, knowledge and belief. Some philosophers actually disagree about whether there are any facts at all, and some philosophers argue that there are moral facts rather than, as is my stance throughout this text, moral opinions. (But I reiterate—just because something's an opinion doesn't mean it can't, doesn't mean it shouldn't, be argued for!)

Furthermore, the requirements for knowledge are still under debate. The standard view is that knowledge is belief that is justified and true; that is, if we believe something to be true, and we are justified in believing it to be true (we have good reason to believe it to be true), and it is indeed true, then we can say we know it. Philosophers have questioned one or more of those conditions. (And we'll get into this a little more in Chapter 6.)

Because established facts are generally uncontestable (they're *established*), people often call opinions "facts"—hoping to manipulate us into uncritical acceptance.

Consider this argument:

??

Let's face facts: the current prime minister has not handled international affairs very well, she's a disaster with the media, and the budget is a mess. It's time for a replacement.

?
these aren't
facts — they sound more
like opinions!

You'll note that it's really a matter of opinion as to whether the prime minister has handled international affairs very well (how are we defining "very well"?), whether she's a disaster with the media (how are we defining "disaster"?), and whether the budget is a mess (how are we defining "mess"?). As opinions, those three claims are contestable, and we may not have to face them after all, let alone agree that it's time for a replacement.

2.9a Practice distinguishing facts from opinions

Identify which of the following are matters of fact (claims that can be known, whether or not they actually are known, to be true or false) and which are matters of opinion.

1. This music is awful!

2. You'll hear many claims about audio systems, but the truth is, nothing sounds as good as live.

     (www.bose.com/auto ad)

3. It's wrong to envy someone else, to be jealous of who they are or what they have.

4. Military recruiters offer $30,000 to sign up, while on average only $7,000 is spent on education per student in public schools.
     (From a pamphlet published by the Global Women's Strike/Phila, philly@crossroadswomen.net www.optoutofwar.net)

5. When Van Morrison visits a recording studio, you can bet your worn-out vinyl copy of *Hard Nose the Highway* he will not leave until he has recorded some seriously astral Irish blues poetry ("Celtic New Year"), tributes to his pop-culture heroes ("Just Like Great") and a lot of mellow, easy-rolling, folk-jazz numbers about the evils of the modern world and the struggle of the poet.
     (Rob Sheffield, review of Van Morrison's "Magic Time," *Rolling Stone*, May 19, 2005)

6. God gets right to the source of most of our problems: SIN. The Bible says, "All have sinned and fall short of the glory of God" (Romans 3:23).

7. On any given day, hundreds of thousands of people are in a rush.

8. People who listen to music during surgery with local anaesthetic experience less stress than those who do not listen to music.

9. No ancient civilization is more commonly associated with the word "collapse" than that of the Maya of Central America. In the ninth century A.D., the Mayan population fell from at least 5 million people to a tenth that size or less . . .
     . . . Typifying the Mayan collapse was a kingdom whose ruins now lie in western Honduras, at a site known as Copán . . .
     Five strands, or major factors, contributing to the downfall of Copán can be tentatively identified. The first strand was simply that population growth was outstripping the available resources. The second strand, already

mentioned, compounding that mismatch, was the array of negative effects that were brought on by deforestation and hillside erosion. The third strand was increased warfare, as neighboring kingdoms fought over their diminishing resources. Bringing matters to a head was a fourth strand: climate change. The worst drought to strike the region in 7,000 years began about A.D. 760 and peaked about 800. By then there were no unoccupied favorable lands to which people could move to save themselves. The ensuing decline in the Mayan population must have come about partly from starvation and warfare, as well as from a fall in the birthrate and in the survival rate of children.

The fifth strand was a failure of the Mayan kings and nobles to address problems within their control. The attention of the leaders was evidently focused on enriching themselves, waging wars, erecting monuments, competing with each other, and extracting enough food and other resources from the peasants to support those activities. Like most leaders throughout human history, the Mayan kings and nobles did not heed long-term problems, if they noticed them at all.

(Jared Diamond, "Collapse," *Natural History*, April 2005)

10. But meetings [between organ donors and recipients] or even a written contract are not for everyone. I've seen cases in which it was not a good idea.

(Lisa Colainni, donor family advocate at the Washington Regional Transplant Consortium, as quoted by Gretchen Reynolds in "Heart to Heart," *O: The Oprah Magazine*, November 2004)

2.10 Deductive and inductive argument

A chapter on the nature of argument would not be complete without a consideration of the distinction between deductive argument and inductive argument. It's a distinction that becomes especially important when you evaluate arguments.

The conclusion of a sound **deductive argument** *necessarily* follows from its premises: as long as the premises are true, the conclusion is true; it cannot be false—and there is no question about it. So even if you "don't agree" with the conclusion, you have to accept it. However, in the case of an **inductive argument**, it's a matter of strength rather than logical necessity: the degree to which you accept the conclusion of an inductive argument *depends on the strength of the argument*.

Another way of saying this is that in the case of a deductive argument, *the conclusion makes explicit what's already implicitly contained in the premises*; it merely articulates the logical implications of the premises. So, in a sense, a deductive argument tells us nothing new about the matter. In the case of an inductive argument, however, *the conclusion goes beyond the information of*

nothing new in conclusion

61

the premises; it articulates new knowledge. In a way, deductive argument is convergent thinking, whereas inductive argument is divergent thinking.

Perhaps now is a good time to emphasize, then, that when you're evaluating an argument, *whether you agree or disagree with the conclusion is irrelevant*; you can't accept an argument just because you agree with the conclusion, and you can't reject an argument just because you don't agree with the conclusion. For example, you can't say "Okay, I accept the premise that alcohol can cause physical and mental birth defects" and "Yes, I accept the premise that fetuses in the uterus get whatever drugs the mother takes," and then say "But I don't accept the conclusion that when a pregnant woman drinks alcohol, she may be causing her baby to have physical and mental birth defects." If you accept the premises, and there has been no error connecting them to the conclusion, you must accept the conclusion.

Quite apart from the logical necessity of this, if you're going to just accept or reject a conclusion according to what you want to believe, regardless of the support, what's the point of having an argument in the first place? If you're going to ignore the evidence, the reasons, the reasoning, what's the point—in thinking about anything? Just believe what you want, just do what you want! See, that's the beauty of all this argument stuff: it's *not* "just a matter of opinion"—*there are clear rules of reasoning that will lead you to clear, defensible, opinions.*

Consider the following example:

> I know that cheating is on the rise. Students can get essays off the internet and most professors don't even know it. I don't think they even read our essays half the time. Or maybe they do but don't think much about whether it's worth an A or a B or whatever. Students who cheat on exams shouldn't be allowed a second try.

You may agree with the conclusion—students who cheat on exams shouldn't be allowed a second try—but you can't accept it *on the basis of this argument* because the premises don't support the conclusion, they don't lead to that conclusion. The first premise merely notes that cheating is on the rise, but how is that relevant to whether or not students who cheat on exams should be given a second try? The next two sentences talk about cheating on essays, not exams, so again there's the question of relevance. If you want to have a defensible opinion about students who cheat on exams, you'll have to come up with premises that actually support that opinion.

Consider the following example:

> It's always better if only one person dies than if five people die, so since the five of us are stuck on this island with no food, it's perfectly acceptable that four of us kill the other one for food.

You might object to the conclusion because it's distasteful (!), but the argument is valid, so *unless you object to one of the premises*, you have to accept the conclusion.

To reiterate, when you're dealing with arguments, it's important not to direct your attention to the conclusion, but rather to the reasoning, to the premises and their relation to the conclusion. When you construct an argument, don't start with the conclusion you want: start with the evidence, the reasons, and go where they lead. Ask yourself what conclusions, if any, can be drawn from what you know. If you can't draw any conclusions, then find out more, increase your knowledge—and in the meantime, suspend your judgment. Similarly, when you evaluate an argument, examine the premises and their relation to the conclusion, not the conclusion.

So how do you examine the premises and their relation to the conclusion? How do you evaluate the argument? In the case of *deductive* argument, if the premises are *true* and the form is *valid*, it's what we call a *sound* argument—and the conclusion is *necessarily* true. No ifs, ands, or buts.

> true premises + valid form = sound argument

In the case of *inductive* arguments, if the premises are *true*, *relevant*, and *sufficient*, the argument is a *strong* argument—and the conclusion is *probably* true. The weaker the argument (typically, the less sufficient the premises), the less probable the conclusion.

> true/acceptable + relevant + sufficient premises = strong argument

Often, but not always, the reasoning in deductive arguments goes from the general to the particular: for example, we might start with the general fact that all fish swim, and conclude that if this particular creature is a fish, this particular creature can swim. Conversely, often, but not always, the reasoning in inductive arguments goes from the particular to the general: for example, we might experiment on one hundred particular people and discover that each of them is disoriented when awakened in the middle of the night by a giggling rhinoceros, so we conclude that, in general, people are disoriented when awakened in the middle of the night by a giggling rhinoceros.

There are two kinds of deductive argument: one is based on categorical logic (also called predicate logic), and the other is based on propositional logic (also called sentential logic or truth/functional logic). Categorical logic deals with, surprise, categories of things. Propositional logic deals with propositions about things. In both cases, the syllogism dominates. A *syllogism* is deductive argument with two premises. Here's an example of a syllogism using categorical logic:

Rationalizing is the very opposite of reasoning; whereas reasoning works from evidence to conclusion, rationalizing works from conclusion to evidence. That is, rationalizing starts with what we *want* to be so and then selectively compiles "evidence" to prove that it *is* so.

Vincent Ryan Ruggerio, *Beyond Feelings: A Guide to Critical Thinking*, 2003

> All dogs are cute.
> <u>Taffi is a dog.</u>
> Therefore, Taffi is cute.

And here's an example of a syllogism using propositional logic:

> If cats think at all, they're thinking alien thoughts.
> <u>Cats do think.</u>
> Therefore, cats think alien thoughts.

Inductive argument is not so easily classified, but we'll consider generalizations, analogies, general principles, and causal reasoning. Generalization involves making a general claim based on specific evidence because of quantitative force (reasoning from an adequately sized study sample to the general case or from the frequency of past or present occurrences to present or future occurrences) or from qualitative similarities (reasoning from a representative study sample to the general case). Arguing by analogy (reasoning from one situation to an analogous situation) will be considered along with generalization based on qualities because both depend on similarities. We'll also consider what is sort of the reverse of generalization: arguments that apply a general principle to a specific case. Causal reasoning involves determining which of several possible explanations is the best account.

As for evaluating arguments, then, remember the following: For *deductive* arguments, if the *premises are true*, and the *form is valid*, you have a *sound argument*, and you can (indeed, you must) *accept the conclusion as certain*.

truth + validity = soundness (certain conclusion)

Note that we're *not* using the word "valid" as it is commonly used, to mean simply "good" (as in "That's a valid point"). Rather, we're using the word as logicians use it, to refer to a correct argument structure. This is addressed in the logic supplements.

For *inductive* arguments, if the *premises are true or at least acceptable*, and *relevant*, and *sufficient*, you have a *strong* argument, and you can *accept the conclusion as probable*. The more acceptable and sufficient the premises, the stronger the argument (the more probable the conclusion).

truth/acceptability + relevance + sufficiency = strength (probable conclusion)

Keep in mind that the strength of an inductive argument depends on what type of argument it is: if it's a generalization, for example, strength depends on sample representation and size; if it's an analogy, strength depends on the relevant similarities, and so on. We'll talk about truth and acceptability in Chapter 6, relevance in Chapter 5, and sufficiency in Chapters 7 and 8.

Why don't the premises of a deductive argument have to be relevant and sufficient? They do—that's built in to validity: if you have a valid form, the premises *will be* relevant and sufficient.

Lastly, it's always important to anticipate objections (often called rebuttals) to the argument at hand, whether you're evaluating an argument or constructing it. Objections—to validity, truth, relevance, or sufficiency—may indicate that the argument should be modified (corrected or strengthened), accepted with reservations, or rejected. All of which is good to know before you invest too much in it—before you go through too much of your life accepting its conclusion!

Review of terms

Define the following terms:

- argument

- premise

- conclusion

- circular argument (an error in reasoning)

- counterargument

- burden of proof

- appeal to ignorance (an error in reasoning)

- fact

- opinion

- deductive argument

- inductive argument

Thinking critically about what you see

Determine whether or not each of the following is presenting an argument (explicitly or implicitly). If it is, articulate the point and the reasons/evidence supporting that point. If not, explain why not.

1.

© Corbis

claim: animals can feel

P 2:

P 2 : It is unjust to keep captive, those that can feel

PC : wrong to captive animals

2.

Background picture © Corbis

P 1: If you work hard deserve a reward

P 2: Drinking sweets makes people feel good

PC : we should drink sweets it we've worked hard

Thinking critically about what you hear

Listen to the audio clip under the Student Resources tab on the companion website at www.routledge.com/textbooks/tittle. Any response?

Thinking critically about what you read

Think critically about each of the following, focusing, at this point in time, on the first two steps in the template—but feel free to go wherever your thought takes you . . . especially if it takes you to steps 5, 6, and/or 7!

Template for critical analysis of arguments

1. What's the point (claim/opinion/conclusion)?

    ■ Look for subconclusions as well.

2. What are the reasons/what is the evidence?

    ■ Articulate all unstated premises.
    ■ Articulate connections.

3. What exactly is meant by . . .?

    ■ Define terms.
    ■ Clarify all imprecise language.
    ■ Eliminate or replace "loaded" language and other manipulations.

4. Assess the reasoning/evidence:

    ■ If deductive, check for truth/acceptability and validity.
    ■ If inductive, check for truth/acceptability, relevance, and sufficiency.

5. How could the argument be strengthened?

    ■ Provide additional reasons/evidence.
    ■ Anticipate objections—are there adequate responses?

6. How could the argument be weakened?

    ■ Consider and assess counterexamples, counterevidence, and counter-arguments.
    ■ Should the argument be modified or rejected because of the counter-arguments?

7. If you suspend judgment (rather than accepting or rejecting the argument), identify further information required.

1. The paradox, say the skeptics, is that HOT-lanes [High Occupancy Toll lanes of traffic that allow drivers without passengers to drive on them for an extra fee] may actually increase car use: by freeing up extra capacity on the freeways, they allow more cars to use them. Nonetheless, simply to get at least some people from A to B quickly, it would surely be sensible to make more HOT-lanes available.

   ("America's Great Headache," no author, *The Economist*, June 4, 2005)

2. I have my own opinion as to which is more important—car or driver—but before voicing it I thought I'd ask some of the experts, starting with newly crowned Champ Car World Series titlist Sébastien Bourdais. "A good driver without a good car is not gonna do anything," said Bourdais. "But a bad driver in a good car is not gonna go anywhere either. So I think it's pretty much a toss-up." . . .

   Former Champ-car driver Chip Ganassi . . . said the balance between car and driver depends on the type of racing. "In some series a great driver can overcome a not-so-good car. In other series a good car can overcome some deficiencies in the driver." In the Nextel Cup, for example, where the rules are quite restrictive and the cars are relatively simple, the driver is much more important. Conversely, in the IRL or Champ Car where you have a highly engineered piece of machinery, if you get the car set up right a lot of guys can drive it—at least at the very top levels of the sport. . . .

   Indy 500 winner Bobby Rahal . . . explained that with the onset of major technological advances, which began a quarter-century ago, the car began to play a greater role in the quest for victory . . .

   World Champion and America's ambassador to racing Mario Andretti says that when you add it all up, it's 50 percent car, 50 percent driver, although some days it may be 70 percent driver, 30 percent car. "A driver contributes more at Monte Carlo than at Indianapolis," said Mario, adding that it also depends on racing conditions. "On a wet day a driver contributes maybe 70 percent of the equation." Andretti said that in the old days when cars were slower and simpler, the driver made a huge difference. "If the car didn't work well you had to *wrassle* with it, but with today's specialized cars, there's only so much a driver can contribute."

   (Joe Rusz, "Pole Position: Car or Driver?," *Road & Track*, February 2005)

3. Parents of severely diseased or defective newborns may reasonably choose not to authorize life-prolonging interventions when one of several conditions obtain: (1) extended life is reasonably judged not to constitute a net benefit to the infant; (2) it is reasonably believed that the infant's condition is such that the capacities sufficient for a minimal independent existence of personhood in a strict sense cannot be attended; or (3) the costs to other persons, especially parents and family, are sufficient to defeat customary duties of beneficence toward a particular human infant.

   (Earl E. Shelp, "Deciding the Fate of Critically Ill Newborns,"
   Born to Die: Deciding the Fate of Critically Ill Newborns, 1986)

4. Most people do not know what sin is. It is generally assumed that sin is doing what one thinks or feels is wrong—or what is viewed as wrong by society generally. But that is IGNORANCE!

And it could be very costly ignorance! The first thing we need to get settled in our minds is this: The living GOD of ALL POWER does not allow us to decide WHAT is sin! He forces us to decide WHETHER to sin! And the PENALTY of sin is DEATH for all eternity! That penalty is REAL! It is an Awful—a FRIGHTFUL fate!

(Herbert W. Armstrong, Worldwide Church of God)

5. Is there an international Islamic threat? Will humanity witness the rise of a "new Comintern" led by "religious Stalinists" poised to challenge the free world and impose Iranian-style Islamic republics through violence, or through an electoral process that enables Islamic movements to "hijack democracy"?

Muslims vary as much in their interpretations of Islam as followers of other faiths with theirs. For the vast majority of believers, Islam, like other world religions, is a faith of peace and social justice, moving its adherents to worship God, obey His Laws, and be socially responsible.

(John L. Esposito, "Political Islam: Beyond the Green Menace," *Current History*, January 1994)

6. The US has rejected the Kyoto Protocol, and they produce at least four times its per capita share of carbon dioxide emissions. They have opposed the establishment of an International Criminal Court (unless its own soldiers and government officials are exempt from prosecution) and helped establish the World Trade Organization as a mechanism for "accelerating and extending the transfer of people's sovereignty from nation states to global corporations" invariably expressing US interests.

(Simon Eassom, quoting Peter Singer, *The Philosophers' Magazine*, 25, 2004)

7. At the root of many of the assumptions about biology and intelligence is the undeniable fact that there have been fewer women "geniuses." The distribution of genius, however, is more a social than a biological phenomenon. An interesting aspect of the lives of geniuses is precisely their dependence on familial, social, and institutional supports. Without schools to accept them, men of wealth to commission their work, colleagues to talk to, and wives to do their domestic chores, they might have gone unrecognized—they might not even have been so smart.

(Sheila Tobias, *Overcoming Math Anxiety*, 1978)

8. We now engage in a wide variety of practices to control, influence, or select the genes and characteristics of offspring. Most of these techniques involve carrier and prenatal screening and operate in a negative way by avoiding the conception, implantation, or birth of children with particular characteristics. But there is a large amount of active genetic selection, albeit at the gross level, that occurs in choosing mates or gametes for reproduction, or in deciding which embryos or which fetuses will survive and go to term.

Cloning does differ in some ways from existing selection technology. Because it actively seeks to replicate DNA, it involves positive choice rather than negative deselection, as occurs with most other means of genetic selection. In addition, it selects or replicates the entire genome (except for mitochondria), rather than focus on the presence or absence of particular genes. Yet neither of these differences are qualitatively different from the genetic selection that now occurs in reproductive medicine. If cloning does not lead to tangible harm to others, it should be no less legally available than existing practices are.

(John A. Robertson, "A Ban on Cloning and Cloning Research is Unjustified," Statement, National Bioethics Advisory Commission, Full Committee Meeting, 1997)

9. I think we have to admit that talk of Santa is a lie and can sometimes do harm. Some kids are bitterly disappointed when their illusion is shattered, and some are morally confused. ("Mom and Dad say not to lie, then do it themselves.") Fortunately, this doesn't happen often. Usually the Santa lie, befitting Christmas, is a white one.

For starters, the lie is only temporary. You tell kids about Santa now, but you'll straighten them out later. The deception isn't forever.

And the deception is a mild one. You don't take a falsehood and call it truth; you take a fiction and call it truth—a smaller distortion. This means the loss of the illusion is gentler. When kids are older they don't lose Santa entirely, they just think of him in a different way.

Finally, the deception is good for kids. Believing in Santa adds magic and excitement to Christmas; the anticipation is keener, the delight sharper. Parental love is fine and even profound, but a guy from the North Pole is far more exotic.

(Thomas Hurka, *Principles: Short Essays on Ethics*, 1994)

10. The Gross Domestic Product (GDP) is the tool economists use to gauge the economy . . . The GDP is the value of all goods and services produced in a country. But the GDP makes no distinction between good and bad activity. It also ignores important parts of the economic engine. [For example,] pollution is counted as economic growth when we spend money to clean it up, [and the] GDP ignores so-called "non-monetary" activity such as the unpaid household and child-rearing work that many women do every day. That's why think tanks such as *GPI Atlantic* are arguing to scrap or at least augment the GDP with something called the Genuine Progress Index (GPI). In contrast to the GDP, which merely measures overall economic production, the GPI adjusts for resource depletion, housework, volunteer work, long-term environmental damage and pollution.

("Grossly Inaccurate," no author, *Sustainable Times*, Spring 1999)

Thinking critically about what you write

Okay, your turn. Write an argument of your own. First, think of some opinion, some claim, you want to argue for. That's your conclusion. Then think of two reasons to accept your claim. Those are your premises. Put your argument in standard form. Be as precise as possible with the way you word everything. Make sure your two premises do indeed give reason to accept your conclusion, your main point. Then write it up in a paragraph. Check it for clarity and coherence. This is best done by coming at it fresh, so put it aside for an hour or a day.

Now, when I say check it for coherence, what I mean is don't make your reader play "Connect the Dots"—articulate the connections between your sentences with words like *because*, *since*, *so*, *therefore*, *consequently*, and so on. If you don't, and they have to connect your dots, two things may happen: they may connect them in a way you didn't intend or they may simply not bother. Either way, they won't have understood your argument.

The easier it is for someone to follow your argument, the better you have written it! Consider the following paragraph:

> Why should she get a lighter sentence because she has kids? Next time I plan on committing a crime, maybe I should get pregnant first. Or at least get a couple of dogs and say, hey, you can't put me in prison, I've got a couple of dogs to look after. It's unfair, when a person's sentence is being considered, to take into account whether there are people depending on that person. The sentence is supposed to be punishment for the crime. Whether or not people are depending on a person doesn't change the fact that the crime was committed. One of the reasons for sentences in the first place is deterrence. Whether or not people are depending on the person is irrelevant. If we give people lighter sentences when they have dependants, crime will be encouraged. People will know that as long as they've got kids, they'll get off lightly. We sentence people to prison in order to protect society. We shouldn't reduce the sentence if the person has dependants. We should extend it. I mean, we should be keeping criminals *away from* children, not letting them have responsibility for and influence over them! Who will look after the kids if she's in jail? Well, if she's a jail candidate, it shouldn't be her in any case! Who will pay the rent and put food on the table if he's in jail? He will! Make him work while he's in jail, so he can continue to pay for his kids' food, clothing, and shelter. (He should continue to pay for his own food, clothing, and shelter too—jail should not be a free ride!)

Could you follow the argument? (Prove it—how many premises are there?)

Now read this version (I've bolded the connecting words):

> Why should she get a lighter sentence because she has kids? Next time I plan on committing a crime, maybe I should get pregnant first. Or at least get a couple of dogs and say, hey, you can't put me in prison, I've got a couple of dogs to look after. It's

unfair, when a person's sentence is being considered, to take into account whether there are people depending on that person. **This is so because, first,** the sentence is supposed to be punishment for the crime, **and** whether or not people are depending on a person doesn't change the fact that the crime was committed. **Second,** one of the reasons for sentences in the first place is deterrence. **Again,** whether or not people are depending on the person is irrelevant. If we give people lighter sentences when they have dependants, crime will be encouraged **because** people will know that as long as they've got kids, they'll get off lightly. **Third,** we sentence people to prison in order to protect society. **So** we shouldn't reduce the sentence if the person has dependants. **On the contrary**, we should extend it. I mean, we should be keeping criminals *away from* children, not letting them have responsibility for and influence over them! **Oh, but** who will look after the kids if she's in jail? Well, if she's a jail candidate, it shouldn't be her in any case! Who will pay the rent and put food on the table if he's in jail? He will! Make him work while he's in jail, so he can continue to pay for his kids' food, clothing, and shelter. (He should continue to pay for his own food, clothing, and shelter too—jail should not be a free ride!)

My guess is you found the second version easier to follow.

Note, in both versions, the use of example in the second sentence. Examples always improve the likelihood of being understood correctly.

Note also the consideration of counterarguments in the last few sentences (from "Oh, but who will look after . . ."). It strengthens your case when you can anticipate and provide adequate responses to objections.

Now, having studied these two examples, go back if you like and improve what you wrote.

Thinking critically when you discuss

Much of what we need to think critically about occurs in the context of conversation. Unfortunately, most of us find it far more difficult to make an argument when we're just talking than when we can write it out; probably this is so because writing enables us to reconsider and revise very easily. Also, most of us find it far more difficult to follow an argument when we're listening to someone than when we're reading what they may have written; our attention span isn't very good and we simply can't hold that much in our mind at once. Not surprisingly, then, most conversations aren't very good for discussing what we think about things. Recall the examples given in Section 2.5.

So, to help you have a *coherent* conversation, a discussion about something that actually goes somewhere (and everyone has good reason to be frustrated with a discussion that doesn't go anywhere), I offer this training exercise: thinking critically about what you hear and say. Like the other "Thinking critically . . ." end of chapter exercises, it will appear at the end of each chapter, but each time it'll be a little more complex, a little more realistic.

73

When someone makes an argument, there are several ways you can respond:

1. You can *ask for clarification*—perhaps you don't really understand how the pieces fit together or perhaps you don't understand what one particular piece means.
2. You can *accept or reject a premise*. There are only three good reasons for rejecting a premise:
   (i) it's simply not true (or acceptable);
   (ii) it's not relevant to the conclusion;
   (iii) it's not strong enough to support the conclusion (it's insufficient).

   Any one of those reasons is reason enough to reject a premise, but in order to accept a premise, all three conditions—truth/acceptability, relevance, sufficiency—must be met.

   Keep in mind that rejecting a premise may or may not require you to reject the conclusion: it depends on whether that premise is the only one or, if not, how important it is (for example, whether all the other premises depend on it).
3. You can *strengthen the argument* either by adding detail or example to a premise, by modifying a premise to make it acceptable, relevant, or sufficient, or by adding a completely new premise that supports the conclusion.

And that's about it. Anything else you might say is pretty much off-topic.

The following chart summarizes your response options: The "(?)" reminds you of option 1, asking for clarification. The "(*)" reminds you of option 3, adding detail or example; the blank rows at the bottom also remind you of option 3, adding premises. The boxes beside each premise are for option 2, indicating whether you accept or reject a premise, and on which grounds: if you find premise 1 true, for example, put a "✓" in the "true/acceptable" column of the premise 1 row; if you find premise 2 irrelevant, put an "✗" in the "relevant" column of the premise 2 row; and so on. Consider each criterion for each premise. The little box in the bottom right corner is for your response to the conclusion—a "✓" or "X" to indicate whether you accept or reject the conclusion (and remember you could accept the conclusion even if you have a few Xs in the premise boxes—perhaps the Xs are for unimportant premises or perhaps you have added some very supporting premises).

	true/acceptable	relevant	sufficient
premise 1 (?) (*)			
premise 2 (?) (*)			
premise 3 (?) (*)			
Therefore, conclusion:			

Finally, there is one more option:

4. You can accept the argument (or not) and *present a counterargument*. Typically, this would be a brand new argument that leads to a conclusion counter to the proposed conclusion, such that they both can't be true—so you'd have to decide which is the stronger argument.

You can use the chart as a sort of shorthand for your response. For example, something like "I know your first premise to be true (or I don't know but I think it's plausible so I'll give you the benefit of my ignorance of the moment). Still, I don't think it's relevant to your conclusion because . . . So, regardless of the sufficiency of your premise, I can't accept your conclusion because you only offer one premise," would look like the following:

	true/acceptable	relevant	sufficient
premise 1: [. . .]	✓	✗ because [. . .]	n/a
Therefore, conclusion: [. . .]			✗

—except that you'd jot in the actual premise, reasons, and conclusion where I've put the brackets. So it'll help if you take notes while you're taking part in a discussion—notes of what others are saying and notes of what you're thinking about what others are saying.

And something like "I challenge the truth of your first premise because [insert counterevidence]. Consequently, whether or not it's relevant and sufficient, it simply can't be called upon as support for your conclusion. Your second premise is acceptable (I'm not exactly sure it's true, but it fits with other stuff I'm sure is true), and it's relevant; however, by itself it's not sufficient for your conclusion, which is stated rather strongly. So I'll either accept a weaker version of your conclusion, or, better, let me add a third premise which I claim is true and relevant, and, together with your second premise, sufficient to support your conclusion as stated" would look like this:

	true/acceptable	relevant	sufficient
premise 1: [. . .]	✗ because [. . .]	n/a	n/a
premise 2: [. . .]	✓	✓	} ✓
premise 3: [. . .]	✓	✓	
Therefore, conclusion: [. . .]			✓

Get the idea?

So, let's start, easy. Arrange yourselves in groups of three. One person initiates the discussion by presenting a very simple argument: one premise leading to a conclusion. For example, someone might start by saying something like "Whether or not you're in class doesn't necessarily indicate whether or not you're learning the material [that's the premise], so I don't think professors should take attendance [that's the conclusion that follows from the premise]." You might articulate an assumed premise about professors' jobs being to measure whether or not students have learned the material. Then the other two people respond, each responding to the argument made by the first person, choosing from the four options and using the chart above.

Then switch and repeat, so each person has a turn initiating with an argument, and each person has two turns responding.

Suggestion: In discussions, it may help to think of yourself, and everyone else, as putting forth positions. The position you put forth at any given time doesn't necessarily have to be the position you personally subscribe to at the moment. In fact, people don't even have to know whether or not you agree with the position you're advocating. That way, people can agree or disagree *with the position*, not with you. (Note, though, that in the real world, there's something terribly dishonest—to yourself and to others—about advocating a position you *don't* subscribe to. And I think it's important that people know when you're doing that.) This is a really good habit to get into; see the ad hominem error covered in Chapter 4 (Section 4.2.1). Also, it enables you to play with all sorts of positions, which is a great way to develop, evaluate, and refine your opinions.

Reasoning test questions

Success on reasoning tests depends partly on mental speed and mental stamina—being able to concentrate, intensely, for the full time allotted. If you're too slow, you won't get all the questions done, and if you "run out of steam" part way through, you won't do well on the questions at the end. So do all of the following questions at one sitting, with no breaks, and time yourself. (Although the number and mix of questions differs from test to test, to give you an idea . . . the Logical Reasoning section of the LSAT has 25 questions and allows you 35 minutes to complete the section.)

For further preparation (test preparation publications, online tutorials, and, perhaps most important, complete sample tests), see the following websites:

www.lsac.org for LSAT preparation
www.ets.org for GRE preparation
www.aamc.org for MCAT preparation
www.mba.com for GMAT preparation

Each of the following is a Logical Reasoning question from an LSAT preparation test; the GMAT has a similar section on each of its tests, and the MCAT also includes such reasoning questions. (The GRE tests reasoning with an essay writing question—see Chapter 5 and the "Thinking critically about ethical issues" supplement on the website.)

1. Prolonged exposure to nonionizing radiation—electromagnetic radiation at or below the frequency of visible light—increases a person's chances of developing soft-tissue cancer. Electric power lines as well as such electrical appliances as electric blankets and video-display terminals are sources of nonionizing radiation.

    Which one of the following conclusions is best supported by the statements above?

    (A) People with short-term exposure to non-ionizing radiation are not at risk of developing soft-tissue cancers.
    (B) Soft-tissue cancers are more common than other cancers.
    (C) Soft-tissue cancers are frequently cured spontaneously when sources of non-ionizing radiation are removed from the patient's home.
    (D) Certain electrical devices can pose health risks for their users.
    (E) Devices producing electromagnetic radiation at frequencies higher than that of visible light do not increase a person's risk of developing soft-tissue cancers.

    (The Official LSAT Prep Test XXI, Section 3, #18)

2. After purchasing a pot-bellied pig at the pet store in Springfield, Amy was informed by a Springfield city official that she would not be allowed to keep the pig as a pet, since city codes classify pigs as livestock, and individuals may not keep livestock in Springfield.

The city official's argument depends on assuming which one of the following?

(A) Amy lives in Springfield.
(B) Pigs are not classified as pets in Springfield.
(C) Any animal not classified as livestock may be kept in Springfield.
(D) Dogs and cats are not classified as livestock in Springfield.
(E) It is legal for pet stores to sell pigs in Springfield.

(The Official LSAT Prep Test XXIII, Section 3, #3)

3   *Francis*: Failure to become properly registered to vote prevents one-third of the voting-age citizens of Lagonia from voting. If local election boards made the excessively cumbersome registration process easier, more people would register and vote.

Sharon: The high number of citizens not registered to vote has persisted despite many attempts to make registering easier. Surveys show that most of these citizens believe that their votes would not make a difference. Until that belief is changed, simplifying the registration process will not increase the percentage of citizens registering to vote.

The main issue in dispute between Francis and Sharon is

(A) whether changing the voter registration process would be cumbersome
(B) why so many citizens do not register to vote
(C) what percentage of those registered to vote actually vote
(D) whether local election boards have simplified the registration process
(E) why the public lacks confidence in the effects of voting

(The Official LSAT Prep Test XXIV, Section 3, #1)

4. Electrical engineers have repeatedly demonstrated that the best solid-state amplifiers are indistinguishable from the best vacuum-tube amplifiers with respect to the characteristics commonly measured in evaluating the quality of an amplifier's musical reproduction. Therefore, those music lovers who insist that recorded music sounds better when played with the best vacuum-tube amplifier than when played with the best solid-state amplifier must be imagining the difference in quality that they claim to hear.

Sound Q quantifiable

Which one of the following, if true, most seriously weakens the argument?

(A) Many people cannot tell from listening to it whether a recording is being played with a very good solid-state amplifier or a very good vacuum-tube amplifier.
(B) The range of variation with respect to the quality of musical reproduction is greater for vacuum-tube amplifiers than for solid-state amplifiers.
(C) Some of the characteristics that are important in determining how music sounds to a listener cannot be measured.

79

(D) Solid-state amplifiers are more compact, use less power, and generate less heat than vacuum-tube amplifiers that produce a comparable volume of sound.

(E) Some vacuum-tube amplifiers are clearly superior to some solid-state amplifiers with respect to the characteristics commonly measured in the laboratory to evaluate the quality of an amplifier's musical reproduction.

(The Official LSAT Prep Test XXI, Section 3, #23)

5. Early in the development of a new product line, the critical resource is talent. New marketing ventures require a degree of managerial skill disproportionate to their short-term revenue prospects. Usually, however, talented managers are assigned only to established high-revenue product lines and, as a result, most new marketing ventures fail. Contrary to current practice, the best managers in a company should be assigned to development projects.

Which one of the following, if true, most strengthens the author's argument?

(A) On average, new ventures under the direction of managers at executive level survive no longer than those managed by lower-ranking managers.

(B) For most established companies, the development of new product lines is a relatively small part of the company's total expenditure.

(C) The more talented a manager is, the less likely he or she is to be interested in undertaking the development of a new product line.

(D) The current revenue and profitability of an established product line can be maintained even if the company's best managers are assigned elsewhere.

(E) Early short-term prospects of a new product line are usually a good predictor of how successful a product line will ultimately be.

(The Official LSAT Prep Test XXII, Section 4, #8)

chapter 3

the structure
of argument

Template for critical analysis of arguments

1. What's the point (claim/opinion/conclusion)?

   ■ Look for subconclusions as well.

2. What are the reasons/what is the evidence?

   ■ Articulate all unstated premises.
   ■ Articulate connections.

3. What exactly is meant by . . .?

   ■ Define terms.
   ■ Clarify all imprecise language.
   ■ Eliminate or replace "loaded" language and other manipulations.

4. Assess the reasoning/evidence:

   ■ If deductive, check for truth/acceptability and validity.
   ■ If inductive, check for truth/acceptability, relevance, and sufficiency.

5. How could the argument be strengthened?

   ■ Provide additional reasons/evidence.
   ■ Anticipate objections—are there adequate responses?

6. How could the argument be weakened?

   ■ Consider and assess counterexamples, counterevidence, and counter-arguments.
   ■ Should the argument be modified or rejected because of the counter-arguments?

7. If you suspend judgment (rather than accepting or rejecting the argument), identify further information required.

3.1 The structure of argument

Arguments come in many shapes—whatever is necessary to make the case. Convergent arguments (sometimes called simple arguments) are those in which one (single) or more (multiple) premises lead to a conclusion; in the case of multiple premises, the premises can be independent of each other (separate) or dependent on each other (linked). Divergent arguments (sometimes called complex arguments) are those in which a single premise diverges into two or more conclusions. And, of course, arguments sometimes need to be multi-structured—because of sub-arguments, an extended argument may incorporate several of the preceding structures, the conclusion of one argument becoming the premise of another.

Don't forget to engage—think while you read!

3.2 Convergent, single

As explained in the opening section of this chapter, an argument consists of a premise leading to a conclusion. So the basic structure would be as follows:

premise

↓

conclusion

However, if you insert a premise and a conclusion, such as the following—

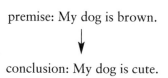

premise: My dog is brown.

↓

conclusion: My dog is cute.

—you'll quickly see that you actually need a second premise:

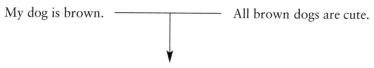

My dog is brown. ——————————— All brown dogs are cute.

Therefore, my dog is cute.

Now the argument makes sense: if my dog is brown, and if all brown dogs are cute, then it follows that my dog is cute. I can *conclude* that my dog is cute. So, to revise the earlier definition, an argument almost always consists of a *set* of premises leading to a conclusion. Notice how there's a single line of reasoning converging to a conclusion; hence, we'll call this argument structure a **single convergent** structure.

Here's another example of a single convergent argument:

> In determining whether animals should have rights, one should not consider whether they are rational or can converse, but only whether they can suffer.
> (Paraphrase of Jeremy Bentham, *The Principles of Morals and Legislation*, 1789)

Creatures that can suffer ——————— Animals can suffer.
should have rights.

Therefore, animals should have rights.

3.2a *Practice identifying single convergent arguments*

Which of the following arguments are single convergent arguments?

1. Having this part-time job will not be detrimental to my studies because the job requires only ten hours a week, leaving over forty-five hours of study time (the recommended three hours outside of class for every hour of class; I have five courses, each of which meet for three hours a week).

2. Having the dog wear a variety of hats on the trip, like those of firefighters, police officers, construction workers, and cowboys, helps reduce road rage.
   (William J. Thomas, *The Dog Rules (Damn Near Everything!)*, 2003)

3. Pesticides can't be that bad for the environment—they make fruit and vegetables look nice.

4. Only those who have already given birth should be allowed to become surrogate mothers, because unless you've gone through it you can't possibly know what it's like, and if you don't know what something's like, you can't possibly give true consent to that something.

5. With all these headaches, who'd even want to be CEO? It's an apt question. Leslie Gaines Ross, chief knowledge officer at Burson-Marsteller, has surveyed executives at Fortune 1000 companies, asking how many aspired for a promotion to the corner office. In 2001, 27 percent said they had no interest in becoming chief executive. By 2004, that number jumped to 60 percent . . . It's important to keep such survey data in perspective: thanks to huge compensation packages and mankind's instinctive appetite for power and

perks, there will always be someone who wants to be the boss. But in this day and age, having the title of boss and having real power aren't necessarily the same thing.

(Daniel McGinn, "Building a Better CEO," *Newsweek*, March 28, 2005)

3.2b Practice diagramming single convergent arguments

Diagram the single convergent arguments of the preceding exercise.

3.2c Practice constructing single convergent arguments

Try constructing your own argument, using the single convergent structure. A diagram is fine.

3.3 Convergent, multiple-separate

When two or more *separate* lines of reasoning lead to the same conclusion, we have a **multiple-separate convergent** argument.

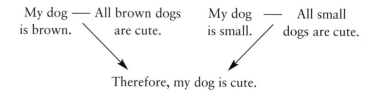

Note that the two arguments are *independent* of each other: if one of them turns out to be a bad argument, you can still accept the conclusion if the other argument is okay. However, you may accept it with less confidence since the overall argument is now weaker, with one less supporting line of reasoning.

Here's another example of a multiple-separate convergent argument:

The province of Quebec has no army. In fact, no Canadian province has an army, since we rely upon the federal government for national defense. At a time when Quebec's place within the Canadian confederation is being questioned, some may ask whether it is not futile for Quebeckers to campaign for the abolition of the army. On the contrary, we believe that the moment could not be better. First of all, we all know that staunch supporters of federalism have not hesitated to use the army against Quebec in the past. ① There is no guarantee that they would not feel tempted to do it again. Secondly, the road to independence may be long and difficult and, during this process, we would still have to pay for the army. ② And finally, since Canada would be our neighbor after independence, it would be in our best interest to

*new
argument?* (3) make sure that Canada adopts a policy of nonviolence, both for Quebec and
for the impact that this nonviolent position could have worldwide. Some may
ask themselves as well whether an independent Quebec should have an army.

(The Committee for the Abolition of the Army,
"Manifesto for the Abolition of the Army," 1992)

*conclusion —
Quebeckers should
support abolition of the
federal army*

Federalists might use
the army against us.

We'd have to pay
for the army.

Nonviolence is in
our best interests.

Therefore, we (Quebeckers) should campaign for
the abolition of the army.

Note that in this case, there are simply independent reasons rather than independent complete arguments that support the conclusion.
And note the annotations—just a reminder to you!

3.3a Practice identifying multiple-separate convergent
arguments

Which of the following arguments are multiple-separate convergent arguments?

C

1. Military air shows should be opposed because they pretend to be educational
    events to teach children and youth about aviation, science, and technology, (1)
    but they're really marketing opportunities for military corporations to peddle
    their deadly products of war; they glorify war machines and romanticize as (2)
    heroes those who wield and use deadly weapons, they promote war as the (3)
    best means of resolving conflicts while totally ignoring peaceful means, they (4)
    associate positive feelings of fun and joy with technology that causes grief
    and misery, and they are ecologically destructive (those warplanes burn more (5)
    fuel per hour than the average US car in a year).

    (*Press for Conversion!* July 2002)

2. Sociologists Candace West and Donald Zimmerman did some extensive
    eavesdropping at various sites around the University of California campus at
    Santa Barbara and found that men interrupt women much more often than
    C they interrupt other men and that they do so more often than women inter-
    rupt either men or other women. In analyzing her tapes of men and women
    who live together, Pamela Fishman found that topics introduced by men
    "succeeded" conversationally 96 percent of the time, while those introduced
    by women succeeded only 36 percent of the time and fell flat the rest of the
    time. Men can and will talk—if they can set the terms.

There are all kinds of explanations for the conversational mismatch between the sexes, none of which require more than a rudimentary feminist analysis. First, there's the fact that men are more powerful as a class of people, and expect to dominate in day-to-day interactions, verbal or otherwise. Take any intersex gathering and—unless a determined counter-effort is undertaken—the basses and tenors quickly overpower the altos and sopranos.

For most men, public discourse is a competitive sport, in which points are scored with decisive finger jabs and conclusive table poundings, while adversaries are blocked with shoulder thrusts or tackled with sudden interruptions. This style does not, of course, carry over well to the conversational private sector. As one male informant admitted to me, albeit under mild duress, "If you're just with a woman, there's no real competition. What's the point of talking?"

(Barbara Ehrenreich, The Worst Years of Our Lives:
Irreverent Notes from a Decade of Greed, 1991)

3. Regarding Judy McGuire's screed on tipping ("Tips on Gratuity," 6/8): Nobody should ever have to tip for a service they are already paying for. It's humiliating for employees to have to put together tips to make rent, and annoying for customers to have to waste time attaching a monetary figure to a worker's performance. In civilized countries (Japan, Italy, etc.) neither waiters nor waitresses nor bartenders nor taxi-drivers sweat customers. And why is that? They're paid a wage they can live on. Which brings us to the real point: The real cheapskates are not the patrons who leave chump on the bar, but the bar owners who fob off on their customers the responsibility for paying their employees.

(T.M. Gendron, Cuernavaca, Mexico, letter to the editor,
New York Press, June 22–28, 2005)

4. I agree that companies should not have to provide benefits to same-sex partners. But then, I don't think they should have to provide benefits to other-sex partners either. Why should a company pay for the upkeep of their employees' partners?

5. The right to a job? Is there such a thing? On what basis? One might say that it's prerequisite for the pursuit of life, liberty, and happiness? Wait a minute— I have a *right* to happiness? How much happiness? (I can imagine that if an employer has to pay Person A $X for A to be happy, then s/he can't hire Persons B, C, or D, which causes them unhappiness, or then the employer will have to raise prices, so neither E nor F will be able to buy the product, which will make them unhappy, not to mention the employer him/herself— perhaps we're confusing the right to X with the right to *pursue* X, or even the right to pursue, *on equal grounds*, X.)

87

3.3b Practice diagramming multiple-separate convergent arguments

Diagram the multiple-separate convergent arguments of the previous exercise.

3.3c Practice constructing multiple-separate convergent arguments

Try constructing your own argument, using the multiple-separate convergent structure (develop two separate lines of reasoning that lead to the same conclusion). Again, a diagram is fine.

3.4 Convergent, multiple-linked

In this case, the multiple lines of reasoning that lead to the single conclusion are *linked* together—hence, the name **multiple-linked convergent** structure.

Consider this argument:

Since the skies are clear tonight, and it's mid-November, when the Earth passes through the Leonid meteors, I'll probably see some meteors tonight.

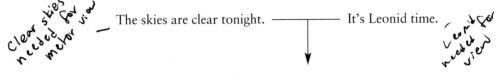

Clear skies needed for meteor view   The skies are clear tonight. ——————— It's Leonid time.   *Leonid for needed view*

So, I'll probably see some meteors tonight.

Notice how the two premises are connected with an arrow. That indicates that they are linked, and *together* they provide support for the conclusion. The skies being clear, alone, wouldn't lead to the conclusion since there might not be any meteors to see. And it being Leonid time, by itself, wouldn't lead to the conclusion since the skies might be cloudy. Only when the two premises are linked together is there support for the conclusion.

Note that in the case of multiple-linked convergent arguments, the link is between two arguments, not, as in the case of single convergent arguments, between one premise and another, the other premise usually being a generalization that makes the first premise relevant to the conclusion. Those generalization premises are also required in the case of multiple-linked convergent arguments. In the example under consideration, we need the additional premise that clear skies are required in order to see meteors for the first premise, the first argument, and we need the additional premise that when the Earth passes through the Leonids they're visible from Earth for the second premise, the second argument. Not only are the premises linked to their accompanying generalization premises, the two arguments—the one about clear skies and the other about it being Leonid time—are linked. They are *dependent* on each other. That means that if one of them turns out to be a bad argument (for example, if one or both of the premises is false—perhaps it's not true that the skies are clear tonight), then the whole argument collapses. *That's* what makes it a multiple-linked convergent argument.

| The skies are clear tonight. | ─┬─ | Clear skies are required to see meteors. | ── | It's Leonid time. | ─┬─ | When the Earth passes through the Leonids, they're visible from Earth. |

Therefore, I'll probably see some meteors tonight.

3.4a Practice identifying multiple-linked convergent arguments

Which of the following are multiple-linked convergent arguments?

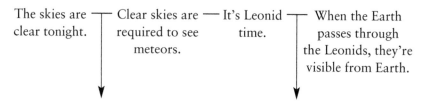

1. When Chessie (the canine I lived with before Taffi) went suddenly blind, she seemed not to know it at first and continued to race around like always. I thought for sure she was going to hurt herself.

2. Whoever is responsible for workplace health and safety should make hiring scabs illegal. When people go on strike, it should be illegal for management to hire replacement workers. It's simply a matter of safety. Replacement workers are unqualified. And in our particular industry, being qualified means knowing how to do the job safely.

3. Life is like a box of chocolates and chances are the key ingredient, coca, was grown and harvested with child labor. More than a quarter of a million children as young as six work in West Africa's cocoa industry, reports the Nigeria-based International Institute of Tropical Agriculture. On Ivory Coast plantations, which supply 40% of the world's cocoa, an estimated 15,000 children are slaves kidnapped by traders or lured with false promises of high pay. For up to 18 hours a day, children use machetes to harvest coca beans from jungle farms. Without masks or other protective equipment, they spray crops with insecticides and pesticides. Farmers claim they rely on underage laborers because they are paid so little for their crops that they cannot afford adult wages. Global chocolatiers like Nestlé and Hershey's have pledged to take steps to end child labor in the industry by 2005. In the meantime, you can sample slave-free chocolate from health food stores or your local fair trade organization.
    (Sarah Cox, "Made by Children, for Children,"
    This Magazine, January/February 2004)

4. Before you decide to enlist, look carefully at what you'll actually be doing—not just your job title. You may find that your job isn't what you thought it would be. The military might not give you the job training and work experience you expect. Jobs with fancy sounding titles often are low skill and non-technical. Many military jobs are so different from civilian jobs that you may not be able to use your training after you leave the military, or you may have to be retrained. The military is not required to keep you full time in the job for which you trained or for the entire time you are in the military. The military's money for education plan (New GI Bill) is not as easy to use as it sounds. It is only after you leave the military that you find out whether you've met all of the requirements. The largest amount of money mentioned in the ads—$50,000—is offered only to those GIs who take jobs the military has a hard time filling.

(American Friends Service Committee, National
Youth & Militarism Program, Philadelphia, 2000)

5. Euthanasia is wrong. First off, it's killing. And killing is wrong. Second, if we make it okay, then doctors and nurses might not try as hard to save you, and then that attitude would carry over to those patients who are not suitable candidates for euthanasia, so it would lead to an overall decline in the quality of medical care.

3.4b Practice diagramming multiple-linked convergent arguments

Diagram the multiple-linked convergent arguments of the previous exercise.

3.4c Practice constructing multiple-linked convergent arguments

Try constructing your own argument, using the multiple-linked convergent structure (think of two or more lines of reasoning that depend on each other to lead to a conclusion). Again, you can present it in a diagram.

3.5 Divergent

Another structure involves one premise that leads to two or more different conclusions (rather than two or more premises leading to the same conclusion). This is called a **divergent** argument, and it is perhaps most common when arguing from a single premise to several conclusions that are consequences of that premise.

Note how, in the following example, the single premise *diverges* into two conclusions:

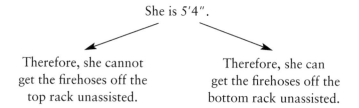

She is 5'4".

Therefore, she cannot get the firehoses off the top rack unassisted.

Therefore, she can get the firehoses off the bottom rack unassisted.

Of course, the argument needs two other premises in order to work: the top rack is 7' off the floor, and the bottom rack is 3' off the floor.

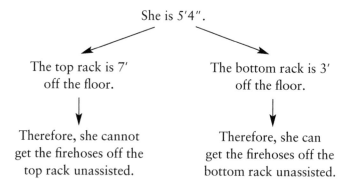

She is 5'4".

The top rack is 7' off the floor.

The bottom rack is 3' off the floor.

Therefore, she cannot get the firehoses off the top rack unassisted.

Therefore, she can get the firehoses off the bottom rack unassisted.

Here's another example of a divergent argument:

Summerhill School is a progressive, co-educational, residential school, founded by A.S. Neill in 1921. One of the unusual features of the school is that all lessons are optional. Teachers and classes are available at scheduled times, but the children can decide whether to attend or not. This gives them the freedom to make choices about their own lives and means that those children attending lessons are motivated to learn.

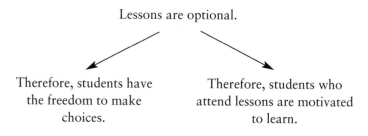

Lessons are optional.

Therefore, students have the freedom to make choices.

Therefore, students who attend lessons are motivated to learn.

Although these two examples had one premise leading to two conclusions, keep in mind that there may be *more than* two conclusions following from a single premise. (Also, note the assumption that being motivated to learn is the only reason children attend lessons!)

3.5a Practice identifying divergent arguments

Which of the following are divergent arguments?

1. Women are much better than men on their feet, they're more coordinated with their feet. That's why they make better dancers. And why they make better soccer players.

2. American foreign policy is almost never analyzed in terms of the psychology of its makers. By unwritten consensus, this influence on public policy has been regarded as too personal and too subjective to be reliable. In fact, the taboo exists because the men who make the policy and analyze it are often uncomfortable with and ill-equipped to understand the role that their personal feelings and values play in decisions of state. As a result, men tend to be not only unwilling to focus on the role that their own psychology plays in their decisions but also only dimly aware that they have distinct psychological biases.

    (Marc Feigen Fasteau, *The Male Machine*, 1975)

3. Since 1995, the Atlantic has been in a period of higher hurricane activity. Scientists say the cause of the increase is a rise in ocean temperatures and a decrease in the amount of disruptive vertical wind shear that rips hurricanes apart. Some researchers argue that global warming fueled by man's generation of greenhouse gases is the culprit.

    Forecasters at the National Hurricane Center say the busy seasons are part of a natural cycle that can last for at least 20 years, and sometimes up to 40 or 50. They say the conditions are similar to those when the Atlantic was last in a period of high activity in the 1950s and 60s.

    It's also difficult to know whether the Atlantic was even busier at any time before record keeping began in 1851. And satellites have only been tracking tropical weather since the 1960s, so some storms that just stayed at sea before then could have escaped notice.

4. Mother Teresa received reportedly 50 million dollars in donations, but it sat in bank accounts. Her hospices continued to re-use needles, dull ones at that. She herself, when she needed medical attention, went to a clinic in California. "With that money she could have built at least one absolutely spanking new, modern teaching hospital in Calcutta without noticing the cost," says Christopher Hitchens.

    (*Free Inquiry*, 16.4, 1996)

5. Lay-offs are often done according to seniority—but should this be the case? Is that morally right? Some associate seniority with loyalty, but are we sure that length of employment at any one company is a measure of the employee's loyalty to that company? Might it be, instead, as is more likely the case today,

a measure of the paucity of other employment opportunities? Or perhaps it is just a measure of the employee's reluctance to take risks, to change directions. Seniority *per se* is merely longevity; it is a measure of quantity, not quality. Quantity *may* affect quality, longevity *may* increase ability and accomplishment; but then again, it may not. (Many a mediocre employee is given a raise year after year just because they've been there one more year. Is it any wonder then that so many employees develop a clock-punching mentality, thinking that just being there, just putting in time, is enough? After all, it is: if they put in enough time, they get that wage increase, those extra holidays—and a stronger guarantee that they'll continue to just be there.)

x
convergent

3.5b Practice diagramming divergent arguments

Diagram the divergent arguments of the previous exercise.

3.5c Practice constructing divergent arguments

Try constructing your own argument, using the divergent structure (think of a premise that leads to two or more separate conclusions). Use a diagram to present your argument.

3.6 Multi-structured arguments

And just to make things really interesting, arguments can involve more than one of the preceding structures.

For example, one of the most common compound structures is a serial or **chain argument**, in which the conclusion of one single convergent argument becomes the premise of a subsequent single convergent argument, and so on.

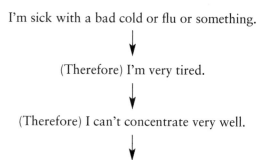

I'm sick with a bad cold or flu or something.

↓

(Therefore) I'm very tired.

↓

(Therefore) I can't concentrate very well.

↓

Therefore, I won't do as well as I otherwise could on this exam.

You see how the second point (being tired) is both the conclusion of the first point (being sick) and the premise for the next point (not being able to concentrate very

93

well). It can be called a subconclusion; that's why the "Therefore" is put in parentheses. And that point is in turn the conclusion of the preceding point, and the premise for the next point (not doing as well as otherwise probably on the exam).

Here's another example of a causal chain:

Participation in interscholastic athletics helps motivate athletes academically, especially the ones on the scholastic borderline, because a specific grade point average is required to maintain eligibility for participation. If the athletes are good enough, they may have a chance to go to college on an athletic scholarship and, while representing their college in sport, attain an education and a degree. This college education can lead to occupational mobility, the attainment of a high-status job, and success in society.

(Andrew W. Miracle, Jr. and C. Roger Rees, *Lessons of the Locker Room: The Myth of School Sports*, 1994)

Student athletes must maintain a specific GPA in order to remain on the team.

↓

(Therefore) They will be motivated to work hard at their academics.

↓

(Therefore) They may get to college on an athletic scholarship.

↓

Therefore, they can attain occupational mobility,
a high-status job, and success in society.

Actually, we might be better splitting the conclusion into three separate conclusions, because those consequences don't necessarily occur together, making this a chain/divergent argument:

Student athletes must maintain a specific GPA in order to remain on the team.

↓

(Therefore) They will be motivated to work hard at their academics.

↓

(Therefore) They may get to college on an athletic scholarship.

↙   ↓   ↘

Therefore, . . .   Therefore, . . . high-   Therefore, . . .
occupational mobility.   status job.   success in society.

94

3.6a Practice identifying causal chains

Which of the following are causal chains?

1. The utopians propose that as more and more people connect to the internet and engage in political conversation, governments will become more accountable to the people, direct citizen input into the political process will become ubiquitous, and viable on-line political communities will form.

(Kevin A. Hill and John E. Hughes, *Cyberpolitics: Citizen Activism in the Age of the Internet*, 1998)

2. Clinton's greatest gift to the Big Three automakers was exempting SUVs from the mileage requirements of regular passenger cars. Because of this exemption, these gas gluttons use up an extra 280,000 barrels of fuel *each day*. That fuel demand is one of the reasons the Bush administration is pushing to drill in the Arctic National Preserve in Alaska. Bush says the drilling will give us an extra 580,000 barrels of oil each day, enough to double the number of SUVs on the road.

(Michael Moore, *Stupid White Men*, 2001)

3. Canadian charities are governed by an archaic, 400-year-old law that prevents them from really playing politics. Because they can only devote 10% of their resources to lobbying, they're being drowned out by big corporations. If we want a stronger democracy, it's about time that changed.

(Bronwyn Drainie, "Dissent Should Be Tax-deductible." *This Magazine*, March/April 2002)

4. The working world has not treated people so well in recent decades, according to Rick Jarow, Professor of Religion at Vassar College. Real wages, adjusted for inflation, are not going up. People are working more and making less than 30 years ago, and they have less vacation. And on a personal level, says Jarow, "most people sacrifice so much of themselves when they go to work."

(Michael Alperin, "Love Your Job," *U.S.1*, June 22, 2005)

5. Money not only can make the difference but can make a huge difference. . . . People make decisions based upon the way they see the world, and the way they see the world is conditioned by the information they have; and money can influence not only the information they have but also the perceptions they have, and therefore influences who wins and loses.

(Richard Wirthlin, Republican pollster, quoted by Elizabeth Drew, *Politics and Money: The New Road to Corruption*, 1983)

95

3.6b Practice diagramming causal chains

Diagram the causal chains of the previous exercise.

3.6c Practice constructing causal chains

Try constructing your own causal chain argument, presenting it with a diagram.

Single convergent structures are not the only argument forms that can be used in combination. In fact, we just saw, in the argument about student athletes, two single convergent arguments and a divergent argument bound up together. Really, the possibilities are endless; it all depends on the argument and how the pieces fit together. Extended arguments often consist not of just single convergent arguments, but of a combination of single and multiple (separate and linked) convergent arguments, which may or may not eventually become a divergent argument.

Here are just two possibilities:

(i)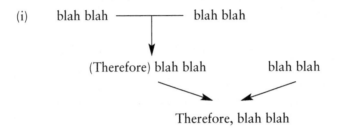

(ii)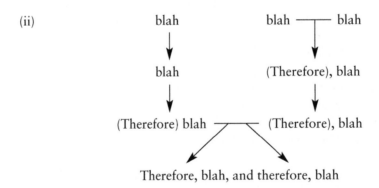

3.6d Practice diagramming multi-structured arguments

Diagram the following arguments; think carefully about whether and how each piece fits into the whole.

1. Competition is the principal mode by which men relate to each other—at one level because they don't know how else to make contact, but more basically

because it is the way to demonstrate, to themselves and others, the key masculine qualities of unwavering toughness and the ability to dominate and control. The result is that they inject competition into situations which don't call for it.

(Marc Feigen Fasteau, The Male Machine, 1975)

2. We should crack down on illegal immigrants. Because they're desperate, they're willing to work for next to nothing. So they take low-skilled jobs away from American citizens and they decrease wages.

3. So Chris Pennell, of AgResearch, a government-owned research firm in New Zealand, is trying to provide [an alternative solution to the problem of birds flying around airports, attracted by the large expanses of grass, and potentially causing great damage]. He proposes to make the grass itself unpalatable . . .

   He now has two symbiotic cultivars that seem to do the business. One of these is cold-tolerant and grows fastest in the winter, the other is heat-tolerant and grows best in the summer. Canada geese—large, grass-eating birds that cause a lot of problems at airports—learn from a single exposure that these grasses are nasty, and will not return to them. Grass-eating insects get the message, too, so insectivorous birds such as starlings have no reason to hang around the new grasses. At least, that is the result of small-scale trials. Dr. Pennell has now made an arrangement with the airport in Christchurch, New Zealand, to see if it works in the real world. If it does, there will be some hungrier, but longer-lived birds around, and passengers will be less likely to be delayed by avian purée in the engines.

("Grassed up," The Economist, June 4, 2005)

4. Advertising informs consumers about products, which enhances competition, which prevents market concentration and stagnation, and it provides the media with financial support, which keeps it free from governmental control, and people approach advertising rationally and therefore it can't be too manipulative, so advertising is okay.

5. The rationale of capitalism is that an unintended coordination of self-interested actions will lead to the production of the greatest welfare of the whole. The logic proceeds thusly: As a natural result of free competition in a free market, quality will improve and prices will decline without limit, thereby raising the real standard of living of every buyer; to protect themselves in competition, sellers will be forced to innovate by discovering new products and new markets, thereby raising the real wealth of the society as a whole. Products improve without limit, wealth increases without limit, and society prospers.

6. I want to show that we need not be afraid of interstellar contact, for unlike the primitive civilizations on Earth that were overpowered by more advanced

technological societies, we cannot be exploited or enslaved. The extra-terrestrials aren't going to come and eat us; they are too far away to pose a threat. Even back-and-forth conversation with them is highly unlikely, since radio signals, traveling at the speed of light, take *years* to reach the nearest stars, and many *millennia* to get to the farthest ones, where advanced civilizations may reside.

(Frank Drake and Dava Sobel, *Is Anyone Out There?*
The Scientific Search for Extraterrestrial Intelligence, 1992)

7. Boredom is a cultural phenomenon unique to Western culture . . . Boredom is a product of culture where individual and communal goals have lost all their significance and meanings, where an individual's attention span is no longer than a single frame in an MTV video: five seconds. In such a culture, one needs something different to do, something different to see, some new excitement and spectacle every other moment. Netsurfing provides just that: the exhilaration of a joyride, the spectacle of visual and audio inputs, a relief from boredom and an illusion of God-like omniscience as an added extra.

(Ziauddin Sardar, *The Cybercultures Reader*, 2000)

8. Should people pray for their team to win? Isn't that asking God to cheat? The rules of a game permit only a certain number of players. If God were to help one side more than the other, wouldn't he be breaking the rules? Wouldn't he be dishonest and illegal?

. . .

And if God were to favor one team more than another, he wouldn't be acting like a father. If we're all his children, shouldn't he treat us equally? Would a decent father like to see some of his children defeat his other ones and make them feel miserable? Would he be proud to be the cause of this?

. . .

Shouldn't we assume that God realizes he shouldn't interfere in games, that he'd be cheating if he guided footballs and baseballs and basketballs, that he'd be unsporting if he provided an athlete with an extra spurt? Spiritual steroids are as dishonest as medicinal ones.

If you were running the universe, would you cheat for your favorite athletes? Of course not. Why would God?

(Dexter Martin, "Asking God to Cheat in Sports,
in *African Americans for Humanism*, 1993")

9. At least since the 1990s, the U.S. has faced a growing shortage of registered nurses. According to the Department of Health and Human Services (DHHS), in 2020 the demand for nurses could exceed the supply by 40 percent if nothing is done to stop this trend. The 20th century has seen recurrent shortages, but this one is different, in part because of an unprecedented

demographic squeeze. The workforce made up of those aged 20 to 35, the prime recruiting pool for nurses, will decline at the same time baby boomers begin to reach retirement and consume medical services at a faster rate. But perhaps a more important factor is the low status of nurses. At one time, low status was far less of a deterrent, but now, when virtually all professions are open to women, nursing has become a relatively unattractive career choice. Moreover, the work is physically demanding: it is so strenuous that nurses generally cannot work much beyond their mid-50s. Indeed, the top concerns of nurses are their increasing workload and long hours.

Furthermore, pay lags behind other occupations that have similar educational requirements: an elementary schoolteacher, for example, earned $14,000 more than a nurse in 2001, according to the DHHS. Registered nurses are leaving the workforce at a faster rate than ever: currently, almost 500,000 RNs do not work in nursing.

Demand for nurses is rising because of population growth, more elderly persons and medical advances that require greater skill. Health industry economics also drives demand. Since 1990, an average of 85 percent of the population have had some form of health insurance and so have been covered, at least partially, for nursing care. At the same time, real per capita disposable income has grown steadily, making it easier to pay for non-covered health care.

Nursing seems to defy the normal laws of supply and demand, given that pay has lagged at a time of higher demand. A possible explanation lies in the superior bargaining power of hospitals—the major employers of RNs—combined with the relative lack of organization of nurses. Only 38 percent of hospital nurses are unionized. Another factor affecting pay is the failure of nurses to develop a strong constituency among the general public. In contrast, schoolteachers have forged strong community bonds through local parent-teacher organizations.

Broadening the recruitment base—nurses are now 86 percent white—would help alleviate the shortage, but long-term solutions most likely will have to deal with the more fundamental nature of the field. In addition to higher wages, the key to resolving the shortage may lie in giving nurses more power over working conditions and over health care decisions now made by physicians.

(Rodger Doyle, "Nurses in Short Supply,"
Scientific American, January 2005)

10. The Christian belief that Christianity is necessary to salvation is morally unjustifiable. Christianity did not come into being instantaneously all over the world. In fact, it spread rather slowly after the death of Christ, involving missionary work even into the nineteenth century. Since there have been millions who died without ever hearing of Christ, the Christian is confronted with a dilemma. Either these people could be saved or they could not. If they

could not, then we are confronted with an obvious example of injustice. Some people were given a chance to be saved, while others were not. The geographical area or historical era in which a person lives does not make any difference in what he deserves. And yet, according to Christianity, people are being treated differently on the basis of factors which do not make any difference in what they deserve. On the other hand, suppose that these people could be saved. Then it follows that the Christian religion is not necessary to salvation. But the fact that Christianity offers salvation is its only excuse for existence, at least according to fundamentalists. Therefore Christianity is worthless. The whole enterprise of sending out missionaries to preach the Gospel has been a foolish waste of time. In fact, if only those who hear and reject the Gospel are damned, then it has imperiled souls rather than saving them.

(B.C. Johnson, *The Atheist Debater's Handbook*, 1983)

3.6e Practice constructing multi-structured arguments

Try constructing your own multi-structured argument. Definitely use a diagram for this one.

Review of terms

Define the following terms:

■ **single convergent structure**

■ **multiple-separate convergent structure**

■ **multiple-linked convergent structure**

■ **divergent structure**

■ **multi-structured argument.**

Thinking critically about what you see

Think critically about each of the following. Again, determine whether or not each of the following is presenting an argument (explicitly or implicitly). If it is, articulate the point and the reasons/evidence supporting that point. If not, explain why not.

1.

Background picture © Corbis

2.

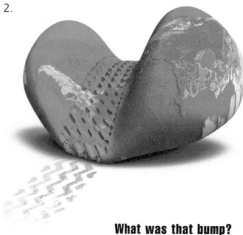

What was that bump?

Courtesy www.adbusters.org

101

Thinking critically about what you hear

Listen to the audio clip under the Student Resources tab on the companion website at www.routledge.com/textbooks/tittle. Any response?

Thinking critically about what you read

Think critically about each of the following, focusing again on the first two steps in the template; pay special attention to the connections between parts of the argument, making a diagram of the structure if it helps you figure out those connections. And, again, feel free to comment and/or evaluate with regard to other steps in the template as well!

1. There are numerous arguments for the legalization of anything, but there are likely an equal or great number of arguments against legalization.

2. Of course climate change is real. Even the insurance industry knows it—they're quite concerned about the increasing number and magnitude of claims because of natural disasters.

3. Consent cannot be truly "informed." Many practicing clinicians report that their patients are unable to understand the complex medical information necessary for a fully rational weighing of alternative treatments. There is considerable research support for this view. A variety of studies document that patients recall only a small percentage of the information that professionals present to them (Meisel and Roth, 1981); that they are not as good decision makers when they are sick as at other times (Sherlock, 1986); and that they often make decisions based on medically trivial factors.

    (Robert M. Arnold and Charles W. Lidz, "Informed Consent: Clinical Aspects of Consent in Health Care," in Warren T. Reich, ed., *Encyclopedia of Bioethics*, 1995)

4. Some evangelical Christians have trouble reconciling evolution and a traditional belief in God as creator and sustainer of the world, but I do not. Within the evangelical tribe, I belong to the Calvinist wing, where a long history exists of accepting that God speaks to humans through "two books" (Scripture and nature), and since there is but one author of the two books, there is in principle no real conflict possible between what humans learn from solidly grounded science and solidly grounded study of the Bible. Of course, if "evolution" is taken to mean a grand philosophical Explanation of Everything based upon Pure Chance, then I don't believe it at all. But as a scientific proposal for how species develop through natural selection, I say let the scientists who know what they are doing use their expertise and whatever theories help to find out as much as they can. On the Bible side, I do not think it is necessary to read everything in early Genesis as if it were written by a fact-checker at the *New York Times*. But as a persuasive basis for believing 1) that God made the original world stuff, 2) that he providentially sustains all natural processes, and 3) that he used a special act of creation

Template for critical analysis of arguments

1. What's the point (claim/opinion/conclusion)?

    ■ Look for subconclusions as well.

2. What are the reasons/what is the evidence?

    ■ Articulate all unstated premises.
    ■ Articulate connections.

3. What exactly is meant by . . .?

    ■ Define terms.
    ■ Clarify all imprecise language.
    ■ Eliminate or replace "loaded" language and other manipulations.

4. Assess the reasoning/evidence:

    ■ If deductive, check for truth/acceptability and validity.
    ■ If inductive, check for truth/acceptability, relevance, and sufficiency.

5. How could the argument be strengthened?

    ■ Provide additional reasons/evidence.
    ■ Anticipate objections—are there adequate responses?

6. How could the argument be weakened?

    ■ Consider and assess counterexamples, counterevidence, and counter-arguments.
    ■ Should the argument be modified or rejected because of the counter-arguments?

7. If you suspend judgment (rather than accepting or rejecting the argument), identify further information required.

(perhaps out of nothing, perhaps from apelike ancestors) to make humans in his own image, the Bible is not threatened by responsible scientific investigations.

(Mark Noll, at: http://www.pbs.org/wgbh/
evolution/religion/faith/statement_02.html)

5. *All I would ask would be that people do not meddle with me when I am busy painting, or eating, or sleeping, or taking a turn at the brothel, since I haven't a wife.*

(Vincent van Gogh, 1853–1890)

Vinnie
my idol
my starry starry night
my symbol of the misunderstood
you are all too easy
to understand.
i've looked at each painting
i've read every letter:
it is a portrait of a young man
as a commercial artist.

you're not trying hard enough to sell
my pretty flowers and sceneries
you scold your brother as he supports you
too incompetent or too greedy or too selfish
to support yourself, to support your own art.

and that bit with the ear—
the madness of genius?
hardly.
a childish tantrum is more likely
or the madness of syphilis.
(chris wind, in *dreaming of kaleidoscopes*, 1994)

6. In 1991 [crop circle] designs started getting more complex. We started to see fractals for the first time including a huge Mandelbrot set which appeared near Cambridge —the home of Benoit Mandelbrot. This formation was interesting because the Mandelbrot Set is a recognizable human mathematical discovery. It would not appear through random wind damage or natural phenomenon. It has intelligence behind it. Therefore, this formation *has* to either be a hoax or a message from intelligent cir-clemakers. What I mean by this is that if you assume the formation is not just the work of silly pranksters, then it is undisputed proof of some kind of intelligent entity—ET?

(Paul Vigay, excerpt from a lecture given at David Kingston's
Dorchester Crop Circle Conference, 4 April 2004, at:
http://www.cropcircleresearch.com/articles/e024-dorchester.html)

7. It seems to me that there is something fundamentally irrational about claiming as your identity aspects of your self that are mere accidents of birth, such as race, sex, and nationality: if you do not choose X, if you have no control over X, then surely you cannot justifiably take any credit or blame for X—nor then can you justifiably take any of the attendant benefits and burdens, rights and responsibilities. It's also a very passive thing, basing your identity on what chance has done to you rather than on what you've done yourself. Perhaps most importantly, it is also unfair, if rights and responsibilities are assigned on such an identity.

8. Since there has been an increase in smoking, it's pretty clear the advertisement campaigns by tobacco companies are succeeding. The anti-smoking lobby should try harder.

9. In the United States, I can't be drafted; in Canada, I am not allowed full combat training; and in Israel, I am not permitted to carry arms in the front lines. I am not a conscientious objector; I am not aged, infirm or feeble-minded. I am a woman.

     Military leaders have a long list of reasons for not drafting, training or arming me: I'd increase military spending because of all those toilets, separate showers and funny-sized uniforms I need; somebody has to stay home to look after the children; I don't have the stamina to storm hills, assault beaches and kill people and, above all, I would distract the true warriors, men.

     Nobody wants to talk about the real reason. War is considered a male sport, despite the fact that bullets and bombs do not kill selectively. And because war is a male sport, I am relegated to the position of cheerleader. The coaches don't quite trust me. And their suspicions are well founded. Draft me and I may refuse to register, choosing instead to fill the jails. Give me combat training and I may refuse to fight. Hand me arms and I may put them down.

     I do not have the same enthusiasm for knocking off human beings as do many of the men in power today. Perhaps I am resentful because I have long been expected to stay home, look after children, knit socks, roll bandages, pray, get pillaged, bombed and raped, instead of being out there at the front having all the real fun. For whatever reason, I'm more interested in the business of living, than in the business of dying, and the military honchos know it.

     I will fight tenaciously in the Warsaw Ghetto and in the Resistance Movement when I'm directly threatened, but I'm not so hot at supporting wars for esoteric reasons like anti-communism, religion or winning. I'm especially lethargic about killing people to prove we're top nation.

     I often put my energy into protesting senseless wars instead of creating or fighting them. And in an era when many military minds think winning a "limited" nuclear war is both possible and desirable, my attitude is not good enough.

     So I'm offered the position of cheerleader, a position which allows me to shout encouragement or disapproval, but permits me no influence over the game. Unfortunately, cheerleaders get killed too. The big game strategy espoused by many of our coaches is leading us all towards a very final playoff match, at the end of which I'll be just as dead as my brothers, husbands, sons and uncles on the field.

If I can't be drafted, I can neither register nor refuse to do so. If I can't receive full combat training, I can neither fight nor refuse to do so. If I can't carry arms, I can neither use them, nor put them down. I can die, though.

And that's not good enough for me. I must get on the field as a full-fledged player. Only then will I share in the decision to keep playing, walk off the field or cancel the game.

(Lyn Cockburn, "Cancel the Game," *Point Blank*, 1986)

10. Although the media and the public spend most of their time focusing on the largest and easiest issues to understand in politics, some of the worst government policies often arise in the lesser-known areas.

One of these areas is the subject of government subsidies to business: direct payments, tax cuts or other benefits given to producers of a particular good or service. One of the worst offenders in terms of federal and state subsidies is the ethanol industry.

On the surface, the arguments that politicians and ethanol-industry advocates use to justify the massive federal and state subsidies for ethanol seem persuasive. One line of argument pushes for the United States to increase ethanol production to achieve energy independence from foreign oil sources. Another argues that ethanol burns cleaner than gasoline and is renewable.

Unsurprisingly, this has resulted in a spurt of political support from politicians who see this as an easy and effective way to cater to farmers and environmentalists. This has resulted in the creation of a tax break for ethanol production that effectively pays producers an extra $0.51 for every gallon of ethanol they produce, as well as mandating ethanol be blended into gasoline.

The problem with current ethanol production arises from the use of corn as the main ingredient in producing ethanol. Right now, the amount of energy used to produce a gallon of ethanol from corn is just a bit less than the amount of energy gained from that ethanol. The process does not produce the excess energy necessary to drive a car or otherwise replace the use of gasoline.

. . .

Regrettably, the ethanol subsidy has had an impact not just in terms of wasteful tax spending but also in the increasingly worrisome inflation of food prices both inside and outside the United States. Since 2005, the price of corn per bushel has tripled, from $2 to more than $6 today. Given the broad uses of corn as feed for meat and dairy animals, as well as in processed foods, the higher price of corn has translated into higher food prices.

. . .

The revealed drawbacks of the ethanol subsidy show what needs to be done: Eliminate the artificial market conditions that spur producers to make it. The current technology for the industrial production of ethanol is not efficient enough to justify the inflation it is causing in food prices. The only responsible step policymakers in

Washington and the states have left is to eliminate the subsidies that continue to drive the ethanol market until better technology is available.

(Andrew Wagner, "Corn Subsidies Distort Market,"
The Badger Herald, April 18, 2008)

Thinking critically about what you write

In this chapter, you constructed six different arguments, each with a different structure: single convergent, multiple-separate convergent, multiple-linked convergent, divergent, causal chain, and multi-structured. That's a lot of ground to have covered. But having covered it will make this end-of-chapter exercise a breeze. Simply go back to Sections 3.2c, 3.3c, 3.4c, 3.5c, 3.6c, and 3.6e, and write up each argument in a short paragraph. That is, just put the premises and conclusions into sentences. Check each paragraph to be sure it makes perfect sense to someone reading it for the first time.

Thinking critically when you discuss

Again in groups of three, one person initiates the discussion with an argument, and the other two people take turns responding to that argument. However, this time, initiate with a slightly more difficult argument, a multiple convergent argument—either with independent premises or with linked premises. (Review Sections 3.3 and 3.4 if you need to.)

Also, especially if you didn't respond with a counterargument last time, try to do so this time. I repeat here the description of this possibility:

4. You can accept the argument (or not) and present a counterargument. Typically, this would be a brand new argument that leads to a conclusion counter to the proposed conclusion, such that they both can't be true—so you'd have to decide which is the stronger argument.

Suggestion: Try not to be bothered by silences. Actually, the more often there is silence, chances are the better your discussion is. It means that people are really thinking about what's been said. And about what they're going to say.

Reasoning test questions

The Verbal Reasoning section of the MCAT "evaluates your ability to understand, evaluate, and apply information and arguments" (*2010 MCAT Essentials*, at: http://www.aamc.org/students/mcat/start.htm). There are seven passages, each about 600 words long, taken from the humanities, social sciences, and natural sciences, and each passage has five to seven multiple-choice questions. You have 60 minutes to answer a total of 40 questions.

Check out the full-length test available online at: http://www.aamc.org/students/mcat/preparing/orderingpracticetests.htm.

107

chapter 4

relevance

contents

Template for critical analysis of arguments

1. What's the point (claim/opinion/conclusion)?

   ▪ Look for subconclusions as well.

2. What are the reasons/what is the evidence?

   ▪ Articulate all unstated premises.
   ▪ Articulate connections.

3. What exactly is meant by . . .?

   ▪ Define terms.
   ▪ Clarify all imprecise language.
   ▪ Eliminate or replace "loaded" language and other manipulations.

4. **Assess the reasoning/evidence:**

   ▪ If deductive, check for truth/acceptability and validity.
   ▪ **If inductive, check for** truth/acceptability, **relevance**, and sufficiency.

5. How could the argument be strengthened?

   ▪ Provide additional reasons/evidence.
   ▪ Anticipate objections—are there adequate responses?

6. How could the argument be weakened?

   ▪ Consider and assess counterexamples, counterevidence, and counterarguments.
   ▪ Should the argument be modified or rejected because of the counterarguments?

7. If you suspend judgment (rather than accepting or rejecting the argument), identify further information required.

4.1 Relevance

In Chapter 3, we saw that three elements could be missing from an argument: one or more premises, the conclusion, or the connection between the premise(s) and conclusion. In the cases we examined that involved a missing connection, what was missing was an *articulation* of the connection. However, more often, what is missing between a premise and the conclusion it is supposed to support is **relevance**. And in that case, the premise doesn't support the conclusion at all; in fact, if a premise isn't relevant to a conclusion, it shouldn't even be considered a premise for that conclusion. Relevance (of the premises to the conclusion) is thus one of the criteria for good arguments. We'll cover the other two—truth or acceptability and sufficiency—later in this text.

To be relevant, the truth of the premise *must make a difference—to the merit of the claim in question (that is, to the conclusion)*. It's important to remember that relevance is not the same as importance of something in and of itself. Rather, relevance is a relational thing: a statement is relevant if it is *important to something else*, namely the proposed conclusion. So when someone (perhaps your professor) dismisses something you say as irrelevant, it's not that what you've said isn't important; it's that what you've said *isn't important to the claim in question*.

Consider this argument:

We should not hire the candidate we just interviewed. We need a good computer programmer. That guy had a ring in his nose for crying out loud!

What does having a ring in one's nose have to do with being a good computer programmer? Absolutely nothing. Whether the premise is true or false (whether he has a ring in his nose or not) makes no difference to the conclusion (to whether he is a good computer programmer), so it's irrelevant.

Now, consider this argument:

We should not hire the candidate we just interviewed. We need a good computer programmer. The application form he filled out online has two mistakes in it!

In this case, whether the premise is true or false makes a difference to the conclusion. If the application form he filled out online *does* have two mistakes, then we have a reason for accepting the conclusion that he would not be a good computer programmer (assuming that (1) mistakes in the online application form indicate a lack of attention to detail, and assuming that (2) being a good computer programmer requires attention to detail), so the premise *is* relevant to the conclusion.

So understanding whether or not something is relevant depends on understanding, first, what the argument is (the issue in contention, the premises, the conclusions).

However, understanding whether or not something is relevant also often depends on the extent of your knowledge: if you don't know anything about X, how can you know whether Y makes a difference to X? For example, in the preceding example, one needed to know that competence at computer programming requires attention to detail. (Knowledge will come in handy again when you're trying to think of, and evaluate, alternative explanations. So you might have to increase your knowledge in order to increase your critical thinking abilities.)

4.1a Practice identifying irrelevant premises

In each of the following arguments, which, if any, of the premises are irrelevant to the conclusion?

1. *Laverly*: Whether or not to abort a fertilized egg is a personal choice, and the law has no right interfering one way or another in personal choices.
   Cevreau: I agree that it's a personal choice, but when personal choices have consequences for others, the law most certainly *does* have a right to interfere!
   Laverly: Okay, but what kind of law—I mean, are you advocating total prohibition or partial prohibition? If the latter, on what basis would you allow abortions?

   [handwritten margin note: missing: judges should not rewrite sacred institutions]

2. Because marriage is a sacred institution and the foundation of society, it should not be re-defined by activist judges.
   (President George W. Bush, State of the Union Address, 2005)

3. "Put yourself there," says Maj. Dylan Moxness. "You're an 18-year-old kid from Tennessee. You don't even understand why these people don't speak English anyway, you're shouting 'Stop!' and the car's still coming at you— you've got to fire."
   (Comment regarding the January 2005 shooting in Iraq by U.S. soldiers at a car accelerating in their direction; their shots killed two adults and injured their five children and one nephew; *Newsweek*, March 28, 2005)

4. Plea bargaining should be abolished. When a defendant agrees to plead guilty and thus not go to court in exchange for a reduced charge or lenient sentence, justice is not being served. Furthermore, it can hardly be called bargaining, since the one party isn't really in a position to bargain—I mean, their only alternative is immediate jail time, even if it's only until the trial, assuming they'll be found innocent.

5. Both suicide and euthanasia are wrong. My body belongs to God, so only He can decide when I should die.

Classes with no definite answer should be offered P-F

6. Since there are no definite answers in ethics, this ethics course will be offered on a pass–fail basis.

beliefs that are half-baked are conducive to tolerance

7. In practice, religious differences are often not problematic [for establishing tolerance and compromise within a society] because when you actually question many people who are officially identified with a religious group, you find their beliefs are a sort of hotch-potch of half-baked and not fully considered ideas all running together in one mind. Talk to members of the Church of England and you find that many of them think there should be gay bishops, although many oppose this; that many support a woman's right to abortion, but some do not; that some of them get drunk, swear, and fornicate as much as anybody else, even though some versions of their religion say they shouldn't engage in that sort of behaviour.

(Piers Benn, "The Identity Trap," *TPM*, 1st quarter 2004)

more violence in public/private than at home

people must be safe and alive n enjoy education

8. Home schooling should definitely be allowed as a substitute for public school and/or private school. For one thing, parents may object to the methods used in public schools. Ditto for the material taught in public school. Also, children are often at risk of violence in public schools. What's wrong with their parents trying to protect them? What good is a public education if you're not alive to benefit from it? People may object, saying that homeschooled kids don't get socialized, but school is not the only social activity available! Last, but not least, teachers have been saying all along that if their class sizes were reduced, or even if they could teach one-on-one, they'd be able to do a much better job. Well, home schooling allows just that: individualized attention!

9. Since there cannot be a gene for every element of our personality, we must have free will.

10. I am absolutely convinced that UFOs have landed here on Earth. I have had strange sensations in my feet and hands for ten years now, and those circles in the fields, remember those? They're landing spots. The grass was burned away by the exhaust. And the pyramids? Who built them? No, sir, there is overwhelming evidence to support my belief. We have been visited by UFOs.

Sometimes what seems irrelevant can be made relevant by filling in a few missing steps. For example, suppose I said that selling unsafe products was wrong because it hurt people (and hurting people is wrong), and you responded by saying that everyone does it. Your statement would be irrelevant because whether everyone does it doesn't affect whether it's wrong—*unless* you *define* "right" as "whatever everyone does." In that case, since everyone does it, it would be right. So, in that case, your statement that everyone does it *is* relevant—but you'd have to provide those missing steps.

4.1b Practice filling in the steps needed to make a premise relevant

Go back to the preceding practice, and for the arguments involving irrelevant premises, articulate a chain of reasoning (however outrageous) that would make the premise relevant. (Don't worry about plausibility at this point—have fun!)

There are a number of specific, and all-too-common, ways in which a statement can be irrelevant to the claim being argued for. I've divided these errors of relevance into four categories, but that's merely for ease of learning; it's more important that you understand the errors than the classifications.

4.2 Errors of relevance: considering the source of the argument instead of the argument itself

Each of the following two errors—appeal to the person and genetic fallacy—involves considering the source of the argument instead of the argument itself. Considering the source instead of the argument is an error because the source of an argument is irrelevant to the merit of the argument; whether an argument is good or bad depends solely on the truth, relevance, and sufficiency of the premises (or, in the case of deductive argument, the truth of the premises and the structure of the argument, the latter of which has relevance and sufficiency "built in").

Note the distinction between the source of an argument (discussed here) and the source of a claim (discussed in Chapter 6). It would be reasonable to consider the source, the reputation of a person for honesty, for example, when evaluating the truth of a claim.

4.2.1 Appeal to the person (ad hominem)

The **ad hominem** error involves *directing your comments toward the person making the argument, rather than toward the argument itself* ("ad hominem" is Latin for "to the person"). Thus, it's generally an error made while *responding* to an argument, rather than while *making* an argument. It's considered an error because who presents the argument is irrelevant to the strength or weakness of the argument. If the argument is a good one, it doesn't matter whether it was put forth by the most respected person in the world or some no-name teenager. Likewise, if the argument is a bad one.

Consider this argument:

> We believe that by educating women and making it easy for them to find jobs in both the economic and the social fields, we have partly helped them on the

road to liberation. We have also set up children's nurseries to enable mothers to go to work without their husbands objecting and insisting that a woman's duty begins at home.

My guess is you think this is a pretty good argument: education and employment can lead to liberation. The argument was made by Saddam Hussein (interview with Fuad Matar 1980, as reported in *The Saddam Hussein Reader: Selections from Leading Writers on Iran*, Turi Munthe, ed., 2002). Does that change anything? No. It's still a pretty good argument! The identity of the person presenting the argument is irrelevant to the merit of the argument.

I think we tend to make this kind of error when we are under the influence of the power of the speaker, whether said power is due to sex, class, race, or employment; we seem predisposed to respect those in power, which includes respecting what those in power say. If you really want to make sure you're evaluating the argument and only the argument, imagine it being said by a child.

Noteworthy errors of this type include our dismissal of thousands of brilliant arguments that happened to be put forward by a woman.

Lastly, an appeal to the person is rather close in nature to an appeal to authority—in both cases, one's attention is on the person making the argument rather than the argument itself. And while an ad hominem is generally considered an error, an appeal to authority is not. See Section 4.3.1 for further discussion on this point.

There are three kinds of ad hominem errors: appeals to the person's character, appeals to the person's practices, and appeals to the person's interests.

(i) APPEALS TO THE PERSON'S CHARACTER

In this case, the comment made about the person (instead of the argument) concerns the person's *character*. The comment can be *positive*, *implying* that the argument is a good one or that it should be accepted. Or, it can be *negative*, *implying* that the argument is a bad one or that it should be rejected. Also, the "comment" doesn't have to be *verbal*: a laugh or some other dismissive *non-verbal* gesture, such as making an incredulous indignant "You're joking, right?" face, can also be an ad hominem.

Here's an example:

> *Tait*: I heard the other day on a radio call-in show, someone said that the insanity defense should be abolished. The real issue is not whether or not someone is insane but whether or not they know what they're doing.
> *Violen*: People who call in to radio shows are such low-lifes. Why aren't they out working in the middle of the afternoon?

Violen's comment concerns the person who made the argument, rather than the argument itself. It is therefore an example of the ad hominem error. Furthermore, the negative comment concerns the person's character (that she or he is a low-life) and suggests that the argument has been dismissed on that basis. Violen should have considered the argument itself before dismissing it.

Here's another example of an ad hominem addressing the person's character:

> *Developer*: We can change our environment, whereas rocks and trees can't. That's why I count more than a rock or a tree. And that's why I have the right to develop a mine or harvest a forest.
> *Environmentalist*: Yeah, but you're a selfish sleazeball.

The developer may well be a selfish sleazeball—but that's irrelevant: it doesn't change the argument—the argument stands or falls whether he's a selfish sleazeball or not! (Note the unstated premise, though, that the capacity to change the environment increases one's moral standing and gives one the right to change the environment.)

It's understandable that we make this mistake because, generally, respected people are respected because of their character; perhaps they even have a reputation for presenting carefully considered arguments. Conversely, people known to be liars or careless thinkers tend to present—well, actually, they tend to present mere claims, not arguments. Nevertheless, considering the person instead of the argument is an error. Even careful thinkers make mistakes.

It's important to distinguish this error from the common practice, in court as well as in everyday living, of "discrediting the witness." When questions asked of witnesses are intended to illustrate that their testimony is less than reliable—perhaps because they have a history of not telling the truth or because they stand to gain some personal benefit by lying—the point is to establish the truth of their testimony. It is not to establish the merit of their argument (presumably they're not even making an argument—they're just reporting what they saw or heard). An ad hominem, on the other hand, is intended to discredit the argument, not merely to question the truth of the premises. It is important, however, to question the truth of the premises, and investigating the credibility of the person presenting the premises *is* relevant to that task—a topic we'll discuss in Chapter 6 when we consider the criterion of truth.

> If you can't answer a man's arguments, do not be discouraged, you can still call him vile names.
>
> Elbert G. Hubbard, *The Notebook*, 1927
>
> The value of an idea has nothing whatsoever to do with the sincerity of the man who expresses it.
>
> Oscar Wilde, *The Picture of Dorian Gray*, 1891

4.2.1a Practice recognizing appeals to the person's character (an error in reasoning)

Which of the following arguments contain an appeal to the person's character? Where applicable, re-craft the argument so it is error-free.

1. *Goverly*: There should be more road signs indicating the distance to the next destination. It's important that people know how far they have to go before they get to wherever they're going. There may be safety concerns.

Willower: You're such a compulsive goal-oriented person, you wouldn't stop to enjoy the scenery even if a volcano erupted right alongside of you!

2. I had also been alerted to the fact that Hovind was under investigation by the I.R.S. for tax fraud and evasion, that he believes income tax is a tool of Satan to bring down the United States, democracy is evil and contrary to God's law, and recommends the infamous anti-Semitic hoax, *The Protocols of the Elders of Zion*, that he received his doctorate from a diploma mill, and that even Ken Ham's creationist organization, Answers in Genesis, disavowed many of Hovind's wackier beliefs in a fascinating web page document entitled "Arguments We Think Creationists Should Not Use."
    (Michael Shermer regarding Kent Hovind prior to engaging in a debate with him, http://ofgodandlogic.com/morality/miracle/index.htm)

3. The "tragedy of the commons" argument, which says that resources are quickly depleted when they are "owned" by everyone because everyone takes what they want, presumes that everyone is self-interested and that that self-interest is very short-term.

4. *Sergimento*: Cancer is increasing, compared to 100 years ago. That proves that there are more carcinogens in our environment.
    Plouffe: Or, since cancer increases with age, maybe it's just that 100 years ago people didn't live long enough to develop cancer.

5. *Smokestack*: You really should stop smoking—it's bad for you!
    Ashtray: You should talk! Look who's smoking at this very moment!

(ii) APPEALS TO THE PERSON'S PRACTICES

A second kind of appeal to the person involves appealing not to the person's character, but to the person's *practices*. This kind of ad hominem is called a *tu quoque* ("tu quoque" is Latin for "you too"): the comment in question typically draws attention to the fact that the person is arguing against something they themselves do. Essentially, this ad hominem exposes the speaker's hypocrisy. While it may be important not to be a hypocrite, one's hypocrisy doesn't affect one's argument one way or another, so the comment is irrelevant—an error.

Here's an example:

McKenzie: You shouldn't go for a run without a warm-up! Don't you know that that's the best way to tear a muscle?
Strider: Look who's talking! I've never seen you stretch before a run!

It may very well be true that McKenzie doesn't warm up before running, but that only proves that McKenzie is making an argument for doing something that she herself doesn't do. It doesn't prove anything about the argument itself. So Strider's comment is irrelevant. If Strider had said instead "Actually, research shows that stretching *after* a run is more effective with regard to preventing injuries than stretching *before* a run," *that* would have been relevant.

Here's another example of an ad hominem addressing a person's practices:

You say it's wrong to hunt, but you eat meat!

In this case, the speaker is responding, presumably, to an argument concluding it's wrong to hunt, but the response concerns the original speaker's practices, specifically his or her practice of eating meat. Instead, the response should have addressed the argument itself; perhaps one of the premises that support the conclusion could have been challenged in some way.

Why do we make this mistake? Perhaps we are simply quick to criticize others. Perhaps we are justifiably concerned with consistency between speech and action.

4.2.1b Practice recognizing appeals to the person's practices (an error in reasoning)

Which of the following arguments contain an appeal to the person's practices? Where applicable, re-craft the argument so it is error-free.

1. *Bocci*: She says I should have the procedure done because it's safe and likely to solve the problem.
   Stanieau: Well, she certainly knows something about medical procedures. After all, she's a nurse.

2. Wasn't it Jefferson who said "All men are created equal"? He was a slave-owner!

3. Of course you'll argue against animal experimentation! You've got a soft spot in your heart for creatures of all kinds!

4. People should be free to govern themselves. And if the people of the United States of America oppose that, they're being hypocritical! They should take another look at their own history!

5. The Pope says, "An institution as natural, fundamental, and universal as the family cannot be manipulated by anyone." This from a man who has no family—no wife, no kids.
   (The quote is from Pope John Paul II, *International Conference on Population and Development: Letter to President Clinton and Address to Dr. Nafis Sadik*, Vatican City, March 18/19, 1994)

(iii) Appeals to the Person's Interests

A third kind of appeal to the person involves appealing to the person's *interests*. Similar to the negative character ad hominem error, this type of ad hominem error discredits the person—in this case, by pointing out some bias based on the person's interests. Such interests may include monetary gain; that is, a person's argument may be dismissed because the person has a monetary interest in advocating such an argument. Interests may also include reputation and status; that is, a person's argument may be dismissed because the person stands to lose their reputation or status if they don't argue for whatever position they're advocating. This fallacy has also been called *poisoning the well*, suggesting that everything that person says is contaminated by their interests.

Here's an example: *(and a last reminder to read with your pen in hand . . . engage!)*

①

Cartier: There should be programs for students who are at risk of dropping out of school before they get their diploma, a program that places them in jobs that don't require a diploma. (Then) they'll know exactly what's in store for them if they give up. ②

① → ②

counter/challenge to ①

Demetrios: I don't know . . . employers don't want that kind of teenager wandering around their factory floor.

not a response to the counter!

Cartier: You're just saying that because *you* don't want that kind of teenager wandering around *your* factory floor!

Cartier dismisses Demetrios' objection on the basis of Demetrios' personal interests, thus committing the error of an appeal to the person. Demetrios' personal interests are irrelevant to the merit of his or her objection. Cartier should have addressed the objection itself—is it a good objection?

Here's another example of an ad hominem addressing a person's interests:

Chang: McDonald's has great food! It's cheap, and fast, and really all those accusations about nutrition, well, you can always order a salad.
Carnegie: You're just saying that because you work there!

Assuming that Carnegie is implying with his or her comment that it's in Chang's best interests to praise McDonald's (perhaps the reasoning is that if Chang criticizes McDonald's, she or he will be reported and fired), then Carnegie has indeed committed the error of an ad hominem. It would have been better if Carnegie had responded instead to the implied relationship between cheap and fast food and great food, for example.

This is a very reasonable mistake to make because while a person's interests do not necessarily affect the argument, one's interests do have the potential to make one biased, and such bias can, for example, lead one to ignore contrary evidence. Even so, the argument stands or falls as presented, independent of the person and his or her interests. It doesn't hurt, however, to make sure the person hasn't misrepresented the truth of the matter (again, we'll consider truth in Chapter 6); check for things like loaded language, as well, which can also be a result of bias arising from certain interests—if an error is present, the argument falls, whether or not it was the person's interests that led to that error.

4.2.1c Practice recognizing appeals to the person's interests (an error in reasoning)

Which of the following arguments contain an appeal to the person's interests? Where applicable, re-craft the argument so it is error-free.

1. *Robinson*: I think the man should have a say in whether or not the woman has an abortion. After all, he's the father.
    Townsmith: Well, he's the *biological* father, a mere sperm-donor—he's not really a father yet.
    Robinson: And if he wants the woman to have an abortion, and she doesn't, he shouldn't have to pay child support. After all, he didn't consent to become a father.
    Townsmith: But you just said he was a father. Make up your mind. And didn't he have sex without a condom? Isn't that tacit consent to creating a child? So of course he should pay child support.
    Robinson: But the woman might have lied, said she was on the pill.
    Townsmith: And you'd believe her? We're talking lots of money here. Twenty years child support. That's an awful lot of trust.
    Robinson: And he shouldn't have to pay if he can't afford it.
    Townsmith: What? If he can't afford it, he shouldn't've created it!
    Robinson: And if he does provide financial support, he should have a say in how that money is spent.
    Dobbin: Hey, until you're actually a father, you don't know what you're ← *must have interest of a father to understand*
    talking about!

2. *Diversky*: In the 1920s, after women scored higher on the first IQ tests, the authors of the test changed the questions.
    Pollitta: Who told you that, a woman?

3. *Hough*: Most miracles are too trivial to have been performed by a god.
    Jaeger: Since when are you interested in miracles?

4. *Harris*: It's my body, so I have the right to decide whether or not to abort!
    Haveras: You're just saying that because now you're pregnant!

5. *Nyung*: Athletes' salaries are way too high. There's no way they deserve that kind of money.

Livres: I don't know . . . doesn't it take into account the fact that they could suffer serious injury? Too, their careers won't last forever.

Nyung: Yeah, well, that's true of people who work in a lot of jobs, but they're not making millions.

4.2.1d More practice with the ad hominem error

Write three arguments that have an ad hominem error, one with an appeal to the person's character, one with an appeal to the person's practices, and one with an appeal to the person's interests. Then rewrite your three arguments so they're error-free.

4.2.2 Genetic fallacy

This is the second error or fallacy that considers the source of the argument rather than the argument itself. And like the appeal to the person (ad hominem), the **genetic fallacy** tends to be an error made while responding to an argument rather than while making an argument. Unlike the ad hominem, however, the genetic fallacy refers not to an individual person, but to a whole *history of origin* (*genesis*): reference is usually made to a historical context, and sometimes to a group that has existed through history. It is an error of relevance because how or when an idea or practice came about has no bearing on the value of the idea or practice (which may well have evolved since its origins). The quality of the argument for that idea or practice depends solely on the evidence and reasoning that make up the argument.

Here's an example:

There is no way we should support eugenics! That idea was advocated by the Nazis in Hitler's Germany, don't forget!

When and where an idea originates has no bearing on, no relevance to, the merit of the idea. Hitler also advocated responsible fiscal planning. He also advocated belief in Christianity. Whether you accept eugenics, or responsible fiscal planning, or Christianity should depend on the arguments for those ideas, not on who happened to present those ideas.

If the speaker had argued against eugenics by appealing instead to our lack of sufficient knowledge and the likelihood of control by ambition and personal gain rather than social justice, that would have been a good, error-free, argument.

Here's another example of the genetic fallacy:

Competition should be discouraged in all its forms. We must remember it is both the fruit and seed of patriarchy!

In this case, the speaker argues for the discouragement of competition partly because of its consequences (it results in male dominance—it's "the seed of patriarchy"), and that's an acceptable argument. But the speaker also argues for the discouragement of competition because of its origin (it's an idea or practice that originates from male dominance—it's "the fruit of patriarchy"), and that's where the genetic fallacy occurs.

I think we're prone to the genetic fallacy because of our tendency to associate things; when things appear to us *together*, we assume some sort of *association* between them. And while certainly there *is* an association—the context or group *is* the source of the argument—the association doesn't affect the merit of the argument.

Hence our inference of "guilt by association"—whether to historical group or currently existing group—is often incorrect. This is especially true if the association in question is not voluntary: attributing racist views to someone who voluntarily belongs to a racist group simply because of that association is more legitimate than attributing racist views to someone whose skin color happens to make them "belong" to a "group" because of that association. A source that is morally bad doesn't necessarily generate an argument that is logically bad.

4.2.2a Practice recognizing the genetic fallacy

Which of the following arguments contain the genetic fallacy? Where applicable, re-craft the argument so it is error-free.

1. ~~I will never get married~~. Did you know that the word "wife" originally referred to those women who were captured, after the invasion and conquest of a neighboring tribe, and brought home to be slaves? Marriage was a degradation!

2. *Ipinswich*: You know, I really think we should do this.
    Nartov: Why, because the idea came to you in a dream?

3. If you have a party, and one of your guests gets drunk and drives home and kills someone, why should *you* be responsible? I mean, just because he came from your place, that doesn't mean you're responsible for what he does when he leaves your place.

4. Benny Proffitt told the crowd at a workshop on religion in public schools that church-state separation comes from the *Communist Manifesto*.
    (Robert Boston, *Close Encounters with the Religious Right*, 2000)

5. *Cohen*: It's perfectly justifiable to prohibit women from working at certain jobs because substances at certain workplaces can harm the fetus after conception.
    Adilmun: But that rule would apply only to women, so it would be sexist. You're arguing for something simply on the basis of sex.

121

4.2.2b More practice with the genetic fallacy

Write three arguments with the genetic fallacy. Then rewrite your three arguments so they're error-free.

4.2.2c Practice recognizing errors of relevance that consider the source of the argument instead of the argument itself

Which of the following arguments consider the source of the argument instead of the argument itself?

Identify the specific fallacy involved:

- appeal to the person (character, practices, or interests)
- genetic fallacy

Where applicable, re-craft the argument so it is error-free.

People gain pride from their origin — *Patriotism ties people to their origin*

Patriotism .. pride is a Character

Interests

1. Patriotism is your conviction that this country is superior to all others because you were born in it.

(George Bernard Shaw, 1856–1950)

2. *Hogan:* If God's responsible for the sudden disappearance of a tumor, why isn't he also responsible for its sudden appearance, huh?

   O'Clair: Oh don't be such a smartass!

3. *Hammond:* Hey listen to this. "Advertisers do one thing—they persuade us to buy products that otherwise we would not buy. If we would buy the products anyway, there would be no point in producers spending the money to purchase magazine space or television time to display ads." Pretty good, eh?

   Signet: Whoever wrote that probably just can't afford advertising. That's why they're trashing it.

   character

   (Quote is from Lisa H. Newton and Maureen M. Ford, eds., Introduction to *Taking Sides: Clashing Views on Controversial Issues in Business Ethics and Society*, 4th edn., 1996)

4. *Luccock:* I was reading an article by Walter Williams, in the 1990 issue of *Society*, and he says the term "African American" has to go. First of all, there is no single African culture. Second, black-skinned people living in the United States generally don't know what part of Africa their ancestors came from. Even if they did, they probably have nothing in common with the people living in that part of Africa. Lastly, they have nothing to gain by discovering or inventing myths about their affinities with Africa.

   Ellmann: Yeah, and I'll bet he's not African-American.

   character

5. We shouldn't pay women to become surrogate mothers—that would be offering an "undue inducement"—someone who hasn't got a lot of money would find it hard to refuse, and that wouldn't be genuine consent. Ditto for paying people for their body parts.

6. Saint Augustine said "Any woman who acts in such a way that she cannot give birth to as many children as she is capable of makes herself guilty of that many murders." He is so full of it.

   – character

7. *Beatty*: I think we should all donate 10 percent of our money to social causes. There are a lot of people out there who are simply less fortunate than us. They work just as hard and are just as deserving, they've just gotten a lot of bad breaks.
   Perkins: You're just saying that because *you* donate 10 percent of your money to social causes.

   – practices

8. The guy's Jewish (or Christian, or Atheist, or White, or Black, or . . .), so of course he denies it. What do you expect?

   – character

9. The owners of the 30 teams that make up the elite National Hockey League (NHL) have locked out the players as part of an effort to make them accept lower salaries. . . .

   Fans can usually be relied on to support players rather than owners in a dispute. This time, however, polls indicate that they are backing the billionaires over the millionaires by a wide margin. Most seem to feel that no one should complain about being paid $1 million or so per year to shoot a puck around a rink. They also know that the players' handsome salaries have a lot to do with the exorbitant ticket prices of $150 or more for the big games.

   Moreover, salary caps seem to be the way professional sports in North American are heading: both the National Basketball Association and the national Football League have adopted them.

   (*The Economist*, October 16, 2004)

10. *Grosset*: If telling the truth endangers the health and well-being of patients, can doctors withhold truth? Can they lie about their patients' conditions? I think so. It would be in the patients' best interests.
    Klinck: But people are more likely to follow treatment if they know truth of the matter.

4.3 Errors of relevance: appealing to an inappropriate standard

Each of the following six errors—appeal to inappropriate authority, appeal to tradition or past practice, appeal to custom, habit, or common practice, appeal to moderation, appeal to popularity, and "two wrongs"—involves appealing to some standard or judgment other than your own, specifically some *inappropriate* standard. They are errors of relevance because, in each case, that other standard or judgment to which you have appealed is irrelevant.

4.3.1 Appeal to inappropriate authority

As the comment in the margin suggests, often it's quite acceptable to appeal to an authority, an expert. The question is, then, how do we tell the difference between an *appropriate* authority and an *inappropriate* authority? Good question. First, an appropriate authority is *qualified*. And how can you determine that, especially since you don't know anything about the issue in question? (That's why you're appealing to an authority in the first place, right?) Generally, education and experience can establish qualification. But even then, you may want to scrutinize the education; there are a lot of "universities" offering "degrees" over the internet for a mere fifty bucks.

Second, *the qualifications must themselves be relevant*. Someone with a degree in botany is *not* an appropriate authority on matters of astronomy, no matter how many doctorate degrees in botany they have from Harvard. Likewise, someone with lots of experience in drama as an actor is *not* an appropriate authority on toothpaste, shampoo, cell phones, automobiles, or investments. So what they think about those issues is irrelevant; for example, what a celebrity with no biochemistry qualifications says about whether a certain toothpaste will prevent cavities is irrelevant to your assessment of that particular claim.

These two points, by the way, provide good reason to cite your sources when making your own arguments—you are providing evidence that your sources, your authorities, are appropriate. This is so even though you don't list their degrees, because you do list the publication from which you obtained your material, and the conventional assumption is that publication in an academic journal, because submitted articles go through a rigorous screening process before they are published, indicates, by itself, an author's expertise. The screening process is typically less rigorous for magazines and newspapers. And as far as websites are concerned, some are more reputable than others. A personal website is least trustworthy because the person can post whatever they want; websites sponsored by legitimate organizations generally screen material before they post it and are therefore more reliable. Even so, check out the tone and the funding—both can indicate bias. When in doubt—or better yet, always—cross-check the material: if

None of us is equipped to establish, independently, most of the claims that we depend on. This is not a bad thing: it means that we can know many more things than we could if left to our own devices.

Mark Battersby, "The Competent Layperson," *Humanist in Canada,* Autumn 2004

124

several apparently legitimate sources say the same thing, reliability increases. We'll come back to this issue when we discuss truth in Chapter 6.

Third, the authority in question should have a *reliable record for accurate and unbiased judgments*. Education and experience alone may not be sufficient; the person may have almost failed all of his or her courses and may have learned nothing from his or her experience!

Here's an example of an appeal to an inappropriate authority:

> My physics professor says the United Nations is just a smiley face, so I don't think I'll apply to become a UN intern after all.

Unless your physics professor is also an expert on political institutions, he is an inappropriate authority with regard to claims about the United Nations; you'd be wise to investigate his claim for yourself before making a decision about that internship!

Here's another example of this particular error:

> According to my financial advisor, it's just as bad for the environment to heat with electricity as it is to heat with oil.

A financial advisor *might* be qualified to say which form of heating is less expensive, but probably not to say which is better for the environment. So whatever he or she has to say on the matter is rather irrelevant.

To sum up, an **appeal to an inappropriate authority** occurs when you accept the judgment of someone who is neither relevantly qualified nor reliably accurate and unbiased.

That said, even an appeal to an appropriate authority involves a lot of trust. That may or may not be a problem for you; it's likely to be more of a problem for the person you're trying to convince (since that person has to trust you *and* the authority you're citing). So try to understand the authority's rationale for the opinion you're stating—and cite the rationale, not just the authority's opinion. It is always better to attend to *what* is said, not *who* says it.

I think we tend to appeal to inappropriate authorities when they have a lot of charisma—we fall for their charm. Perhaps that's why such people make this appeal. Also, we generalize and assume, incorrectly, that if someone is an expert in one field, she or he will be an expert in another field—or at least won't lie about being an expert in another field.

4.3.1a Practice recognizing appeals to inappropriate authority

Which of the following arguments contain an appeal to an inappropriate authority? Where applicable, re-craft the argument so it is error-free.

1. ✓ The guy at the shoe store said these are the best shoes for distance running, so I figured, hey, they cost a little more than I wanted to spend, but I don't want to end up with knee problems a few months from now.

2. ≁ Dr. Bob said that you shouldn't be completely honest about yourself during the initial stages of a relationship. Too much information can be overwhelming. He says to wait until a certain level of trust has developed before you're completely truthful.

3. ✗ If our President says this is the right thing to do, well that's good enough for me!

4. As a practicing physician, I am convinced that boxing should be banned.

   First, boxing is a very visible example that violence is accepted behavior in our society—outside the ring as well as inside. This sends the wrong message to America's youth, and at a time when so many kinds of violence are on the rise, it is a message we should stop.

   Second, boxing is the only sport where the sole object is to injure the opponent. Think about what a knockout really is: It is a cerebral concussion that knocks the victim senseless! Boxing, then, is morally offensive because its intent is to inflict brain injuries on another person. And it is medically indefensible because these injuries so often lead to irreversible medical consequences, such as subdural hematoma, nonfatal acute intracranial hemorrhages, "punch drunk syndrome," progressive neurological disorder and serious eye conditions.

   (Robert E. McAfee, "Ban Boxing," *USA Today*, 1999)

5. Brains are beautiful. Usually a reference to intellect, but for Deborah Hyde, M.D., neurosurgeon, the brain's physical contours are enthralling. "The anatomy is so beautiful. I just find it a turn-on."

   Her brain is turned on by . . . well, brains and other finer things. After surgery that starts before dawn, Dr. Hyde may head out for lunch and shopping. En route, Lincoln LS provides stimulation for all the senses. Its heated and cooled leather-trimmed front seats are pleasing to the touch year-round. A reflex-quick aluminum suspension keeps the ride smooth and steady. The clarity of the THX Certified Audio System helps induce a harmonious brain state, no matter how snarled the traffic. And its cabin, trimmed in American walnut burl and satin nickel, flashes through the optic nerve and stimulates the occipital cortex. Pleasure is registered.

   The reaction? "I love this car." Dopamine is released, producing a feeling of well-being. Dr Hyde adds, "Current research suggests that the nucleus accumbens is very important in pleasure. It's not the cortex, where cognitive thought occurs. It's deeper in the brain, where feeling is."

Thus, it's possible luxury may be perceived before it reaches the cortex—before you can 'think' it, you are already enjoying it. And craving more. "There's so much going on neurally that it's conceivable that we never experience the same thing the same way twice."

The brain: mind-boggling. But whatever mysteries that lie within its folds, there's no better stimulation for the brain of a driver than an empty road, a full tank of fuel and energizing music over the sound system. But be aware: the pleasures of the road are extremely habit-forming. Go online for an inside view of all the ways the Lincoln LS has been designed to tickle your neurons.

("The Pleasure Neuron," an advertisement for the Lincoln LS., *Inc. Magazine*, May 2005)

4.3.1b *More practice with appeals to inappropriate authority*

Write three arguments that have an appeal to an inappropriate authority. Then rewrite your three arguments so they're error-free.

4.3.2 Appeal to tradition or past practice

One day a woman was about to cook a roast. Before putting it in the pot she cut off a small slice. When asked why she did this, she paused, became a little embarrassed, and said she did it because her mother had always done the same thing when she cooked a roast. Her own curiosity aroused, she telephoned her mother to ask why she always cut off a little slice before cooking her roast. The mother's answer was the same: "Because that's the way my mother did it." Finally, in need of a more helpful answer, she asked her grandmother why she always cut off a little slice before cooking a roast. Without hesitating, her grandmother replied, "Because that's the only way it would fit in my pot."

(Ellen J. Langer, *Mindfulness*, 1989)

Traditions usually start for a reason. That reason may be a good reason. But it may, at some point, no longer be important—or, more importantly, it may no longer be relevant. Times change. The present may not be similar to the past—at least not in the particular way that matters. So when you make an **appeal to tradition or past practice** to support your claim (your belief or action), you're *assuming* that the reason for the tradition in the first place is still a good reason. If your assumption is correct, why not just appeal to the reason instead? And if it's not correct, then why are you appealing to that reason, albeit indirectly? It's irrelevant!

Here's an example:

Witches cackling on broomsticks has always been part of Halloween! I'm not going to give in to those who say it's offensive to the Wiccan religion!

The speaker is appealing to a tradition to support her decision to include images or costumes of witches cackling on broomsticks in Halloween celebrations; she or he is therefore making an appeal to tradition. Whether or not Halloween has always been celebrated that way is irrelevant to whether it should now be celebrated that way. It would be far better if she had reasons other than tradition to support her decision—and if she would respond to the arguments made by those who claim it's offensive.

Here's another example of an appeal to tradition:

> Why are you so upset when I squeeze the toothpaste tube in the middle instead of rolling it up from the end? It's just the way I do things. I've always done it that way. And I'm certainly not about to change now!

Again, the speaker is appealing to past practice to justify current practice. It would be better if other, more relevant, reasons could be offered: perhaps it's easier that way; perhaps the amount of toothpaste that remains unused with that method is negligible; perhaps he or she is not lucid enough in the morning to care about efficiency . . .

This error is similar, then, to an argument by analogy: you are implying that the past is *like the present*. But for an argument by analogy to be a good one, the two things being compared must be *similar in the relevant aspects* and *not dissimilar in any relevant aspect*; otherwise, it's a weak or false analogy (see Section 7.3.1).

Keep in mind that this particular error involves an appeal to "the way we've always done it"—whether that's formally referred to as a "tradition" or just considered "past practice." As the latter, perhaps "precedent" is the word that will be used. In fact, a whole part of our legal practice consists of exactly this appeal: lawyers make their cases *based on precedent*, and judges make decisions that follow the decisions that have been made previously. That has always struck me as amazing. How can lawyers and judges not see that their whole system is based on an error in reasoning? Well, they'd maintain that it's not. The only precedents that count are those in which the critical elements of the past case are similar to those of the present case; so their appeal to precedent is more an appeal to consistency, through analogical reasoning. Even so, they're depending on the first decision being correct. What if the cases *are* similar, with regard to the critical elements, but the first judge made a bad call? Then all the judges after him or her are just repeating his bad call . . .

Perhaps part of why we fall for this particular error is that we're a little insecure: who are we to say all those people who have followed tradition are wrong, and we alone are right? Also, traditions seem to have some authority over us; traditions become respected, even revered. But we shouldn't be swayed by that appeal to our emotion—we should think very carefully about what we revere! Lastly, nostalgia seems to be part of our psychological make-up: we idealize the past, including judgments made during that past.

A noteworthy example of this type of error? Consider all the people—medical personnel, friends, family—who, through their use of pink and blue, their unconscious appeal to that tradition, imply that whether it's a boy or a girl is *the most* important thing about a child's birth; as a consequence, almost all of us have been forced into a sexual apartheid from birth.

4.3.2a Practice recognizing an appeal to tradition or past practice

Which of the following arguments contain an appeal to tradition or past practice? Where applicable, re-craft the argument so it is error-free.

1. The company has always done it this way. So I suggest you keep your new-fangled ideas to yourself and follow established procedure. ✗

2. Why do I want to be a police officer? My dad was in the force. So was his dad before him. ✗

3. My parents spanked me and their parents spanked them. ✗

4. In recent years, a flood of books and articles has advanced the notion that all is well with the environment, given credence to this anti-scientific "What, me worry?" outlook . . . One reason the brownlash [anti-science] messages hold so much appeal for many people, we think, is the fear of further change. Even though the American frontier closed a century ago, many Americans seem to believe they still live in what the great economist Kenneth Boulding once called a "cowboy economy." They still think they can figuratively throw their garbage over the backyard fence with impunity. They regard the environmentally protected public land as "wasted" and think it should be available for their self-beneficial appropriation. They believe that private property rights are absolute (despite a rich economic and legal literature showing they never have been). ✓

   (Paul R. Ehrlich and Anne H. Ehrlich, "Brownlash: The New Environmental Anti-Science," *The Humanist*, November/December 1996)

5. As we've seen with the Jets debacle, however, "infrastructure" can be an awfully flexible term when it comes to stadium finance. A recent study by Rutgers professor Judith Grant Long found that the average pro sports stadium costs the public 40 percent more than the stated price tag—and that figure has risen in recent years, thanks largely to undercounted "land and infrastructure" costs. ✗

   "If the Mets plan goes through," says Long, "it's safe to assume that the actual deal, post-approval, will involve public costs far higher than the initial reports."

   (Neil DeMause, "A Queens Ransom," *Village Voice*, June 15–21, 2005)

4.3.2b More practice with appeals to tradition or past practice

Write three arguments that have an appeal to tradition or past practice. Then rewrite your three arguments so they're error-free.

4.3.3 Appeal to custom, habit, or common practice

This is similar to the appeal to tradition, but what's being appealed to is less formalized: it's not so much an appeal to tradition as an **appeal to custom, habit, or common practice**. The problem is the same, however: the reason for the custom, habit, or common practice may not be relevant to the action being currently proposed; the situation or circumstance that gave rise to the habit may have since changed in some important way or disappeared altogether. If the reason *is* still relevant, then appeal to the reason, not the mere fact that you always do it that way. If the reason is *not* relevant, then you don't have any support for what you're proposing.

Here's an example:

Of course I open doors for women. It's just habit!

If that's the only reason you can offer for your action, you're making an appeal to custom. It may well be habit to open doors for women, but that's irrelevant to whether or not you should be doing so. If you open doors for women because they're too weak to open their own doors, that's a better argument—you've provided a relevant reason.

Here's another example of an appeal to custom:

Of course we kill and eat our elderly. It's our way!

And quite possibly it's a good thing. But not just because it's your way. You'd have a stronger argument if you had other, relevant, reasons for killing and eating your elderly.

Common practice is, by definition, what everyone does. To this extent, an appeal to common practice is very much like an appeal to popularity (see Section 4.3.5a), and that might go some way toward explaining why we fall for this error. Too, habits are familiar, and we like what's familiar. Psychology has proven that. (However, psychology has also shown that we have a fondness for variety, for something different, so a converse fallacy might be called an "appeal to novelty." It would be an error in reasoning in a similar way: whether or not something is new has no bearing on, no relevance to, its merit.) Furthermore, as a habit, the practice in question has, by definition, been repeated. So we're being sucked in to the power of repetition. Perhaps we should call this error an "appeal to inertia"!

Lastly, as with all appeals to standards other than our own, it's simply easier to let someone else do our thinking: someone started doing it this way, they must have had a good reason, or at least I'll just assume that they did, and I'll assume that this situation is the same as that situation. Perhaps a noteworthy error of this type is "When in Rome, do as the Romans do."

4.3.3a Practice recognizing an appeal to custom, habit, or common practice

Which of the following arguments contain an appeal to custom, habit, or common practice? Where applicable, re-craft the argument so it is error-free.

1. It takes 21 pounds of grain to produce a pound of meat. Millions are starving. ✓ Put two and two together: if North Americans ate just 10 percent less meat in a year, there'd be enough grain to feed 65 million people.

2. It is common practice to pay men more than women; we will not depart from ✗ that standard.

3. [M]any of the prochoice movement's writers and intellectuals would have us ✓ believe that the early fetus . . . is nothing more than a dewy piece of tissue, to be excised without regret . . . Yet . . . [a] pregnant woman . . . doesn't call the growth inside her an embryo or fetus. She calls it a *baby*.
   (Jason DeParle, "Beyond the Legal Right: Why Liberals and Feminists Don't Like to Talk about the Morality of Abortion," *Washington Monthly*, 1989)

4. There are diminishing returns from money, or, as economists would say, there is diminishing marginal utility. The more dollars you have, the less you benefit from an extra dollar. ✓

   Let's say you're poor, a single mother living on welfare. An extra thousand dollars will make a large difference to your quality of life. Now imagine that you're Paul Reichmann. An extra thousand dollars won't get noticed, and even if it does, won't significantly affect your well-being.

   Given this trend, if we have extra funds to distribute we do best by giving them to those who have least. And if we take from the rich to give to the poor—as we do if we combine progressive taxation with welfare payments— we do more good than harm. The losses to the rich are smaller than the gains to those who started with less.
   (Thomas Hurka, *Principles: Short Essays on Ethics*, 1994)

5. *Anasi*: The rape shield law should be tossed out! It's important to know ✗ whether the woman who's accusing some man of rape is in the habit of saying yes.

131

Hubert: How is that relevant? She could've said no on the occasion in question.

Anasi: Yeah, but unless we've got a witness or circumstantial evidence, it's just her word against his. So either we have to decide who is more likely to tell the truth, which we probably can't do since we don't know either of them. Or we have to decide which story is more likely.

Hubert: You mean if she's in the habit of saying yes, she probably said yes that night.

Anasi: Right.

Hubert: Okay, and if he's in the habit of forcing women, he probably forced that night.

Anasi: Right. The past history of both people should be admissible in court.

Hubert: But people can change.

Anasi: Sure, but hey, that's what a reputation is for. I mean, come on, if I've got a reputation for being the most non-violent person in the world, if no one has *ever* seen me become in the least aggressive, I think that should be admissible in court if I'm accused of rape one day!

Hubert: And if I tend to say yes to men I've just met …

Anasi: You got it.

Hubert: But that's basing a conclusion on past practice.

Anasi: No, it's basing a conclusion on character.

4.3.3b *More practice with appeals to custom, habit, or common practice*

Write three arguments that have an appeal to custom, habit, or common practice. Then rewrite your three arguments so they're error-free.

4.3.4 Appeal to moderation (or lack of)

Another error of relevance is the **appeal to moderation (or lack of)**: this is an error because where an argument falls on the scale of moderation—whether toward the middle or toward either of the two extremes—is irrelevant to its quality. And yet we often seem to favor moderate or extreme views, probably as a result of our individual psychological disposition—and not, as is preferable, as a result of any intrinsic value of the view itself.

(i) AN APPEAL TO MODERATION (ALSO CALLED THE FALLACY OF THE GOLDEN MEAN)

Sometimes, we seem to automatically think that views in the middle of a given spectrum are preferable to views at the extreme—for no other reason than that they're in the middle. But that by itself is generally insufficient reason for accepting any particular view. Where a position falls on any given spectrum is irrelevant to the merit of that position. One could argue that a moderate view will please more people than an extreme view and on that basis argue for it, but that's invoking quite a different reason—that it will please more people—than simply that it is moderate.

Here's an example:

Down with anarchists! Extremists aren't the answer!

This is an appeal to moderation: the speaker is rejecting anarchy because of its presumed extremism, implying support for a more moderate position simply *because* it's more moderate. It would have been a better argument if specific reasons for rejecting anarchy or anarchists had been given.

Here's another example of an appeal to moderation:

When you go to an interview, it's best to appear neither too poor, nor too well-off.

In the absence of anything further, we are justified in assuming that the moderate position described is held merely because it's moderate. It would have been much better to have given other reasons, such as if you appear poor, interviewers will think you're not capable, and if you appear well-off, interviewers will think you don't need or want the job.

Perhaps we make this mistake because we think "moderate" means "reasonable" and "extreme" means "unreasonable." But what is, after all, a "moderate" view? Or an "extreme" view? If we mean by "extreme" "all or nothing," then many "zero-tolerance" policies are extreme—and yet there are probably very good reasons for accepting such policies.

People who are middle-of-the-road people, personality-wise, life-wise, will probably gravitate toward this error.

Perhaps a noteworthy example of this error is the view, in its many iterations, that it is good when things are in balance (when the extremes have equal influence or equal time).

4.3.4a Practice recognizing an appeal to moderation

Which of the following arguments contain an appeal to moderation? Where applicable, re-craft the argument so it is error-free.

1. We are standing in a pool of gasoline. Tom says we should not light any matches. Dick says we should light all the matches we have. I propose a compromise: let's light half of the matches in our possession.

2. Taxpayers have a right not to be offended by what their tax dollars buy, so art intended to appear in public places should be mild and inoffensive.

3. I heard that she had a heart attack right in the middle of the marathon. See, it just goes to show that a little moderation wins the day. Too little exercise and you get fat; too much exercise and you put such a strain on your body, it's not made for that, all these elite athletes that can barely get through a season without injury.

4. "When it comes to sentencing," says the judge, "I tend to favor neither the minimum nor the maximum sentence."

5. The more we understand the human genome, the more genetic testing will be required by employers, insurance companies, and the government. We should just leave it all alone. If that means you end up with a genetic disease, well, que sera sera.

4.3.4b *More practice with appeals to moderation*

Write three arguments that have an appeal to moderation. Then rewrite your three arguments so they're error-free.

(ii) AN APPEAL TO THE EXTREME

And sometimes, we seem to automatically think that views at the extreme are preferable to views in the middle—again, for no other reason than that they're extreme. Sometimes radical or drastic measures may be best, but they must be deemed best not merely *because* they're radical or drastic, but because they achieve the goals we want to achieve. Again, where a position falls on any given spectrum is irrelevant to the merit of that position.

Here's an example:

The time for compromise is over. We must simply scrap everything and start over from scratch.

In this case, the speaker is claiming as support for the claim of scrapping everything and starting over its status as extreme (or more precisely, its status as not a compromise). It would have been a better argument if the speaker had given specific reasons for scrapping everything and starting over from scratch (perhaps nothing was salvageable; perhaps that would be the most efficient approach).

Here's another example of an appeal to the extreme:

Extreme sports are the best! Because they're extreme!

In this case, the speaker appeals to the nature of the sports as extreme in order to justify endorsing said sports. That is, the very fact that they're extreme is taken as sufficient support for endorsing them. If the speaker had endorsed extreme sports because of their danger, or their thrill, that would have been a better, error-free, argument.

People who are "out-there" people, who like to take risks, who don't know the meaning of the word "moderation," probably gravitate toward this error.

4.3.4c Practice recognizing an appeal to the extreme

Which of the following arguments contain an appeal to the extreme? Where applicable, re-craft the argument so it is error-free.

1. I say we should treat people equally. No exceptions. All this affirmative action and special parking spaces for wheelchairs and fragrance-free workplaces, it's all gotten out of hand. We don't have to go to such extremes—a little common sense would go a long way here. ✗

2. If you're going to do this at all, you have to do it all the way. Anything else is wimping out. ✗

3. Surely just because many of our products will be in households with children, we are not obligated to childproof everything we make! The parents must take responsibility for the safety of their children! ✓

4. I think you'll find that people are most unhappy if they're at either end of the spectrum—lower class and upper class. Middle-class people seem to be the happiest. Perhaps that's because they have enough money to meet their basic needs, but not so much money they worry about the responsibility that comes with it.

5. We believe it is time that the lodging industry "just say NO" to the Gideons . . . If hoteliers wish to serve customers in possible crisis, it would be far more useful to compile a list of local secular resource numbers: the police, battered woman's shelter, Red Cross, mental health hotline, nearby hospitals, etc. In fact, the bible itself offers not just gruesome bedtime reading (blood is splashed on nearly every page), but potentially violence-inciting and lethal advice. Murderers, child molesters, rapists, sexists, racists and even slaveholders have turned to bible verses to justify crimes. Jesus promotes self-mutilation, the terrifying myth of hell, and the dangerous, primitive belief that sickness results from "demons." The bible also offends by its often pornographic and bloodthirsty language. Why align your association with this image, and insult customers of other faiths, or no faith?
    (Excerpted from letter written by Annie Laurie Gaylor, Freedom from Religion, Inc., to Kenneth F. Hin, Executive Vice President, American Hotel & Motel Association, February 14, 1989)

4.3.4d More practice with appeals to the extreme

Write three arguments that have an appeal to the extreme. Then rewrite your three arguments so they're error-free.

4.3.5 Appeal to popularity (or lack of)

This error considers the number of people supporting an argument to be relevant to the quality of the argument when, in fact, it's not. Whether a million people are convinced by an argument or whether only one person is so convinced is irrelevant to the quality of the argument; only the truth, relevance, and sufficiency of the premises can determine the quality of an argument.

We seem to favor popular or unpopular views, again probably as a result of our individual psychological disposition—and not, as is preferable, as a result of any intrinsic value of the view itself.

This is an appeal to an inappropriate standard of judgment in that we're considering a group of people—either the majority or the minority—to be an appropriate authority when, in fact, we have no evidence of their qualifications or reliability with regard to accurate and unbiased judgments.

(i) APPEAL TO THE MAJORITY (ALSO CALLED THE BANDWAGON FALLACY)

In this case, we are appealing to the authority of the many; we accept the majority view—simply *because* it is the majority view. But the majority isn't always right! Large numbers of people are quite capable of making poor judgments.

Here's an example:

> A lot of Muslims don't read the Koran, and they still call themselves Muslim, so I don't see why I can't call myself a Muslim too. I still believe Allah is the Only God and Mohammed is his messenger.

The speaker is appealing to what is done by the majority (assuming that "a lot" is the majority) in order to support what he or she is doing. But the number of people who support a particular position is irrelevant to the merit of that position. It would have been better if the speaker had given other reasons for calling her- or himself a Muslim, reasons independent of what other people do or don't do.

When you support your claim by saying something like "Everyone does it" or "Everyone agrees," you're implying that the opinion of the majority carries weight. As just suggested, the majority has been known to be wrong. But even if they're right, the fact that they *are* right isn't a *reason* in *support* of your point; it's merely an observation—that others agree with your point. As such, it's neither here nor there; it's irrelevant. You're better off finding out *why* the majority agrees and then using that reason to support your point.

THE FAR SIDE BY GARY LARSON

**"Okay, Williams, we'll just vote. ... How many
here say the heart has four chambers?"**

Here's another example of an appeal to the majority, this one typical of advertisements:

What are you waiting for? You don't want to be left out! On sale now!

The company is appealing to our desire to be part of the (presumably) majority crowd—everyone else has one, so we should want one too! But note that the reason used to convince us to buy the product is merely that most people have bought the product.

We probably fall for this error because of our desire to conform; one philosopher has called this error "the fallacy of mob appeal"—the term suggests that it appeals to whatever it is that makes us want to get carried away in or with a crowd, perhaps the pack mentality of our animal brain? Or maybe we just assume that other people think clearly and carefully about their decisions, so if most people think X, it's probably true. (Of course, if most people think like we do, that *other* people think clearly and carefully—who's thinking clearly and carefully?) A noteworthy example of this error might be our belief in "majority rule."

4.3.5a Practice recognizing an appeal to the majority

Which of the following arguments contain an appeal to the majority? Where applicable, re-craft the argument so it is error-free.

1. Everyone knows that it's wrong to steal.

2. Hey, I'm not the only one who believes in UFO abductions!

3. I deserve an extension on this assignment because everyone else did.

4. A focus on "Islamic fundamentalism" as a global threat has reinforced the tendency to equate violence with Islam, to fail to distinguish between illegitimate use of religion by individuals and the faith and practice of the majority of the world's Muslims who, like adherents of other religious traditions, wish to live in peace. To equate Islam and Islamic fundamentalism uncritically with extremism is to judge Islam only by those who wreak havoc—a standard not applied to Juadaism and Christianity. The danger is that heinous actions may be attributed to Islam rather than to a twisted or distorted interpretation of Islam.

   (John L. Esposito, "Political Islam: Beyond the Green Menace," *Current History*, January 1994)

5. *Municom*: Why should business have any more social responsibility than private citizens?
   Curran: Because they have that much more power! Power entails responsibility.
   Municom: But they're not particularly qualified to solve social problems. Besides, no one elected them to run society.
   Curran: And yet they do.
   Municom: So what do we do, take away the power of business or require it to comply with certain social solutions?

4.3.5b More practice with appeals to the majority

Write three arguments that have an appeal to the majority. Then re-craft your three arguments so they're error-free.

(ii) APPEAL TO THE MINORITY, APPEAL TO THE AUTHORITY OF THE ELITE

In this case, we are appealing to the authority of the few; we accept the minority view—simply *because* it is the minority view. We assume the majority, the masses, are wrong; only the few, an elite, know what's right. But a small number of people are just as capable of making a poor judgment as a large number of people! Don't look at the numbers; look to the reasons!

Here's an example:

Most people vote Liberal or Conservative. That's why I'm voting Green.

This is an appeal to the minority: few people vote Green, so I'm going to vote Green. The mere fact that few people endorse the Green party is taken as sufficient reason to support the Green party. But again, the number of people who support a given position is irrelevant to the merit of that position.

Here's another example of the appeal to the minority, and again, this one's typical of advertisements:

Only the very few buy a Scalera. Will you be one of them?

This is an appeal to our desire to be part of an elite; note that no reason is given for buying a Scalera except that few people do.

We probably fall for this error because of our desire to be special—one of the enlightened outsiders, rather than one of the masses.

4.3.5c *Practice recognizing an appeal to the minority*

Which of the following arguments contain an appeal to the minority? Where applicable, re-craft the argument so it is error-free.

1. Many are called. Few are chosen. Be one of them.

2. Affirmative action is justified because it will achieve a representative work-force: there will be the same proportions of minorities in all sectors of the workforce as there are in the population at large. Also, seeing members of minority groups in positions of power and responsibility will change people's attitudes about people who belong to such minority groups. And of course, there's the compensation for past injuries argument, though those compensated are not those who were injured (at least not directly) and those doing the compensating are not those who did the injuring (again, not directly).

3. Very few individuals have need of a researcher's services, so I think you should reconsider your plan to become a researcher-for-hire.

4. Everyone's got a PC, so I'm going to buy a Mac.

5. It seems to me that most first-year students take Psych. I think I'm going to take Anthropology instead.

4.3.5d More practice with appeals to the minority

Write three arguments that have an appeal to the minority. Then rewrite your three arguments so they're error-free.

4.3.6 "Two wrongs"

This is another error more often made in response to an argument than while constructing an argument. When someone makes an argument against doing something, for example, and you respond, "But other people are doing it!" you've committed the **"two wrongs" fallacy**: you are suggesting that "two wrongs make a right." The fact that other people are doing it (a sort of appeal to popularity) is irrelevant to whether or not it is morally acceptable. Two wrongs generally make, well, two wrongs.

Here's an example:

> I appreciate your advice to stick to the issues, but my competitor is engaged in a smear campaign against me, going to the media to publicize personal transgressions that are, admittedly, moral transgressions, but are, I maintain, irrelevant to my political competence. So I think it's perfectly acceptable for me to engage in a similar campaign.

The speaker is saying that certain behavior (engaging in a smear campaign) is acceptable *because* someone else is engaging in that same behavior. If the candidate had said something like "If I don't respond in a similar fashion, people will think that my competitor is morally pure and I'm the only one who's ever done something morally reprehensible," that would have avoided the "two wrongs" fallacy.

Here's another example of the 'two wrongs' fallacy:

> *Forst*: Hey, you just cut off that other car!
> *Luzzaro*: Yeah, well he cut me off first!

Luzzaro defends his position by pointing out that someone else has done the same thing—two wrongs don't make a right!

Note, however, that if you are suggesting that the other "wrong" is actually right, and because your action is similar in relevant ways, your action is, therefore, also right, then that's *not* the "two wrongs" fallacy. Such an argument would be an argument by analogy (see Section 7.3). However, if that is the case, you really should articulate the complete argument, explaining why the action in question is right; a simple reference to someone else doing it hardly makes the point you're apparently intending to make. And, if you *can* explain why the action is right, then you really don't need to refer to the other person's behavior at all; your action would be right whether or not someone else is doing something similar.

Another subtlety to be aware of is this: if you are suggesting that an action is right if and when it is *in response to* other people doing it, that's different. In that case, it's not simply *that* they're doing it that matters; it's that their doing it changes the situation such that your doing it is now acceptable. For example, a business may justify lowering their wages by saying "Other businesses are doing it!" If they were just making some sort of excuse for their action, then they're committing the "two wrongs" fallacy. However, if they meant to be saying something like "When other businesses lower their wages, they unlevel the playing field and we no longer have fair competition; I can make things fair again, however, by also lowering my wages; and there's nothing wrong, indeed there's something very right, about trying to create fair competition." If *that's* what they meant, then they're *not* committing the "two wrongs" fallacy. In this way, two wrongs *may* make a right.

Another example might be hitting in self-defense. One might claim the second hit is a case of "two wrongs": the first person did wrong by hitting you, so you also do wrong by hitting, perhaps thinking "two wrongs make a right." However, the first hit is offensive, whereas the second hit is defensive; so unless you believe self-defense to be wrong, that second hit isn't a wrong—so there can't have been two wrongs.

The "two wrongs" fallacy is an appeal to an inappropriate standard of judgment in that you are considering some other person to be an authority on the matter—otherwise, why should their judgment be invoked to support your own judgment? Sometimes, however, this error is more a case of false analogy (see Section 7.3.1): you mistakenly believe that the other case is similar to your case in the relevant respects, so consistency demands that if the action is acceptable in that case, it is acceptable in your case.

We probably make this error out of sheer laziness—it's an excuse for simply doing what we want to do.

4.3.6a Practice recognizing the "two wrongs" fallacy

Which of the following arguments contain the "two wrongs" fallacy? Where applicable, re-craft the argument so it is error-free.

1. It is appropriate to use wickedness against the wicked.

   (Hindu proclamation)

2. An eye for an eye.

   (Christian proclamation)

3. They're traveling with the ball and committing all sorts of fouls, so I don't see why we shouldn't follow suit.

4. *Rogers*: A student's right to free speech doesn't stop when she enters the school. So if she wants to say a prayer, whether she's meeting others in

a classroom or whether she's on stage making a valedictorian speech, she should be allowed to do so.

Bruck: And would you say the same if she wanted to make a racial speech rather than a religious speech?

5. In order to change anything, you need media attention, and the media pays attention only to violence. And if the violence we do to get that media attention is less than the violence we're trying to stop, then yes, I say it's okay!

4.3.6b More practice with the "two wrongs" fallacy

Write three arguments that have the "two wrongs" fallacy. Then rewrite your three arguments so they're error-free.

4.3.6c Practice recognizing errors of relevance that appeal to an inappropriate standard

Which of the following arguments involve an appeal to inappropriate authority? Identify the specific fallacy involved:

- appeal to inappropriate authority
- appeal to tradition or past practice
- appeal to custom, habit, or common practice
- appeal to moderation (or lack of)
- appeal to popularity (majority or minority)
- 'two wrongs'

Where applicable, re-craft the argument so it is error-free.

1. *custom* You will address your superiors as "Sir," whether they're male or female. That is correct procedure. Is that understood?

2. *majority* "Look," Ted said, "you may enjoy putting me down, but the fact is, lots of people think there will be more extreme weather, including more hurricanes and tornadoes and cyclones, in the future."

   "Yes, indeed, lots of people think so. But scientific studies do not bear them out. That's why we *do* science, Ted, to see whether our opinions can be verified in the real world, or whether we are just having fantasies."

   (Michael Crichton, *State of Fear*, 2004)

3. *moderation* I don't know. Jiles says the union is right, and Wos says management is right. The truth is probably somewhere in the middle.

4. *2 wrongs* I know it's wrong to let my kids eat junk food. But if they're going to eat chips, they may as well drink soda too.

5. Drug use—especially heavy drug use—destroys human character. It destroys dignity and autonomy, it burns away the sense of responsibility, it subverts productivity, it makes a mockery of virtue.

> (William J. Bennett, "Drug Policy and the Intellectuals," from an address at Harvard in 1989)

6. If we say that since animals have no capacity for moral judgment, they have no rights, then we must also say that newborns and psychopaths have no rights.

7. Hey, a slide rule was good enough for my predecessors, so it's good enough for me. You can keep all your new-fangled calculators and computers and what have you!

8. Never follow the masses. It's as simple as that.

9. My doctor says my blood pressure is too high—I'm too stressed. He says I should put in less overtime at work and spend more time at home.

10. You know, she's trying to be a size 0. A little extreme, don't you think?

4.4 Errors of relevance: going off-topic

Each of the following four errors—paper tiger, red herring, non sequitur, and appeal to emotion—involves going off-topic, and if you're off-topic, you're making comments that are irrelevant. The errors may be committed as intentional diversionary tactics, or they may simply reveal the respondent's inability to stay on the issue (perhaps because they don't understand what the issue is).

4.4.1 Paper tiger (also called the straw man fallacy)

The **paper tiger** error involves responding to an argument that is not the argument that was presented. As mentioned above, such a response could be an honest mistake: it may be that the respondent simply doesn't understand the original argument—subtleties and complexities may be missed, so the respondent ends up addressing a simplified version of the original argument. However, often the respondent is intentionally misrepresenting the other person's argument—presumably because it's easier to dismiss as misrepresented (a paper tiger is easier to defeat than a real tiger). Sometimes the misrepresentation is a gross simplification; sometimes it's an extreme version of the original argument; sometimes it's an argument that's completely unrelated to the original argument. Either way, since the argument being responded to is not the argument that was made, the response is irrelevant.

Here's an example:

> *Union representative*: We'd like a 5 percent wage increase effective September 1 of this year, and hereafter, annual increases equal to the cost of living increase.
>
> *Management representative*: Hey, I'd like a lot more money too, everyone would like to be rich. Gee, it'd be nice to afford dinner out every night, and a new car every year, but this is the real world. We can't afford to give everyone everything they want.

In this case, the management rep has committed the paper tiger fallacy by responding to an exaggerated version of the union rep's argument: the union didn't ask to be rich, nor did he or she ask management to give everyone everything they wanted. The management rep's response may be a very good response to the argument responded to—but it's irrelevant to the argument that was actually presented.

Here's another example of the paper tiger error:

> *MacNeil*: Could I have next Wednesday off to celebrate my divorce? I understand it's company policy to allow wedding leave, so I figure it should also be policy to allow divorce leave.
>
> *MacDonaugh*: Of course not! The company can't afford to give employees a day off whenever they request one!

MacDonaugh responds to what was *not* MacNeil's argument: MacNeil did not just request a day off; she asked for a particular day off for a particular reason, suggesting consistency with current company policy. Had MacDonaugh responded to her suggestion of consistency, perhaps by arguing that divorces were somehow different from weddings with respect to needing or deserving a day off, that would have been okay. As it is, MacDonaugh's response is irrelevant (irrelevant to the argument presented).

People often commit this error because they're unable to respond to the real argument—and they're unwilling to admit that. If they simplify the argument, perhaps it's because they don't understand the real argument. Or maybe they just weren't paying attention. If they take the original argument to a ridiculous extreme, perhaps it's because they don't accept its conclusion and making the person look ridiculous (an ad hominem error, of course) is seen as a way to have the argument dismissed.

It's important that we don't get suckered in by this mistake. When someone attacks a position that you didn't put forth, don't be led into defending that position; just neatly sidestep by saying something like "You're quite right—but I didn't argue for that position."

4.4.1a Practice recognizing paper tigers

Which of the following arguments contain the paper tiger fallacy? Where applicable, re-craft the argument so it is error-free.

1. *Nash*: We should uphold the separation of church and state; it should not be mandatory to say the Pledge of Allegiance—complete with the line "under God" at the beginning of day in public schools.
   Schwarz: You will rot in hell! Try to stop people believing!

2. I cut into his monologue. "Hey, I didn't do this, *Chester*. You can rant and rave all you want, but the place was fine when I left. I locked up and put the key back through the mail slot like Bucky suggested. Ray Rawson was here. If you don't believe me, you can ask him."

   "Everybody's innocent. Nobody did nothing. Everybody's got some kind of bullshit excuse," Chester groused.

   (Sue Grafton, *L is for Lawless*, 1995)

3. *Newlove*: Because of animal research, we have vaccines against diphtheria, polio, measles, mumps, whooping cough, rubella, and smallpox. We simply can't do everything with computers and tissue cultures. For example, we can't develop medication for high blood pressure that way.
   Ditsky: Yeah, but high blood pressure in humans has social causes. It's caused by stress, for example, from working too hard. You can't duplicate that in a rat. In the United States, 17–22 million animals die per year because of animal research.
   Newlove: Yeah, but a lot more die when we clear just one acre of forest for cattle for your hamburgers.

4. "Anyway, what are you doing trying to turn some of our open land into a mall?"

   "What mall? Look here, what are you talking about? We're making an inquiry about the extra water MWD is offering, because it makes sense, it saves us money. That's part of our job on the council. Now as to this other thing, if someone is exploring the possibilities of a multi-use center, what's the problem? Are you saying we shouldn't try to create jobs here in El Modena?"

   (Kim Stanley Robinson, *Pacific Edge*, 1990)

5. Most feminists will reluctantly admit that, at least in sports, the difference in performance between women and men is a result of innate factors and not social conditioning. No amount of political indoctrination will transform a female athlete into a respectable linebacker for the National Football League. This then places the feminist in the curious position of arguing that innate factors account for the profound difference in male/female performance in sports but in absolutely nothing else.

   (Robert Sheaffer, "Feminism, The Noble Lie," *Free Inquiry*, Spring 1995)

4.4.1b *More practice with paper tigers*

Write three arguments that have a paper tiger. Then rewrite your three arguments so they're error-free.

4.4.2 Red herring

According to one of several stories about the origin of this fallacy's name, in order to prevent their land from being wrecked by fox hunters, farmers used to drag a red herring across the likely path of fox heading their way in order to direct the chase away from their land (presumably the hunting dogs would rather catch a red herring than a fox). So basically a **red herring** is a distraction. And, as a distraction, whatever it is that's said is irrelevant to the argument at issue. Like the paper tiger, then, this is an error of response. And, again like the paper tiger, the red herring indicates an inability or an unwillingness on the part of the respondent to engage in the argument at issue.

Here's an example:

> *Pitkin*: I can't accept the plan. We'd be causing too much environmental damage. And given that our product is, in truth, not that essential, such damage is not ethically justified.
> *Kerr*: But if we don't cut down those trees, someone else will, you know that.

Kerr's comment may well be true. But whether or not someone else cuts down the trees is irrelevant to whether or not it's morally acceptable for *them* to do it. (Unless they're defining "morally right" as "that which someone else will do"—but that's unlikely.) Kerr's comment is a red herring.

Here's another example of a red herring:

> *Hoogland*: I don't like this limited advertising campaign you're proposing. We should advertise steel-toed construction boots to a female target audience as well. If we don't, it's unjustified discrimination to women currently working on construction sites. And, it's harmful to all the little girls who see in the ads only men working in manual trades—their future job prospects will be limited by their narrowed imaginations.
> *Worley*: I know lots of women who work in construction.

Worley may well know lots of women who work in construction, but what does that have to do with whether or not the proposed advertising campaign would be discriminatory and harmful? Nothing. Worley's comment is irrelevant. It's a red herring—either he or she doesn't understand what Hoogland has said or he or she can't counter Hoogland's argument and, for some reason, wants to draw attention away from it.

Why do we commit this error? As just suggested, perhaps it's a way of avoiding an argument because it's a good one and we don't want to accept its conclusion!

4.4.2a Practice recognizing red herrings

Which of the following arguments contain a red herring? Where applicable, re-craft the argument so it is error-free.

1. *Brewster*: Have you ever looked closely at those school crossing signs? Note that the boy is taller. Taller suggests older which suggests more mature, wiser. And just in case you miss this not-so-subtle suggestion of male authority, look, he has his hand on the little girl's shoulder, guiding, protecting, patronizing. It will be there for the rest of her life.
   Wiebe: But boys *are* taller!
   Brewster: Not at that age!
   Wiebe: Okay, but if it were the other way around, if the girl were taller and she had her hand on the boy, guiding him across the street, you'd say "Look, they're teaching girls that it's their job to nurture, that it's a woman's job to look after men!"

2. Simply put, the state has rights that the private individual does not. In a democracy, those rights are given to the state by the electorate. The execution of a lawfully condemned killer is no more an act of murder than is legal imprisonment an act of kidnapping. If an individual forces a neighbor to pay him money under threat of punishment, it's called extortion. If the state does it, it's called taxation. Rights and responsibilities surrendered by the individual are what give the state its power to govern. This contract is the foundation of civilization itself.
   (Edward I. Koch, "Death and Justice," *The New Republic*, 1985)

3. Concern for the morals and health of young soldiers preparing for World War I prompted the surgeon general of the United States to initiate a massive effort to close down all houses of prostitution near training camps.
   (Robert T. Francoeur, *Taking Sides: Clashing Views on Controversial Issues in Human Sexuality*, 3rd edn., 1991)

4. *Rubinsky*: Hip hop deserves far more serious attention than it has received. It's an innovative hybrid of sound-based poetics and blues improvisation.
   Whitt: I heard that a lot of hip hop artists just pretend to be from the Black ghetto.

5. Fairfax, VA—The National Rifle Association's Political Victory Fund (NRA-PVF) has endorsed George W. Bush for President of the United States.

"NRA stands with President George W. Bush on November 2nd," said Wayne LaPierre, NRA executive vice president. "If you believe in freedom and want to preserve the Second Amendment for future generations, vote to re-elect President Bush and Vice President Cheney.

"In the United States we have a long tradition of hunting and sport shooting," stated LaPierre. "President Bush and Vice President Cheney both love to hunt and fish. They know the Constitution gives people the personal right to bear arms. And, they want to pass the values of our Nation on to a new generation."

(Press release from the National Rifle Association posted on the NRA website, dated Wednesday, October 13, 2004)

4.4.2b More practice with red herrings

Write three arguments that have a red herring. Then rewrite your three arguments so they're error-free.

4.4.3 Non sequitur

"Non sequitur" is Latin for "it doesn't follow"—so a **non sequitur** is any statement that doesn't follow from whatever it was it was presumed to have followed from. Most often it refers to a conclusion that simply doesn't follow from the given premises. It is an error of relevance in that the premise, since it doesn't lead to the conclusion, is irrelevant to it. It's also an error of logic: all invalid deductive arguments (see the logic supplements) are non sequiturs.

Here's an example:

Different cultures have different beliefs about what's right and wrong, so there is no objective right and wrong.

That there is no objective right and wrong doesn't follow from the fact that different cultures have different beliefs about what's right and wrong. That would be like saying there's no objective truth about Tregebov's height because one person thinks she's 5′3″ and another person thinks she's 5′1″.

Here's another example:

All Communists believe the good of the whole is more important than the good of any one individual. You also seem to believe that, so I can't but conclude that you're a Communist!

Again, the conclusion doesn't follow from the premises. While it may be true that all Communists believe that the good of the whole is more important than the good of any one individual, it's not the case that *only* Communists believe that (at least, that wasn't indicated as a premise of the argument). It's quite possible that the "you" in the example is one of the not-Communists to believe that the good of the whole is more important than the good of any one individual.

I imagine this error is most often made because of careless thinking—we simply don't take the time and energy to think through carefully the connection we thought existed between the premise and conclusion.

4.4.3a Practice recognizing non sequiturs

Which of the following arguments contain a non sequitur? Where applicable, re-craft the argument so it is error-free.

1. Because a society is measured by how it treats the weak and vulnerable, we must strive to build a culture of life.

    (President George W. Bush, State of the Union Address, 2005)

2. *Host*: I certainly hear what you're saying. What do you think of President Reagan's economic plan?

    Caller: President Reagan's what?

    Host: His economic plan.

    Caller: Well, I really haven't been too involved in it, because we live in the suburbs . . .

    (Dave Barry, "Radio's Air Heads," in
    Dave Barry's Bad Habits, 1985 [1982/83])

3. *Babcox*: I think the government should take responsibility for our runaway population growth, since it's apparent that individuals have not.

    Reid: So you're a communist!

4. Most murders are committed by someone known to the victim. This means that most murders cannot be prevented by the police.

5. The amazing discovery of the image of "Mother" Teresa in a cinnamon bun in Nashville, Tennessee prompted one of the intellectually challenged to declare: "This should be another example to the people of this planet that God is indeed watching us and Judgment Day is approaching faster than people realize."

    (*The Canadian Atheist*, Summer 1997)

4.4.3b More practice with non sequiturs

Write three arguments that have a non sequitur. Then rewrite your three arguments so they're error-free.

4.4.4 Appeal to emotion

We've already discussed (Section 2.1) how using emotion to persuade is not using argument; that kind of appeal to emotion is not an appeal to reason. However, as already suggested (Section 1.1), emotion *can* have a valid role in argument: an emotional response may constitute a premise. In order to count as a supporting premise, however, the emotional response must be relevant to the conclusion. Recall the example of a child being afraid of the dark; that fear, along with the premise that children who are afraid should be comforted, leads to the conclusion that we should comfort said child.

If, however, the **appeal to emotion** simply expresses an emotional reaction *to* a claim, it doesn't provide support *for* the claim; it's thus irrelevant to the claim. That's the error in reasoning we're talking about here: the use of an emotional response *to* a claim as reason to accept or reject said claim. We may be outraged by an argument, or more precisely, by the conclusion of an argument, but that's irrelevant to whether or not the argument should be accepted. At best, our emotion might indicate that we should examine the matter closely—we may find we have *good reason* for the emotion, reason which can then properly serve in the argument. But otherwise, if the argument is good, then its conclusion should be accepted, outrage aside. Alternatively, we may be quite excited by an argument, but we shouldn't let that convince us—we should look at the evidence, look at the reasoning.

Here's an example:

> You actually grind up animal parts and eat them? That's disgusting! You shouldn't do that!

Whether or not one finds the grinding up and eating of animal parts to be disgusting is irrelevant to the merit of the practice; one's emotional response is insufficient reason for rejecting (or accepting) a claim.

I suppose we make this error because we do get emotional about arguments. And that's okay. But ignore the emotional reaction; focus on the argument. Or better, deal with the emotion separately, first maybe, and *then* deal with the argument. In fact, when you deal with the emotion, when you examine it, you may discover another reason for or against the conclusion in question.

Alternatively, perhaps we appeal to emotion because we can't appeal to reason—perhaps there are no good reasons in support of the opinion or action we're advocating, or perhaps we're just not aware of them.

There are those who disagree with this stance. Consider the following excerpt from an essay by Leon Kass, Chair of the President's Council on Bioethics (despite having not a degree in Ethics or even Philosophy, but, instead, degrees in Science and Medicine):

> Revulsion is not an argument; and some of yesterday's repugnances are today calmly accepted—though, one must add, not always for the better. In crucial

cases, however, repugnance is the emotional expression of deep wisdom, beyond reason's power fully to articulate it. Can anyone really give an argument fully adequate to the horror which is father-daughter incest (even with consent), or having sex with animals, or mutilating a corpse, or eating human flesh, or even just (just!) raping or murdering another human being? Would anybody's failure to give full rational justification for his or her revulsion at these practices make that revulsion ethically suspect? Not at all. On the contrary, we are suspicious of those who think that they can rationalize away our horror, say, by trying to explain the enormity of incest with arguments only about the genetic risks of inbreeding.

The repugnance at human cloning belongs in this category. We are repelled by the prospect of cloning human beings not because of the strangeness or novelty of the undertaking, but because we intuit and feel, immediately and without argument, the violation of things that we rightfully hold dear. Repugnance, here as elsewhere, revolts against the excesses of human willfulness, warning us not to transgress what is unspeakably profound.

(Leon R. Kass, "The Wisdom of Repugnance,"
The New Republic, June 2, 1997)

What do you think? Is repugnance sometimes the emotional expression of deep wisdom? If so, how do we determine when it is and when it is not? And, what if you feel repugnance at cloning, but I don't? Is it right or wrong then? In short, is emotional response sufficient reason for accepting or rejecting a claim? I like what you're saying, it makes me happy, so I'll accept it; I don't like what you're saying, it angers me, so I'll reject it? (You can tell that I endorse the view that unless one can provide rational justification for a belief or action, one should suspend judgment about the merit of said belief or action!)

4.4.4a Practice recognizing appeals to emotion

Which of the following arguments contain an appeal to emotion? Where applicable, re-craft the argument so it is error-free.

1. Look at what you're wearing! I'm so embarrassed! Why must you always embarrass me? Go back into the house and change!

2. You're saying we should pass legislation that would force industry to make all of their products meet certain energy use ceilings—not only during use, but also during production and disposal? That's outrageous!

3. Putting the national flag in your window shows you feel proud of your country. It is good to feel proud. So it is good to put your national flag in your window.

4. I need an A to get into law school. So, you should give me an A.

5. One big question is "How offensive is offensive?" One way to decide this is according to the "reasonable person" standard. But one of the problems with this is that a reasonable man may react quite differently than a reasonable woman: for example, suppose there is someone walking behind you at night who changes sides of the street every time you do—if you're a woman, you might reasonably fear attack, but if you're a man, you might reasonably just think that some idiot can't make up his mind which side of the road he wants to walk on.

4.4.4b More practice with appeals to emotion

Write three arguments that have an appeal to emotion. Then rewrite your three arguments so they're error-free.

4.4.4c Practice recognizing errors of relevance that go off-topic

Which of the following arguments go off-topic?
Identify the specific fallacy involved:

- paper tiger
- red herring
- non sequitur
- appeal to emotion

Where applicable, re-craft the argument so it is error-free.

1. In an episode of *Boston Legal*, a developer is contesting the classification of salmon as an endangered species by adding farmed salmon to the numbers (when that's done, it appears that salmon are not in danger of becoming extinct) in order to be allowed to proceed with a development project which will detrimentally affect the nearby salmon population. The opposition contests his inclusion of farmed salmon in the numbers. The developer says at one point something like "Is a *fish* going to hold up my city?"

   red herring

2. Now, as for parental leave, why should that be a right—with or without pay? I mean if Person A gets a year off to go have a kid, why shouldn't B get a year off to go write music? Is there something special about kids? Let's face it—almost anyone can make a kid, but few people can write music; some kids grow up to be real nasty, but I've seldom heard of music doing any real damage—well, okay, except for country. Is there something special about kids, something that obligates an employer to provide some benefit to

employees? If anything, shouldn't society as a whole bear the burden of maintaining the species? (And I'm not suggesting for a minute that maintaining the species is necessarily a good thing.)

non-sequitur

3. We are an organization of Christian men of science, who accept Jesus Christ as our Lord and Savior. The account of the special creation of Adam and Eve as one man and one woman and their subsequent fall into sin is the basis for our belief in the necessity of a Savior for all mankind. Therefore, salvation can come only through accepting Jesus Christ as our Savior.

(Marcel LaFollette, ed., *Creationism, Science, and the Law: The Arkansas Case*, 1983)

non-sequitur

4. *Stennet*: You know, if you object to animals in a zoo, you should also object to animals as pets.
Tittle: But Taffi is so cute!

emotion

5. *Potts*: The government should not get involved in censorship. People can decide for themselves what they want to see and what they don't want to see. After all, we're adults. Let the marketplace decide. They respond to us—if we don't buy it, it won't get made.
McQuilkin: As long as the marketplace doesn't force images upon us. Pornography is often on the front cover. Which is often in the front window.
Potts: Okay, so some control over display might be warranted. But no control over the images themselves.
McQuilkin: But women can't even agree about which pictures are pornographic.

6. *Patters*: Homosexuality is wrong.
Conti: But homosexuals don't choose to be the way they are; they're born that way.

paper tiger
non-sequitur

7. Well, your conclusion would certainly make a lot of people happy.

8. The aim for which we were fighting the War was the loftiest, the most overpowering, that man can conceive: it was the freedom and independence of our nation, the security of our future food supply, and—our national honor: a thing which, despite all contrary opinions prevailing today, nevertheless exists, or rather should exist, since peoples without honor have sooner or later lost their freedom and independence, which in turn is only the result of a higher justice, since generations of rabble without honor deserve no freedom. Any man who wants to be a cowardly slave can have no honor, or honor itself would soon fall into general contempt.

(Adolf Hitler, *Mein Kampf*, 1925)

153

9. One potential invasion of privacy involves monitoring job performance. After all, how else can management be sure it has a quality workforce—by rumour? Surely first hand evidence is preferable. But what, exactly, should this evidence include? Monitoring the employee's phone calls? Reading the employee's email messages? I think not. It's unreasonable to demand, and indeed unhealthy to expect, that all phone calls and email messages be bereft of anything personal. Given that, it would be a personal invasion to monitor calls and messages. Wouldn't it be more effective to respect people's privacy and trust them to do their jobs well? Treat someone like an irresponsible, cheating kid and soon enough they'll act like one.

10. *Mitton*: A classic case of worker safety is the asbestos thing. The Johns Manville Company became aware of the adverse health effects of asbestos exposure in the 1930s but did nothing to inform its workers. Are they therefore more at fault than the company that unawares causes harm to its workers? Does knowing make you more responsible? If so, companies may refuse to thoroughly investigate matters, enabling them to later plead ignorance and therefore innocence.

  Boresen: It could take years before one knows for sure though. Is the company supposed to test its materials and procedures for decades before opening?

4.4.4d More practice recognizing irrelevant comments

Listen to or watch one hour's worth of a talk show, and make a note of every irrelevant comment. Identify as many specific fallacies as you can. (Note that before you can determine what's irrelevant, you have to determine what's relevant. And before you determine what's relevant to the issue, you have to determine what the issue is—what's the argument about? *Is* there an argument, a point, being made?)

Review of terms

Define the following terms:

- relevance

- appeal to the person (ad hominem)

- genetic fallacy _— history / origins_

- appeal to inappropriate authority

- appeal to tradition or past practice

- appeal to custom, habit, or common practice

- appeal to moderation (or lack of)

- appeal to popularity (or lack of)

- "two wrongs" fallacy

- paper tiger _— straw man_

- red herring _— distraction_

- non sequitur _— bad deduction_

- appeal to emotion.

Highlight the five errors that are typically made in response to an argument rather than while constructing an argument.

Thinking critically about what you see

Think critically about each of the following. In particular, consider relevance. Are the signs relevant to the implied claim being made by the protest? What is the relevance of the corporate logos in place of the stars?

155

1.

© Marilynn K. Yee/The New York Times/Redux

2.

© Courtesy www.adbusters. org

Thinking critically about what you hear

Listen to the audio clip under the Student Resources tab on the companion website at www.routledge.com/textbooks/tittle. Any response?

Thinking critically about what you read

Think critically about each of the following, focusing, first, on the first two steps in the template. At this point, you should be able to extract the outline for each argument: indicate,

Template for critical analysis

1. What's the point (claim/opinion/conclusion)?

   ■ Look for subconclusions as well.

2. What are the reasons/what is the evidence?

   ■ Articulate all unstated premises.
   ■ Articulate connections.

3. What exactly is meant by . . .?

   ■ Define terms.
   ■ Clarify all imprecise language.
   ■ Eliminate or replace "loaded" language and other manipulations.

4. Assess the reasoning/evidence:

   ■ If deductive, check for truth/acceptability and validity.
   ■ If inductive, check for truth/acceptability, relevance, and sufficiency.

5. How could the argument be strengthened?

   ■ Provide additional reasons/evidence.
   ■ Anticipate objections—are there adequate responses?

6. How could the argument be weakened?

   ■ Consider and assess counterexamples, counterevidence, and counter-arguments.
   ■ Should the argument be modified or rejected because of the counter-arguments?

7. If you suspend judgment (rather than accepting or rejecting the argument), identify further information required.

perhaps with some sort of diagram, the individual premises and conclusions, and their relationship to each other. Then, as per this chapter, check the reasons and evidence for relevance, part of the fourth step. And, again, if you can think of what would strengthen or weaken the argument, say so!

1. A man who had moved to Hialeah, but continued to vote in Miami: "I've always felt more in tune with things in Miami than anywhere else. Look, I'm an American citizen and I feel you don't violate the law when you vote. It's my right as an American citizen."

    (Dave Barry, *Dave Barry Hits Below the Beltway*, 2001)

2. Norm Brodsky knows that unions do quality work and that hiring local people is good for a business's reputation in the community ["Why the Union Can't Win," March]. He says that before he met with the representatives from Local 361, he was considering hiring a few union guys, as a gesture of goodwill—but after the business manager for Local 361 was gruff with him, that went out the window. The lack of sales technique on the part of Local 361's representative was an affront to the author's entrepreneurial sensibilities.

    (Robert Cavanaugh, Exton, PA, *Inc .Magazine*, May 2005)

3. You know, without Christ, without Jesus, we have no hope. Why? Well, because we know that the standard of God's righteousness is Law, a law of the Ten Commandments, a law of statutes and judgments. And which God gave unto Moses on Sinai, saying this is thy righteousness, O Israel.

    (David Koresh, of the Branch Davidians, best known for the Waco, Texas, incident, 1993, at: http://www.serendipity.li/waco/koresh.html)

4. Question asked in June 29/05 issue of *am New York* "What do you think of New York City's chances of winning the 2012 Olympic Games?"

    "Outside of Paris we have an excellent chance. Hopefully our perseverance over recent setbacks with the stadium deal will convince the Olympic Committee that we deserve the games." Leonard Wilson, age 20

    "My impression of New York City is that after 9/11 the city made such an effort to be strong that it deserves to win the games." Marion Strack, age 47

    "I think there is a great chance for us. The athletes work hard and need to relax after the games, and where can you find better nightlife than in New York?" Chancel Torres, age 16

    "According to the papers our chances are very slim, but the versatility of the city might carry us through in the end." Jim Behrens, age 44

    "We have a lot of enthusiasm for the Olympics. I'm new to the city and I'm always shocked by the diversity of people here. And New Yorkers are much friendlier than their stereotype." Ruchi Pancholy, age 22

5. Until Harrah's Casino in Reno, Nev., fired Darlene Jespersen in August 2000, she had been a model employee for more than 20 years. As a bartender in the casino's sports

bar, Jespersen consistently received "highly effective" ratings. Her supervisor nominated her in 1996 for a special employee award. Loyal customers wrote her fan mail, and she still gets teary-eyed remembering her regulars.

But in spring 2000, Harrah's introduced a "personal best" policy that required women beverage servers to, among other things, wear makeup—foundation or powder, mascara, blush and lipstick. The makeup had to be applied precisely the same way each day, in order to match a baseline photograph held by the supervisor. Males, in comparison, were required *not* to wear makeup. Jespersen, who felt uncomfortable having to "doll" herself up in an ultra-feminine way, said no to cosmetics and was fired.

She filed a federal sex-discrimination suit under Title VII of the 1964 Civil Rights Act, arguing that the makeup policy posed a bigger burden on women than men and that it perpetuated harmful gender stereotypes. "I don't think it makes a woman any more professional," she said. "I think it should be a woman's choice."

(Lucia Hwang and Michele Kort, "Judicial Worst," *Ms.*, Spring 2005)

6. We certainly don't want a society in which the *average* wage paid to *all* women equals the *average* wage paid to *all* men because that would be a society which would have eliminated the role of motherhood. The career of motherhood is not recorded or compensated in cash wages in government statistics, but that doesn't make it any less valuable. It is the most socially useful role of all. We don't even want a society in which the average wage paid to all *working* women equals the average wage paid to all working men, because that would be a society in which working wives and mothers would be working in paid employment all their lives for as many hours a week as men. Most wives do not do this now, and they don't want to do it. By working fewer hours in the paid labor force, wives and mothers can give more time to their families and to the role of motherhood.

We want a society in which the average man earns more than the average women so that his earnings can fulfill his provider role in providing a home and support for his wife who is nurturing and mothering their children. We certainly don't want feminist pressure groups to change public policy in order to force us into a society in which all women are locked into the work force on a lifetime basis, because that would mean forfeiting their precious years and hours as a mother.

(Phyllis Schlafly, "Government Intrusion in the Workplace," in "Statement Submitted to Committee on Labor and Human Resources," United States Senate, in *Hearings on Sexual Discrimination in the Workplace*, 97th Congress, 1st Session, April 21, 1981)

7. *Question*: "I am a newly anointed thirtysomething, and I recently purchased a black three-quarter-length slim-fitting overcoat. I like it tremendously and favor it over the dowdy full-length version sported by our nation's finest accountants and lawyers. I do, however, have a concern that it may not be formal enough for some occasions. I would think yes with a sport coat, maybe (but risky) with a suit, and no with a tux. Is this correct?"

Answer: "Does it look bad to you? We're having a mod moment here, so the rules are in semi-abeyance if you're cutting a dashing figure. If it's a chic-looking coat, you can wear it with a tux, even if it hits you above the knees. And what's wrong with a black-tie car coat? It's not like you're going to walk to the ball; the coat is just for getting you from the carriage to the cloakroom. Besides, you're 30 now, and you can make a statement if you want to."

(Glenn O'Brien, "The Style Guy," *GQ*, June 3, 2005)

8. Advertisers who sell to children are asking the most impressionable and least experienced members of the audience to make complex and reasoned consumer judgments. In order to make a meaningful purchase decision, the child, whose skills of analysis and judgment are still in a developmental stage, must answer an intricate series of questions: Is the product as it appears in the TV commercials? Is the product more desirable than other products in its category? Does the desire or need for the product justify its price? Does the product have limitations or potential harmful effects which should be considered? Is the price a reasonable and/or affordable one?

At every step of the consumer reasoning process, the child is at a disadvantage. Analysis of child-oriented commercials suggests that children are given little true consumer information, few facts about the price, durability, or nutritional value of a given product. . . .

. . .

Since most young children do not comprehend an advertiser's motives, they lack the reasonable skepticism which adults exhibit when evaluating commercials. Research findings have revealed that as many as half of all preschool children believe that all commercials are true in a literal sense. Findings such as these reflect the child's incomplete conception of the world. The geocentric nature of the young child as described in cognitive development theory suggests that he cannot see into the minds of others and that he cannot imagine that others see the world differently than he does.

. . .

It is believed that advertising directed to very young children is inherently deceptive and unfair and should be stopped.

(Peggy Charren, "Should We Ban TV Advertising to Children? Yes,"
National Forum: Phi Kappa Phi Journal, Fall 1979)

9. In the wake of the embarrassing Harriet Miers nomination, it is time to ask: Shouldn't feminists—the source of the mandate for a female Supreme Court justice—be disqualified from *any* influence on public affairs? An exchange in the Yale alumni magazine provides the perfect vehicle for analyzing the lunacy of feminist ideology and its unfitness for the real world.

In May, the magazine ran several articles on religion at Yale, provoked by the university's decision to sever ties between its chapel and the Congregationalist Church (now known as the United Church of Christ). The magazine's cover showed a close-up of four smiling clergymen sharing a laugh against the backdrop of Yale's neo-Gothic arches. The caption read: "So, a minister, a priest, a Buddhist, and a rabbi walk into a university . . . no joke: religion at Yale."

This image was more than two female Yale graduates could bear. "I was ashamed at the cover of last month's alumni magazine," wrote Danielle Elizabeth Tumminio in a letter to the editor. Demonstrating the deconstructive interpretive skills she undoubtedly picked up as an undergraduate, Tumminio went on: "[T]his image sends the message that Yale as an academic and spiritual center has not progressed far from the days when only men could take books out of the library, enroll in classes, and graduate with diplomas that gave them the privilege to lead congregations. . . . [I]t waters down religion at Yale to a patriarchy in which students are asked to conform to the God of the old boys' network."

The Rev. Clare Robert, a divinity school graduate, was equally distraught: "I couldn't believe my eyes when I saw the latest issue of your magazine," she wrote. "I believe an apology is in order." To the Rev. Robert, Yale's cover shows the failure of "30-plus years of feminism and feminist theology." She asks incredulously: "Didn't anyone look at that front cover of four clergymen and see how unrepresentative it is of Yale, of the people in the pews, and even the campus ministries these men supposedly represent?" Inevitably, Robert also took offense at the article's title: "Gods and Man at Yale." A more "sensitive" editor, she admonished, would have amended the title to "Gods and (Wo)Man at Yale"—and literary style be damned.

The world learned last January that the neurasthenic streak in today's feminists has become so strong that they collapse at the mere mention of scientific hypotheses that displease them (as befell MIT biologist Nancy Hopkins upon hearing Harvard president Larry Summers aver to possible sex differences in mathematical ability). Now it turns out that the neo-Victorians cannot even tolerate the sight of men together without breaking out into shame and dismay.

Tumminio and Robert's elicitation of the "patriarchy" from the magazine's cover is a heavy burden to place on one light-hearted photo—especially since the photo happens to be true. It depicts Yale's four university chaplains—Protestant, Jewish, Buddhist, and Catholic—who just happen to be men. Contrary to Robert's assertion that the picture is "unrepresentative" of Yale, it is perfectly representative of the leaders of Yale's main religious communities and is a wholly unremarkable way of introducing the topic at hand.

The irony is that despite their gripe about the cover, Tumminio and Robert implicitly acknowledge that there is nothing remotely "patriarchal" about Yale. Women have a "prominent role" in spiritually nurturing Yale students, Tumminio notes, and serve in large numbers on the divinity school faculty. "Womanist and feminist theology" features prominently in Yale's "religious traditions," says Robert.

The suggestion that the alumni magazine's editors are insensitive to women is equally delusional. This is the same magazine that enthusiastically follows every latest development in Yale's women's and gender studies program, as well as in its queer studies initiatives. In the issue in which Tumminio's and Robert's letters appear, the renowned-alumnus slot goes to Debbie Stoller, the editor of *Bust* magazine ("For

Women With Something to Get Off Their Chests") and author of *Stitch 'n Bitch Nation*, which inspired an international network of women's knitting groups.

But feminism is above all else insanely narcissistic and hermetically sealed off from reality. The truth doesn't matter. The fact that the university chaplains *are* male is irrelevant. Feminists such as Tumminio and Robert insist that they must see the female image everywhere, and if they don't, they find solace in something far more satisfying: perpetual injury and rage. Actual equality and access to every social institution count for nothing; one lousy picture, however accurate, triggers an eruption of grievance.

So what is a poor photo editor to do? He has a pleasant image of Yale's university chaplains for a series about the range of religious experience at the college. His problem: The chaplains are men. He knows that this will cause a furor. But what is the proper ratio of male to female that will prevent a feminist wound? If fifty-fifty is always required, does he keep the four chaplains and add four female associate chaplains? If so, the picture will be impossibly crowded. If, on the other hand, he starts jettisoning a chaplain here and a chaplain there in order to reduce the male population, who goes first? The editor's instinct, of course, will be to throw out the Catholic and the Protestant, since they are most associated with the oppressive Western tradition. But here, the sensitive photo editor breaches another mandate: racial representation. Turns out Yale's Protestant chaplain is black. Note that the racial "inclusiveness" of the magazine's cover photo mattered not one iota to the censors, demonstrating that feminists will kick their "people of color" allies in the chops in an instant in their pursuit of female hegemony.

The easiest solution, obviously, is to get rid of the university chaplains entirely and find an all-female photo. And if this picture runs, the editor will receive not one letter from an incensed male reader complaining that he did not see himself "represented" on the cover. Until the feminists can develop a similar degree of immunity to the terrible traumas that daily life inflicts, they should nurse their fragile egos at home and not even think of engagement in anything as bruising as Supreme Court politics.

(Heather MacDonald, "God and (Wo)man at Yale,"
The Weekly Standard, October 17, 2005)

10. In September, *Adbusters* entered into high-level negotiations with the Fox Broadcast Corporation. We wanted to do what any burger, beer, SUV or shampoo company can do every day in America: buy 15, 30 or 60 seconds of airtime. The answer came as no surprise: "You might understand, for a broadcast TV network things like boycotting television and anti-consumerism might not go over very well with our other advertisers," said Tim Souris of the broadcast standards department. Fox, he said, makes an effort not to rock the boat.

. . . So up the ladder we went to Darlene Lieblich, executive director of broadcast standards. The Fox policy comes from the top, she said—"the Fox über-mensch." Product ads are okay, and advocacy ads are not. Case closed.

. . .

What we needed was a network with guts, so we went knocking on doors at MTV. We showed Jackie Soriano, the director of commercial clearance, a set of eight TV spots about everything from anti-consumerism to voodoo economics to television addiction. "We can't advertise something that's too controversial," said Soriano. But is it controversial to point out, for example, that 52 percent of a Big Mac's calories come from fat? It's a fact: we got the information from McDonald's own website.

MTV: As I said, we're a network and we are loyal to our advertisers. We cannot accept advertising that disparages our major advertisers.

Adbusters: And isn't having all the information important when the public makes a decision?

MTV: They do have all the information. They know what they're eating. We do make the public aware, absolutely. But anything controversial, we cannot accept.

Adbusters: And you feel the basic health information about a product is controversial?

MTV: Like I said, it is up to the fast food chains to decide whether or not they want to expose the public to that.

Adbusters: To know all the health information of food—is that not important to know?

MTV: Sir, all I can tell you is that it would be up to McDonald's to tell you how terrible their food is for you.

Thinking critically about what you write

Below you will find an outline for an argument. Present the argument in a clear and coherent paragraph using complete and connected sentences. Note that the outline includes the anticipation of an objection and a reply to that objection.

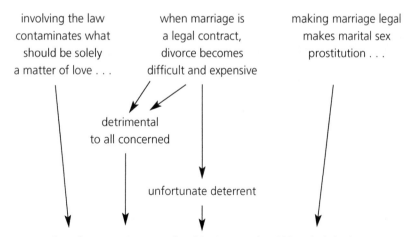

involving the law contaminates what should be solely a matter of love . . .

when marriage is a legal contract, divorce becomes difficult and expensive

making marriage legal makes marital sex prostitution . . .

detrimental to all concerned

unfortunate deterrent

Therefore, marriage as a legal institution should be abolished.

BUT without the legal obligation, care for the children that result from the marriage is at risk—stability, financial support . . .

When you have finished, double-check that you have connected your dots. This is best done by putting it aside for a day or so and then coming back to it; points you thought were clear when (because) they were very much in your mind may not be so clear when you're coming at it anew—which is how other people will be coming at it. Another good thing to do is once you've written your argument, go ask someone to read your paragraphs and tell you honestly whether they followed you; if not, you probably need to connect your dots more explicitly.

Thinking critically when you discuss

Again meet in groups of three, one person initiating the discussion with an argument, and the other two people taking turns responding to that argument. Choose from the same repertoire of responses as you used last time, but since we've just covered all those errors of relevance, be particularly attentive to the relevance of the premises as per response 2(ii):

1. Ask for clarification—perhaps you don't really understand how the pieces fit together or perhaps you don't understand what one particular piece means.
2. Accept or reject a premise. There are only three good reasons for rejecting a premise:

    (i) It's simply not true (or acceptable).
    (ii) It's not relevant to the conclusion.
    (iii) It's not sufficient enough to support the conclusion.

    Any one of those reasons is reason enough to reject a premise; in order to accept a premise, all three conditions—truth/acceptability, relevance, sufficiency—must be met.
    Rejecting a premise may or may not require you to reject the conclusion: it depends on whether that premise is the only one or, if not, how important it is (for example, whether all the other premises depend on it).
3. Strengthen the argument either by adding detail or example to a premise, by modifying a premise to make it acceptable, relevant, or sufficient, or by adding a completely new premise that supports the conclusion.

And here's the chart again:

	true/acceptable	relevant	sufficient
premise 1 (?) (*)			
premise 2 (?) (*)			
premise 3 (?) (*)			
Therefore, conclusion:			

Suggestion: Disagreement is bound to occur, and when it does, it helps to deal with it in a mature fashion. It's especially impressive if you can do that before you're 30. When someone disagrees with you, think of them as shining a spotlight on something, and recognize that it's to your advantage to take a good look: maybe that particular reason *is* a bad one, and maybe you can strengthen it or maybe you should find another reason, or maybe you should reject the claim that reason was supposed to have supported.

Reasoning test questions

1. A program instituted in a particular state allows parents to prepay their children's future college tuition at current rates. The program then pays the tuition annually for the child at any of the state's public colleges in which the child enrolls. Parents should participate in the program as a means of decreasing the cost of their children's college education.

   Which of the following, if true, is the most appropriate reason for parents *not* to participate in the program?

   (A) The parents are unsure about which public college in the state the child will attend.
   (B) The amount of money accumulated by putting the prepayment funds in an interest-bearing account today will be greater than the total cost of tuition for any of the public colleges when the child enrolls.

(C) The annual cost of tuition at the state's public colleges is expected to increase at a faster rate than the annual increase in the cost of living.

(D) Some of the state's public colleges are contemplating large increases in tuition next year.

(E) The prepayment plan would not cover the cost of room and board at any of the state's public colleges.

(GMAT® mini test #2)

2. Most adults in country X consume an increasing amount of fat as they grow older. However, for nearly all adults in country X, the percentage of fat in a person's diet stays the same throughout adult life.

The statements above, if true, most strongly support which one of the following conclusions about adults in country X?

(A) They generally consume more fat than do people of the same age in other countries.

(B) They generally eat more when they are older than they did earlier in their adult-hood.

(C) They generally have diets that contain a lower percentage of fat than do the diets of children in country X.

(D) They tend to eat more varied kinds of food as they become older.

(E) They tend to lose weight as they become older.

(The Official LSAT Prep Test XXII, Section 4, #12)

3. The caterpillar of the monarch butterfly feeds on milkweed plants, whose toxins make the adult monarch poisonous to many predators. The viceroy butterfly, whose cater-pillars do not feed on milkweed plants, is very similar in appearance to the monarch. Therefore, it can be concluded that the viceroy is so seldom preyed on because of its visual resemblance to the monarch.

Which one of the following, if it were discovered to be true, would most seriously undermine the argument?

(A) Some predators do not have a toxic reaction to insects that feed on milkweed plants.

(B) Being toxic to predators will not protect individual butterflies unless most members of the species to which such butterflies belong are similarly toxic.

(C) Some of the predators of the monarch butterfly also prey on viceroys.

(D) The viceroy butterfly is toxic to most predators.

(E) Toxicity to predators is the principal means of protection for only a few butterfly species.

(The Official LSAT Prep Test XXIII, Section 2, #8)

4. *Antinuclear activist*: The closing of the nuclear power plant is a victory for the anti-nuclear cause. It also represents a belated acknowledgment by the power industry that they cannot operate such plants safely. ✓

    Nuclear power plant manager: It represents no such thing. The availability of cheap power from nonnuclear sources, together with the cost of mandated safety inspections and safety repairs, made continued operation uneconomic. Thus it was not safety considerations but economic considerations that dictated the plant's closing.

    Which one of the following, if true, most strongly supports the activist's claim of victory?

    (A) The plant had reached the age at which its operating license expired.
    (B) The mandate for inspections and repairs mentioned by the manager was recently enacted as a result of pressure from antinuclear groups.
    (C) The plant would not have closed if cheap power from nonnuclear sources had not been available.
    (D) Per unit of electricity produced, the plant had the highest operating costs of any nuclear power plant.
    (E) The plant that closed had been able to provide backup power to an electrical network when parts of the network became overloaded.

    (The Official LSAT Prep Test XXI, Section 2, #23)

5. When a stone is trimmed by a mason and exposed to the elements, a coating of clay and other minerals, called rock varnish, gradually accumulates on the freshly trimmed surface. Organic matter trapped beneath the varnish on stones of an Andean monument was found to be over 1,000 years old. Since the organic matter must have grown on the stone shortly after it was trimmed, it follows that the monument was built long before the arrival of Europeans in the Americas in 1492.

    Which one of the following, if true, most seriously weakens the argument?

    (A) Rock varnish itself contains some organic matter.
    (B) The reuse of ancient trimmed stones was common in the Andes both before and after 1492.
    (C) The Andean monument bears a striking resemblance to monuments found in ancient sites in western Asia.
    (D) The earliest written reference to the Andean monument dates from 1778.
    (E) Rock varnish forms very slowly, if at all, on trimmed stones that are stored in a dry, sheltered place.

    (The Official LSAT Prep Test XXIII, Section 3, #19)

167

chapter 5

language

Template for critical analysis

1. What's the point (claim/opinion/conclusion)?

   - Look for subconclusions as well.

2. What are the reasons/what is the evidence?

   - Articulate all unstated premises.
   - Articulate connections.

3. **What exactly is meant by . . .?**

   - **Define terms.**
   - **Clarify all imprecise language.**
   - **Eliminate or replace "loaded" language and other manipulations.**

4. Assess the reasoning/evidence:

   - If deductive, check for truth/acceptability and validity.
   - If inductive, check for truth/acceptability, relevance, and sufficiency.

5. How could the argument be strengthened?

   - Provide additional reasons/evidence.
   - Anticipate objections—are there adequate responses?

6. How could the argument be weakened?

   - Consider and assess counterexamples, counterevidence, and counter-arguments.
   - Should the argument be modified or rejected because of the counter-arguments?

7. If you suspend judgment (rather than accepting or rejecting the argument), identify further information required.

Good language—language that is clear and neutral—facilitates critical thinking. Language that is unclear and slanted gets in the way of critical thinking; quite simply, it makes it harder to do.

After all, words have meanings. They stand for objects, qualities, quantities, concepts. Different words generally mean different things. But sometimes different words mean the same thing. And sometimes the same word can mean different things. (Is it any wonder we occasionally misunderstand each other?) Choosing which words to use, and choosing how to put those words together, is tremendously important; your choices affect your meaning.

So this chapter is not just about language, for language is merely the way we convey our thinking. This chapter is about clear thinking. And it's about expressing that thinking in a neutral way—without deception, manipulation, or similar interference with people's autonomy, their rational assessment of what you've said.

5.1 Clarity

As you've probably learned from the last chapter, it's important to be clear. If a person's argument isn't clear, it won't be understood—at least, it won't be understood as intended; and if it's not understood, it can't be assessed.

5.1.1 Precise diction

Clarity is largely a matter of being *precise*, of choosing the perfect word, the word that means *exactly* what you mean, what you think. For example, suppose someone says "Sure, I might've said some not so nice things about you, but I didn't hurt you!" What exactly is meant by "some not so nice things"? Are we talking about racist slurs or did the person just say you're never on time? If the former, it's doubtful the person wasn't hurt—unless only "physical injury" was meant by the word "hurt."

Rolling Stone published a list of "Rock Immortals" (May 19, 2005), but judging by the letters which followed, some of which are presented below, their definition of "immortal," of what makes someone "immortal" for the purposes of their list, was not at all clear:

Thank you for "The Immortals II". I'm grateful for the reflections on Diana Ross. There is a strong case for her place in the civil-rights movement. The Supremes truly were "America's Sweethearts" at a time when African-Americans were still mainly playing maids and butlers on TV and in film.

(Donald King)

So is it socio-political contribution or popularity (as sweethearts) that makes them immortal?

> Your list of Rock's 100 immortals was brilliant. But I'm puzzled by the omission of B.B. King. Listen to the three-minute opening guitar solo on "How Blue Can You Get?" from *Live in Cook County Jail* and tell me it was performed by a mere mortal!
>
> (Alex Hinds)

Or is it their godlike-ness?

> How could Pink Floyd be left off this list? *Dark Side of the Moon* is the second-best-selling album of all time. It has been on the *Billboard* music charts for an unprecedented 740 weeks.
>
> (Steve Richmond)

Here it's the music, not the musician, that's immortal—as measured by longevity of sales.

> The omission of Talking Heads is glaring. Their blend of art, punk, Third World rhythms, and American R & B and funk has had my hips shaking and my soul satisfied since I was a kid.
>
> (Quinn Callicott)

. . . suggesting that immortality is defined by the positive effect on one person? Hmm . . .

> Since R.E.M. have been on the cover of your magazine as the best band in America, shouldn't that grant them a position among your hallowed immortals?
>
> (Mike Shara)

Okay, here we're back to popularity, this time as measured by appearance on the cover of *Rolling Stone*.

> After reading "The Immortals," I realized its flaw: You chose only people within the music industry to vote. Next time leave it up to the fans—those of us who run to the stores with our last money to buy albums, stand in line to see live shows and cry as we rock out to our heroes.
>
> (Daniel Labbie)

Good point. Even if *Rolling Stone did* provide a clear definition, their results have limited value perhaps because they asked only one small group which bands met that definition.

Precise diction, or word choice, depends, then, on having a reasonably large vocabulary. You can't use a word you don't know. Maybe "ubiquitous" is exactly what you mean, exactly what you have in mind, but if you don't know that there is a word for what you have in mind, and that that word is "ubiquitous," you can't use it.

So part of being precise is avoiding *vague words*, words that have no clear meaning. When you use a fuzzy word, you will be expressing a fuzzy thought. For example, the claim "This is a good book" is imprecise because the word "good" is too vague—what exactly do you mean by "good"? The claim "A lot of people were there" is equally imprecise—how many is a lot?

Ambiguous words are also worth mention here, although they're not necessarily imprecise; they are unclear, however, because they have more than one meaning. For example, on an episode of the television show *Commander in Chief*, the President (played by Geena Davis) tells a staff member, "I don't want to hear that torture was used—am I understood?" It later becomes clear that she meant torture should be banned; however, the staff member understood her to be giving tacit permission to torture without informing her—presumably so she could later claim, if need be, that she didn't know. Both interpretations are valid: the phrase "I don't want to hear about it" could be understood both ways. And in this case, the ambiguity, the lack of clarity, led to extremely serious consequences.

Another part of being precise is avoiding *exaggeration*. For example, if it's not the case that *everyone* does X, don't say it is!

5.1.1a Practice recognizing and improving imprecise diction

Which of the following contains imprecise diction? Rewrite the problematic sentences to be clear.

1. "For Smarter Intelligence"—heading of a letter to the editor about the failure of the FBI and CIA to act on information they had.

   (*Time*, May 17, 2004)

2. What it is, however, is a convenient list of products designed, crafted, and produced by Americans for Americans in America (I realize that sounds a little redundant).

   (posted on the Free Republic website, at: http://www.freerepublic.com/focus/f-news/1542841/posts, accessed January 15, 2010)

3. Israeli Prime Minister Ariel Sharon suffered a minor stroke but his condition was improving, a hospital spokesman said Sunday.

   (CNN website December 18, 2005, at: http://rss.crossmap.com/article/israeli-prime-minister-sharon-hospitalized-after-stroke/story52621.htm, accessed January 15, 2010)

4. People often underestimate the commitment in merging two lives together. The reason we fight most about money is because it's the most measurable. Sure, compromises also need to be made when it comes to issues of time, space and affection, but with money the give and take is quantifiable.

(Dr. Phil's website, at:
http://www.drphil.com/articles/article/32, accessed January 15, 2010)

5. Are children of older parents at greater risk?

6. Make a fresh start! Set goals and achieve your dreams with a little help from the cosmos.

(msn.astrology)

7. I pledge allegiance to the flag of the United States of America . . .

8. The California Highway Patrol is turning to the classroom for a new driver education program the agency hopes will lower a sobering statistic: Teen drivers are involved in automobile collisions at a higher rate than any other segment of the motoring public. The program, called Start Smart, will begin early in 2006 and bring together the CHP and newly licensed teen drivers, along with their parents or guardians, to discuss ways to prevent the young adults from developing bad – read: aggressive – driving behaviors that lead to injuries and fatalities.

(Posted on the Free Republic website, at: http://www.freerepublic.com)

9. History is a required course in the tenth grade.

10. This organization is dedicated to strategic wildlife management.

5.1.1b *More practice recognizing and improving imprecise diction*

Find five examples of imprecise diction. Consider textbooks, newspapers, magazines, websites, radio, television, and so on. Rewrite them with a more precise word.

It starts at the gate: "We'd like to begin the *boarding process*." Extra word. "Process." Not necessary. Boarding is sufficient. "We'd like to begin the boarding." Simple. Tells the story. People add extra words when they want things to sound more important than they really are. "Boarding process" sounds important. It isn't. It's just a group of people getting on an airplane.

To begin their boarding process, the airline announces they will *pre-board* certain passengers. And I wonder, How can that be? How can people board before they board? This I gotta see. But before anything interesting can happen I'm told to get on the plane. "Sir, you can get on the plane now." And I think for a moment. "*On* the plane? No, my friends, not me. I'm not getting *on* the plane; I'm getting *in* the plane! Let Evel Knievel get on the plane, I'll be sitting inside in one of those little chairs. It seems less windy in there."

Then they mention that it's a *nonstop flight*. Well, I must say I don't care for that sort of thing. Call me old-fashioned, but I insist that my flight stop. Preferably at an airport. Somehow those sudden cornfield stops interfere with the flow of my day. And just about at this point, they tell me the flight has been delayed because of a *change of equipment*. And deep down I'm thinking, "broken plane!"

Speaking of potential mishaps, here's a phrase that apparently the airlines simply made up: *near miss*. They say that if two planes almost collide it's a near miss. Bullshit, my friend. It's a near hit! A *collision* is a near miss.

[WHAM! CRUNCH!]

"Look, they nearly missed!"

"Yes, but not quite."

. . .

"Please continue *to observe the No Smoking sign until well inside the terminal*." Folks, I've tried this. Let me tell you it is physically impossible to observe the No Smoking sign, even from just outside the airplane, much less from well inside the terminal. In fact, you can't even see the *airplanes* from well inside the terminal.

(George Carlin, *Napalm & Silly Putty*, 2001)

5.1.2 Precise grammar

However, choosing the right word is only part of being precise. Having the right grammar is equally important.

Consider the following four sentences:

Only I drank one beer.
I only drank one beer.
I drank only one beer.
I drank one beer only.

Four sentences, four different meanings. Which do you say when the police question you, suspecting you are driving under the influence?

"Only I drank one beer" means "*Only I*—no one else drank one beer."

"I only drank one beer" means "I *only drank* the beer—I didn't do anything else with it, like buy it."

"I drank only one beer" means "I drank *only one*—not two, not three, only one."

"I drank one beer only" means "I drank one beer *only*; that's all I did; I didn't do anything else."

Sometimes one sentence can have two (or more) different meanings:

After the woman saved her daughter, she went to work as usual.

Who went to work, the woman or the daughter? There's nothing grammatically incorrect about the sentence; it's just ambiguous—it has two meanings. The only way to fix something like that is to re-craft the sentence altogether:

After saving her daughter, the woman went to work.

Consider this statement: "I don't know anybody who believes in dirty air or dirty water" (Irving Shapiro, former chair of the board of the Du Pont Company). What does that mean? What does it mean to *believe in dirty air*? Does he mean, instead, "I don't know anybody who believes dirty air exists"? Or does he mean "I don't know anybody who thinks dirty air is a good thing"? The sentences "I believe in God" and "I believe in freedom," although grammatically identical, mean two different things: in the first case, "believe in" means "believe it exists," whereas in the second case, "believe in" means "believe it is a good thing."

Speaking of God, here's another example, one that's a little more complicated. We have often heard Friedrich Nietzsche's phrase "God is dead." But what exactly does it mean? What, exactly, do those three words put together like that mean? Vincent Ryan Ruggiero suggests the following possibilities, each of which is far more precise than "God is dead": People no longer *want* to believe God exists. People are no longer *able* to believe God exists. People are no longer *certain* God exists. People no longer *act* as if God exists. People no longer *care* whether God exists. People no longer *accept* some particular conception of God. People are no longer *satisfied* with the limitation of traditional expressions of belief in God's existence. Given the many plausible possibilities, you can see how easily you could be misunderstood if you simply said "God is dead."

Lastly, if grammar fails you, consider using emphasis (through italics or underlining, for example) to make your meaning clear. But be judicious; and be sure you're using such emphasis *not* as an emotional punch, but as a cue to your meaning.

5.1.2a *Practice recognizing and improving imprecise grammar*

Which of the following contain imprecise grammar? Rewrite the problematic sentences to be clear.

1. When driving through fog, what should you use?

2. *Berzins*: Mary had a little lamb.

   Vanderholt: Wow, genetic engineering has advanced more than I thought.

3. What is the difference between a flashing red traffic light and a flashing yellow traffic light?

4. I could care less.

5. She said that the proposal to build a security wall along the Canadian-American border indicates a lack of understanding about what the real challenges are of the Canadian-American border.

6. A Conservative government would consider abandoning the United States as Canada's main trading partner if the two countries can't quickly resolve the softwood lumber dispute, Stephen Harper said Saturday. The Tory leader said the future of the North American Free Trade Agreement depends on the United States agreeing to honor a ruling that it should repay at least $5 billion in illegal softwood duties collected since 2002.

   (Michelle Macafee, *National Post* website,
   December 17, 2005, at: http://www.nationalpost.com)

7. The higher the profits, the better the company.

8. Randy Thomas, arguably the Washington Redskins' best offensive lineman, fractured his right leg early in the fourth quarter yesterday and will miss the rest of the season. Thomas will have surgery today to repair the break in his fibula.

   (*Washington Times*, December 19, 2005)

9. All men are created equal.

10. However, more elaborate versions of this particular argument exist, and notably that developed in the book, *Dismay*, which, for reasons that will later become apparent, is of particular interest to us.

5.1.2b More practice recognizing and improving imprecise grammar

Find five examples of imprecise grammar. Consider textbooks, newspapers, magazines, websites, radio, television, and so on. Rewrite them so their meaning is more precise.

5.1.3 Repetition

Sometimes repetition can increase clarity. For example, one might explain a difficult concept in more than one way to be sure it's understood.

However, sometimes repetition decreases clarity. Consider this statement:

I admire your invention because it's practical, innovative, and original.

You might reasonably think that I have three reasons for admiring your invention, but since innovation is the same as originality, I have been redundant. Since I have said the same thing twice, I actually have only two reasons.

Saying the same thing twice is most a problem, however, when you say it once as your conclusion and once as your premise, which is—a circular argument (Section 2.4). Consider the following:

Travel faster than the speed of light is impossible because it can't happen.

Saying that travel faster than the speed of light is impossible is the same as saying it can't happen, so the speaker has said the same thing twice. He or she has actually said "Travel faster than the speed of light is impossible because it's impossible." You can see how the "because" there doesn't make sense at all; the speaker has given no "because," no reason in support of the claim.

Here's another example of repetition that's actually circular:

Unjustified discrimination is wrong because it's making judgments unfairly.

Insofar as unjustified discrimination is defined as making judgments unfairly, the argument is "X is wrong because it's X"—in which case the speaker has assumed ahead of time the very point he or she was supposed to be proving and has, in fact, provided no reason for claiming X is wrong.

So when you find you've said the same thing twice (which can be hard to see when you use different words), double check: are you just being redundant or did you say what you said once as your conclusion and once as your premise? If the latter, you've made a circular argument.

5.1.3a Practice recognizing repetition

Which of the following contain repetition? Of those, which contain circular arguments?

1. We should do something about the increase in crime, because more and more people are shooting each other.

2. I believe X because that's just my faith, it's what I believe.

3. Euthanasia is wrong because it violates and goes against the sanctity of life.

4. If the government gives you money to send your kids to private school, well, they're no longer private schools, are they? They're public schools, if public money is used to support them.

5. Presidents who are tall and have a reputation for being highly charismatic tend to have mistresses. Presidents who are tall and charismatic also tend to be better performers and to be rated as great or near great in surveys of political scientists. All of these findings are statistically significant, indicating that they could not have occurred by chance. Therefore, Presidents who are tall and charismatic are more likely to have mistresses and to be effective.
   (William D. Spangler, "Lives and Loves of Tall, Charismatic Presidents," *New York Times*, February 16, 1992)

6. I find this kind of thinking so hard—because it's just so difficult!

7. This is an example of what I call "random art"—see how the paint spatters are placed at random on the canvas?

8. Externalities are those sorts of expenses outside our sphere of responsibility such as the cost of dealing with the product once the consumer is through with it and waste disposal. So, we're not responsible for externalities.

9. We have no free will: we have no choice but to do what we do, because we always follow our strongest motive—the strongest motive is the one we can't help but follow.

10. I watched the World Cross-Country championships the other day. Kenya won, but Ethiopia was a close second. It was a good race, but I could have done without all those bank commercials. But then it occurred to me: one of the biggest and most powerful financial institutions has staged a race, dangled

$100,000 at the finish line, and now watches representatives of two starving countries compete for it. (How sick is that?)

5.1.4 Detail

In addition to precision, *detail* is often the way to clarity. Referring to a "tree" may well be exactly correct: you mean a tree, not a bus; you're not confusing the two. (Not today anyway.) But referring to a "young, healthy, aspen" is even more exactly correct; the added detail adds clarity. Thus, the ability to be clear depends on the ability to notice. Someone who isn't paying much attention won't notice it's a young, healthy aspen. But it also depends on knowledge. If you can't tell an aspen from a cedar, well, you can't provide that detail.

It's this ability to attend to detail that enables us to make distinctions. Since to me, they're all just trees, I'm not qualified to make decisions about whether or not they should be cut down in order to maintain the health of the forest. It won't even occur to me to ask "*Which* trees?" (I *can* give an opinion about whether cutting them down will decrease the *beauty* of the forest, however.) To give another example, someone who doesn't know much about color may call the carpet in my room red, but someone who *knows* about color can differentiate between fuchsia, magenta, scarlet, crimson, cerise—and can, therefore, correctly identify it as fuchsia.

The same is true with abstractions. Someone who doesn't know much about euthanasia, abortion, and capital punishment will not be able to differentiate between the different kinds of killing—justified and unjustified, deliberate and accidental, coercive and consensual, and so on. To those who don't know, they're all trees, it's all red, it's all killing, case closed. It may not even occur to them to ask "How?" or "When?" or "Why"—questions which are important to those who can, or try to, make distinctions.

And our language, your language, has to be up to making these distinctions. That's why, when you acquire knowledge about a subject, you also acquire what's sometimes called a specialized vocabulary. The additional words enable you to think about, to discuss, the precise and detailed features of the subject.

5.1.4a Practice recognizing the need for detail

Which of the following need more detail in order to be clear? (Identify specifically what elements need more detail.)

1. The question with which to start my investigation is obviously this: Is there enough to go around? Immediately we encounter a serious difficulty: What is "enough"? Who can tell us? Certainly not the economist who pursues "economic growth" as the highest of all values, and therefore has no concept of "enough."
   (E.F. Schumacher, *Small is Beautiful: Economics as if People Mattered*, 1999 [1973])

2. In a famous study of children's aggression, children were observed while at play. However, the toy available for play was a Bobo doll, a life-sized doll with a weighted bottom such that when one strikes it, it falls over but always rebounds back to an upright position. How many and how often children hit the doll was taken to be some measure of their aggression. But as one researcher noted, "What else can one do to a self-righting Bobo doll except hit it?" Touché. What if the "toy" available had been a tray of water serving as a doll's swimming pool? Nevertheless, the study may have been enlightening, if only to show that it's the opportunity for aggression that is the critical factor.

3. But the fact is, the United States of America *was* conceived and brought forth by Christians, and history tells us that story in no uncertain terms . . . Anyone who reads about the values upon which this nation was founded understands perfectly well that this was, from the start, a Christian nation.
(D. James Kennedy, *Character & Destiny*, 1994)

4. With respect to the state's important and legitimate interest in potential life, the "compelling" point is at viability. This is so because the fetus then presumably has the *capability of meaningful life outside the mother's womb* . . . If the state is interested in protecting fetal life after viability, it may go so far as to proscribe abortion during that period *except when it is necessary to preserve the life or health of the mother.*
(From Roe v. Wade, 1973)

5. If there is any one single concept that organizes the passions and actions of men as a gender, I would propose that power is a likely candidate. From the private fantasies of boys becoming men and later of men acting out their internal scripts, being powerful and having power takes a high position. Seldom is powerlessness a preferred and admired quality in the male.
(Joseph A. Kuypers, *Men and Power*, 1999)

6. I read somewhere that 82 percent believe in heaven, whereas only 28 percent believe in evolution. Well, if the theory of heaven had as much detail as the theory of evolution and was, therefore, more difficult to follow, those percentages would be a lot more equal!

7. Strikes are always caused by greedy unions. What's sad about this is the negative impact strikes have on the public. The fact that unions will inconvenience the public at the drop of a hat is further evidence that workers are selfish.
(An example of "Media Think Truisms," from James Winter, *Democracy's Oxygen: How Corporations Control the News*, 1997)

8. This book presents a detailed program for teaching academic skills—reading, language, arithmetic—to your preschool child, an endeavor that may seem

intimidating to you. There are three reasons for teaching academic skills to your preschool child. These are:

(1) If your child learns these skills as a preschooler, your child will be smarter than the average child and will be in a position to learn new skills at a faster rate.

(2) The schools are not well designed to teach every child academic skills. If you leave the teaching to the schools, your child may be a school failure and may learn to hate school and academic work.

(3) Perhaps most important, teaching your child is a very nice and natural thing to do. The most basic relationship among humans is the transmission of knowledge from parent to child. Parents teach other important skills, such as dressing and eating. They direct the child's activities. Academic skills are important, and the child will be engaged in them for a lifetime. When the skills are taught in a home-teaching situation, the child is shown that the parent is interested in these skills and that they are part of the parent–child relationship.

(Siegfried and Therese Engelmann, *Give Your Child a Superior Mind*, 1966)

9. *Mowbray*: Why do you say that television should not be allowed in the courts? Where is the evidence that if court trials are televised, they'll be less fair?

Doyle: Well, to the extent that television is by definition entertainment, court trials that are televised will be turned into entertainment. This alone suggests that said court trials would *not* be fair.

Mowbray: But what about magazines and newspapers in which court reports appear? Are they not entertainment?

Doyle: Well, two wrongs . . .

Mowbray: Besides, only the notorious trials are broadcast.

Doyle: So? Is that supposed to be a red herring?

Mowbray: We have a right to observe, to witness, justice in action. They're *our* courts! It's *our* money!

Doyle: Okay, but can't you just go in person and watch if you want to?

Mowbray: No, a lot of people can't. Not without great expense.

Doyle: Well, not everyone would be able to get the court television channel either.

Mowbray: Right. So every station should broadcast every trial.

Doyle: That's impossible. Do you know how many trials are going on at any given moment?

Mowbray: Okay, so they edit a bit.

Doyle: No way. Either we get the whole trial or none of it. Imagine what parts would be left out and why. That would *really* make things unfair.

Mowbray: Okay, but won't everyone behave better if they know they're being watched?

Doyle: Maybe. Then again, have you ever seen the Canadian parliamentary proceedings? They're televised, and I swear my high school student council meetings were conducted with more maturity. In any case, they may behave better. Or they may just behave differently. Perhaps knowing they're being watched, they'll put on a charade, they'll play it up.

10. [The] feminist movement is sexually harassing the role of motherhood and dependent wives (homemakers) [by] Affirmative Action for women. Affirmative Action in favor of women is grievously unjust to everyone, but most especially to the dependent wife and mother in the home whose breadwinner-husband is denied a job, a raise or a promotion he deserves or has earned, which is given instead to a less qualified woman, perhaps even to one who is the second wage-earner in the family.

(Phyllis Schlafly, "Government Intrusion in the Workplace," from "Statement Submitted to Committee on Labor and Human Resources," United States Senate, in *Hearings on Sexual Discrimination in the Workplace*, 97th Congress, 1st Session, April 21, 1981)

5.1.4b More practice recognizing the need for detail

Find five examples of lack of detail that prevent critical thinking. Consider textbooks, newspapers, magazines, websites, radio, television, and so on. Can you suggest the kind of detail that's needed?

5.1.5 Beware of manipulation

In the hands of many advertisers and other disreputable folk, lack of clarity—usually through lack of precision or lack of detail—is a tool, a way to manipulate us into accepting a claim that has no support at all. Lack of clarity prevents critical assessment—and as a critical thinker, you can't let them get away with that! Consider the ever-popular claim that Brand A is ten times better, or that Product Y gives you so much more. Better than what? Last year's product? Brand B's product? More what? More grief? Incomplete comparisons are completely useless—for rational assessment. They are use*ful*, however, for persuading the thoughtless. And for avoiding lawsuits—falsely claiming that Brand A is ten times better than Brand B might land Brand A in court. (And anyway, what exactly is meant by "better"? Ten times faster is okay; that's a clear quantitative comparison that we can understand—if we're given the baseline. But ten times *better*?)

5.2 Neutrality

The effects of loaded language, as well as of various visual, aural, and other elements of presentation, may be intentional. In that case, someone is trying to manipulate us. But the effects may, instead, be unintentional. In that case, we're still being prevented from thinking critically about what's being said—it's just accidental, rather than deliberate. Either way, beware.

5.2.1 Loaded language

Like clear language, neutral language facilitates critical thinking. Language that is not neutral—language that is biased, that is "loaded" with value judgments—hinders critical thinking. **Loaded language** does this either by totally distracting us and thus preventing us from thinking critically (we simply accept the implied judgment), by "merely" getting in the way and making us work harder to pay attention to the argument (so we may overlook something important like the absence of sufficient evidence), or simply by appealing to our emotion instead of to our cognition.

Using neutral language is harder than it might seem. Imagine you're a newspaper reporter, reporting something as straightforward as a motor vehicle accident. You begin with "A serious accident occurred——." Well, right away you're in trouble: Who says it's serious? How serious *is* serious? Serious to whom? You've inserted a value judgment. In addition, you've assumed it was an accident. My guess is you didn't speak to the drivers. Maybe it was intentional. So you try again. To say "A *ran into* B" is to say it in rather aggressive terms. "A *hit* B" is just as bad. "*Car* A hit *Car* B" is a little better. "Car A *collided with* Car B" is better yet, but still you're suggesting that A is to blame (because it did the doing—the colliding or whatever); maybe Car B *got in the way of* Car A. "Car A and Car B collided" is better still, but only "Car A and Car B occupied the same space at the same point in time" is *really* neutral.

Now consider the difficulty of reporting an event involving something a little more complicated than inanimate objects—people, for example. Consider the statement, "The fight continues between the Board and the Union . . ." To call it a *fight* is to describe a whole set of attributes (animosity, competition, and so on) which may or may not be present. And, in any case, I don't think everyone agrees on when an interaction involving those attributes actually becomes a *fight*—again, you're inserting a value judgment. "The struggle to find a common ground continues . . ." is better, but still, you've called it a struggle—you've again put some sort of negative spin on it. To say "The negotiations continued . . ." is perhaps most neutral. But you'd better stop there: even to add "for yet another day" would be to suggest that it's going on too long—another negative spin, another value judgment.

We even have a loaded word to describe loaded words: euphemism. What is a euphemism but a word or phrase that has a positive spin even though it really refers to something rather negative; a euphemism is a camouflage word, a deceptive word. For example, consider "let go" compared to "fired." If we're the person doing the "letting go," we may choose to say "You're being let go" instead of "You're fired" because it's apt to be less emotionally inflammatory, and we don't want to face the other person's anger and distress. So we manipulate his or her behavior to suit our own interests—simply by choosing certain words over others, by choosing to use loaded language. Too, somehow, being let go has a "Well, that happens" feel to it, whereas being fired makes us more apt to question the justice of the decision (yes, it is someone's decision, not something that just happens). Thus, our disposition to question, to challenge, to *think critically* about the matter at hand has been affected by the words used.

Here's another example of loaded language that we hear a lot: "disturbing the natural balance." "Disturbing" has a negative feel to it, whereas "natural balance" has a positive feel to it. So we get the idea that "disturbing the natural balance" is a bad thing to do. So if someone wanted us to disagree with whatever action is being described, they might call it "disturbing the natural balance" rather than the more neutral "altering the existing distribution" (let alone "improving" or "rectifying" the existing distribution)—and presto! We're on their side without even hearing their arguments.

Consider, lastly, the terms "pro-life" and "pro-choice": both were no doubt coined in order to gain agreement (without having to engage in the messy business of presenting and evaluating reasons and evidence), for who could be *against* life or *against* choice? However, since someone can be both "pro-life" and "pro-choice" (someone can endorse the view that whether or not to abort is the woman's choice *and* at the same time endorse the view that it's wrong to choose to abort), those two terms don't really define the debate. A more accurate pair of words would be "pro-abortion" and "anti-abortion." But since "abortion" has become a loaded word, one with a negative feel, describing the debate in those terms would be unfair: saying you're "pro-abortion" would sound like you're "pro-murder." Equally unfair, but illustrative, would be describing the debate as "for compulsory childbearing" and "against compulsory childbearing" (thanks to Lucinda Cisler, "Unfinished Business: Birth Control and Women's Liberation," in *Sisterhood is Powerful*, 1970).

Sometimes loaded language does more than distract or give an emotional push in one direction or another. Sometimes it clears the way for attitudes and behaviors that should otherwise most certainly be questioned. For example, sexist language routinely excludes half the species. When you hear the word "piano man"—quick, what did you picture, a man or a woman? That's why we changed "fireman" to "firefighter," "mailman" to "letter carrier," "chairman" to "chair" and so on. What we imagine limits what we do. Racist, classist, heterosexist, and theist language similarly maintains the existing power hierarchies by excluding or belittling those the speakers want to keep invisible or insignificant.

And sometimes loaded language is a blatant lie. For example, *is* "the moral majority" a majority? Did they take a poll of the entire nation's residents, asking who agreed with the opinions they advocate? And is it moral? By what standards?

Some of mankind's most terrible misdeeds have been committed under the spell of certain words or phrases.

James Bryant Conant in his Baccalaureate Address at Harvard University, June 17, 1934

Poor people used to live in slums. Now "the economically disadvantaged" occupy "substandard housing" in the "inner cities." And a lot of them are broke. They don't have "negative cash flow." They're broke! Because many of them were fired. In other words, management wanted to "curtail redundancies in the human resources area," and so, many workers are no longer "viable members of the workforce." Smug, greedy, well-fed white people have invented a language to conceal their sins. It's as simple as that.

. . .

The CIA doesn't kill anybody, they "neutralize" people. Or they "depopulate" an area. The government doesn't lie, it engages in "disinformation." The Pentagon actually measures nuclear radiation in something called "sunshine units." Israeli murderers are called "commandos," Arab commandos are called "terrorists." The contra killers were known as "freedom fighters." Well, if crime fighters fight crime and firefighters fight fire, what do freedom fighters fight?

. . .

But it's all right, folks, because thanks to our fear of death, no one has to die; they can all just pass away. Or expire, like a magazine subscription. If it happens in the hospital, it will be called a terminal episode. The insurance company will refer to it as negative patient-care outcome. And if it's the result of malpractice, they'll say it was a therapeutic misadventure.

To be honest, some of this language makes me want to vomit. Well, perhaps "vomit" is too strong a word. It makes me want to engage in an involuntary, personal protein spill.

(George Carlin, *Napalm & Silly Putty*, 2001)

5.2.1a Practice recognizing and rewriting loaded words or phrases

Identify each of the following as value-positive, value-negative, or neutral. Then write two more versions, one in each of the other two ways.

1. employment opportunity

2. bribe

3. tree butcher

4. failure

5. affirmative action

6. volunteer work

7. under-developed countries

8. white-skinned

9. small business

10. unborn baby

5.2.1b More practice recognizing and rewriting loaded words and phrases

Find five examples of loaded words or phrases. Consider textbooks, newspapers, magazines, websites, radio, television, and so on. (In particular, you might want to compare right-wing and left-wing accounts of the same event; such a comparison is sure to uncover some loaded language.) Rewrite them with neutral substitutes.

Not only single words or phrases, but also whole styles of speech can be loaded. Surely you have heard someone speak in an excessively academic way, sounding almost burdened by their many doctorate degrees. "Consider for instance," says David Cogswell, "some comfortable English professor defending Russian totalitarianism. He cannot say outright, 'I believe in killing off your opponents when you can get good results by doing so.' Probably, therefore, he will say something like this: 'While freely conceding that the Soviet regime exhibits certain features which the humanitarian may be inclined to deplore, we must, I think, agree that a certain curtailment of the right to political opposition is an unavoidable concomitant of transitional periods, and that the rigors which the Russian people have been called upon to undergo have been amply justified in the sphere of concrete achievement'" (David Cogswell, *Chomsky for Beginners*, 1996).

Likewise, you have surely heard "officialese," that obnoxious kind of talk that sounds so, well, so official! Such styles of speech can be intimidating: speakers can make what they're saying sound so incredibly complex you can't possibly understand it or so incredibly legitimate you won't even question it. Both inhibit critical thinking. And both are persuasive, quite apart from—and that's the problem—the arguments therein.

Excessive use of rhetorical questions is also manipulative. Recall that a rhetorical question is by definition one that is not intended to be answered, and that's usually because the speaker assumes you know the answer; she or he assumes *everyone* knows the answer because she or he assumes there is only one answer—the answer she or he has in mind. Thus, as a style of speech, rhetorical questions short-circuit critical thinking; we as listeners/readers are predisposed *not* to consider *other* possible answers.

Newspeak is the name for the language that the government used to hide what it was doing. Using techniques such as oversimplification, euphemism, misrepresentation, abbreviation, blurring and reversal of meaning, Newspeak makes language so meaningless that it cannot be used to communicate—or even to understand—the activities of the state.

On Orwell's novel *1984*, quoted from David Cogswell, *Chomsky for Beginners*, 1996

To acquire immunity to eloquence is of the utmost importance to the citizens of a democracy.

Bertrand Russell, *Power*, 1938

5.2.1c Practice recognizing and rewriting loaded styles of speech

Rewrite each of the following in (a) an overly pretentious full-of-importance style, and (b) an overly complicated you-can't-possibly-understand style.

1. The Rolex Daytona is an excellent watch.

2. The attack was successful.

3. They lied.

4. This is a good car.

5. Try this one instead.

5.2.1d Practice recognizing and rewriting loaded language

Identify the loaded language in the following. Rewrite each using neutral language.

1. "Well, girls, do you think you can do better second half?" (coach to his losing boys' basketball team)

2. Terminator Fluid fights bad breath!

3. "Can I help with the housework?" (husband says to wife)

4. "You are instructed to manage the release of the data effectively, to minimize any potential negative commercial impact," internal memo, giant pharmaceutical company.
   (*Adbusters*, "Bad Pharma," November/December 2005)

5. The land has been allowed to become overgrown by invasive species, including weeds.

6. The 2006 Infiniti M45 Sport: The G35's bigger, better, faster brother. . . . A quick look at the numbers shows the 4000-lb M45 is no slouch, blazing to 60 mph in 5.3 seconds and through the quarter mile in 13.8 sec. at 101.6 mph. It accomplishes this with fluid ease, the engine and transmission working together seamlessly to deliver smooth, linear acceleration through the powerband. These times are almost identical to those of the last BMW 545i Sport we had at our office, putting it in good company. Factor in a price difference of around $10,000 (the M45 Sport starts just under $50K), and this latest Infiniti looks poised to hassle the 5 Series much as the G35 challenged the 3 Series.
   (Kim Wolfkill, "2006 Infiniti M45 Sport," *Road and Track*, 2005)

187

7. Wherever you look, trade tensions are on the rise. America and the European Union are squealing about surging textile imports from China; both are slapping on "safeguard" quotas to stem the flow. China is furious and has retaliated by scrapping voluntary export taxes on its textile exporters. Meanwhile Americans and Europeans are, once again, spitting at each other about subsidies to Boeing and Airbus.

("The Key to Trade and Aid," *The Economist*, June 4, 2005)

8. Conservatives, like Americans generally, have no wish to return to the days of black smoke billowing out of smokestacks. But they do believe common sense can be brought to bear in dealing with the environment: that it is possible to protect the environment without sacrificing the freedoms for which America stands.

(John Shanahan, "Environment," in Stuart M. Butler and Kim R. Holmes, eds., *Issues '96: The Candidate's Briefing Book*, 1996)

9. My heart breaks for that tiger and for all the animals languishing in makeshift cages and filth-ridden enclosures. If humans were being kept in such conditions, the phrase "torture chamber" would surely apply. Animals are indiscriminately denied their basic freedoms, and in some cases are subjected to pain, neglect, and cruelty . . . Animals are displayed in undersized, substandard exhibits that do little to satisfy their full range of biological and behavioral needs. Zoo animals tend to be warehoused for months or years with little to occupy their time. They become lethargic, obese, bored, frustrated or even insane . . . Many zoos still obtain significant numbers of animals from the wild. They are not the conservation institutions they claim to be.

(From a letter from the World Society for the Protection of Animals regarding zoos)

10. Consider the most recent State of the Union Address, at: http://www.whitehouse.gov.

5.2.2 Visual effects

Like verbal language, visual language can be loaded: what we see, and how it is presented, can influence how we respond.

With regard to print materials, consider *placement*. For example, in newspapers, front page placement suggests the story placed there is far more important than the one on the back page; the same goes for top placement, compared to bottom placement.

Consider *size*. For example, how much space is allotted to a story usually influences us: we get the impression that the stories that get a lot of space are more important than the ones that get just a little space. And we haven't even read them yet. For example, the *Washington Post* featured 25 page one stories to Bill Clinton's Lincoln Bedroom sleepovers and donor coffees, but only 12 page one stories to Dick Cheney's backroom meetings with polluters (Todd Gitlin, "The Great Media Breakdown," *Mother Jones*, November/December 2004; source cited for the information was Lexis-Nexis as of September 14, 2004).

Even *font style* can predispose us one way or another. Large block type can be intimidating; italicized script can be misleadingly personal. What effect would using this font for this textbook have?

With regard to images, there's so much more. Camera operators are masters of the visual effect. Consider *camera angle*: notice, for example, that when we are intended to respect a character, the camera "looks up" at him or her. Consider *camera distance*: close-ups, for example, suggest intimacy—we are drawn to identify with the character, to *feel* favorably toward that character; distance is often used to suggest power and wisdom (especially when panoramic) or insignificance, depending on the context. (But note the word "feel"—all of this is non-rational persuasion, we're not *thinking* about any of this, about what the character has done, for example.) Consider *lighting*: is it sharp (suggesting things are real) or fuzzy (suggesting they're imagined or, at least, not definitely real). Consider *color*: the bright gets our attention; the dull escapes our notice.

© Corbis

© Corbis

© Corbis

Lastly, consider *context*: what else is in the frame? Advertisers depend on association and so juxtapose images very carefully. Show a toothbrush next to a party, and presto, we have the impression that there's something exciting and fun about that toothbrush! And, perhaps more important, notice what is *not* in the frame—what *aren't* we seeing? And, again, consider placement in that context: what's in the foreground and what's in the background?

Context changes everything. What you don't know *can* hurt you—or at least it can prevent you from fully understanding, and therefore assessing, what's presented to you.

Context can be linear as well: notice the sequence of images, whether in a magazine, or, more effectively, on video (television, film, and so on). What follows what? Much is implied about X by what comes before and after X.

Of course context matters when you're dealing with just words as well. Consider the following:

> To suppose that the eye with all its inimitable contrivances for adjusting the focus to different distances, for admitting different amounts of light, and for the correction of spherical and chromatic aberration, could have been formed by natural selection, seems, I freely confess, absurd in the highest degree.
> (Charles Darwin, *On the Origin of Species*, 1859)

It sounds like Darwin's saying natural selection is absurd. But what he goes on to say changes that. Here's a more complete excerpt (note, in particular, what I have emphasized):

> To suppose that the eye with all its inimitable contrivances for adjusting the focus to different distances, for admitting different amounts of light, and for the correction of spherical and chromatic aberration, could have been formed

by natural selection, seems, I freely confess, absurd in the highest degree. When it was first said that the sun stood still and the world turned round, the common sense of mankind declared the doctrine false; but the old saying of Vox populi, vox Dei, as every philosopher knows, cannot be trusted in science. Reason tells me, that if numerous gradations from a simple and imperfect eye to one complex and perfect can be shown to exist, each grade being useful to its possessor, as is certainly the case; if, further, the eye ever varies and the variations be inherited, as is likewise certainly the case; and if such variations should be useful to any animal under changing conditions of life, *then the difficulty of believing that a perfect and complex eye could be formed by natural selection, though insuperable by our imagination, should not be considered as subversive of the theory.*

(Charles Darwin, *On the Origin of Species*, 1859)

Whenever you read quoted material, keep in mind that it's probably an excerpt, an incomplete part of a whole. And the rest of that whole may determine the meaning of the part you're reading.

And, of course, like words, the images themselves—whether in newspapers, books, or magazines, or on websites or television—can be "loaded." Notice the details: dress, setting, props, and so on. Some images can also be outright lies: body proportions can be changed, facial features can be deleted or added, bits and pieces of a scene can be put together to indicate that something happened when, in fact, it did not, and so on. Other images just present the pieces in a way that *suggests* a certain something without coming right out and presenting it.

5.2.2a Practice recognizing loaded visual effects

How do the following manipulate or predispose us one way or another?

1.

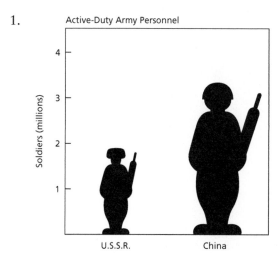

From Zachary Seech, *Open Minds and Everyday Reasoning*, 2E. © 2005 Wadsworth, a part of Cengage Learning, Inc. Reproduced by permission. www.cengage.com/permissions

2.

© Corbis

3.

© Corbis

4.

© Corbis

5.

© Shelley Eades /
San Francisco Chronicle

5.2.2b More practice recognizing loaded visual effects

Find five examples of loaded visual effects. Peruse textbooks, newspapers, magazines, websites, radio, television, and so on.

5.2.3 Aural effects

Like the written word, the spoken word can predispose us to agree or disagree with a claim, independent of the reasoning being presented.

Consider *pitch*. Low-pitched voices carry more weight in our culture than high-pitched voices. And a serious tone implies that something serious is being conveyed. Once, when visiting Sweden, I saw a television weather report delivered by a young man wearing jeans and shirt. He presented the forecast quite casually, as if it were no big deal—and I thought, *well, it's not*! I mean, it *has* rained before. I realized then just how often people in North America try so hard to appear important.

Another aural effect that influences us is the *pace* of speech. Something said slowly seems to have greater significance than something said quickly. It's as if the words themselves were heavy and so take effort to say; somehow the impression given is "This is hard work, important work." And consider pauses. The grave pause absolutely *commands* attention, invokes the utmost respect. Remember your parents saying "Don't   you   ever   do that   again!" Unfortunately, as adults, we still fall for that. Listen, again, to news anchors and political leaders; but also listen to the guy in the meeting who seems to be taken more seriously and given more air time than the rest of you.

And think about *tone*. Consider flabbergasted indignation, that over-the-top combination of visual and aural effects that suggests the claim in question is simply too ridiculous to take seriously. What a way to dismiss an argument—without an argument! On the other hand, a smiling face and tone often says "Agree with me, I'm being reasonable." It's just another way *not* to pay attention to the argument.

And visual effects combine with aural effects not only in facial expression. The whole body is important. Again, in our culture, something said by a male body seems to get more respect, seems to have more authority, than something that's said by a female body. Note the voice-overs in advertisements: when is a male voice used and when is a female voice used? Also, tall bodies get more respect than short bodies (though this difference matters more for male bodies than for female bodies). Attractive bodies get more respect than unattractive bodies (and this one matters more for female bodies than for male bodies). Old bodies get more respect than young bodies (but only up to a point; the bodies can't be too old). And seemingly fit bodies get more respect than seemingly unfit bodies. And bodies in lab coats and suitcoats especially get our respectful attention. Take a good look at television news anchors, for which an aura of authority is preferred. And go look at presidential candidates—and presidential candidate winners.

> The examiner's manner [the manner of the cross-examiner in a courtroom] is often more important than the substance of his questions. His or her approach may be verbal, tonal, or silent altogether. A grin, eyebrow lift, or "listen-to-that" shrug towards bench or jury box may invite emotional conspiracy. The dismissing of a witness with "That will be all!" in triumphant tone may pretend that damaging testimony was instead a coup. Another device is to address a witness as "Sir" or "Madame" in a heavy sneer that, if verbalized outside the courtroom's permissive ground, would approach slander.
>
> (Anne Strick, "Requiem for the Adversary System," in Anne Strick, *Injustice for All*, 1976)

> To say it still another way: Entertainment is the supra-ideology of all discourse on television. No matter what is depicted or from what point of view, the overarching presumption is that it is there for our amusement and pleasure. That is why even on news shows which provide us daily with fragments of tragedy and barbarism, we are urged by the newscasters to "join them tomorrow." What for? One would think that several minutes of murder and mayhem would suffice as material for a month of sleepless nights. We accept the newscasters' invitation because we know that the "news" is not to be taken seriously, that it is all in fun, so to say. Everything about a news show tells us this—the good looks and amiability of the cast, their pleasant banter, the exciting music that opens and closes the show, the vivid film footage, the attractive commercials—all these and more suggest that what we have just seen is no cause for weeping. A news show, to put it plainly, is a format for entertainment, not for education, reflection or catharsis.
>
> (Neil Postman, *Amusing Ourselves to Death*, 1985)

Unfortunately, in argument the one who talks longest, loudest, and last often comes out looking like "the winner," even though he or she may not have argued at all. This is because . . . no one has answered the argument— . . . no one has actually shown that the argument is weak or unlikely.

S. Morris Engel, *With Good Reason*, 1999

Lastly, in advertisements, as well as television programs of all kinds, the sound-track and sound effects are designed to elicit or magnify certain responses—generally not including critical response. Imagine a sitcom without a laugh track. Listen to a stand-up comic in an empty room. You might be amazed at how much you suddenly *don't* find all that funny—which is to say, at how much your response is influenced by the aural effect of hearing other people laugh.

5.2.3a Practice recognizing loaded aural effects

1. Compare the speaking styles of your various professors. Can differences account for why you tend to accept what some say more readily than what others say?

2. Pay attention to how your fellow students speak in class. Do you notice any of the aural effects described above?

3. Incorporate one of the aural effects described above into your speaking (for example, lower your voice or speak with grave pauses). Did you notice any difference in how what you said was received?

5.2.3b More practice recognizing loaded visual and aural effects

For the following exercises, to attend to the aural, try closing your eyes; to attend to the visual, try muting the volume.

1. Watch fifteen minutes of a television drama, and make a note of *every* time you're being manipulated by some visual or aural effect—consider the camera work (angle, distance, lighting), the casting (who was chosen for which parts, that is, what they look like), the acting (how the lines are spoken, what body language is used), the soundtrack, the sound effects, and so on. (You might also watch a few minutes of a television sitcom, paying attention to how often the laugh track is played.)

2. Watch fifteen minutes of a television newscast, and make a note of *every* time you're being manipulated by some visual or aural effect—notice the bodies, the faces, the clothing, the voices, and so on.

3. Watch five television advertisements, and make a note of *every* time you're being manipulated by some visual or aural effect—notice the placement, size, and context of the various bits of the image, the music, the narrator's voice, and so on.

5.2.4 Other effects

Quite apart from the discussion of repetition earlier (Section 5.1.3), sheer repetition is powerful. So beware of repeated words and phrases; it may be that if someone says something often enough, we'll come to agree with him or her. We do show a tendency to like what's familiar. But it's a completely non-rational response—you haven't thought about it!

You can make people believe anything if you just say it often enough.

Sheri S. Tepper, *Gibbon's Decline and Fall*, 1997

195

In closing, it might be valuable to note that people who pay a lot of attention to form (appearance) may do so because they're unable to understand, and hence assess, substance. They can't tell the difference between a formula for catnip and a formula for an AIDS vaccine, or an explanation about why we keep killing each other that is nonsense and one that has merit. Consequently, they take their cues from whether the formula or explanation is typed on letterhead or written on a napkin (it doesn't take much skill or knowledge, or energy, to tell the difference between letterhead and a napkin). So the more we develop the skill and knowledge to understand and critically assess matters of substance, the less we'll be influenced by matters of form.

5.3 Definition

Some of the greatest controversies would cease in a moment, if one or other of the disputants took care to mark out precisely, and in a few words, what he understands by the terms which are the subject of dispute.

Antoine Arnauld, *The Art of Thinking,* 1662

How many a dispute could have been deflated into a single paragraph if the disputants had dared define their terms.

Aristotle (384–322 BCE)

As you have no doubt noticed by this point, definitions are important. Much discussion tends to be wasted because, it turns out, hours later, the discussants are talking about different things. A common comment, at the beginning of a discussion (or, alas, well after the beginning), is "It depends on what you mean by . . ." True enough. If, as some philosophers say, definitions are merely how we use our words, then it's particularly important to specify how indeed we're using them. For example, if we're arguing about value differences between lower and middle classes, perhaps we should start by defining 'lower class' and 'middle class'—are there some annual income figures we can use for that? If someone else insists on a different definition, fine, we're just not arguing about the same thing then.

If, however, the argument is *about* how best to define something, like "death" or "speech," then we can't be so cavalier about someone's different definition. The definition of "death," for example, has significant implications for our policies about organ transplant, and the definition of "speech" bears on whether certain gestures such as flying the national flag upside down are protected by the First Amendment about speech. A similar point can be made about all sorts of important words, like "life," "person," "religion," "freedom," "self-defense". . .

Words that are used in specialized contexts usually have very specific meanings that are quite different from their common meanings. For example, we generally consider "depressed" to mean "sad," but psychologists have a much more precise definition of the word: people diagnosed as suffering from major depression must have experienced five or more of the following symptoms during the same two-week period—depressed mood most of the day, diminished interest or pleasure in all, or almost all, activities, significant weight loss, insomnia, psychomotor agitation, fatigue, feelings of worthlessness, diminished ability to concentrate, and recurrent thoughts of death. So if your argument is about depression in the context of psychology, you'd better know how psychologists define it.

Here's another example of a word in a specialized context having a very specific meaning: according to the U.S. Bureau of Labor Statistics, a person is not "unemployed" unless he or she has actively looked for work in the previous month. So the unemployment figures released by the Bureau do *not* indicate how many people are currently out of work (which is what you probably thought, right?).

Definition is important not only when we're using specialized terms, but also when we're using unfamiliar, vague, abstract, or controversial terms. Dictionary definitions typically indicate merely how a word is customarily used. Generally, such definitions are useful only as starting points for using the word in argument. The dictionary definition of "person," for example, as "a human being, an individual" is not very helpful when we're trying to decide if a fetus is a person for the purposes of deciding whether abortion is morally acceptable (given the premise that ending the life of a person is morally unacceptable). Also, dictionary definitions can be circular (a bad thing): a "humorist" is defined as "one whose writing or conversation is characterized by humor." A thesaurus, a special dictionary that provides synonyms, can also be useful as a starting point, but often words presented as synonyms have subtleties in emotional value that can be quite important. For example, I just looked up the word "love" in my Microsoft Word thesaurus and was given both "worship" and "be fond of."

So if we can't rely on the dictionary, what *can* we rely on? What *is* a good definition for the sake of argument? Basically, it's a definition that is agreed upon by all the people concerned. And if, when you construct a definition, you consider each of the following three elements—genus and species, necessary and sufficient conditions, and inclusiveness and exclusiveness—you'll increase your chances of figuring out whether people *are* in agreement.

Calvin and Hobbes ©1995 Watterson. Dist. by UNIVERSAL UCLICK. Reprinted with permission. All rights reserved.

5.3.1 Genus and species

If you define a word by specifying its **genus** and its **species**, you will end up with a good definition. The genus refers to the larger group to which a thing belongs, and the species (also called "differentia") refers to the features that set this particular thing apart from others in that larger group.

So a "triangle" can be defined as a "polygon with three sides." "Polygon" would be its genus, the larger group to which it belongs (polygons are multi-sided closed shapes, including rectangles, octagons, triangles, and so on); "with three sides" would be its species, the feature that sets triangles apart from other polygons (no other kind of polygon has three sides—rectangles have four sides, octagons have eight sides, and so on).

Here's another example of a genus-species definition: a piano is a musical instrument (its genus) that is played by pressing keys that in turn hit strings (its species). Note that if there is another musical instrument that is played by pressing keys that in turn hit strings (a harpsichord? no, its keys pluck strings), then the species would have to be refined a bit more.

5.3.1a Practice identifying genus and species

Identify the genus and species, when given, in the following definitions.

1. dog—a four-legged animal

2. water—liquid composed of two parts hydrogen and one part oxygen

3. murder—the killing of a human being with malicious forethought

4. banff—that facial expression which is impossible to achieve except when having a passport photograph taken (Douglas Adams and John Lloyd, *The Meaning of Liff*, 1983)

5. planet—an object that has a mass between that of Pluto and the Deuterium-burning threshold and that forms in orbit around an object that can generate energy by nuclear reactions

5.3.1b Practice defining by genus and species

Define the following terms using the genus and species approach.

1. community

2. curiosity

3. poem

4. angel

5. human

5.3.2 Necessary and sufficient conditions

Definitions should also articulate necessary and sufficient conditions.

Necessary conditions are those conditions or attributes that *must be present* in order for something to fall within your definition. For example, in order to be considered a hat, an article must be intended to be worn on the head; that is a necessary condition—if it isn't intended to be worn on the head, it can't be a hat.

Note, however, that while necessary conditions are necessary, they are not sufficient; that is, other elements are required for that something to qualify as whatever you're defining. For example, being intended to be worn on the head isn't all that's required before we call something a hat; if it were, we'd call headphones hats. For something to be called a hat, more is involved than that it be intended to be worn on the head.

Sufficient conditions are those conditions or attributes that if present are *all that is required* for something to fall within your definition. Unlike necessary conditions, sufficient conditions are, well, sufficient—nothing else is required. For example, in order for an animal to count as a vertebrate, it must have a spine. That's all it takes. It doesn't have to have four legs, or fur, or anything else. Having a spine is all it takes; the condition of having a spine is sufficient.

Sometimes, two or more conditions may be jointly sufficient. For example, one might define as a sufficient condition of being "dead" the cessation of brain activity *and* the cessation of independent cardiovascular function. It's not enough for just your brain to have stopped functioning, nor is it enough for just your heart and lungs to have stopped, but if both conditions occur, then you are considered dead.

Conditions can be necessary or sufficient or both. That is, something can be necessary but not sufficient (it's necessary that something be intended to be worn on the head in order to be a hat, but being intended to be worn on the head is not all it takes), sufficient but not necessary (if a paint is red, that is sufficient for it to be called a primary color paint, but being red is not necessary—being blue also makes the paint a primary color paint), or both necessary and sufficient (having a spine is required before something is called a vertebrate and it happens to be all that's required).

Considering borderline cases, by the way, can help you really get a grip on your definition—they have a way of highlighting those necessary and sufficient conditions. For example, when trying to define "person," you might carefully consider embryonic and comatose human beings (and Taffi). Neither embryos nor the comatose have desires, the ability to think, or the ability to communicate, but they both have human DNA. Taffi, however, does have desires, the ability to think, and the ability to communicate, but she doesn't have any human DNA. So, is it *necessary* that something have human DNA before we call it a person? If so, Taffi's not a person. Is it *sufficient* that something have human DNA in order to be called a person? If so, then embryos and the comatose are persons. And the piece of human flesh sitting in the Petri dish? (It has human DNA . . .)

5.3.2a Practice identifying necessary and sufficient conditions

Identify the necessary and sufficient conditions, when given, in the following definitions.

1. *Thesen*: You need skill to get a job.
    Santoz: Oh yeah, then why don't I have one?! I have skills coming out of my ears!

2. There is no such thing as "safe sex."

3. Any sexually explicit material counts as pornography.

4. To succeed in the world it is not enough to be stupid, you must also be well-mannered.

    (Voltaire, 1694–1778)

5. Sergeant John Bruhns is sharply critical of soldiers who go AWOL. 'I feel that if you are against the war, you should at least be man enough to stay put and fight for what you believe in,' he says.

    (David Goodman, "Breaking Ranks," *Mother Jones*,
    November/December 2004)

5.3.2b Practice defining by necessary and sufficient conditions

Define the following terms by specifying necessary and sufficient conditions:

1. consent

2. intoxicated

3. cruel and unusual punishment

4. terrorist

5. fair

5.3.3 Inclusiveness and exclusiveness

Lastly, your definition should be neither too broad (too inclusive), nor too narrow (too exclusive).

Definitions that are *too broad* are *too inclusive*—they include more than you want. Put the other way, they are not exclusive enough—that is, they do not exclude enough. For example, suppose we defined a chair as "something you can sit on." The problem with this definition is that it's too broad; tables, beds, lawns, houses, and people would count as chairs, according to our definition, because you can sit on them. Suppose we modify our definition to "a piece of furniture intended to be sat upon." This one is better because by specifying "a piece of furniture," we exclude lawns, houses, and people. And by specifying "intended to be sat upon," we exclude tables and beds. However, our definition is still too broad because it would include couches. How about "a chair is a piece of furniture intended to seat one"?

Definitions that are *too narrow* are *too exclusive*—they exclude more than you want. Put the other way, they are not inclusive enough—that is, they do not include enough. Suppose we had revised our definition of a chair to say it's "a four-legged piece of furniture intended to seat one." That would have been too narrow because it would exclude bean bag chairs.

Here's another example to consider with regard to being too broad or too narrow:

> New Jersey students will soon say goodbye to soda and other lunchtime junk foods under a new school nutrition policy announced Monday by Acting Gov. Richard J. Codey . . . Under the New Jersey plan, soda, candy and foods listing sugar as the first or principal ingredient will be banned from school cafeterias. Snacks and drinks with more than eight grams of total fat per serving and two grams of saturated fat will be banned, and cafeterias will have to restrict amounts of foods with trans fats.
>
> (*The New York Times Metro*, June 7, 2005)

The problem with this definition is that it's too broad. Critics of the New Jersey new policy point out that under its terms (it defines unhealthy foods as those with more than eight grams of total fat per serving) "things like cheeses, nuts, peanut butter" could be excluded.

Note that a definition can at the same time be both too broad and too narrow:

> Basketball is a ball game played in a gym.

That definition is too broad because it also includes volleyball (a ball game played in a gym), and it's too narrow because it excludes basketball games played on outdoor courts.

As you work with definitions, whether you're on the receiving end or the presenting end, keep in mind that this element of definition, perhaps more than the other two, has *power*: what or who is included and what or who is excluded can have terribly significant consequences. The definition of "crime" makes the difference in who gets imprisoned and who does not; the definition of "poverty" determines who gets financial assistance and who does not; the definition of "refugee," "endangered species," "pass/fail"—you get the idea. Pay careful attention!

5.3.3a Practice identifying and correcting definitions that are too broad or too narrow (or both)

Which of the following definitions are too broad or too narrow (or both)? Correct them.

1. Pizza is a food item consisting of a bread crust, topped with cheese, tomato sauce, and a variety of meats and/or vegetables.

2. A book consists of a bunch of pages.

3. A leaf is a green thing that hangs from tree branches.

4. A tunnel is a hollow space dug out in the ground that has an entrance and an exit.

5. A "conscientious objector" is a person who objects to participation in all forms of war, and whose belief is based on a religious, moral or ethical belief system.

6. "Rape" is doing anything sexual to someone who doesn't want it.

7. "Domestic terrorism" refers to activities that (A) involve acts dangerous to human life that are a violation of the criminal laws of the U.S. or of any state, that (B) appear to be intended (i) to intimidate or coerce a civilian population, (ii) to influence the policy of a government by intimidation or coercion, or (iii) to affect the conduct of a government by mass destruction, assassination, or kidnapping, and (C) occur primarily within the territorial jurisdiction of the U.S.

   (*U.S. Criminal Code* at *18, U.S.C.2331*)

8. A hero is someone who does something for someone else at great expense to him- or herself.

9. Computers cannot produce something novel; they can merely rearrange what they've been given. That is why I say they cannot think.

10. In a memo issued Monday, the NBA set forth a "minimum" dress code starting with the 2005–2006 season. The following highlights are excerpted from the memo:

    (1) General Policy: Business Casual Players are required to wear Business Casual attire whenever they are engaged in team or league business. "Business Casual" attire means:

    - A long or short-sleeved dress shirt (collared or turtleneck), and/or a sweater.

- Dress slacks, khaki pants, or dress jeans.
- Appropriate shoes and socks, including dress shoes, dress boots, or other presentable shoes, but not including sneakers, sandals, flip-flops, or work boots.

(2) Exceptions to Business Casual

There are the following exceptions to the general policy of Business Casual attire:

a. Players In Attendance At Games But Not In Uniform

Players who are in attendance at games but not in uniform are required to wear the following additional items when seated on the bench or in the stands during the game:

- Sport Coat.
- Dress shoes or boots, and socks.

(3) Excluded Items

The following is a list of items that players are not allowed to wear while on team or league business:

- Sleeveless shirts.
- Shorts.
- T-shirts, jerseys, or sports apparel (unless appropriate for the event (e.g., a basketball clinic), team-identified, and approved by the team).
- Headgear of any kind while a player is sitting on the bench or in the stands at a game, during media interviews, or during a team or league event or appearance (unless appropriate for the event or appearance, team-identified, and approved by the team).
- Chains, pendants, or medallions worn over the player's clothes.
- Sunglasses while indoors.
- Headphones (other than on the team bus or plane, or in the team locker room).

(as reported on espn.com news service, "NBA adopts
'business casual' dress code," October 17, 2005)

5.3.3b Practice constructing good definitions

Define the following terms. Check your definitions for genus and species, necessary and sufficient conditions, and inclusiveness and exclusiveness.

1. spoon

2. paper

3. tree

4. toy

5. sweet

6. excellence

7. mature

8. freedom

9. Hispanic-American

10. religion, cult

5.3.4 Equivocation (an error in reasoning)

Once you have defined a term, implicitly or explicitly, you can't change it in the middle of your argument. If you do, you're guilty of equivocation. **Equivocation** is an error of reasoning that occurs when you use the same word to refer to different things in an argument. So on the one hand, it's an error of definition—you're changing your definition in the middle of an argument and you can't do that. (Well, you *can*, but then you'd be abandoning one argument and starting another.)

On the other hand, equivocation is an error of clarity, because if you were precise about the words you were using, the error wouldn't occur: you would have chosen one word for X and then a different word for Y.

Consider the following argument:

> Your supervisor is your superior, and someone who's superior is someone who's better than others, so your supervisor is better than you.

At first glance, this seems like an acceptable argument, X meaning "your superior":

1. Your supervisor is X.
2. Being X means being better than you.
Therefore, your supervisor is better than you.

However, "superior" in the first premise means "organizational superior" or "superior in the hierarchy," whereas "superior" in the second premise means "better." So the argument is really this:

© Claudio Muñoz

1. Your supervisor is X.
2. Being Y means being better than you ("you" is included in "others").
Therefore, your supervisor is better than you.

Had the two premises actually been talking about the same thing, the argument would have been perfectly good. But, equivocation has occurred: the meaning of the word being used has changed from premise one to premise two. Hence, the two premises are *not* talking about the same thing, and the conclusion does *not* follow from them.

Here's another example of equivocation:

If it were true that life is a matter of the survival of the fittest, athletes wouldn't be dying from heart attacks.

The argument in standard form would be this:

1. The fittest survive.
2. Athletes are the fittest.
Therefore, athletes should survive.

However, the word "fittest" in the first premise, likely referring to the phrase "the survival of the fittest," means those that most fit their environment, those that have best adapted to their environment. However, the word "fittest" in the second premise likely refers to physical fitness, to muscular and cardiovascular strength and resilience. Again, the meaning of a word has changed through the course of the argument, so the argument is erroneous. (There is actually another error of equivocation here in that "fittest" in the context of "survival of the fittest" refers to a species as a whole, but "fittest" in the second premise seems to be referring to individual members of the species.)

While perhaps not exactly equivocation, it is especially important to beware of changing definitions when a case is made for an increase or decrease in some condition, such as poverty, crime, or mental illness. Often over the years the definition of those terms changes. For example, if the level of income under which people are considered to be living in poverty is lowered, it will seem as though poverty has decreased, whereas in fact, it may well be that the number or percentage of people making less than a certain amount of money has remained the same; it's just that since the cut-off level has changed, people once considered poor are not now considered poor.

5.3.4a Practice identifying the error of equivocation

Which of the following arguments contain the error of equivocation?

1. Scobie is an asset to this firm. All assets can be liquidated. Therefore, Scobie can be liquidated.

2. If practice makes perfect, why do lawyers who've been in practice for years lose cases?

3. It used to be that a husband's income was sufficient for a family to be middle-class. Nowadays, both husband and wife have to work just to have a decent house and a vacation every year. That just goes to show that men's real wages have decreased over the years.

4. Men often resort to violence to resolve a conflict even when it's not life-threatening. Most animals would just leave the scene. Clearly we are not the superior species.

5. Most prisoners in the United States are Christian. So religious instruction obviously does not improve morality.

6. How, then, should the United States formulate a foreign policy? Every action taken abroad should reflect the purpose behind the creation of the government: namely, to serve the interests of American society and the people who live in it. Washington's role is not to conduct glorious utopian crusades around the globe. It is not to provide a pot of cash for the secretary of state to pass out to friendly regimes to increase United States influence abroad. It is not to sacrifice the lives of Americans to minimize other people's sufferings.

In short, the money and lives of the American people are not there for policy-makers, or even the president, to expend for purposes other than defending the American community.

(Doug Bandow, "Keeping the Troops and the Money at Home," *Current History*, January 1994)

7. Indeed, given that there is a developmental continuum from embryo to fetus to infant to child, it is logically sound to extend policies about child abuse post-birth to pre-birth: "To begin legal protection and comprehensive obligations toward human beings only at birth, is to assume that the most vulnerable period of all human life, the period during which the foundations of childhood and adulthood health are laid, is discontinuous with and of no influence on those later stages" (Edward W. Keyselingk, *The Unborn Child's Right to Prenatal Care*, 1984). On this basis, the state may be justified in regulating the behavior of the (biological) parents.

8. Nobody's perfect. And I'm nobody.

(bumper sticker)

9. It is clear there are laws of nature. For example, objects dropped off tall buildings fall down rather than fall up. If there are laws, there must be a law-maker. Who then has set these laws? Why, the supreme lawgiver, God!

10. Regarding proposed legislation governing surrogacy in the United States, under which if the surrogate mother miscarries prior to the fifth month of pregnancy, no compensation other than medical expenses will be paid. If she miscarries after this time, 10% of the fee plus medical expenses would be paid . . . Of course this makes it clear that the baby is a product. You don't deliver the goods, you don't get paid. But there is another point to be made here. If the woman miscarries prior to the fifth month of pregnancy, does the physician who examined her not get paid? Does the physician who inseminated her not get paid? Does the psychiatrist who screened her not get paid? Does the lawyer who arranged the surrogate pregnancy lose out on his money? Not on your life.

They all get their money. But there is no need to pay the woman. And most people don't notice anything amiss in this arrangement. They really don't know what you are talking about when you object to it. You can't rent a *cow* in this country for five months for free. But you can rent a woman.

(Personal communication from Gena Corea, author of *The Mother Machine*, to Marilyn Waring, September 5, 1986)

5.3.4b Practice making an argument without equivocation

Construct three arguments that exhibit the error of equivocation. Reconstruct the arguments so they are error-free.

Review of terms

Define the following terms:

- ◼ **loaded language**

- ◼ **genus and species**

- ◼ **necessary and sufficient conditions**

- ◼ **inclusiveness and exclusiveness**

- ◼ **equivocation.**

Thinking critically about what you see

Again, think critically about each of the following. Pay special attention to any language that is used.

1.

© Agilent Technologies, Inc., 2005. Reproduced with permission. Courtesy of Agilent Technologies, Inc.

2.

© Corbis

Thinking critically about what you hear

Listen to the audio clip under the Student Resources tab on the companion website at www.routledge.com/textbooks/tittle. Any response?

Thinking critically about what you read

Think critically about each of the following, paying special attention to clarity, loaded language, and definition.

You may want to consult the template again; steps 1 and 2 should be routine by now; don't forget to consider relevance (the only part of step 4 we've covered to this point); and before you make a final decision about accepting the argument, work through steps 5, 6, and 7.

1. Americans are a free people, who know that freedom is the right of every person and the future of every nation. The liberty we prize is not America's gift to the world, it is God's gift to humanity.

      (George W. Bush, Jr., State of the Union Address, 2003)

2. A survey reported in the December 27, 2004 issue of *Sports Illustrated* listed the average number of households in a region that tuned in each week to various sports concluding that "the most watched sport on television continues to be pro football . . ."

      ("What Fans Watch")

Template for critical analysis

1. What's the point (claim/opinion/conclusion)?

    ■ Look for subconclusions as well.

2. What are the reasons/what is the evidence?

    ■ Articulate all unstated premises.
    ■ Articulate connections.

3. What exactly is meant by . . .?

    ■ Define terms.
    ■ Clarify all imprecise language.
    ■ Eliminate or replace "loaded" language and other manipulations.

4. Assess the reasoning/evidence:

    ■ If deductive, check for truth/acceptability and validity.
    ■ If inductive, check for truth/acceptability, relevance, and sufficiency.

5. How could the argument be strengthened?

    ■ Provide additional reasons/evidence.
    ■ Anticipate objections—are there adequate responses?

6. How could the argument be weakened?

    ■ Consider and assess counterexamples, counterevidence, and counter-arguments.
    ■ Should the argument be modified or rejected because of the counter-arguments?

7. If you suspend judgment (rather than accepting or rejecting the argument), identify further information required.

3. There are now more than 4,400 biotech firms in the world, the vast majority still privately owned. America, the birthplace of modern biotech, continues to tower over the field, accounting for more than half of all publicly-traded firms and almost $43 billion in revenues last year, including from such giants as Amgen and Genentech. America's success is reflected in growing investment: the industry there raised almost $17 billion from public and private markets in 2004, almost five times as much as in Europe.

("From Seed to Harvest," *The Economist*, June 4, 2005)

4. I have to be honest: I really don't think Britney is that bad. Sure she made some mistakes, but who doesn't when they are in their early 20s? We only know what the tabloids say about her, which is most likely a bunch of lies. From everything I have heard, she is a sweet, fun-loving girl who does have high morals. The fact is that she is married now and probably will have a child soon. I am sure she has the same dreams that we did: to be married and to have children. Give the girl a break! I, for one, am glad to see her on the cover!

(Posted on *Redbook*'s online message board by jess0521 and printed in March 2005 issue of *Redbook*)

5. I see it with the executives within the studio area. The other day, I saw a woman producer who was really quite powerful; and she railroaded, walked all over this guy, who was far less successful and powerful than her. She just behaved as if this man wasn't there because her position was more powerful than his. And it was much more disconcerting because it was a woman doing it. It was unfeminine, you know?

(Adrian Lyne, quoted by Susan Faludi in *Backlash: The Undeclared War Against American Women*, 1991)

6. Thousands participated in the June 3 Gay Pride parade in Jerusalem, faced with protesters and the condemnation of the city's mayor, Ha'aretz reported. Jerusalem Mayor Uri Lupolianski, in a radio interview on June 4, decried the downtown parade, according to media reports. "To carry out an insulting parade—I don't call that pride," Lupolianski told reporters. "In a place like Jerusalem, this is an ugly phenomenon, which need not happen." He said the event was inappropriate in a "sacred city," Ha'aretz reported. "This parade is not only ugly, it's also a provocation," Lupolianski said in the interview. "It's not appropriate for the city, and it offends the sensitivities of its residents. Even people distant from Jerusalem must grasp that this is a sacred city for the Jewish people, and the world as a whole. This isn't Paris, and it isn't London. I'm not talking about what a person does privately in his home—a parade in public is something else . . . If somebody has some sort of deviant trait, it doesn't mean that he has to raise its banner in public.

(*New York Blade*, June 11, 2004)

7. It would be futile to attempt to discuss the question as to what race or races were the original standard-bearers of human culture and were thereby the real founders of all

211

that we understand by the word humanity. It is much simpler to deal with this question in so far as it relates to the present time. Here the answer is simple and clear. Every manifestation of human culture, every product of art, science and technical skill, which we see before our eyes to-day, is almost exclusively the product of the Aryan creative power. This very fact fully justifies the conclusion that it was the Aryan alone who founded a superior type of humanity; therefore he represents the archetype of what we understand by the term: M A N. He is the Prometheus of mankind, from whose shining brow the divine spark of genius has at all times flashed forth, always kindling anew that fire which, in the form of knowledge, illuminated the dark night by drawing aside the veil of mystery and thus showing man how to rise and become master over all the other beings on the earth. Should he be forced to disappear, a profound darkness will descend on the earth; within a few thousand years human culture will vanish and the world will become a desert.

(Adolf Hitler, *Mein Kampf*, 1942 [1939])

8. Americans are constantly told that their health care is the best in the world. In terms of research, technology and advances in surgery, the boast is undoubtedly true. In other ways, it is hard to justify. At any one time, more than 43m Americans under the age of 65 have no health insurance (the elderly are covered by Medicare, a federal insurance programme). The infant mortality rate for black Americans runs at 14 per 1,000 live births, double the rate for white Americans and over four times the rate in Japan. Indeed, in a 2000 study of the effectiveness of health-care systems around the world, the World Health Organization ranked America only 37th (France came top).

(From "Headaches for All," posted November 14, 2004
on Physicians for a National Health Program website, at:
http://www.pnhp.org/news/2004/november/headaches_for_all.php)

9. In an effort to avoid potential conflicts, it is required that Chrysler Corporation be alerted in advance of any and all editorial content that encompasses sexual, political, social issues or any editorial that might be construed as provocative or offensive. Each and every issue that carries Chrysler advertising requires a written summary outlining major theme/articles appearing in upcoming issues. These summaries are to be forwarded to PentaCom prior to closing in order to give Chrysler ample time to review and reschedule if desired . . . As acknowledgment of this letter we ask that you or a representative from the publication sign below and return to us no later than February 15.

(From a letter sent by Chrysler's ad agency, PentaCom, a division of BBDO
North America, to at least fifty magazines, as presented in Russ Baker, "The
Squeeze," *Columbia Journalism Review*, September/October 1997)

10. Laws that operate on the basis of race require definitions of race. Because of the Court's decision today, our statute books will once again have to contain laws that reflect the odious practice of delineating those qualities that make one person a Negro and make another white. Moreover, racial discrimination, even "good faith" racial discrimination,

is inevitably a two-edged sword. "[P]referential programs may only reinforce common stereotypes holding that certain groups are unable to achieve success without special protection based on a factor having no relationship to individual worth" (*University of California Regents v. Bakke, supra*, 438 U.A., at 298, 98 S.Ct., at 2753, opinion of Powell, J.). Most importantly, by making race a relevant criterion once again in its own affairs, the Government implicitly teaches the public that the apportionment of rewards and penalties can legitimately be made according to race—rather than according to merit or ability—and that people can, and perhaps should, view themselves and others in terms of their racial characteristics. Notions of "racial entitlement" will be fostered, and private discrimination will necessarily be encouraged.

(Potter Stewart, "The Constitution and Discrimination," from Dissenting Opinion, *Fullilove v. Klutznick* 448 U.S. 448, 1980)

Thinking critically about what you write

Can you make any sort of argument from the following bunches of statements (facts and opinions)? That is, in each case, where do these facts and opinions take you, what claim or claims do they support, what claim or claims follow from these facts and opinions? Don't assume that all of the bits are relevant to the same conclusion. Don't assume they're all equally important.

Write up the two arguments you would make (you'll likely find you've got about 500 words each). Feel free to add bits that, if true, would strengthen your arguments.

1.
- over 90 percent of the violent crime committed in the U.S. is committed by men
- we raise our boys differently than we raise our girls
- how we're treated as kids generally affects how we behave as adults
- men typically have more testosterone than women
- men kill other men more often than they kill women
- handguns are prohibited in England and their violence rate is lower than ours, but it was lower even *before* the prohibition
- the average 18-year-old has seen 16,000 simulated murders and 200,000 acts of violence on TV (according to *Mother Jones*, November/December 2004)
- Myriam Miedzian says that "Many of the values of the masculine mystique, such as toughness, dominance, repression of empathy, extreme competitiveness, play a major role in criminal and domestic violence and underlie the thinking and policy decisions of many of our political leaders" (*Boys Will be Boys: Breaking the Link between Masculinity and Violence*, 1991)

2.
- about half of all pregnancies in the U.S. are unplanned; that's over 3 million unintended fertilized eggs (from http://www.agi-usa.org/pubs/fb_induced_abortion.html)

- we require teachers of children to undergo formal training
- what parents do or don't do to and with their kids can have very serious consequences
- plumbers have to have a license
- most people think that our children are more important than our toilets
- genetic disease can be passed on through the genetic material in sperm and ova
- the use of drugs, from crack to alcohol, during pregnancy can cause the newborn to experience excruciating pain and to have birth defects
- the fetus is a potential human being, so it should have potential rights, not actual rights
- parents are responsible for the physical, emotional, cognitive, and social development of a human being

When you have finished, double-check to be sure you have defined your terms well and avoided loaded language.

Suggestion: Until you internalize the process, it might help to imagine a reader (or a bunch of them) looking over your shoulder as you write and asking questions—what do you mean by that? and that? isn't going from that bit to this bit a bit of a jump? what about the idea that . . .?

Thinking critically when you discuss

Okay, this time arrange yourselves in groups of four.

Also, after each person responds to the initial argument, anyone can respond to what anyone has said. That is, the third person might respond to whatever the second person said in response to the initial argument, or vice versa; also, whoever made the initial argument can respond to the two responses to that argument. But use the same repertoire of responses (see the list and chart given at the end of Chapter 2).

And, since we've just spent a chapter on language, pay special attention to the words that are used! Also, be sure all the important words are defined to everyone's satisfaction!

Suggestion: It might help if you paraphrase what the preceding speakers said before you say your bit. Not only does that help everyone stay on track (something that becomes more difficult as more people take part in the discussion), it also keeps the misunderstandings to a minimum.

In fact, feel free to make notes during the discussion: as mentioned previously, our society isn't much of an aural one anymore and our listening skills have become pretty minimal (in terms of attention span and retention capacity). Besides that, it's not easy to follow an argument if it has more than one or two premises leading to a conclusion. And it's especially difficult to follow if it *doesn't* follow—that is, if the premises are irrelevant. Making notes not only helps you follow what's being said, it also helps you remember what you plan to say if something occurs to you while you're listening. If you don't write it down, you'll spend your mental energy trying to remember what you're going to say and you'll stop listening to what's being said!

Freethinkers are those who are willing to use their minds without prejudice and without fearing to understand things that clash with their own customs, privileges, or beliefs. This state of mind is not common, but it is essential for right thinking; where it is absent, discussion is apt to become worse than useless.

Leo Tolstoy, *War and Peace*, 1862

Reasoning test questions

The GRE no longer has multiple-choice questions that test logical reasoning. Instead, there is an "Analytical Writing Section" which consists of two essay writing tasks, each scored on a scale of six: a 45-minute "Present Your Perspective on an Issue" task and a 30-minute "Analyze an Argument" task. Details are available at the ETS website (www.ets.org); download "An Introduction to the Analytical Writing Section of the GRE General Test" (it's free).

According to the "Introduction," the "Present Your Perspective on an Issue" task "assesses your ability to think critically about a topic of general interest and to clearly express your thoughts about it in writing"—see the section entitled "Understanding the Issue Task" for details about how you are expected to go about doing that! (You might want to do that before you proceed here; if you do, also check out "Preparing for the Issue Task.")

The following is a sample prompt for the "Present Your Perspective on an Issue" task; these are the only instructions you're given. Go ahead and see how you do!

■ ■ ■

Present your perspective on the issue below, using relevant reasons and/or examples to support your views.

In our time, specialists of all kinds are highly over-rated. We need more generalists—people who can provide broad perspectives.

chapter 6

truth and acceptability

Template for critical analysis of arguments

1. What's the point (claim/opinion/conclusion)?

   ■ Look for subconclusions as well.

2. What are the reasons/what is the evidence?

   ■ Articulate all unstated premises.
   ■ Articulate connections.

3. What exactly is meant by . . .?

   ■ Define terms.
   ■ Clarify all imprecise language.
   ■ Eliminate or replace "loaded" language and other manipulations.

4. **Assess the reasoning/evidence:**

   ■ If deductive, check for truth/acceptability and validity.
   ■ **If inductive, check for truth/acceptability**, relevance, and sufficiency.

5. How could the argument be strengthened?

   ■ Provide additional reasons/evidence.
   ■ Anticipate objections—are there adequate responses?

6. How could the argument be weakened?

   ■ Consider and assess counterexamples, counterevidence, and counter-arguments.
   ■ Should the argument be modified or rejected because of the counter-arguments?

7. If you suspend judgment (rather than accepting or rejecting the argument), identify further information required.

6.1 Truth and acceptability

A good argument has premises that are true or at least acceptable. That criterion is the focus of this chapter.

6.1.1 Truth

While philosophers typically leave the establishment of **truth** to others (those working in social science, natural science, and so on), our arguments, nevertheless, depend on truth. For example, we might argue that because affirmative action programs that require the hiring of members of a certain group just to fill a quota result in feelings of low self-worth on the part of those hired and feelings of resentment on the part of those not, such programs should not be implemented. Whether or not such programs *do*, in fact, result in feelings of low self-worth on the part of those hired and feelings of resentment on the part of those not *is* important to our argument; indeed the truth of that premise is essential to the strength of the argument. But it's not *our* job to figure that out—we leave that to psychologists to establish.

To be more specific about the role of truth in argument, recall that *in order for a deductive argument to be sound*, two criteria must be met: the structure must be valid and *the premises must be true*. So the role of truth in deductive argument is quite clear: unless the premises are true, you need not—and indeed you should not—accept the conclusion. (Validity is addressed at length in the logic supplements.)

In order for an inductive argument to be strong, three criteria must be met: the premises must be relevant, *they must be true*, and they must be sufficient. (Relevance was discussed in Chapter 4, and sufficiency will be discussed in Chapters 7 and 8.) So, again, truth is a requirement. Note, however, that we speak of strong and weak arguments in the case of induction, whereas we speak of valid and invalid arguments in the case of deduction. When an inductive argument is *strong*, its conclusion is accepted with more or less certainty, rather than simply accepted or rejected.

Given the importance of truth, it is somewhat paradoxical—or at least ironic—that scientists spend more time proving things to be false than proving them to be true. In order to understand why, you must understand the difference between verification and falsification. If we can show X to be true, we have verified X; if we can show X to be false, we have falsified X. A claim is **verifiable** if we can describe conditions under which we can show it to be true; a claim is **falsifiable** if we can describe conditions under which we can show it to be false. It is far easier to falsify a claim than to verify it. For example, to prove that the statement "All swans are white" is false, all we need is one black swan; to prove the claim to be true, on the other hand, we'd have to find and examine every swan in existence.

Every swan. Because to verify a claim, not only do we have to gather the supporting evidence, we also have to eliminate all competing claims. Supporting evidence is consistent with the hypothetical claim, of course, but it may well be consistent with other hypothetical claims as well. For example, a white swan does indeed support the claim that "All swans are white," but it also supports the claim that "Some swans may be black." So we'd somehow have to eliminate that competing claim. And the only way we can do that is find *every* swan. That's why disconfirming evidence (even a single counterexample) is more valuable than confirming evidence: disconfirming evidence proves that the claim is false, but confirming evidence doesn't prove that it's true—it merely proves that it could be true. In fact, some theorists argue that it's actually impossible to prove anything since there's always a chance there's some disconfirming evidence out there we haven't yet come across. Certainly negative claims are virtually impossible to prove: how would you prove "She did not see him" to be true? (Now, how would you prove it to be false?) This is why, recall (see Section 2.7), the burden of proof is on the person who makes the positive claim.

All of this applies, however, only to empirical claims. An empirical claim is one that can be tested—verified or falsified by empirical evidence, evidence subject to measurement by one sense or another. And note the phrase "*measurement* by one sense or another"—we may not be able to see, hear, smell, touch, or taste magnetism, but we can devise tests and/or instruments that will register its existence somehow in a way we can see, hear, smell, touch, or taste. (We'll get into this in more detail in Section 6.3.)

An appeal to ignorance (see Section 2.8) involves mistaking a lack of falsification for verification; basically, when one makes an appeal to ignorance, one is saying, "We don't know that it's not true (we have no falsification), therefore it is true (we have verification)." For example, if someone said that since we haven't found any black swans, we can conclude they're all white, an appeal to ignorance would have been made: the person has taken the lack of falsification as verification.

The appeal to ignorance thus assumes that our current knowledge is complete (and completely correct): if we have no knowledge that A is not true, the appeal to ignorance implies, there must be no such knowledge (because we know everything there is to know)—so A is true.

6.1.2 Acceptability

Although less robust than truth, acceptability is often more difficult to determine. Even so, there are three categories of claims for which we use the standard of acceptability.

The first category includes instances in which the claim is indeed true or false, but *it is unlikely, for practical reasons, that we will be able to establish whether it's true or false*. On the one hand, this may be because of *the magnitude of the task*, as is the case with generalizations of a universal nature describing large populations. For example, to establish the universal generalization that all mosquitoes are beige, we'd have to find and examine every single mosquito in existence, a task of such magnitude, it is unlikely to be performed. Whether or not such generalizations are acceptable will depend instead on the arguments supporting them (see Section 7.2). On the other hand, we may be unable to establish whether the claim is true or false because of *the limitations of our understanding*. In this case, we have to rely on others with greater understanding, so acceptability becomes a matter of establishing trust, usually based on credibility. Whether or not others' claims of truth or falsity are acceptable becomes a matter of whether or not they are an appropriate authority (see Sections 4.3.1 and 6.4.3).

The second category in which we use acceptability rather than truth includes instances in which *it is impossible, even in theory, to determine truth (though there is some truth to the matter)*. Predictions fall into this category because we can't know the future. While it is actually true or false that "X will occur," we can't know (today, at least) whether "X will occur" is true or false. Predictions are acceptable to the extent that their supporting arguments are strong (see Section 8.3). But perhaps the greater part of this category consists of causal reasoning: we never actually *see* something cause something else. We see X happen and then we see Y happen, but we never see X *causing* Y. Whether causal statements are acceptable will depend on the arguments supporting them (see Chapter 8).

If the claim is, at least in theory, true or false, as in these first two categories, a general measure of acceptability is that of *plausibility*. And plausibility can be addressed by asking two questions. First, "Is it *possible*?" (Of course, if one believes in miracles, however, then even the impossible is plausible.) Second, "Is it *reasonable*?" (Good for you, though, if you're saying "Define 'reasonable'!") An even higher standard than plausibility is *probability*: is the claim not just possible, but probable? If so, it is even more acceptable.

The more knowledgeable one is about the issue in question, the more able one is to determine the plausibility of various claims, and hence their acceptability, because one will be able to measure the claim against a wealth of background knowledge, claims already established as true or acceptable. Keep in mind that determining relevance and sufficiency also requires knowledge: if you don't know anything about the issue, you won't be able to identify what is and is not relevant, nor will you be able to think of counterexamples, alternative causes, and so on.

The third category in which we use the criterion of acceptability rather than truth includes claims of a non-empirical nature. In particular, statements about what is beautiful (aesthetic propositions) as well as statements about what is morally right or wrong (ethical propositions) fall into this category. While such statements cannot be proven to be true or false, they are nevertheless very important in argument and indeed life. And we need some way of judging their relative merit if only because such claims are often mutually exclusive. For example, we can't accept both "X is wrong" and "X is right" without contradiction. Arguments for aesthetic and ethical propositions usually invoke a general principle as a premise: aesthetic propositions usually invoke some principle of design (balance, contrast, unity, color, line, timbre, and so on), artist intent, or audience impact, and ethical propositions usually invoke some principle involving values, rights, or consequences. It is these general principles that enable us to make judgments about acceptability. For example, to the extent a work of art displays balance and unity, we might accept the claim that that work of art is beautiful. To the extent an action respects rights or minimizes painful consequences, we might accept the claim that that action is right.

Another approach to determining acceptability, which can be used in all three cases, is to *consider the implications of the claim*. First, does X flatly contradict other stuff you know to be true? If so, you can judge the claim unacceptable. (Or reconsider that other stuff you thought you knew to be true!)

Second, if X is true, what follows? And is what follows acceptable? For example, consider the tabloid headline, "Aliens Kidnap Trailer Park Boys!!!!!" And let's assume that it will be impossible to establish whether or not it's true, so we need to use the standard of acceptability instead. Let's consider the implications of the claim. If it's true that aliens kidnapped trailer park boys, what else would have to be true? Well, that there *are* aliens, and that they are more intelligent than us: after all, we haven't discovered other life forms (they have), nor have we traveled to the other life forms' home planet (they have), nor have we managed to kidnap the other life forms (they have). Is all of that possible? Perhaps. Reasonable? Maybe. Probable? Okay, there I think I draw the line.

6.1.2a Practice determining whether truth or acceptability applies

For each of the following claims, indicate whether they should be evaluated for truth or acceptability. If the former, indicate what would verify or falsify the claim.

1. With the proper meditation techniques, I can invoke an out-of-body experience, one in which my astral body separates from my physical body and floats above for a few moments before departing on an astral journey.

2. Overall, in the United States, in public testing sites, 32% of the people who test positive don't come back for their results.
   (Dr. Bernard M. Branson, of the Divisions of H.I.V./AIDS Prevention at the Federal Centers for Disease Control and Prevention, quoted by Richard Pérez-Peña in *The New York Times*, June 6, 2005)

222

Acceptability

3. This painting is exquisite!

4. The U.S. has twice as many shopping malls as high schools. *Truth*
(*Mother Jones*, November/December 2004)

5. Paying taxes is morally indefensible. *Acceptability*

6. I am having a vision: tomorrow you will be offered a job you can't refuse. *Acceptability*

7. God created human beings. *Acceptability*

8. Tom created new toys. *Truth*

9. Particles of rock, sand, and mud, which are collectively called sediment, settle in layers at the bottoms of rivers, lakes, and oceans, and as the sediments accumulate, they bury shells, bones, leaves, pollen, and other bits and pieces of living things. With the passing of time, the layers of sediments are compacted by the weight of overlying sediments and cemented together, and the buried plant and animal remains become fossils within the sedimentary layers. Since sedimentary rocks are formed particle by particle and layer by layer, the layers end up stacked one on another; thus, in any sequence of undisturbed sedimentary rock, the layers increase in age the further down they are. Geologists have divided time into four very broad segments: the Precambrian, up to 540 million years ago; the Paleozoic, 540—250 million years ago; the Mesozoic, 250—65 million years ago; and the Cenozoic, 65 million years ago to the present. (Certain elements decay and turn into other elements at a known and constant rate, so by measuring the amount of decay, geologists can determine the age of the rock; for example, it takes 5,700 years for carbon to half-decay into nitrogen, it takes 1.3 billion years for potassium to half-decay into argon, and so on.) So the fossil record provides evidence for the theory that animal life forms have developed along a certain trajectory: invertebrates developed first, as invertebrate fossils are found in the Precambrian layer of rock; then fish and reptiles started showing up, in the Paleozoic time period; mammals and birds don't appear until the Mesozoic.
(Based on John Pojeta, Jr. and Dale A. Springer, "Evolution and the Fossil Record," American Geological Institute, at: http://www.agiweb.org/news/evolution/index.html)

10. There were four main causes of the Mexican War. First, the annexation of Texas: Mexico said it would regard annexation of Texas as an act of war. Second, the boundary dispute: the United States maintained that the southern border of Texas was formed by the Rio Grande, but Mexico argued that the traditional boundary was at the Nueces River farther north. Third, the California question: United States President Polk clearly wanted to expand

the United States to the Pacific Ocean by taking control of California and lands in the Southwest—a prime example of the 'manifest destiny' mentality. Fourth, the monetary claim issue: the United States had extracted a promise from the Mexican government to pay $3 million to cover the claims of American citizens who had lost property during turmoil and revolution; Mexico defaulted on those payments and the American creditors pressed their government for action.

(From http://www.u-s-history.com/pages/h322.html)

6.1.2b *More practice with the standards of truth and acceptability*

List five claims you most definitely do not believe at the moment. For each, indicate what would make you consider the claim to be true or acceptable.

6.1.2c *Still more practice with the standards of truth and acceptability*

For each of the following, indicate which claims need to be verified in order for the conclusion to be acceptable; alternatively, indicate what falsification would lead you to reject the conclusion. Also, consider whether each claim is plausible (possible and reasonable) or probable, consider its implications, and, if applicable, indicate questions that need to be answered before you accept it.

1. People don't refrain from killing their neighbors because they don't want to risk the penalty. They just don't want to kill their neighbors. So punishment isn't a deterrent.

2. There should be "girls only" schools because girls speak up in class more often when there are no boys around. And, of course, they're not interrupted by boys when they do so. They become more assertive; they become more sure of themselves. And when not distracted by attractions or animosities—especially when the fear of appearing too smart is removed—they focus more on the subject matter and actually become quite good, even at subjects traditionally thought of as "boy" subjects (math, engineering, law, and so on). In fact, I read that students from girls only schools score higher on tests like the SAT and GRE than those at mixed schools.

   People say that eventually they'll have to live in a world with males, so they should get used to it. But isn't it better if they meet the challenges of constant silencing and put-downs when they're mature and they've developed the confidence and skills to insist on equal consideration?

   People also say that segregation perpetuates significant differences that underlie sexism, so if we endorse such segregation, we'll never become a sex blind society. But I'm not convinced that differences underlie sexism; after all, men are quite different from each other. I think it's something else.

3. Of course, most parents aren't thinking of the "higher" good at all. They send their children to college because they are convinced their young benefit financially from those four years of higher education. But if money is the only goal, college is the dumbest investment you can make . . .

If a 1972 Princeton-bound high-school graduate had put the $34,181 that his four years of college would have cost him into a savings bank at 7.5 percent interest compounded daily, he would have had at age 64 a total of $1,129,200, or $528,200 more than the earnings of a male college graduate . . .

In fact there is no real evidence that the higher income of college graduates is due to college. College may simply attract people who are slated to earn more money anyway; those with higher IQs, better family backgrounds, a more enterprising temperament.

(Caroline Bird, *The Case Against College*, 1975)

4. Chlorine monoxide is a derivative of an important family of synthetic chemicals that are known as chlorofluorocarbons (CFCs). They have enjoyed wide use for decades as coolants in refrigerators and air conditioners, propellants in aerosol spray cans, blowing agents in the manufacture of plastic and rubber foam products and as solvents in the production of electronic equipment.

Once released into the atmosphere, CFCs drift upward until they reach the ozone layer, which begins in the stratosphere [and protects the Earth by blocking out most of the sun's harmful ultraviolet light]. As long as they remain in their original molecular form, CFCs are harmless. But intense ultraviolet radiation can break the CFC molecule apart, producing chlorine monoxide and setting off a series of reactions that destroy ozone. [Cooper elsewhere in her article describes the effects of excessive UV radiation, including cataracts, cancer, weakened immune systems and hence decreased ability to ward off infectious diseases, and disrupted photosynthesis leading to reduced crop yields.] . . .

Ozone-destroying chemicals are extremely stable, so they last in the atmosphere for many decades. That means that even if production of all CFCs and halons stopped today, the chemicals already in the atmosphere would go on destroying ozone well into the 21st century.

(Mary H. Cooper, "Ozone Depletion," *CQ Researcher*, April 3, 1992)

5. [T]he whole notion of the ozone layer as something fixed and finite, to be eroded away at a faster or slower rate like shoe leather, is all wrong to begin with—it's simply not a depletable resource; . . . even if it were, the process by which CFCs are supposed to deplete it is highly speculative and has never been observed to take place; and even if it did, the effect would be trivial compared to what happens naturally . . .

[O]zone is all the time being created in the upper atmosphere. . .

If ozone were depleting, UV intensity at the earth's surface would be increasing. In fact, actually measurements show that it has been decreasing—by as much as 8 percent in some places over the last decade. . . .

. . . CFCs don't rise in significant amounts to where they need to be for UV-C photons to break them up . . .

[Regarding the suggestion that a thousand times more chlorine has been measured over the Antarctic than models say ought to be there] . . . The measuring station at McMurdo Sound [in the Antarctic] is located 15 kilometers downwind from Mount Erebus, an active volcano venting 100 to 200 tons of chlorine every day . . .

[A]n unexpectedly low value in the Antarctic winter-spring ozone level was reported by the British scientist Gordon Dobson in 1956—when CFCs were barely in use . . .

An increasing rate of UV-induced skin cancer means that more people are receiving more exposure than they ought to. It doesn't follow that the intensity of ultraviolet is increasing as it would if ozone were being depleted. (In fact, it's decreasing, as we saw earlier.) Other considerations explain the facts far better, such as that sun worship has become a fad among light-skinned people only in the last couple of generations, or the migrations in comparatively recent times of peoples into habitats for which they aren't adapted: for instance, the white population of Australia. (Native Australians have experienced no skin-cancer increase.)

(James P. Hogan, "Ozone Politics: They Call This Science?" *Omni*, June 1993)

6.2 How do we define truth? (theories of truth)

Philosophers have several theories of truth; what follows are very simplified versions of four of them.

6.2.1 Subjectivism

One commonly hears phrases like "Well, it's true for me; it may not be true for you." Although such statements seem to present a view of the nature of truth, one called subjectivism, which we'll talk about in a minute, I think more often such statements are just a careless way of saying one of three things—none of which actually involve the nature of truth.

First, the speaker could mean "It's been my experience; perhaps you haven't experienced the same thing." And that's almost too trivial to point out. After all, it's not at all unusual for you to have experienced quite a few things I have never experienced and vice versa. But *experience* is not the same thing as *truth*. A winter's day may seem bitterly cold to you, but just mildly cold to me. Does that mean there are two different truths about the temperature, yours and mine? Of course not. It just means that we experience things, even the same things, differently.

Second, the speaker could mean "I'm aware of evidence for X being true; you may not be aware of evidence for X being true." But *awareness* of a truth is not the same as the truth itself. Whether one is aware of evidence for X being true does not change whether or not X is in fact true. Whether one *thinks* X is true has no effect on whether X *is* true. (Our minds are simply not that powerful!) (Good thing!) Similarly, we sometimes hear it said of people of a different time and place, "It was true for them," when what is really meant is "They *thought* it was true."

A third more correct meaning of "It's true for me" is "I think this evidence indicates that X is true (and you do not)." But the issue of contention here is not what's true, but what the evidence indicates about what's true.

Those three possibilities notwithstanding, it may well be that the speaker truly means that truth is subjective—that what is true, that whether X is true, is up to the individual. This theory of truth, subjectivism, stands in opposition to objectivism, according to which truth is independent of any particular subject or person. Very few people really subscribe to this theory of truth as it's very hard to defend: basically, it proposes that *if you believe it's true, it is*. Okay, I believe you're dead. Gee, you're still alive. Why didn't that work? Another way to discredit subjectivism is to follow its implications (recall the previous section), one of which is that given the subjective nature of truth, X and not-X can both be true: X may be true for you, and not-X may be true for me. But most people's brains reject that possibility: a chair can't have arms and not have arms at the same time.

As you might imagine, this critique [postmodernism] began to annoy real, practicing scientists. Physicists were particularly irritated, since they deal with things like gravity, speed and mass, which are kind of hard to shrug off as "subjective" (especially if you've ever been in, say, a car crash).

Clive Thompson, *This Magazine*, May/June 2004

6.2.2 The coherence theory

According to the coherence theory of truth, *something is true if it fits with other things we hold to be true*. For example, we might consider it plausible that a fish jerking in the air at the end of a line with a hook in its mouth is feeling pain, given several other things we know to be true: fish begin to suffocate when they're out of the water, suffocation makes us panic, we often jerk about when we're panicked, fish have nerve endings in their mouths, nerve endings conduct pain, pain often causes us to jerk about, and a metal hook caught in our mouth would be painful.

Perhaps the most obvious problem with this theory is that those other things we hold to be true may, in fact, not be true. Those who subscribe to this theory, and only this theory, risk living in delusion. It's a coherent, self-contained delusion, but it's a delusion nevertheless (at least from the correspondence theory point of view!).

Plantinga's Epistemically Inflexible Climber

[C]onsider the Case of the Epistemically Inflexible Climber. Ric is climbing Guide's Wall, on Storm Point in the Grand Tetons; having just led the difficult next to last pitch, he is seated on a comfortable ledge, bringing his partner up. He believes that Cascade Canyon is down to his left, that the cliffs of Mount Owen are directly in front of him, that there is a hawk gliding in lazy circles 200 feet below him, that he is wearing his new *Fire* rock shoes, and so on. His beliefs, we may stipulate, are coherent. Now add that Ric is struck by a wayward burst of high-energy cosmic radiation. This induces a cognitive malfunction; his beliefs become fixed, no longer responsive to changes in experience. No matter what his experience, his beliefs remain the same. At the cost of considerable effort his partner gets him down and, in a desperate last-ditch attempt at therapy, takes him to the opera in nearby Jackson, where the New York Metropolitan Opera on tour is performing *La Traviata*. Ric is appeared to in the same way as everyone else there; he is inundated by wave after wave of golden sound. Sadly enough, the effort at therapy fails; Ric's beliefs remain fixed and wholly unresponsive to his experience; he still believes that he is on the belay ledge at the top of the next to last pitch of Guide's Wall, that Cascade Canyon is down to his left, that there is a hawk sailing in lazy circles 200 feet below him, that he is wearing his new *Fire* rock shoes, and so on. Furthermore, since he believes the very same things he believed when seated on the ledge, his beliefs are coherent.

(Alvin Plantinga, *Warrant: The Current Debate*, 1993)

It is, however, valuable to check for coherence when you are considering claims of truth; recall that in the last section, one test for acceptability was whether the claim contradicted other claims known to be true. So coherence is important— it's just not sufficient.

6.2.3 The correspondence theory

According to this third theory of truth, the correspondence theory, *if X accords with the way things are, X is true.* This is the view taken throughout this text. For example, I may claim that "It's raining." If it is indeed raining, then my claim is true.

There is a possible circularity with this theory, however, one that is perhaps more easily seen when stated thus: if X accords with the facts, it's true. And what are facts? Those things that are true. So is the theory just saying "If it's true, it's true"?

6.2.4 Pragmatism

According to Charles S. Peirce, one of the founders of pragmatism, "In order to ascertain the meaning of an intellectual conception one should consider what practical consequences might conceivably result by necessity from the truth of that conception; and the sum of these consequences will constitute the entire meaning of the conception" (*Collected Papers of Charles Sanders Peirce*, 1935). The pragmatist looks at the effects of a thing, the consequences, in order to determine the meaning of a thing. Thus, according to the pragmatist theory of truth, *if X works, it's true*. William James, another founder of pragmatism, said "On pragmatistic principles, if the hypothesis of God works satisfactorily in the widest sense of the word, it is true" (*Pragmatism*, 1907).

One of the problems with this view is the definition of "works." What exactly does James mean? Well, James says, further "True ideas are those that we can assimilate, validate, corroborate, and verify. False ideas are those that we can not."

Another "problem" with pragmatism—though this is more likely to be a problem with misunderstanding pragmatism—is that it can be reduced to mere expediency. Is that a satisfactory way of determining what's true and what's not?

> Suppose Epimenides of Crete says to you, "Cretans are always liars." Is his statement true or false?

6.3 How do we discover truth?

Having established the importance of truth, let's go on now to consider how we find out whether or not something is indeed true.

6.3.1 Innate ideas and/or experience and/or reason?

Early philosophers believed that we are born with certain ideas already in our minds—**innate ideas**. Among these were the ideas of truth, beauty, perfection, and so on. Since we now know that the cognitive structures of a newborn are insufficient for idea comprehension, let alone judgments of truth and falsity, this opinion is generally not held by contemporary philosophers. A baby may seek food and may cry when hungry, but the former is an instinct or reflex behavior and the latter an emotional response, rather than a case of the baby *knowing it requires food*. (This should have you asking "But how do we know we know—

what conditions must apply for us to say we *know* something?" Good. See the box on Gettier's "Smith and Jones.")

The alternative view is that we obtain all of our ideas through experience, a view called **empiricism**. Basically, empiricism holds that we discover the truth about things as we go. So if you could not see, hear, touch, smell, or taste anything, you would not know anything about the world.

experiences

A third possibility is that we are born not with ideas but with a certain cognitive framework within which, as it matures, we will process our experience. Immanuel Kant identifies this framework as a system of categories, but we may well simply describe the framework as the laws of thought that our brain seems hardwired to follow. The law of non-contradiction, which states that a thing and its opposite can't both be true, is an example: we generally find it impossible to believe that a dog can be both barking and not barking at the same time.

This view, called **rationalism**, that we can know things without experience, by use of our reason alone, is given further support by the things we consider true by definition. In this category are mathematical truths: for example, we don't seem to need any actual experience in order to know that the proposition "2 + 2 = 4" is true; its truth depends solely on the way we have defined the individual terms of the proposition ("2," "+," "=," and "4") and our reasoning about those terms as defined.

Gettier's "Smith and Jones"

Suppose that Smith and Jones have applied for a certain job. And suppose that Smith has strong evidence for the following conjunctive proposition: (d) Jones is the man who will get the job, and Jones has ten coins in his pocket. Smith's evidence for (d) might be that the president of the company assured him that Jones would in the end be selected, and that he, Smith, had counted the coins in Jones' pocket ten minutes ago. Proposition (d) entails: (e) The man who will get the job has ten coins in his pocket. Let us suppose that Smith sees the entailment from (d) to (e), and accepts (e) on the grounds of (d), for which he has strong evidence. In this case, Smith is clearly justified in believing that (e) is true.

But imagine, further, that unknown to Smith, he himself, not Jones, will get the job. And, also, unknown to Smith, he himself has ten coins in his pocket. Proposition (e) is then true, though proposition (d), from which Smith inferred (e), is false.

[Does Smith *know* that the man who will get the job has ten coins in his pocket?]

(Edmund L. Gettier, "Is Justified True Belief Knowledge?" *Analysis*, 23.6, 1963)

With this thought experiment, Gettier is challenging the standard account of knowledge, which says that one knows X if (1) one believes X to be true; (2) one is justified in believing X to be true; and (3) X is indeed true. Smith *believes* it is true that the man who will get the job has ten coins in his pocket; he is *justified* in believing it to be true (on the basis of the president's assurance and his counting Jones' coins and his then "putting two and two together"); and it is indeed *true* that the man who will get the job has ten coins in his pocket. Nevertheless, Gettier suggests, it is clear that Smith does not *know* that the man who will get the job has ten coins in his pocket, for it is Smith himself who gets the job and not, as he had thought, Jones, and he didn't know that he himself had ten coins in his pocket.

In a similar case, Gettier shows the problem (a justified belief that happens to be true even though it was derived using what turns out to be a false premise) can arise not only with conjunctive propositions (those involving *and*), but also with disjunctive propositions (those involving *or*). So what's wrong with the standard account?

6.3.2 Random personal experience

Given that our starting point for knowing the truth about reality is empirical experience, there are two possible sources for empirical information: our own day-to-day experience, which is generally a random sort of thing, and something more methodical like surveys and experiments.

Our own experience of the world is generally obtained through our senses and reasoning about our sensory experience, as the rationalists claim. Intuition and faith can also be included here.

There are several points about personal experience—whether our own or that of others—that we should be aware of, most of which indicate its limitations with regard to claims to truth:

- Our personal experience is usually a *random* affair. So it shouldn't be called upon for any kind of complete or cohesive picture of the world. It's just bits and pieces, here and there.
- Personal experience is an experience that has happened to *one* person. As such, how can it be verified? It will always just be that person's word that whatever happened to the person did in fact happen. And people do sometimes lie. Whether I appeal to my senses, my intuition, or my faith, when I say "X happened to me, it's true," why should anyone believe me? Additionally, even if we had conclusive evidence corroborating the person's claim of some personal experience, to generalize from what happens to one person is very unwise. What grounds would I have for claiming on the basis of it happening to me that it happens to everyone? That's why we dismiss anecdote (personal stories) so quickly. Consider the oft-heard and endless

231

variations of "Well, it's happened to me"—for example, "It's not wrong for parents to hit their kids, my dad hit me every now and then, and I can't say that it did me any harm." Fine. It may not have done you any harm. (However, you can't know that for sure, since you have no basis for comparison: if your dad hadn't hit you, maybe you would've turned out to be a *better* person, in which case being hit *did* do you some harm—you'll never know.) But, that's just you. On what basis do you extend your experience to the whole world in order to make that sweeping all-inclusive claim "It's not wrong for parents to hit their kids"?

Keep in mind that while personal experience is insufficient for proving a generalization, it *is* sufficient for *dis*proving a generalization: all it takes is one example to disprove any claim about all, every, never . . .

- Even if it were okay to generalize from random and singular experience, the nature of personal experience is such that it almost always involves *interpretation*: we almost always make some assumptions between the experience and our description of it. Recall my example of seeing a building (Section 2.3): that's what we say we see, but actually, we see only two walls—we just assume there's a whole building there. I may see flashes of light in an arc out my window as I'm driving one night and say I saw a UFO—but of course maybe what I saw was the reflection of the headlights of passing cars, somehow getting into my line of sight via my driver's side window and my rear-view mirror.

- But even before interpretation gets in the way, our own *sensory perception deficits* may get in the way: for example, how good is our eyesight and our hearing? What I see looks like fuzzy hair. But is it really? Everything at a distance looks fuzzy to me, even when I'm wearing my glasses!

- And then there are the *environmental conditions* under which we are perceiving whatever it is we're perceiving: is there sufficient light, do we have an unobstructed view, is there background noise masking whatever we think we hear, et cetera?

- And there's our observational *skill*. Most of us are not trained to observe. We are not scientists. We are not even police officers or classroom teachers. We're amateurs. (Police officers are trained, for example, to identify the make and model of a car by its rear-light configuration. Most of us, on the other hand, can maybe identify its color.)

- Our *emotional state* may also have an influence: are we paying close attention (we can't pay close attention to everything all the time) or are we distracted, or perhaps tired. Sometimes we miss things; sometimes we get it wrong.

- Our *cognitive state* also has the potential to interfere: we generally see what we want to see. That's just the way we're built, and usually it's a good thing. But our brains are wonderful things, and they can play all sorts of tricks on us: consider hallucinations, whether drug-induced or stress-induced. Remember, just because it *seems* real doesn't mean it *is*.

"I have certain, positive knowledge from my own direct experience. I can't put it any plainer than that. I have seen God face to face." With these words, the fictional theologian Palmer Joss defends his religious convictions in Carl Sagan's 1985 novel, *Contact*. Joss argues for the existence of his Christian god on the basis of personal revelation. And Joss is not alone. Many theists rest their faith on the apparently solid foundation of personal religious experiences. Some receive visions. Others hear a comforting voice. Almost all experience a "sense of presence" or a feeling of "unity with the universe." . . .

To completely counter this argument for the existence of god(s), some alternative explanation must be given for the religious experience. Researchers in the fields of psychology and neuroscience have begun to uncover the biological mechanisms that might give rise to feelings of revelation in healthy adults . . .

. . . Dr. Michael Persinger of Laurentian University has devised a machine that generates a particular kind of magnetic field around the head, producing "microseizures" in the temporal lobes of the brain. Healthy people who have experienced this induced brain activity have reported such things as a feeling of floating, deformations of the body, strong emotions, a "sensed presence," and specifically religious dreamlike hallucinations.

Persinger's experimental work arose after years of research into the neurological basis of religious experiences . . . In brief, religious experiences are seen as the result of "temporal lobe transients" (TLT)—short-lived rate increases and instability in the firing patterns of neurons in the temporal lobe. . . . [These powerful TLT events may naturally result from a number of factors, including . . . loss of oxygen to the brain, and changes in blood sugar. These biological conditions may be caused by crisis situations, prolonged anxiety, near-death contingencies, high altitudes, starvation and fasting, diurnal shifts, and other physiological stressors.] . . .

. . . In a typical experiment, the subject is isolated from sounds and the eyes are covered. A helmet equipped with solenoids is strapped to the head. While reclining in this state of partial sensory deprivation, currents are induced in the subject's brain through the generation of patterned extremely low frequency milligauss magnetic fields in the solenoids. The subject is asked to describe any experiences aloud, and this monologue is recorded.

. . . When temporal cortical areas are targeted for stimulations, subjects often report dreamlike visions (often with mystical or religious content), a "sense of presence" and strong emotions . . .

. . . Given these results, the skeptic may present the believer with a simple question: How do you know that your religious experience is not a simple trick of your brain—the unfolding of a perfectly-natural temporal lobe transient? How can you trust such an experience when, through science, we can convincingly mimic the face of God?

(David C. Noelle, "Searching for God in the Machine," *Free Inquiry*, Summer. 1998)

233

- Lastly, our *memory* is not picture-perfect, and the more time passes, the more the details fade. Yesterday I knew the license plate I saw was MHX 338; next week I won't remember whether it was MHX or HMX.

6.3.3 Methodical investigation: the scientific process

Scientific investigation seeks to overcome the weaknesses of random personal experience as a way of knowing.

- *Scientific investigation is methodical*, not random. Scientists figure out what they want to know or what they need to know (perhaps additional information is required to establish a claim), and then they go about investigating that very thing (as opposed to finding out about only what they happen to run across). So through scientific investigation, we tend to get a more complete picture of reality.

  An important part of the scientific method is that scientists *isolate the phenomenon* that's being investigated in order to be sure that that's the thing that is indeed being investigated. For example, suppose they're interested in observing the effect of diet on heart fitness; in order to be sure the results they observe aren't due to something other than diet, such as exercise, they make sure that all of their study participants have the same exercise—they control all the variables except the one they're investigating. In fact, a *control group* is often established as a basis for comparison with the *experimental group*. For example, let's say they have a hundred people in their study, and they make sure that all the other things that could affect heart fitness—such as exercise, age, and so on—are the same. Then, if all of their participants are put on a diet high in fat, for example, and every one of them experiences a decline in heart fitness, they might conclude that fat leads to a decrease in heart fitness. But maybe the participants would have experienced such a decline even without the high-fat diet; maybe just getting one year older (suppose their study lasted a year) is sufficient for heart decline to occur. So what they do is establish a control group—a second group of people, identical to the first except that they are *not* on a diet high in fat. Then if the first group (the experimental group) experiences a decline in heart fitness and the second group (the control group) does not, they can be even more certain that it is the fat that leads to a decrease in heart fitness.

  It's important to choose the right group for comparison. For example, one often comes across statements like this: women who have an abortion are more likely to get breast cancer than women who carry a pregnancy to term. That may be true. But the supposed protection from breast cancer comes from carrying a pregnancy to term, so women who never get pregnant are at just as much risk as those who have an abortion. It's not that abortion increases one's risk; it's that a full pregnancy reduces one's risk. So the proper comparison is not between those who abort and those who do not, but between those who experience a full pregnancy and those who do not.

- *Scientific evidence represents the experiences of more than one person—both with regard to the data itself and to the obtaining of that data.* Surveys, for example, include the experiences of many people—the more, the better (to a point; see Section 7.2.2). So generalizations made from survey results are more trustworthy than generalizations made from just one person's experience. And experiments, for example, are designed to be conducted by anyone skilled in the techniques involved. Replication (see below), another hallmark of scientific investigation, further ensures that evidence comes from a number of people.

- *Scientists are careful to separate their observations from their interpretation of their observations.* In fact, in the standard scientific report, those two elements are in different sections: observations are in the "Results" section, and interpretation of the observations is in the "Discussion" section. Sometimes there is disagreement about the validity of the results. There may be concern expressed about the equipment used in the experiment or, more often, about the design of the experiment; for example, in an experiment involving pH levels of rainwater, perhaps all of the water samples were taken at the beginning of a storm when pH levels are atypical. However, most disagreement concerns how to best interpret the results. This can be tricky, and scientists are quite careful to consider and eliminate for good reason as many alternative interpretations as possible.

- The influence of sensory perception deficits, emotional states, and cognitive states is minimized by *the use of instruments* for measurement. Instruments can record all sorts of things, such as time, space, distance, heat, the presence of specific substances, and so on, and they do so independent of any one person. This means that the measurements are objective and they thus provide corroboration for our personal experience ("It feels hot, doesn't it feel hot to you?"). Problems resulting from lack of skill are minimized since scientists are *trained observers*, whether they're psychologists and sociologists observing people or chemists and biologists observing beaker contents and microscope slides. They know what to look for. And they know that looks can be deceiving. Lastly, *environmental conditions are carefully optimized* so that accurate observations and measurements can be made. Keep in mind, however, it is possible that a scientist's bias may cause him or her to misread instruments (especially when they're not as straightforward as needles on a dial—consider slides under a microscope, for example). In order to protect against subjective contamination, good science involves *replication*: evidence is generally not accepted until it has been obtained again and again, by different people. If the results of an experiment can't be replicated—if

Men who have excessive faith in their theories are not only ill-prepared for making discoveries; they also make poor observations.

Claude Bernard, *Introduction to the Study of Experimental Medicine*, 1865

235

someone else does the same experiment and doesn't come up with the same results—the conclusions drawn on the basis of the results are generally not accepted.

- Unlike most of us going about our business throughout the day, scientists publish their discoveries, *exposing their claims of truth to public scrutiny.* This increases their reliability, compared to personal experience, since errors—whether in procedure, measurement, or interpretation—are apt to be noticed. They can then be corrected in subsequent investigations.

People who dismiss science and/or its results often do so because they don't understand how much work is involved in order to establish those results. The actual steps someone follows when making a scientific investigation are as follows:

1. Identify the issue of investigation. For example, you might seek to determine what is the case or why something is the case. Typically, you start with a broad definition or description of the problem to be investigated, and then narrow the focus as details are learned.

2. Become familiar with relevant existing knowledge. This is done in order to build upon it or to identify the gaps that need to be filled. This step is often harder than you might think; you might make mistakes about what's relevant and what's not. After all, at this point, you don't know much about what you're investigating. (That's why you're investigating it.)

3. Develop a hypothesis—a conjecture, a tentative explanation or prediction—specifying what would verify or falsify the hypothesis. Often the hypothesis involves a prediction. And it's likely you'd seek to falsify rather than verify your hypothesis (see Section 6.1.1). In addition to knowledge (gained at step 2), imagination and creativity are required to develop a hypothesis. For example, if you can't directly test A you'll have to get creative. Perhaps if A is true, then B is true, and you can directly test B . . . And to be sure that A is the case, rather than C or D, you'll have to be able to imagine C or D . . . Perhaps what is the case isn't even in that alphabet!

4. Steps 2 and 3 tend to develop into a feedback loop rather than staying in a two-step line: the more you learn, the more you'll refine your hypotheses. That's why it's often best to start with a "working hypothesis"—something subject to change!

5. Test the hypothesis by designing and conducting a reproducible experiment that will provide the specified conditions of verification or falsification, following established methods of investigation.

6. Formulate conclusions based on the evidence, conforming to established standards of proof and sufficiency. This typically includes consideration of alternative explanations and compatibility of the proposed explanation with other well-established hypotheses.

As you can see, science is not a matter of simply sitting in an armchair, speculating about things for a few days, then writing down one's ideas. For example, just getting to step 4—the actual experiment—may take years. Likewise, the experiment itself, which is often a conceptually-linked series of experiments, may take years.

For example, consider this brief description of research that might eventually lead to sight for blind people:

> Brenda Coles and her colleagues at the University of Toronto minced up eyes donated from deceased people and cultured the cells. They found that about one in 500 cells from the black ring around the iris could divide indefinitely and adopt the full variety of retinal cell types . . . When transplanted into embryonic mice or chicks, the stem cells turned into cells of the type found in that animal at that stage of development. Their next experiment, Coles says, is to transplant the cells into mice with degenerating retinas to see if they restore function and later to figure out how to activate and manipulate them.
> (*Scientific American*, January 2005)

Given the years of investigation, it would take a certain sort of arrogance or ignorance to just dismiss any claim Coles might eventually make about eyes and the sense of sight.

In the case of formal, large-scale research, just to receive the funding for the research, the person (or people—usually there's a whole team involved) has to prepare extensive reports that identify the issue, summarize everything that's known to date about the issue, explain and justify the hypothesis (or hypotheses—often there are several), and describe the experiment (or experiments—again, often there are several) in detail, the expected results, and the anticipated impact of the results. Committees of experts review the research plan. If it meets their criteria, it gets approved. Then the research has to be done. A year or two later, or five or ten years later, it is described in a report. The report is then reviewed by a few selected experts in the field who determine whether the work is sound. If they determine that it is, the report gets published for everyone in the field to see, and criticize, and repeat to double-check.

Still, science isn't always as value-neutral as we like to think. Scientists are human, after all, and their personal view of the world no doubt has some influence on their work. Certainly, as suggested above, the method *minimizes* subjective distortion of measurement, and public scrutiny compensates for subjective distortion of interpretation. But what about before the method and interpretation are even under way? What about personal bias at step 1—identifying the issue of investigation? Certainly, funding determines what gets investigated, and often the potential for profit determines funding. This explains much of pharmaceutical research. And what about the role of personal beliefs? I find this especially prevalent in animal research: those who do not believe animals have emotion are

What we need is not the will to believe, but the will to find out.

Bertrand Russell
(1872–1970)

Scientists are the paradigm of the good citizen. They're staunch believers in meritocracy and wildly suspicious of authority—hell, they're practically anarchistic in orientation. A scientist will never accept any argument on face value, no matter who yells it at them or how powerful that person is. The inverse is also true: If an unknown grad student at a minor school discovers data that upends accepted wisdom, it doesn't matter if she's a total nobody; smart scientists will always accept her conclusions, even if it means changing their most basic beliefs.

Clive Thompson, "Science Fiction," *This Magazine*, May/June 2004

237

more likely to interpret, for example, the licks of a dog as submission rather than affection. (What experiment could distinguish between the two?)

Keep in mind, too, that there is a difference between good science and bad science. Some science is better than no science at all because the former pays attention to evidence. As long as you appeal to one fact or one reason in support of your claim, you are using the scientific process, if only in a very rudimentary way. The "no science" approach makes claims with no regard to evidence, for or against the proposed claim: evidence is simply irrelevant to someone who rejects the scientific process. But bad science may be even worse than no science at all. Pretending to have evidence when you don't, falsifying your results, ignoring or not investigating results that may challenge the hypothesis you want to prove—all of these are the marks of bad science.

That said, it's important to distinguish between scientific *process* and scientific *progress*. The two are completely separate. And whether the scientific process leads to progress depends on what is done with the results of the scientific process, the scientific investigation. And decisions about what should be done are usually matters for ethical investigation; ethical reasoning is perhaps the most important kind of critical thinking we can do, and we'll cover it in Chapter 8.

Semmelweis and childbed fever

As a simple illustration of some important aspects of scientific inquiry let us consider Semmelweis' work on childbed fever. Ignaz Semmelweis, a physician of Hungarian birth, did this work during the years from 1844 to 1848 at the Vienna General Hospital. As a member of the medical staff of the First Maternity Division in the hospital, Semmelweis was distressed to find that a large proportion of the women who were delivered of their babies in that division contracted a serious and often fatal illness known as puerperal fever or childbed fever. In 1844, as many as 260 out of 3,157 mothers in the First Division, or 8.2 percent, died of the disease; for 1845, the death rate was 6.8 percent, and for 1846, it was 11.4 percent. These figures were all the more alarming because in the adjacent Second Maternity Division of the same hospital, which accommodated almost as many women as the First, the death toll from childbed fever was much lower: 2.5, 2.0, and 2.7 percent for the same years. In a book that he wrote later on the causation and the prevention of childbed fever, Semmelweis describes his efforts to resolve the dreadful puzzle.

He began by considering various explanations that were current at the time; some of these he rejected out of hand as incompatible with well-established facts; others he subjected to specific tests.

One widely accepted view attributed the ravages of puerperal fever to "epidemic influences," which were vaguely described as "atmospheric-cosmic-telluric changes" spreading over whole districts and causing childbed fever in women in confinement.

But how, Semmelweis reasons, could such influences have plagued the First Division for years and yet spared the Second? And how could this view be reconciled with the fact that while the fever was raging in the hospital, hardly a case occurred in the city of Vienna or in its surroundings: a genuine epidemic, such as cholera, would not be so selective. Finally, Semmelweis notes that some of the women admitted to the First Division, living far from the hospital, had been overcome by labor on their way and had given birth in the street: yet despite these adverse conditions, the death rate from childbed fever among these cases of "street birth" was lower than the average for the First Division.

On another view, overcrowding was a cause of mortality in the First Division. But, Semmelweis points out that in fact the crowding was heavier in the Second Division, partly as a result of the desperate efforts of patients to avoid assignment to the notorious First Division. He also rejects two similar conjectures that were current, by noting that there were no differences between the two Divisions in regard to diet or general care of the patients.

In 1846, a commission that had been appointed to investigate the matter attributed the prevalence of illness in the First Division to injuries resulting from rough examination by the medical students, all of whom received their obstetrical training in the First Division. Semmelweis notes in refutation of this view that (a) the injuries resulting naturally from the process of birth are much more extensive than those that might be caused by rough examination; (b) the midwives who received their training in the Second Division examined their patients in much the same manner but without the same ill effects; (c) when, in response to the commission's report, the number of medical students was halved and their examinations of the women were reduced to a minimum, the mortality, after a brief decline, rose to higher levels than ever before.

Various psychological explanations were attempted. One of them noted that the First Division was so arranged that a priest bearing the last sacrament to a dying woman had to pass through five wards before reaching the sickroom beyond: the appearance of the priest, preceded by an attendant ringing a bell, was held to have a terrifying and debilitating effect upon the patients in the wards and thus to make them more likely victims of childbed fever. In the Second Division, this adverse factor was absent, since the priest had direct access to the sickroom. Semmelweis decided to test this conjecture. He persuaded the priest to come by a roundabout route and without ringing of the bell, in order to reach the sick chamber silently and unobserved. But the mortality in the First Division did not decrease.

A new idea was suggested to Semmelweis by the observation that in the First Division the women were delivered lying on their backs; in the Second Division, on their sides. Though he thought it unlikely, he decided "like a drowning man clutching at a straw" to test whether this difference in procedure was significant. He introduced the use of the lateral position in the First Division, but again, the mortality remained unaffected.

At last, early in 1847, an accident gave Semmelweis the decisive clue for his solution of the problem. A colleague of his, Kolletschka, received a puncture wound in the finger, from the scalpel of a student with whom he was performing an autopsy, and died after an agonizing illness during which he displayed the same symptoms that Semmelweis had observed in the victims of childbed fever. Although the role of micro-organisms in such infections had not yet been recognized at the time, Semmelweis realized that "cadaveric matter" which the student's scalpel had introduced into Kolletschka's blood stream had caused his colleague's fatal illness. And the similarities between the course of Kolletschka's disease and that of the women in his clinic led Semmelweis to the conclusion that his patients had died of the same kind of blood poisoning: he, his colleagues, and the medical students had been the carriers of the infectious material, for he and his associates used to come to the wards directly from performing dissections in the autopsy room, and examine the women in labor after only superficially washing their hands, which often retained a characteristic foul odor.

Again, Semmelweis put his idea to a test. He reasoned that if he were right, then childbed fever could be prevented by chemically destroying the infectious material adhering to the hands. He therefore issued an order requiring all medical students to wash their hands in a solution of chlorinated lime before making an examination. The mortality from childbed fever promptly began to decrease, and for the year 1848 it fell to 1.27 percent in the First Division, compared to 1.55 in the Second.

In further support of his idea, or of his hypothesis, as we will also say, Semmelweis notes that it accounts for the fact that the mortality in the Second Division consistently was so much lower: the patients there were attended by midwives, whose training did not include anatomical instruction by dissection of cadavers.

The hypothesis also explained the lower mortality among "street births": women who arrived with babies in arms were rarely examined after admission and thus had a better chance of escaping infection.

Similarly, the hypothesis accounted for the fact that the victims of childbed fever among the newborn babies were all among those whose mothers had contracted the disease during labor; for then the infection could be transmitted to the baby before birth, through the common bloodstream of mother and child, whereas this was impossible when the mother remained healthy.

Further clinical experiences soon led Semmelweis to broaden his hypothesis. On one occasion, for example, he and his associates, having carefully disinfected their hands, examined first a woman in labor who was suffering from a festering cervical cancer; then they proceeded to examine twelve other women in the same room, after only routine washing without renewed disinfection. Eleven of the twelve patients died of puerperal fever. Semmelweis concluded that childbed fever can be caused not only by cadaveric material, but also by "putrid matter derived from living organisms."

(Carl Hempel, *Philosophy of Natural Science*, 1966)

6.4 How do we evaluate claims of truth?

If the claim in question is the *conclusion* of an argument, then evaluating it is a matter of evaluating the argument. If it's a deductive argument, and the premises are true and the form is valid, the conclusion must be true: that's all there is to it. Inductive arguments are trickier, but still, if the premises are true, relevant, and sufficient, the conclusion can be accepted as true.

So what if the claim in question is a *premise* of an argument? How do we evaluate its truth? Well, it depends on the kind of claim it is. If the claim is a matter of personal testimony, we can make certain inquiries to determine its acceptability (see Section 6.4.1).

Empirical claims, especially of a specialized nature, are best evaluated by experts in the relevant field. For example, there have been at least 26 different claims that a certain piece of fabric is the shroud of Turin—the burial cloth bearing an imprint of the face of Jesus Christ. Obviously, only one of those claims can be true. How can we determine which one? Well, we look at the evidence. Well, not "we" exactly—I'm not an archaeologist or a historian, so I wouldn't know what to look at—but someone out there does. As it turns out, at least one of the claims was rejected because the weave in one supposed shroud had a herringbone pattern that was not manufactured until the Middle Ages. As it also turns out, though, the Gospel accounts of Jesus' burial refer to several shrouds and a separate napkin over his face—in which case *none* of the shrouds could be *the* shroud because only the small napkin would bear the imprint of his face.

If an empirical claim is presented as the result of some study, though, we can examine the study to determine whether it was designed and conducted according to good scientific practices. Some of what constitutes good scientific practices has already been covered (Section 6.3), but we'll look at a few more things below (Section 6.4.2).

If the claim is presented as common knowledge, but it's not part of *our* common knowledge, we can always just "look it up"—we can check some reputable source (Section 6.4.3).

In all cases, however, one solid test for truth or acceptability is that of *non-contradiction*: if the claim contradicts other truths, it simply can't be true or acceptable. For example, if it's true that glass shatters when hit, then the claim that glass does not shatter when hit can't be true.

And in all cases, it's wise to consider the claim *in context*: who says so, why do they say so, on what basis do they say so, what else do they say . . . (Conversely, be wary of any claims presented out of context or without any context!)

Finally, remember that we need not accept or reject a claim; we can decide to suspend judgment pending further specified information.

241

6.4.1 Evaluating personal testimony

The weaknesses of random personal experience, identified in the previous section (6.3), give us some direction as to evaluating personal testimony—whether our own or that of others. The following questions give us further direction:

Is the claim based on personal sensory experience or something like intuition or faith? There are specific questions one can ask about the former, but how does one test the truth or acceptability of the latter? Of course, there may be some sensory basis for intuition or faith—perhaps one experiences a headache when intuition strikes or perhaps one hears God's voice. But even then, most of the following questions can't apply. But those that do apply—about interpretation, emotional and cognitive states, and credibility—are critical.

How much of the claim is tainted by interpretation? That is, is the claim a pure description of sensory experience ("I heard a squeak") or have assumptions been made ("I heard a mouse cry in desperate alarm")? Have any unwarranted assumptions been made? Have any details been omitted as unimportant? Even decisions about what's important and what's not are a matter of interpretation.

How good is the person's sight, hearing, smell, and/or taste? Is the person near-sighted? A little hard of hearing?

What were the conditions at the time? Visibility? View? Noise level? Was there enough time to have seen what was reportedly seen? Consider whether or not the person had the opportunity to obtain the evidence she or he claims to have.

Is the person particularly observant? Was she or he paying sufficient attention at the time? Did she or he use any tools, training, or knowledge that would increase accuracy of perception?

What was the person's emotional state? Might stress, drugs, haste, or coercion have influenced his or her perception?

What was the person's cognitive state? Might it have influenced his or her perception? Consider the person's wants, needs, and expectations, all of which can predispose us, consciously or unconsciously, to see or hear something incorrectly.

How long ago did it happen? Is it likely that memory of the event has faded or become distorted, by the mere passage of time or by intervening events?

How credible is the person? Has the person given incorrect reports before? Does she or he have a reputation for being truthful? Completely truthful?

Lastly, is there any corroborating or contradicting evidence to support the personal testimony? For example, were there other witnesses?

It's possible for two people to witness the exact same event, but walk away with completely different perceptions. Anyone who's ever had casual sex can attest to this.

Chris Gudgeon and "Sugar" Roy Carboyle, *You're Not As Good As You Think You Are: A Demotivational Guide,* 1997

To conclude this section, consider my claim, "It's raining outside." Actually, in the interests of precise language and avoiding redundancy, I think we can change that to just "It's raining." In fact, we can probably do better than that since it is most certainly raining *somewhere*—let me claim "It's raining here and now." Is that true? "How do you know?" you may well ask.

I might respond, "I just have this feeling that it is—I have good intuitions," or I might say, "I believe—I have faith—that it *is* raining!" Will either of those statements convince you? I doubt it. So I might say, "I can see the rain!" (And I might point out that I've got my glasses on.) I might open the window and say, "I can hear it!" I might reach out my arm and report, "I can feel it!" Yeah, well, maybe you're nuts, you say. Fair enough. I look around the classroom. Can't you all see the rain? Can't you hear it? Can't you feel it? Yeah, well, maybe we do—but maybe we're all nuts.

Okay. I go outside and bring in a very wet dog. Look. It's been standing outside, tied to the bike rack by a very bad dog owner. It's wet. Therefore, it's raining. Nope. Not good enough. It could have had a pail of water tossed at it. Quite possibly by the aforementioned dog owner.

Okay, I proceed to bring in three other dogs, oddly enough each tied to one of three other bike racks at three different locations on campus. All are wet. I point to the grass. It too is wet. I point to the earthworms squiggling across the pavement and say that past experience has shown that earthworms crawl out of their earthly holes when it rains.

Okay. It's not conclusive proof, but until a better explanation is proposed for the similar reported experience of everyone in the class, the simultaneous wetness of the three dogs, the grass, and the appearance of earthworms, you'll accept my claim that it's raining here and now.

So you see the problem with personal testimony, with "It's so because I say it's so"? And the advantage of obtaining corroborating evidence that exists independently of the person making the claim?

6.4.1a Practice determining whether personal testimony is acceptable

How acceptable do you consider each of the following? Articulate your reasons, of course.

1. My eyeball and eye socket were recently destroyed by someone playing a "harmless" prank with a paintball gun. Parents should remember that paintball guns are exactly that: guns and not toys.

2. I lowered my vibrations to be able to come to Earth and pay off a debt I owed to a girl in a previous lifetime—a karmic debt.
    (Omnec Onec, a visitor from Venus, speaking at the
    World UFO Congress held in Tucson in May 1991)

243

3. I had cancer, then I started taking megadoses of vitamin C and a month later the disease was gone. Miracle cure!

4. Yes, that's the man! [says a person pointing out the only tall, bald, black-skinned man in a police line-up]

5. After 9/11, someone told the *New York Times* that her house was still standing because of the protection afforded by a statue of Buddha on her property; houses not similarly protected had been erased, she pointed out.

6.4.2 Evaluating studies (surveys, experiments, numbers)

There are two parts to evaluating studies: evaluating the evidence and evaluating how the evidence is used. The second part usually involves inductive argument leading to generalizations and causal claims—we'll address these issues in Chapters 7 and 8. As for evaluating the evidence, much depends on the study in question. Nevertheless, there are some general questions we can become familiar with; some apply to all kinds of studies, some mostly to surveys, and some mostly to experiments. Lastly, evidence often involves numbers, so we'll cover some basics in that area as well.

Here are some general questions to ask with regard to any study, in order to evaluate the truth or acceptability of its evidence:

How old is the study? Some things change, so some studies become less acceptable as they age. It all depends, of course, on what you intend to do with the evidence.

Who conducted the study? Consider the level of expertise, as well as the possibility of bias that may have distorted the results (through flaws in design or errors in measurement) or the conclusions.

Who funded the study? Consider, again, the possibility of distorting bias.

Were the instruments (tools and/or techniques) both valid and reliable? Validity in this context means that the instruments do, in fact, measure what they're supposed to measure. A reading test, for example, should measure only reading ability and not also reasoning ability. Reliability in this context refers to the consistency with which the instruments measure what they're supposed to measure. For example, a speedometer that indicates 40 miles per hour one day and 60 miles per hour another when the car is actually moving at the same speed each day is not a reliable instrument.

Is the evidence consistent with other established knowledge?

What state of affairs would contradict the evidence? Is that state of affairs known to be true? Is that state of affairs likely? Is it at least possible? (Note the degrees there—the more likely it is that contradicting evidence exists, the less likely it is that the evidence in question is true.)

Was the study replicated? If so, were the same results obtained? The more often this has occurred, the more acceptable the results. That said, researchers who acknowledge failure to replicate results indicate an honesty that warrants attention; they are perhaps unlikely to suppress counterevidence.

Does the nature of the study support its conclusions? For example, some studies on non-human animals are not applicable to humans, so to make conclusions regarding humans on the basis of such studies would not be warranted. (We'll address this kind of conclusion—a generalization—in greater detail in Section 7.2.) Always be careful to separate the results from the researcher's interpretation of those results.

Are you reading about the study first-hand as described by the researchers themselves or second-hand as described by someone who might have misinterpreted or omitted certain bits? If the latter, how qualified is the person in the field of study concerned?

SURVEYS

Here are some questions to consider with regard to surveys (questionnaires, polls, and so on):

What questions are asked? What questions are not asked? Clearly what is asked will determine what is found out. If you don't ask about something, you won't find out about that something. So although the evidence obtained may well be true, it may not be complete—and in that way, the evidence may misrepresent reality.

What is the order of the questions? Context matters. A question about the importance of a government-funded healthcare program asked after a question about recent injuries and illnesses may elicit different responses than if it had been asked after a question about increased taxes anticipated to fund the program. And, more simply, questions asked at the end of a survey might receive sloppier answers (or less clear, less complete, perhaps even less honest answers) than those asked at the beginning—people get tired!

How are the questions worded? Recall the section on loaded language (Section 5.2.1). Loaded language in questions can be just as manipulative as loaded language in statements. Consider the difference between these three versions of the "same" question:

One of the rules in this business is that the question determines the answer.

Janice Ballou, quoted by E.K. Coughlin, "Researchers Practice the Science and Art of Public Opinion Polling," *Chronicle of Higher Education,* 1990

Does the American government spend too much money on homeland defense?

Does the American government spend too much money on war?

Does the American government spend too much money going to other countries and killing the people who live there?

When options are given, are all the possibilities covered? The absence of "so-so" might lead to many false "yes" and "no" responses. Most people don't want to sound like idiots or psychopaths, so if they're not given a sort of "none of the above" option, they may feel compelled to provide a dishonest response.

When are respondents asked? Are they busy and in a rush? Is it just after an event that will temporarily intensify their opinion? For example, asking about people's opinion of capital punishment right after a brutal murder is reported in the news might result in different findings than if the question was asked a year after the murder. Such factors will affect the accuracy of the evidence.

How are respondents asked? In person? By phone? By mail? Again, these variables are likely to affect the truthfulness and the completeness of the answers, your evidence. In the first and second cases (in person and over the phone), the interviewer's body language and/or tone of voice can influence answers. Sometimes people are more honest when they can write out their answers in the privacy of their own home than when they have to say them to someone face-to-face. On the other hand, sometimes people respond at greater length when they're talking to someone than when they're required to write it out. And yet, giving an answer on-the-spot doesn't enable the memory process to come into full play. Whether or not you pay your respondents is another factor than can influence the answers you get.

Who are the respondents? Who is asked, as well as who answers (note that they are not the same bunch of people), affects the extent to which the evidence will justify generalizations. As mentioned above, we'll address this in the next chapter (Section 7.2), but for now, know that any survey with a self-selected sample (that is, the only responses obtained are from people who choose to respond) is bound to be unrepresentative, and so generalizations will be unjustified. People may choose to respond to a questionnaire for all sorts of reasons, but often it's a reason that matters in some way to the results: perhaps only those who are happy with whatever the questionnaire is about will bother to respond; or perhaps only those who are extremely unhappy will respond; or perhaps both groups will respond, but those who have no strong feelings one way or the other will not. A survey with a simple random sample is also apt to be unrepresentative; for example, if every fifth person on the subway during rush hour is surveyed, the opinions of those who drive to work, or bike to work, or don't have a job will not be included.

Check "yes" if you agree that Americans ought to be able to smoke anytime anywhere they please, and the wimpy anti-smoking nuts should shut up and take up knitting. Check "no" if you think the anti-smoking fruitcakes have a right to impose their will on the rest of the nation and ban smoking in public places—even if it violates the Constitution of this great nation.

Daniel McDonald and Larry W. Burton, *The Language of Argument*, 1999

How many respondents are there? How many potential respondents were there (that is, how large is the target population)? The opinion of "two out of three dentists" isn't very indicative of anything if only six dentists were asked!

Who conducted the poll? Was it a reputable polling company?

Who funded the poll? Was it a company whose interest in certain results may have biased the results?

Are the conclusions drawn fairly from the actual results? To conclude that people are pleased with a certain situation because only 10 percent indicated they have had a problem is unwarranted: they may not have had a problem, but they may be aware that others have problems and so are not at all pleased with the situation. Perhaps even more troubling, to conclude that people actually do or think as they say they do or think when surveyed is not necessarily warranted. People may intentionally or unintentionally misrepresent their actions and thoughts.

6.4.2a Practice determining whether survey results are acceptable

How acceptable would you consider the results of each of the following? Articulate your reasons, of course.

1. Twenty-two thousand readers responded [to a 1994 *Consumer Reports* survey about the effectiveness of psychotherapy]. Of these, approximately 7,000 subscribers responded to the mental health questions. Of these 7,000 about 3,000 had just talked to friends, relatives, or clergy, and 4,100 went to some combination of mental health professionals, family doctors, and support groups [for stress or other emotional problems]. Of these 4,100, 2,900 saw a mental health professional: psychologists (37%) were the most frequently seen mental health professional, followed by psychiatrists (22%), social workers (14%), and marriage counselors (9%). Other mental health professionals made up 18%. In addition, 1,300 joined self-help groups and about 1,000 saw family physicians. The respondents as a whole were highly educated, predominantly middle class; about half were women, and the median age was 46.

   (Martin E.P. Seligman, "The Effectiveness of Psychotherapy: The *Consumer Reports* Study," *American Psychologist*, December 1995)

2. Anyway, Dr. Kaplan sent questionnaires to people who requested mail from the [Vampire Research Center], and forty responded that, yes indeed, they are vampires.

   (Dave Barry, "Junkyard Journalism," in *Dave Barry's Bad Habits*, 1985 [1982/83])

247

3. According to the June 12–18, 2003, Gallup Poll, American women do not appear to be bitter or disgruntled about their status in society, or about the opportunities they have had in their lives. The first item in the poll asked "Are you very satisfied, somewhat satisfied, somewhat dissatisfied, very dissatisfied with the way women are treated in society?" and 69 percent were very satisfied or somewhat satisfied.

4. More than half of Americans will develop a mental illness at some point in their lives, often beginning in childhood or adolescence, researchers have found in a survey . . .

(*The New York Times*, June 7, 2005)

5. Question: What do you think has/should have the most influence on the values of young people today?

	Has (%)	Should have (%)
TV and movies	34	1
Parents	20	74
Young people	19	1
Musicians and music videos	10	0
Celebrities and athletes	6	1
Teachers	5	9
Political leaders	2	1
Religious leaders	1	11
Military leaders	1	0

Survey by Mellman & Lazarus for Massachusetts Mutual Life Insurance Co., September 1991, as in Everett C. Ladd, "The Myth of Moral Decline," *The Responsive Community*, 4.1, 1993/1994.

6. According to a 1977 study of gun crime inmates in a Florida prison, only 8.8 percent acquired a handgun for crime purposes. 87% acquired it for self-defense, hunting or target practice, etc.

(Sam Fields, "Handgun Prohibition and Social Necessity," *St. Louis Law Review*, 23, 1979)

7. In a study of 1,297 telephone operators, researchers found that the typical ill operator was a married woman, widow, or divorcee who had hoped to be a housewife and mother. Deprived of her husband's support by death, desertion, or incompatibility, she had been forced to continue working, often while rearing small children. The healthiest operators, on the other hand, tended to be single women with little drive toward marriage and whose ambitions did not go much beyond the modest satisfaction of their jobs.

("Down with Love," *Scientific American*, January 2005, quoting something that appeared in their January 1955 issue)

8. Web Poll: What should the Bush administration's top economic priority be? 48% said reducing the cost of providing health care. This month's poll: What is your biggest challenge in doing business overseas?

(From the website of *Inc. Magazine*, www.Inc.com)

9. Top Five Neighborhood Problems:

Staten Island

1. Potholes
2. Traffic congestion
3. Dangerous intersections
4. Too much growth, over-building
5. Soot or air pollution

Queens

1. Potholes
2. Too much growth, over-building
3. Illegal conversion, lack of enforcement
4. Traffic congestion
5. Dangerous intersections

Manhattan

1. Street noise
2. Litter or garbage
3. Soot or air pollution
4. Rats or rodents
5. Drugs or drug dealing

Brooklyn

1. Litter or garbage
2. Potholes
3, Drugs or drug dealing
4. Vandalism or graffiti
5. Dangerous intersections

Bronx

1. Drugs or drug dealing
2. Vandalism or graffiti
3. Environmental health problems

4. Street noise
5. Youth violence or gangs

> (According to "a joint study about the main quality-of-life complaints among New Yorkers released by the non-profit Citizens for NYC and Baruch College's eTown Panel," as reported in *am New York*, June 23, 2005)

10. Studies show that external rewards can lower your performance, especially if creativity is involved. Intrinsic interest in something—doing it for its own sake—declines when people are given an external reason for doing it. Philip Slater, *Wealth Addiction*, says "Using money as a motivator leads to a progressive degradation in the quality of everything produced." Rewards encourage people to focus only on getting the task done, as quickly as possible, without taking risks that might be fun but that might lead to failure. Turning a task into a means to an end changes the way it's perceived—it's no longer seen as an end in itself.

Last month our ongoing Scientific Correctness Survey posed the question: Are citizens of earth being kidnapped by aliens from outer space? The significance of the "alarming frequency with which they are being sent back" was raised. Several votes said that people were being kidnapped "not in adequate quantities." Our supplemental question asked "Should we require that schoolchildren be taught to protect themselves against extraterrestrial abductors?" 28% of the respondents said 'yes' and 35% said 'no'. Why a whopping 37% don't care is anyone's guess.

(*Scientific Correctness: Cosmic Kidnapping Results in The Mini-Annals of Improbable Research*, 1997)

Our Scientific Correctness Survey in mini-AIR 1996-06 asked you to settle, once and bureaucratically for all, the question, "Does reality exist?" We had 139 comprehensible responses. Of these, 42% believe reality exists, while 31% believe it does not. From those who believe reality exists, we learn that it is "over priced", "over rated" and "a military secret". From those who believe reality does not exist, we learn that it "used to" and is "all done with mirrors". One person admits to being undecided, two voted both ways, four people feel their reality exists but ours does not, and seven are agonizing over the definitions of various words. A descendant of René Descartes answered the question with "I think so." Jim Livingston feels that "Reality exists when it is really necessary." Carson Bays expressed a view held by many readers: "Yes, except in New Jersey." And Dennis McClain-Furmanski believes the answer to the question can be determined by locking a physicist and a cat in a box with two slits in it. He has a particular physicist in mind but needs help getting said physicist into the box.

("Correctness Survey Results: Reality—Yes or No?," *The Mini-Annals of Improbable Research*, August 1997)

EXPERIMENTS

Although there are many different kinds of experiments, the questions listed below apply to the majority of them, and should be asked in most cases in order to assess the acceptability of the results:

Was the experiment a lab experiment or a field experiment? The former is more controlled, which is good because the variables can be truly isolated. However, that greater control may make the experiment less applicable to the real world because variables do not occur in such isolation in real life. Much depends, of course, on what is studied—for example, quartz or cats?

Was there a control group? As suggested in the previous section (6.3), a control group—in which all elements are identical to the experimental group except the element that is being tested—is necessary in order to be sure that any observed effects are due to the element being tested. This is why observational studies (studies in which one or more groups are simply observed, with regard to any number of phenomena and their associations) are often less conclusive about causation than experiments.

If applicable, was it a "double-blind" study? When a study involves two groups of people, one of which receives a certain drug, for example, the other of which receives a placebo, it is important that neither the participants nor the experimenters know who is getting the drug and who is getting the placebo because such knowledge can influence the results: the experimenters, who might really want the drug to work, might unconsciously exaggerate the observed benefits; the participants, who might also really want the drug to work, might "try harder" to get better, either by following instructions more closely, perhaps with regard to diet and activity, or simply by maintaining an optimistic outlook (one's mental attitude can affect one's physical health). So the potentially confounding variables are not controlled and if indeed those who receive the drug get better, the experimenters couldn't conclude that the reason was the drug rather than the diet, activity, attitude, and so on.

Was the test group, if applicable, sufficiently large and sufficiently representative (see Sections 7.2.2 and 7.2.3)? Again, much depends on what is studied. The more variation there is among individual bits of the study material, the more important sample size and representation will be. (Quartz or cats?) Also, note the importance of representativeness in biological experiments.

The
General Surgeon
has determined that breathing
is dangerous to your health.
This conclusion
was drawn from a survey
of 100 Canadian rats
that have died
within the past 5 years.
All were
habitual breathers.

© Gibson Greeting Cards, Inc.

6.4.2b *Practice determining whether experiment results are acceptable*

How acceptable would you consider the results of each of the following? Articulate your reasons, of course.

1. Research shows that 75 percent of all stomach aches go away after taking "Go Away!"

2. Researchers at the University of Washington in Seattle had 19 people follow an eating program that provided 30% of calories from protein and 20% from fat with no calorie restrictions. The participants ate an average of 441 calories a day less on the 30%-protein diet than they did on the 15%-protein diet they were on before the program began. They dropped 11 pounds in 12 weeks.

"Protein definitely reduces appetite both in the short term and the long term," says lead researcher Scott Weigle of the University of Washington School of Medicine.

(Nanci Hellmich, "Protein is the New Diet Hook,"
USA Today, October 16, 2005)

3. I've kept accurate records: a lot of ships have disappeared in the Bermuda Triangle! It's an evil place!

4. In 1993 . . . ABC sent a male and female, Chris and Julie, on an "experiment" to apply in person for jobs several companies were advertising. Chris and Julie were both blonde, trim, neatly dressed college graduates in their 20s, with identical resumes indicating management experience . . . [W]hen the company recruiter spoke with Julie, the only job he brought up was a job answering phones. A few minutes later, the same recruiter spoke with Chris. He was offered a management job.

(Manual G. Velasquez, *Business Ethics:
Concepts and Cases*, 4th edn., 1998)

5. The crime rate in Orlando, the home of Disney World, is higher than the crime rate in Atlantic City, the home of many casinos, even though they both have about 30 million visitors per year. This shows that casinos do not, in fact, attract criminals or otherwise increase crime.

6. The Canadian Department of Indian Affairs and Northern Development spent $80,000 to determine the effect of oil spills on polar bears. The procedure involved immersing three polar bears in a container of crude oil and water. One polar bear died after licking oil from her fur for 12 hours. A second polar bear was killed for "humane reasons" after suffering intense pain from kidney failure. The third survived after suffering from severe infection that was caused by injections that the bear was given through her oil-stained skin by veterinarians who were attempting to treat her for the kidney and liver damage that was caused by her immersion in oil.

(See *The Province* and *The Vancouver Sun*,
March 28, 1980 and April 8, 1980)

7. So on Friday before the holiday weekend he came up with a press release received on December 9 from Newark-based UMDNJ Medical School: "Researchers Find 'Game Boy' is an Effective Approach for Treating Anxiety in Children About to Undergo Elective Surgery." . . .

. . . Anuradha Patel, principal investigator on the study, thought hand-held video games might ease severe anxiety in children about to undergo elective surgery.

Patel and her cohorts, pediatric anesthesiologists, had tried various stress relieving activities, from watching television, to reading, to using coloring books, but nothing really worked. An alternative, an anti-anxiety drug called midazolam, can produce a "drug hangover" that lasts longer than the effect of the anesthesia itself.

Patel hoped video games could substitute for drugs. She tapped the services of an Eagle Scout to collect Game Boys for a randomized controlled study. Some children had only their parents to help them cope with their anxiety. Others, also accompanied by their parents, were given the drug, and a third group, also accompanied by parents, was given a Game Boy about 30 minutes before anesthesia.

You guessed it. Those with Game Boys remained calm, while the drugged group showed an anxiety increase of 7.5 percent, and the control group was 17.5 percent more anxious.

("Between the Lines," *US#1*, June 1, 2005)

8. To determine the most effective means for treating German pilots who had become severely chilled from ejecting into the ocean, or German soldiers who suffered extreme exposure on the Russian front, [Dr. Sigmund] Rascher and others conducted freezing experiments at Dachau. For up to five hours at a time, they placed victims into vats of icy water, either in aviator suits or naked; they took others outside in the freezing cold and strapped them down naked. As the victims writhed in pain, foamed at the mouth, and lost consciousness, the doctors measured changes in the patients' heart rate, body temperature, muscle reflexes, and other factors. When a prisoner's internal body temperature fell to 79.7°F, the doctors tried rewarming him using hot sleeping bags, scalding baths, even naked women forced to copulate with the victim. Some 80 to 100 patients perished during these experiments.

    ("NOVA Online," at: http://www.pbs.org/wgbh/
    nova/holocaust/experiside.html#free)

9. Suspecting a professor of an anti-Hispanic bias, particularly toward male students, based on grades received by students in his classes during previous years (for example, never had a Hispanic male student received a grade higher than B-), the class of '06, along with the cooperation of the professor, conducted the following experiment. Every assignment in the current year's course was to be submitted as a Word document, identified only by a number; a student from another course would collect each batch of assignments and record the student's name and identifying number, before giving the assignments to the professor for grading. A similar procedure was followed for in-class tests and the final examination. When the final grades were tabulated, students and professor discovered a bias (on average, Hispanic male students received lower grades than Hispanic female students and all non-Hispanic students), though not as much as anticipated.

NUMBERS

Numbers can be intimidating. But they don't have to be. And it's important to understand how numbers can mislead us into thinking something is true or acceptable when it is not. Numbers seem so objective—who can argue with 2 + 2 = 4? But there are numbers and there are numbers. When faced with results that include numbers, consider the following questions:

Are the results expressed in absolute numbers or ratios (usually percentages)? If the number of flying squirrels in your township increases by 100 percent (a ratio), you might think you're going to have to duck the next time you go outside to look at the stars. But if there were only two of them to begin with, now there are four; that's an increase of just two (an absolute number). No need to duck. So, look for context. Ask "Out of how many?" whenever you're given numbers so you can calculate the percentage. And ask "How many is that?" whenever you're given percentages so you know the numbers.

Are the numbers unrealistically precise? We tend to be more willing to believe numbers when they're very exact than when they're not. As a result, fake precision is often used to manipulate us. Question numbers that seem improbably precise.

When an average is given, determine whether it is the mean, mode, or median? The mean is what most people call the average; it's obtained by adding all the numbers and dividing by how many there are. The mode is the most often occurring number. The median is the number in the middle: there are as many numbers above it as there are below it.

Consider the following information about annual income in three fictional countries, each of which has five inhabitants:

Half of the people in the world are below average.

Country A ($)	Country B ($)	Country C ($)
10,000	7,000	4,000
9,000	6,000	4,000
3,000	5,000	3,000
1,500	4,000	1,000
1,500	3,000	1,000

Note that the average income, meaning the mean, in both A and B is the same: $5,000. But in Country A, two people are really rich and the rest have incomes below average; in Country B, the wealth is spread out pretty evenly. This illustrates two points: one, often the mean isn't very informative (in particular, it doesn't tell us anything about how the numbers are distributed);

two, the mean can be influenced by just a few extreme values (very high or very low).

Note, further, that the mode for Country A is $1,500, Country B doesn't have a mode, and Country C has two modes, $1,000 and $4,000.

Note, lastly, that the median is the same for both A and C: $3,000. And yet, the two countries are quite different with respect to both equitable distribution and overall wealth as indicated by incomes.

So it seems that in this case, neither the mean, nor the mode, nor the median is very informative. What would be informative? Statements to the effect that in Country A, X percent are in the $0–$3,000 range, Y percent are in the $4,000–$7,000 range, and so on would be of value. Or a graph:

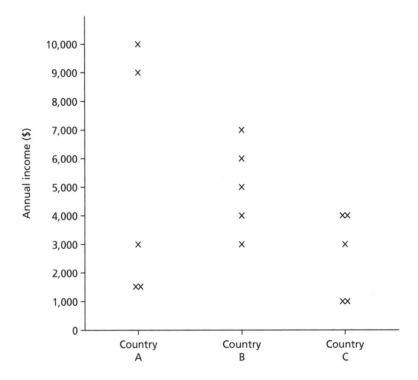

One can see at a glance the highs and lows and concentrations.

Keep in mind that "on average" means just that. Consider this comment about the finding that women who have used birth control pills take about eight months on average to conceive once they've stopped taking said pills: "But remember that this finding is just an average. There are plenty of women who get pregnant the month after they stop taking the Pill . . ."! (Janis Graham, "Does the Pill Make You Fat?" *Redbook*, March 2005).

What is the margin of error? When you are presented with any statistical finding, such as "24% of the people surveyed believed X," the margin of error should always be provided.* The margin of error is the largest plausible difference between the given results of a study and reality. For example, if results are accurate to two percentage points (if that's the margin of error), then a given result of 24 percent could actually be anywhere from 22 percent to 26 percent (two percentage points below and above the given, or the given plus or minus 2 percent). So if in the preceding year, that same figure was 22 percent (also with a 2 percent margin of error), there could have been no actual increase (if last year's 22 percent was actually 22 percent and this year's 24 percent was also actually 22 percent) or there might have been an increase of 6 percent (if last year's 22 percent was actually 20 percent and this year's 24 percent was actually 26 percent). The larger the sample is in relation to the population, the smaller the margin of error. So, also, the higher the margin of error you're willing to live with, the smaller your sample need be.

What is the level of confidence? This should also be provided and considered.*

The level of confidence is usually expressed as a percentage (for example, 90 percent), sometimes in decimal form (for example, .90). It indicates the likelihood that the given results do in fact reflect reality. For example, if results are accurate within a margin of 5 percent and with a level of confidence of 90 percent, that means that the researchers are 90 percent certain that those results, plus or minus 5 percent, reflect the target population. Put another way, it means that 90 percent of other samples taken in the same way are expected to be accurate also within a margin of 5 percent. The larger the sample, the higher the confidence level. So, also, the less confident you are willing to be, the smaller the sample you need.

If a comparison is given, is it complete? If you read that something is now ten times greater, you don't know much. Greater than what? Greater than it was yesterday? Greater than it is somewhere else?

With respect to comparison, has equivocation occurred? That is, are apples being compared to apples? Consider the many variations of the claim "Product X has fewer grams of fat per serving than Product Y." If the size of a serving of Product X is 175 ml and the size of a serving of Product Y is 250 ml, the comparison is misleading indeed.

Are graph increments correct? Take a close look at the following graph:

---

*Researchers calculate their margin of error and level of confidence according to charts prepared by statisticians that indicate both margin of error and level of confidence for various sample sizes relative to various population sizes, assuming simple random procedures. A sample of 1,200 is generally considered sufficient by social scientists.

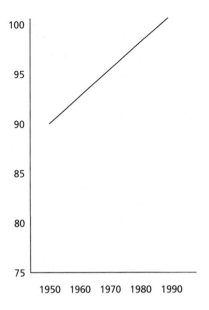

The increase (of whatever it is) looks reasonably steep. But notice that the y-axis (the vertical scale) *starts* at 75. If it had started at zero, the increase would appear considerably less steep:

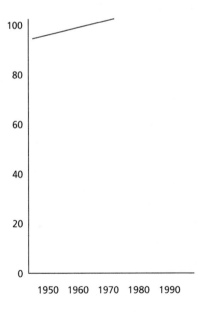

Another kind of distortion occurs when one increment takes up one inch of space at one end of the graph, but at the other end, the same increment takes up two inches of space.

Here's another example illustrating the need to pay attention to scale: a pH value of 7 is neutral, but there's a tenfold difference between each unit, so a pH of 6 is ten times more acid than a pH of 7, and a pH of 5 is a hundred (not twenty) times more acid than a pH of 7, and so on.

You're not convinced? You need another reason to try our demotivational program? How about this. *Successful people are less happy.* It's true. Psychologists have proved it. Okay, a psychologist proved it. Granted, *proved* may be too strong a word. Let's just say that a psychology student we met at a party said that he'd read somewhere that successful people are less happy.

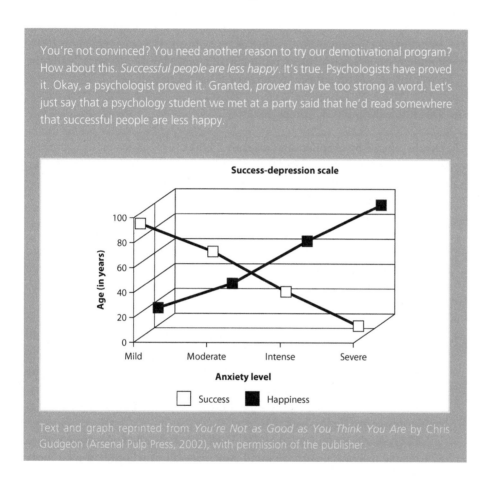

Text and graph reprinted from *You're Not as Good as You Think You Are* by Chris Gudgeon (Arsenal Pulp Press, 2002), with permission of the publisher.

6.4.2c Practice determining whether "the numbers" are acceptable

How acceptable would you consider each of the following? Articulate your reasons, of course.

1. The President won over 80 percent of the vote, showing overwhelming support by the people.

2. Psychologist Terry Orlick discovered that 90 percent of the children he surveyed would rather play on a losing team than warm a bench on a winning team. Winning was actually at the bottom of their list—they wanted fun and excitement, they wanted to improve their skills and be with their friends.

3. We consider the risk to be minimal: less than .01 percent suffered side-effects.

4. We have over a dozen satisfied customers in your neighborhood.

5. 14 million documents were classified as secret by the U.S. government in 2003. 8 million were classified as secret in 2001 (*Time*, May 17, 2004). Clearly the government is getting more secretive or it has more to hide.

6. This headache pill is 3.7 times better!

7. Deaths caused by occupational disease: 25,000
Deaths caused by crime: 24,000
Other physical harm caused by occupational disease: 15,000
Other physical harm caused by crime: 1,000,000
So one is as likely to die by some occupational disease as by crime.

8. According to studies by the American Association of University Women and the Institute for Women's Policy Research, women with four-year college degrees still earn 72 percent as much money as comparably educated men (as reported in *Ms.*, Spring 2005).

9. Eight out of ten Lotto winners have one amazing thing in common—they all had high levels of vitamin C in their systems when they won their millions!

     That's the finding of a stunning news study published here last week by a renowned sociologist, Dr. Michael Valsing.

     The study has indisputably linked large doses of vitamin C to what is commonly called "good luck."

     The research team headed by Dr. Valsing sent detailed questionnaires to 671 people in France, Australia and America—all of whom had won more than $4 million in lotteries . . .

     "[O]ther than the vitamin C, none of the winners ate the same foods. The only thing their diets had in common was the vitamin C," [reports Dr. Valsing.]

     . . . Dr. Valsing says he has no idea why the taking of vitamins should have an effect on good luck. But his associates have what they think is a plausible theory: They deduced that science has shown that everyone has some degree of psychic ability. But it remains undeveloped in most people.

     It could very well be that something in vitamin C has an effect on the part of the mind that receives telepathic thought waves. In other words, these people's ESP abilities may have been temporarily heightened, allowing them to "tune in"—so to speak—to what numbers would come up in the lottery.

(Ann Victoria, "Shocking Study Reveals . . . Vitamin C Can Help You Win the Lottery!" *The Weekly World News*, February 1, 1994)

10. However, there is strong evidence that racial profiling does not work. In fact, where racial profiling has been studied in the context of law enforcement, such as in the United States, it has been found by some scholars to be neither an efficient nor effective approach to fighting crime. Studies in the United States have consistently found that while minorities (African American and Latino persons) were targeted more, the chance of finding contraband when their cars were searched was the same or less than White persons. In several studies, minorities were found to be statistically significantly less likely to have contraband found following a search. For example, a 2001 U.S. Department of Justice report on 1,272,282 citizen-police contacts in 1999 found that, although African Americans and Hispanics were much more likely than White persons to be stopped and searched, they were about half as likely to be in possession of contraband.

(http://www.ohrc.on.ca/english/consultations/racial-profiling-report_5.shtml#_TOC55791618)

6.4.3 Evaluating sources

Sometimes, often, we can't figure it out ourselves—we have to trust others when they present evidence as fact or hypotheses as best explanations. So when is our trust well-placed? Whether we're considering our source to be the person who authored the report containing the evidence in question or the journal, magazine, book, newspaper, television show, radio show, or website in/on which the report is presented, several questions should be asked:

Is the source given? This has to be the first question. If no source is given, you can't evaluate the source. That alone might be cause for suspicion about its merit.

Is the source qualified? Qualifications can be measured by academic degrees, field experience, and so on. Basically, we're trying to determine whether the person has the knowledge or skill we lack. (Of course, if we don't know enough to figure it out, how do we know what someone else needs to know in order to figure it out . . .?)

Are the qualifications relevant? A report on a cure for cancer written by a fashion magazine columnist might be suspect.

Is the source impartial? Are there any conflicts of interest (usually involving personal gain such as continued funding or employment) that might lead to

Most of us rarely give any thought to cleaning our tongues. Yet each year more than 34 million Americans develop physical problems that could easily have been prevented with adequate tongue hygiene, according to statistics that recently came to us in a dream.

Dave Barry, *Dave Barry's Gift Guide to End All Gift Guides*, 1994 the suppression of certain evidence or, in some other way, to the misrepresentation of the truth? For example, an article on the effectiveness of a certain drug published in a magazine owned by the company that makes that drug isn't likely to be very impartial. Also, is there any possibility that coercion has been used? The greater the investment, the more pressure company executives might put on researchers to come up with "favorable" results. Even routine payment for an expert opinion can be coercive in that it may pressure the person to express a particular opinion.

Is the source thorough, especially in a way that leads to fair representation? For example, suppose your source is radio or television (talk shows can be particularly problematic in this regard). Who's been invited and who's not been invited? We can't hear from someone if they're not there! How much time is given to each guest? Disproportionate time allotments may affect our perception of relative worth and/or render the guest's contribution necessarily incomplete. What questions are asked and what questions are not asked? Does the wording of the question push the answer in one direction or another? Has important contextual information been provided by the host, if not by one of the guests? And is the show edited? You'll never know what parts of whose answers were deleted. Advertisements and political speeches also typically suppress evidence and so are suspect sources. So too are news stories: detail is often left out, especially detail about the history of a current event and the connections between one event and another—such information is important if one wants to understand the "why" as well as the "who, what, where, when, and how."

Has the report (article, story, and so on) undergone peer review? Most academic journals send out the reports submitted to them for publication to people qualified in the field (the author's "peers") for evaluation. These experts read the reports carefully and provide their opinions as to whether or not the study was carried out correctly—in short, whether or not it is good science. Thus, evidence obtained through shoddy research is unlikely to be published. Such independent examination acts as a kind of "gate-keeper": if it's in a "refereed" journal, we are more justified in accepting it. This also applies to many book publishers and some websites.

On most websites, however, "anything goes"—anyone can post anything. Consequently, the possibility of fiction appearing as fact is high. Don't be taken in by appearances. The site may look professional, but all that takes is a skilled web designer. Check the credibility of the website: read the "About Us" page, do some independent research about the organization or person hosting the website. Consider potential bias: ".com" sites are often (but not always) for-profit sites; ".org" and ".edu" are typically (but not necessarily) not.

However, although the presence of gate-keeping generally increases acceptability, its absence need not decrease acceptability. In fact, gate-keeping often amounts to censorship, and researchers reporting "unpopular" results may be

People who've never read an encyclopedia are surfing the net, voraciously. Why? The net is the same as the encyclopedia: it provides a hodgepodge of information. But it's different from the encyclopedia in one important way: *it doesn't have the credibility of scholarship*. Sure, it looks better—it's got lots of colors, and it's got lots of pictures, and they're even moving around, and there's all those links, and you feel so important sitting there with your mouse *controlling* everything—but can you tell the difference between facts and lies? Can you tell the difference between unsupported ranting and supported ranting? Surfing the net doesn't make you informed; it merely gives you the illusion of being informed. And it certainly doesn't make you smart. If anything, because it slips you ten incompatible views before breakfast, it makes you stupid.

denied publication no matter how good their science is. Although more common in the arts (consider independent music labels and independent book publishing), some scholars have also resorted to self-publishing in order to be heard. Megacorporations increasingly own book publishers, magazines, and newspapers, and since their overriding interest is profit, they routinely refuse to publish anything that will upset the advertisers who pay them (and pay them a lot of money).

Has the source been around for a while? Does it have a reputation for being informed and impartial? True, reputations can sometimes be undeserved, but as a general rule . . . However, while a good reputation is a good thing, the absence of a good reputation is not necessarily a bad thing. Perhaps the source hasn't been around long enough or been subject to the right kind of critics to have had a reputation, good or bad, established.

Is the source presenting the original publication of the evidence or is it presenting a quote or a summary? Quotes are, by definition, out of context and that can result in misrepresentation. Summaries are, by definition, incomplete and that can be a problem; the omitted detail may include an important qualification of a generalization, for example. Also, the author gets the chance to correct the original publication before it goes to print, but not so with quotes and summaries. Always check the original; otherwise, you're trusting someone else to have copied correctly.

6.4.3a Practice determining whether sources are acceptable

How acceptable would you consider each of the following sources? Articulate your reasons, of course.

1. A yearlong examination of death-record data from across the nation conducted by *The Washington Post* indicated that "there have been approximately 1,367

killings of pregnant women or new mothers since 1990 . . . 67% of the women were killed with guns, often at home and usually by husbands or boyfriends. [The victims] spanned a wide range of ages, races, cultures and socioeconomic backgrounds, including: a minister's wife, a Navy petty officer, a waitress, a college student, a business woman, a high school athlete and an immigrant housekeeper."

(As reported in *Ms.*, Spring 2005)

2. If your wife does not obey you, first give her notice, then separate your bed from her, then beat her.

(The Koran, Chapter 4, Verse 34)

3. During my years in family court, I have seen a dramatic deterioration in the lives of adults and children. At the same time, there has been a dramatic increase in expensive public programs. We are spending a fortune and the result is failure. The recipients of these monies are in the same or worse shape than before, and the consequences are all around us: more and meaner delinquents, more unwanted children, more abused children, more dysfunctional adults, more teenage pregnancies. By shifting the emphasis from individual responsibility to government responsibility, we have infantilized an entire population.

(Judge Judy aka Judy Sheindlin, *Don't Pee on My Leg and Tell Me It's Raining*, 1997)

4. You will be earning up to $1,000 a day in just days! Pay your bills! Get out of Debt! Spend time with your family. Buy your dream home. Let me show you how I do it! I put $1,000++ in my account every day and so can you! Fill in the form below and press "Get More Info" button. Start today and your world will be different tomorrow!

(http://waterhousereport.com/ns10.htm)

5. President Bush is calling on Congress to develop legislation that will offer temporary worker status to undocumented men and women now employed in the United States and to those in foreign countries who have been offered employment here. The legal status would expire after 3 years (with the ability to be renewed). Temporary workers then must return home or apply for a green card under existing law, unlike the blanket amnesty that was enacted in 1986. . . .

Giving criminal aliens any type of legitimate status or legal benefits (jobs) is amnesty. Bottom line: Now is NOT the time to even mention a program like this. It will only encourage a rush of new criminal aliens hoping to take advantage of this "program."

What is very frustrating for me is that the ag business won't stop fighting for this idea. Economic freedom is a republican principle but instead of fighting for economic freedom in terms of reduced regulation, relaxed child-labor laws, and a reduced minimum wage the farmer (and many Republicans) would prefer to fight for access to foreign citizens.

They would rather that money earned in this country be sent to Mexico. They would rather that our culture be diluted. They would rather that we continue to put more and more Spanish translations on everything. . . .

Don't tell me about "jobs that Americans won't do" either. I'll drive my kids to the fields in the morning and guess what, they don't speak Spanish!

They also don't send 50% of their wages to another country and they don't rape 12 year old girls. (Don't ask me for the stats, you idiot, just read my archives) . . .

(Daniel Sherwood, "Daniel's Political Musings," excerpts from his blog entries of February 2 and 3, 2006, at http://danielisright.blogspot.com/)

6.4.4 Evaluating images

You may have heard the saying, "Seeing is believing." Pretend you haven't. Because not only can our eyes deceive us (Section 6.4.1), but so too can imaging technology. Here are some questions to consider with regard to images (photographs, web images, and so on):

Is the lighting consistent? Or are there "mixed message" shadows, shadows indicating that the sun must be in two different places at once? Color and contrast will also differ when the lighting differs, such as when part of the picture was taken outside and part of it inside with a flash.

Are there inconsistencies in the sharpness of the various objects in the picture? This might be especially apparent at edges. An object with sharper edges than everything else has probably been inserted into the photograph.

Are there errors in perspective or scale? If a map, for example, doesn't consistently use the same scale (100 miles per inch, for example), you'll be seriously misled about how far it is from point A to point B.

Are there any anachronisms in the picture, things that are out of place time-wise? For example, suppose you're presented with a photograph of two students in Plato's Academy, sitting at their desks, writing with ball-point pens. (Actually, there are two anachronisms there—did you get the second one?*)

Are there contradictions to known facts in the picture? Such as a fifty-pound hummingbird hovering in the corner?

Is context missing? Is there material outside the frame that would lead to a different interpretation of the picture? In this case, the picture itself may not be fake in any way, but its presentation out of context may be misleading.

---

*Not only were ball-point pens not invented by Plato's time—neither was photography!

6.4.4a Practice determining whether images are acceptable

How true or acceptable would you consider each of the following images? Articulate your reasons, of course.

1.

© Corbis

2.

Actress and anti-war activist Jane Fonda speaks to a crowd of Vietnam veterans as activist and former Vietnam vet John Kerry listens and prepares to speak next concerning the war in Vietnam (*Washington Post*).

3.

© Getty Images

4.

© Corbis

5.

6.5 Errors of truth

Basically, any false premise is an error of truth. For example, consider this argument:

> Many terrorists who kill innocent men, women, and children on the streets of Baghdad are followers of the same murderous ideology that took the lives of our citizens in New York, in Washington, and Pennsylvania. There is only one course of action against them: to defeat them abroad before they attack us at home.
>
> (President George W. Bush, June 28, 2005)

Quite apart from the lack of relevance of the first sentence to the second sentence (the presumed conclusion drawn from the evidence presented in the first sentence), the second sentence is simply not true: there is *not* only one course of action against them. We could act to defeat them when they attack us at home. Or we could fight them, abroad or at home, and *not* defeat them.

There are several specific false premises that are quite common, four of which we'll cover in this section. False analogies are also common, but we'll deal with that error in Chapter 7 when we discuss analogies. And there are several errors of truth involving causation, but we'll deal with them in Chapter 8, when we deal with causal reasoning. Lastly, an appeal to ignorance (covered in Sections 6.1.1 and 2.8) might also be considered an error of truth.

However, before we get to the four errors of truth, mention should be made of suppressed evidence, especially counterevidence—which is not so much an error of truth as an error of sufficiency (and so will be dealt with at greater length in Chapters 7 and 8). When evidence is suppressed, the truth of the matter as presented is incomplete. Now of course, one can hardly be expected to present the complete truth in every case; every article would have to be a full-length book.

So the problem is less with the evidence or the source of the evidence than it is with the person who makes use of that evidence: when we use an incomplete truth as a premise, we're reasoning to a conclusion on insufficient grounds.

For example, suppose I argue that elk often move in herds because there's safety in numbers: when there's more of them, more vigilance will occur overall, so the presence of wolves will be more easily detected. You might respond by presenting evidence that counters the claim that there's safety in numbers: wolves are more likely to attack large groups because that's where the vulnerable elk are (the injured, the very young, and the very old). Unless I anticipate that objection—that is, unless I present the counterevidence and deal with it somehow (I might argue that while the chance of attack is greater in large herds, the chance of any one elk's death is less, because there are so many more of them—so, there *is* greater safety, for the individual elk, in numbers)—I'll be arguing to a conclusion on the basis of incomplete evidence, incomplete truth.

6.5a *Practice recognizing counterevidence*

Which of the following, if true, would be counterevidence to the given evidence?

1. [H]igh schools across the U.S. are taking soft drinks out of their vending machines because, they say, they want to encourage better eating habits. But they're replacing them with something that's even worse: flavored milk drinks . . . These strawberry and chocolate concoctions are full of fat, cholesterol, sugar, and sodium—far more than in the soft drinks they replace—and the milk in them is associated with a host of health problems, including diabetes, obesity, cancer, and heart disease.

    ("Dump the Dairy," *Animal Times*, Spring 2004)

    (A) Flavored milk drinks are higher in calcium and vitamins than soft drinks.
    (B) Flavored milk drinks cost more than soft drinks.
    (C) Water is preferable to both flavored milk drinks and soft drinks.

2. Crop circles are UFO landing sites.

    (A) A certain fungus dehydrates grass in a circular pattern.
    (B) Engineering principles support the likelihood that space vehicles will be circular.
    (C) Crop circles have been found mostly in the United States.

3. The public school system is a monopoly, and we all know that monopolies don't produce good results because there's no competition, and without competition, the monopoly has no incentive to strive for quality or efficiency. That's why private schools are the way to go.

(A) Privatizing the school system passes the expense of education onto the individual.

(B) Countries whose students routinely outperform ours have public education systems.

(C) Competition is the best motivator.

4. How can we explain getting involved in a gang or cult? Simple. Desire for recognition, for feeling special, chosen, accepted.

(A) Many gangs and cults have a rite of passage that prospective members must pass before they're considered members.

(B) Some people join gangs for protection.

(C) Many people who join cults have low self-esteem.

5. In 2004, the Nobel Peace Prize was awarded to Wangar Maathai, a Kenyan environmentalist-turned-politician, for planting 30 million trees. Although some question the award, her supporters say it was well-deserved. Conflict often springs from competition for water or fertile land. As deserts expand and populations soar, such competition can turn violent. The war in the Darfur region of western Sudan, for example, has its roots in the struggle between black farmers and Arab pastoralists over a slab of increasingly arid soil. By reforesting Kenya, M. Maathai has made it less likely to go the way of Sudan. And the way she did it—by paying peasant women to plant seedlings in their own villages—empowers women, and so promotes peace even more.

(*The Economist*, October 16, 2004)

(A) A better solution to diminishing water and fertile land would be a decrease in population.

(B) It is most often men, not women, who initiate and engage in war.

(C) Skirmishes over pasture are common, but wars are more often the result of struggles for political power; for example, a group of guerrillas rebelled against an oppressive regime, which responded by slaughtering the rebels' ethnic kin.

6.5b Practice "constructing" counterevidence

What would constitute counterevidence to the following claims or arguments?

1. It is clearly beneficial for American companies to set up shop in developing countries. Such companies benefit from the cheap labor provided by such countries, and the countries benefit from the jobs that are provided.

269

2. Stem cell research is clearly a good thing. Embryonic stem cells can be grown to produce organs or tissues to repair or replace damaged ones. Skin for burn victims, brain cells for the brain damaged, spinal cord cells for quadriplegics and paraplegics, hearts, lungs, livers, and kidneys could be produced.

3. The vaccination for hepatitis B was introduced in 1991, but there has been no decline in the disease, proving that vaccinations don't always work.

4. Everything in the world shows evidence of intelligent design.

5. Women should not serve in the military. As Brian Mitchell points out, "Physical limitations make it impossible for many women to live up to the boast that they perform as well as men. The Marine Corps does not train women to throw hand grenades because a test of female Marines found that barely half of them could throw a hand grenade far enough not to kill themselves."

(Brian Mitchell, "Should Military Women Serve in Combat? Con," *The American Legion Magazine*, May 1990)

6.5.1 The either/or fallacy

This error (also known as the black-and-white fallacy or a false dichotomy) occurs when a person presents two options as if they're the only options—when in fact they're not. It can also occur when a person presents two options as if you can't choose both (when in fact you can), or as if both can't be true (when in fact they can). In other words, it involves presenting two options as if they're exhaustive and/or mutually exclusive when they're not.

Here's an example of the either/or fallacy:

Anyone who seeks political office is after either the power or the glory.

Well, no, they might actually be after making the world a better place. The speaker has presented the two possibilities as if they exhaust the possibilities (so this is an exhaustive either/or), when, in fact, they don't.

This kind of reasoning is often used to manipulate us into taking a particular position. That position is presented as the only alternative to another, opposing and distasteful, position. Sometimes, however, this error is not the product of a manipulative mind, but of a simple mind that can only see the world in black and white, a mind that simply can't handle the many shades of grey that exist.

Here's another example of the either/or fallacy:

Look, you have to choose: chocolate or vanilla!

Isn't it possible to have both? In this case, the speaker has presented two options as if one must choose between the two, as if choosing one excludes choosing the other (so this is an exclusive either/or), when, in fact, one can choose both.

Perhaps we fall for this erroneous reasoning because of a lack of imagination: we fail to imagine options other than the two that are presented to us (or we fail to imagine a way whereby we can have our cake and eat it too. After all, what good *is* a cake if we can't eat it?).

6.5.1a Practice recognizing the either/or fallacy

Which of the following arguments contain an either/or fallacy? Where applicable, re-craft the argument so it is error-free.

1. "Would you like plastic or paper?" the grocery store clerk asks.

2. Dr. Phil's Life Law #1: You either get it or you don't.
    (http://www.drphil.com/articles/article/44)

3. "Sink or swim!"

4. Wanted: Dead or Alive.

5. We either deal with terrorism and this extremism abroad, or we deal with it when it comes to us.
    (General John Vines, as quoted by
President George W. Bush, June 28, 2005)

6.5.1b More practice with the either/or fallacy

Write three arguments that have an either/or fallacy. Then rewrite your three arguments so they're error-free.

6.5.2 The fallacy of composition

What is true for individual parts is *not necessarily* true of the whole formed by those parts. When you claim that it is, you commit the fallacy of composition.

Here's an example of the fallacy of composition:

> Every single musician in this orchestra is a virtuoso, so I expect to be blown away by their performance of Beethoven's Fifth.

Well, you might be disappointed: just because they are excellent individual musicians, it doesn't follow that they will play well together.

I think we tend to make this error because we fail to consider how complicated reality can be; parts and wholes are not always related in straightforward ways. Sometimes the sum of the whole is greater than its parts, and sometimes it is less. In any case, it's usually different!

6.5.2a Practice recognizing the fallacy of composition

Which of the following arguments contain the fallacy of composition? Where applicable, re-craft the argument so it is error-free.

1. Of course this is a great paper! Every single article in it is great!

2. The days get longer in summer. So of course summer is the longest season of the year.

3. Every part of this flower is made of glass, so this flower is made of glass.

4. I will bring you many beautiful flowers tomorrow; you will be able to make a beautiful bouquet!

5. Is Congress ineffective? Is it non-responsive to your interests? The solution is to elect better members of Congress!

6.5.2b More practice with the fallacy of composition

Write three arguments that contain the fallacy of composition. Then rewrite your three arguments so they're error-free.

6.5.3 The fallacy of division

What is true of the whole is *not necessarily* true of the individual parts. When you claim that it is, you commit the fallacy of division. (You'll note that this fallacy is the "flip side" of the previous fallacy.)

Here's an example of the fallacy of division:

This is such a large hotel! I'm sure we'll have plenty of space in our rooms!

The hotel as a whole may be large, but that doesn't mean that its individual parts—its rooms, for example—are also large!

It is important not to make this error especially when we're talking about people: individuals seldom have all the attributes of whatever whole or group they are part of.

6.5.3a Practice recognizing the fallacy of division

Which of the following arguments contain the fallacy of division? Where applicable, re-craft the argument so it is error-free.

1. This committee has consistently come up with creative solutions. I don't understand why your individual performance is so lack-lustre.

2. My team has won every game it's played this season. I'll put any one of my players against any one of yours any day!

3. I don't understand why the anthology was such a failure. Nothing but excellent poems were included.

4. If you use only the best-tasting ingredients, *any* casserole you bake will taste fantastic!

5. My bicycle is in my apartment, so every part of my bike must be in my apartment.

6.5.3b More practice with the fallacy of division

Write three arguments that contain the fallacy of division. Then rewrite your three arguments so they're error-free.

6.5.4 The gambler's fallacy

This error involves a mistaken understanding about reality; specifically, it involves a belief that previous occurrences affect probability of current occurrences, when in fact that's simply not true.

When you toss a coin, for example, there are only two possible ways it could land ("heads up" or "tails up"), and each way has an equal chance of happening. So the chance of it landing, say, "heads up" is 1 in 2. (And 1 in 2 is equal to 50 in 100, which is why people say the chances are "50–50." They may also say there's a 50 percent chance of it landing "heads up"—50 percent means 50 per 100.) Now the thing is this: the coin has an equal chance of landing either way *every time you toss it*. If you think that the chances change the more often you toss it—suppose you've tossed it ten times in a row and you've always gotten "heads," so you figure the chances of getting "tails" are increasing with every toss—well, you're wrong: you've fallen for the gambler's fallacy. Yes, in the long run, the coin should land as often "heads" as it lands "tails"—but "in the long run" equals "infinity"! So landing "heads" ten times in a row, or all day, or all week, or all year—all of that may be but a blink of an eye. The next time you toss it, it still has a 50–50 chance of being "heads" again.

Here's an example of the gambler's fallacy:

> After the Safety Lecture comes the takeoff, which is terrifying until you realized that the pilot has probably taken off thousands of times without a mishap, which means that the odds of a mishap occurring get better every time.
>
> (Dave Barry, *Dave Barry's Bad Habits*, 1985)

The odds of a mishap occurring do *not* get better every time; each time they are the same (and dependent on a number of variables, such as the pilot's competence, the weather conditions, and so on).

I think we make this error because it seems so right: it *is* very unlikely that "heads" will keep turning up—"tails" has *got* to turn up, our luck *must* change soon. In the long run, that's true. But who's to say the change will happen today, tomorrow, or within the next decade?

It's important that we don't make this error because our lifetime is considerably less than an eternity. A noteworthy error of this type? Visit Las Vegas. Or your corner store's lottery ticket counter.

6.5.4a *Practice recognizing the gambler's fallacy*

Which of the following arguments contain the gambler's fallacy? Where applicable, re-craft the argument so it is error-free.

1. *Belsito*: I notice you're buying ten tickets today instead of your usual five.
    Naljiwan: That's right. I haven't won this month yet, so I figure my day's coming. And I'm being smart about it, gonna make it count, gonna make the most of my winning day!

2. Okay, this time I'll get a basket. I mean, I've missed every one so far, so the odds are good that this will be the one that makes it.

3. The older I get, the less apt I am to have an accident because with every passing day, my driving record gets better and better.

4. Of course the chances of making a mistake increase the longer I work because the longer I work, the more tired I become!

5. Ten applicants were shortlisted—I'm one of them! And, it turns out, there are five positions, not just one. And, the news gets better, I just found out that three applicants have been eliminated. So at first I thought my chances were one in ten, but then they were fifty–fifty, and now they're even better!

6.5.4b More practice with the gambler's fallacy

Write three arguments that contain the gambler's fallacy. Then rewrite your three arguments so they're error-free.

6.5.4c Practice recognizing errors of truth

Which of the following arguments contain one or more fallacies of truth? Identify the specific fallacy involved:

- the either/or fallacy
- the fallacy of division
- the fallacy of composition
- the gambler's fallacy
- an appeal to ignorance.

Where applicable, re-craft the argument so it is error-free.

1. *Security Manager*: We note that there are very few personal email messages being sent by employees, so we're going to extend our surveillance program from email communications to phone communications.
   Smart Employee: But you have no way of knowing how many personal email messages were sent before surveillance began—so you can't conclude that the surveillance "worked."
   Security Manager: Yes, well, we don't know that it *doesn't* work.

2. You're not going to get every question on the test right, so of course the more you get in a row right, the greater the chance the next one will be wrong, so you shouldn't leave the big questions for the end! That's when your chances of getting one wrong are highest! Do the ones that count the most at the beginning!

3. If you don't get married, you'll be a lonely old spinster.

4. The university is very well-known, which is why I'm surprised there are so many unknown professors here.

5. You have taken the most mundane of objects, and used the most mundane of colors, and yet, your painting is stunning.

6. The only way the planet will sustain itself is if each country becomes self-sustaining.

7. I don't profess to be able to understand this at all. I never got past high school chemistry, so I couldn't possibly understand this science. But I want to say

275

that this is the most dangerous research ever conducted in the United States, and it should be prohibited.

(Senator on DNA research, as reported by Paul Berg, "Bio Brain Backs Stem Cells," *Discover*, April 2005)

8. The Bush administration claimed that the December 2002 UN report regarding Iraq's weapons of mass-destruction was incomplete. Of course it was. The United States had removed over 8,000 pages of information implicating twenty-four American corporations and government agencies that had provided Iraq with not only biological and chemical weapons, but also with material for nuclear weapons.

(Michael I. Niman, "What Bush Didn't Want You to Know about Iraq," *The Humanist*, March/April 2003)

9. The power goes out at least once or twice each winter. Winter is almost over, and it hasn't yet gone out, so I'm prepared: I'm saving my work every minute—I'm serious!

10. I submit that justice is, or should be, a truth-seeking process. The court has a duty to the accused to see that he receives a fair trial; the court also has a duty to society to see that all truth is brought out; only if all the truth is brought out can there be a fair trial. The exclusionary rule [that evidence seized through illegal search and seizure may not be presented in court] results in a complete distortion of the truth.

(Malcolm R. Wilkey, "The Exclusionary Rule: Why Suppress Valid Evidence?" *Judicature*, November 1978)

Review of terms

Define the following terms:

- **truth**

- **acceptability**

- **verifiability**

- **falsifiability**

- **subjectivism**

- **coherence theory of truth**

- **correspondence theory of truth**

- **innate ideas**

- **empiricism**

- **rationalism**

- **absolute numbers**

- **percentages**

- **mean**

- **mode**

- **median**

- **margin of error**

- **level of confidence**

- **the either/or fallacy**

- **the fallacy of composition**

- **the fallacy of division**

- **the gambler's fallacy.**

277

Thinking critically about what you see

Think critically about each of the following. Are there any reasons not to accept them as true or acceptable?

1.

Hospital survival rates

Table 1	Survived	Died	Total	Survival rate
Mercy Hospital	750	250	1000	75%
Charity Hospital	840	160	1000	84%

From "Hazards of Irrationality" by Michael Clark, *The Philosophers Magazine*, no. 26, 2nd quarter, 2004. Reprinted with permission.

Are you better off going to Charity Hospital?

2.

© The Metropolitan Museum of Art / Art Resource, NY

Thinking critically about what you hear

Listen to the audio clip under the Student Resources tab on the companion website at www.routledge.com/textbooks/tittle. Any response?

Thinking critically about what you read

Think critically about each of the following, paying special attention to truth and acceptability.
You may want to consult the template to be sure you're applying all of the skills you've acquired to this point.

Template for critical analysis of arguments

1. What's the point (claim/opinion/conclusion)?

    - Look for subconclusions as well.

2. What are the reasons/what is the evidence?

    - Articulate all unstated premises.
    - Articulate connections.

3. What exactly is meant by . . . ?

    - Define terms.
    - Clarify all imprecise language.
    - Eliminate or replace "loaded" language and other manipulations.

4. Assess the reasoning/evidence:

    - If deductive, check for truth/acceptability and validity.
    - If inductive, check for truth/acceptability, relevance, and sufficiency.

5. How could the argument be strengthened?

    - Provide additional reasons/evidence.
    - Anticipate objections—are there adequate responses?

6. How could the argument be weakened?

    - Consider and assess counterexamples, counterevidence, and counter-arguments.
    - Should the argument be modified or rejected because of the counter-arguments?

7. If you suspend judgment (rather than accepting or rejecting the argument), identify further information required.

1. A recent study found that 50 percent of men commit sexual assault within a week of their viewing pornographic movies, proving once again that pornography is bad for women!

2. Twenty-four out of the twenty-five jobs ranked worst in terms of pay and working conditions by the Jobs Related Almanac have one thing in common: they are all 95 percent to 100 percent male. This proves that men have *not* arranged everything to be so wonderful for themselves as feminists suggest.
   (Based on Robert Sheaffer, "Feminism, The Noble Lie," *Free Inquiry*, Spring 1995)

3. Why do you keep pushing me to get married? Each year, two million Americans get married, and one million get divorced. That means that half of all marriages fail! It's not like I'm not all grown up unless I'm married—is *that* what you think? That marriage is some rite of passage to adulthood?

4. It's quite clear to me that the sun moves around the earth and not the other way around. I *see* the sun rise in the east, move across the sky, and then fall in the west out of sight as it goes around the other side. Furthermore, I am standing here on Earth and I tell you it's not moving! I'm not the least bit dizzy!

5. A neurotoxic poison, mercury, is especially worrisome to developing fetuses. A nation-wide study reveals that a significant number of women of child-bearing age have too much of the metal in their systems. Researchers at the University of North Carolina at Asheville based their results on hair samples from nearly 1,500 people of all ages. As hair grows, it incorporates mercury from the bloodstream. Interim results from the Greenpeace-commissioned survey released October 20 revealed that one fifth of those studied had mercury levels above the EPA recommendation of one part per million in hair. The investigators report no other pollutant has anywhere near this high a percentage of the U.S. population with exposure levels above federal standards. The biggest sources of airborne mercury are coal-fired power plants. The investigators will gather an estimated 5,000 samples or more in total and issue their final report in March.
   (Charles A. Choi, *Scientific American*, January 2005)

6. Nothing about contraception should be taught in schools. There is no question that it will encourage sexual activity.
   (Phyllis Schlafly, *New York Times*, October 17, 2002)

7. Hebrews 11:1 says, "Now faith is the substance of things hoped for, the evidence of things not seen." The *evidence* of your healing is the fact that you claimed it in the name of Jesus Christ, and your *faith* will stand in the place of your total healing until Satan turns loose of the symptoms and he will because he *must*.
   (Austin Miles, *Setting the Captives Free*, 1990)

8. Economists seem to assume that economic growth is a good thing. Why? If it means everyone will get more, then okay. But in Canada, for example, between 1991 and 2001, per capita real economic growth increased 25 percent. Hourly wages increased 1.4 percent. Okay, but maybe those workers got more through government spending

(because government revenues increased due to taxes on the wealth created by that economic growth)—more health care, more education, and so on. In 1990/91 per capita spending by government was about $3800; in 2000/02, it was $3879—a bit of an increase, but nothing near 25 percent. So who exactly benefits from economic growth? (Based on Ellen Russell, "Let Them Eat Pie," *This Magazine*, September/October 2005)

9. In recent years, anthropologists have reevaluated the perspective of "man the hunter," which long served as a model of the origins of human society . . . Using this model, primatologists and anthropologists . . . had reasoned that hunting, a male activity, was a creative turning point in human evolution—that it required intelligence to plan and to stalk game, and to make hunting and other tools. It also required social bonding of men, the use of language to cooperate in the hunt, and then the distribution of meat and the development of tools for hunting and cutting the meat. According to Washburn and Lancaster in Lee and De Vore's *Man the Hunter*, "In a very real sense our intellect, interests, emotions, and basic social life—all are evolutionary products of the success of the hunting adaptation." . . . The question is, what merit is there to the model and the explanations derived from it?

   Among others, Frances Dahlbert in *Woman the Gatherer* suggests the account can only be considered a "just-so story" in the light of new scholarship. Beginning in the 1960s, research on primates, on hunter-gatherer societies, and archaeological and fossil records made this story obsolete. For example, the paleo-anthropological myth of man the hunter was deflated when the "killer ape" of Robert Ardrey's *The Hunting Hypothesis*, the presumed australopithecine forebear of humans, turned out to be predominantly vegetarian . . . A greater challenge to the man the hunter model came from Sally Linton in Sue Ellen Jacobs's *Women in Cross-Cultural Perspective*. Linton attacked the validity of theories of evolution that excluded or diminished women's contributions to human culture and society. She noted that women contribute the bulk of the diet in contemporary hunting and gathering societies, that small-game hunting practiced by both sexes preceded large-game hunting practiced by men, and that females as well as males probably devised tools for their hunting and gathering and some sort of carrying sling or net to carry babies. According to this view, the collaboration and cooperation of women was probably as important to the development of cultures as that of men.

   (Cynthia Fuchs Epstein, "Inevitabilities of Prejudice," *Society*, 23.6, 1986)

10. *Ipellie*: Immigrants take jobs away from Americans.

    Sileilka: Nonsense. They either take the jobs Americans turn down or they get the jobs Americans can't do. One in three engineers working in the United States is an immigrant. Over half of all scientists graduating with doctorate degrees from American universities are immigrants.

    Ipellie: Yeah but I just read a study indicating that public assistance to the 19.3 million immigrants who have settled here since 1970 will cost us $42.5 billion.

    Sileilka: What about the taxes they'll have paid though? Immigrants tend to come to the U.S. when they are young and working; I read that over their lifetimes, they'll each pay about $20,000 more in taxes than they use in services.

Ipellie: Well, the study I mentioned—the $42.5 billion in public assistance was what they'll cost us *after* subtracting their taxes, which, the study says, will be $20.2 billion.

Sileilka: Okay, but how much will public assistance to the how many million native-born Americans cost us? You've got to compare. The 1990s census reveals that about 6 percent of native-born Americans are on public assistance versus 7 percent of foreign-born. That's not that much of a difference.

Thinking critically about what you write

Suppose you wanted to persuade (not manipulate) someone that "X" ("X" being some claim), what arguments would you make? That is, write your own letter to the editor or op-ed column. Aim for about 750 words.

Important note: When you start with the conclusion, you're actually thinking backwards, which is not necessarily a good idea. (It's better to start with the evidence, as in the previous chapter's writing exercise.) The question should always really be not "*What* argument should I make to prove X?" but "*Can* I make an argument to prove X?" And you should always consider the possibility that the answer will be "no"—that is, you may discover that there is insufficient support for X. In which case, you should abandon that X and argue for another, more defensible, claim.

Thinking critically when you discuss

Keep your group size to four, but this time, see how you handle a free form discussion: have someone start the discussion with some sort of claim (hopefully backed by a line of reasoning) and go from there. What's the claim? What's the argument? Is it a good argument? Why or why not? Consider counterarguments. Since we've just covered truth and acceptability, you might pay special attention to those elements, but also consider relevance and sufficiency. If you exhaust the issue, have someone else start another discussion on another issue.

Suggestion: Resist the temptation to just spew. That's lazy. Not to mention inconsiderate. Don't expect someone else to do the hard work of trying to make some order out of your mess. Straighten out your thoughts before you open your mouth and articulate exactly how what you say is relevant to what's just been said.

Reasoning test questions

The Verbal Reasoning section of the MCAT "evaluates your ability to understand, evaluate, and apply information and arguments" (*2010 MCAT Essentials* http://www.aamc.org/students/mcat/start.htm). There are seven passages, each about 600 words long, taken from the humanities, social sciences, and natural sciences, and each passage has five to seven multiple-choice questions. You have 60 minutes to answer a total of 40 questions.

Check out the full-length test available online at: http://www.aamc.org/students/mcat/preparing/orderingpracticetests.htm.

chapter 7

generalization, analogy, and general principle

Template for critical analysis of arguments

1. What's the point (claim/opinion/conclusion)?

   ■ Look for subconclusions as well.

2. What are the reasons/what is the evidence?

   ■ Articulate all unstated premises.
   ■ Articulate connections.

3. What exactly is meant by . . .?

   ■ Define terms.
   ■ Clarify all imprecise language.
   ■ Eliminate or replace "loaded" language and other manipulations.

4. **Assess the reasoning/evidence:**

   ■ If deductive, check for truth/acceptability and validity.
   ■ **If inductive, check for** truth/acceptability, relevance, and **sufficiency.**

5. How could the argument be strengthened?

   ■ Provide additional reasons/evidence.
   ■ Anticipate objections—are there adequate responses?

6. How could the argument be weakened?

   ■ Consider and assess counterexamples, counterevidence, and counter-arguments.
   ■ Should the argument be modified or rejected because of the counter-arguments?

7. If you suspend judgment (rather than accepting or rejecting the argument), identify further information required.

7.1 Sufficiency

Now that we're about to start the section on inductive argument, it's a good time for a review: an *inductive argument* differs from a deductive argument in that its *conclusions are more or less probable* rather than certain. A strong inductive argument is one in which the premises are true or acceptable, relevant, and sufficient. The more acceptable, relevant, and sufficient the premises are, the stronger the argument is. We've already addressed the first two criteria (Chapters 6 and 4, respectively). **Sufficiency** (sometimes called adequacy) refers to the degree of support provided by the premises for the conclusion. Factors that affect the degree of support vary according to the kind of inductive argument, so we'll discuss sufficiency as we go along.

For now, let's consider this example: suppose we argue that since a certain product hurts people, it is morally wrong to sell it. Now suppose that using the product will cause only mild harm, or suppose that using it will cause harm in only one in a million cases. One could say the premise is insufficient; it's true, and it's relevant, but it's not strong enough to support the conclusion (that it's wrong to sell it). Perhaps that premise *is* strong enough, however, to support another conclusion—that the product should be sold under restricted circumstances, such as only to adults. Or perhaps the premise is almost strong enough . . . suppose the product hurts mostly children; perhaps both premises together are strong enough to support the conclusion that it should be sold only to adults.

As you can see, sufficiency is a matter of degree, and it's sometimes difficult to determine how strong is strong enough. Certainly, the more sweeping the conclusion and the more certain the conclusion, the more demanding we should be with regard to sufficiency. Perhaps this will serve as a general definition: *a premise or a series of premises is sufficient when their truth or acceptability and relevance make the conclusion more probable than alternative conclusions.* Certainly counterevidence (Section 6.5) and counterarguments (Section 2.5) will have to be considered when one assesses sufficiency.

Furthermore, additional information may be required before one is willing to grant sufficiency. There is no general rule about when additional information is required; it depends on how sufficient you need or want your premises to be, which, in turn, depends on how sweeping or certain the conclusion is.

Probability is the guide of life.

Joseph Butler, *Analogy of Religion*, 1736

7.1a Practice identifying when and what additional information is required

Which of the following arguments consists of insufficient support? That is, for which of the following arguments would you require additional information? Specify the nature of the additional information required.

1. Hydrogen is the most common element in the universe. So hydrogen fuel cells are definitely the wave of the future. We're already running out of oil—it's time to convert now! They're bound to be better than the fossil fuel engines that are currently running our cars.

2. I know firsthand that drinking water helps your skin, wards off infection, and prevents bloating, and I can feel it when I don't get enough.

   (Stacy Lenher, "Health: What Are You Waiting for?,"
   O: The Oprah Magazine, June, 2005)

3. An American manufacturer of woolen sweaters goes to Congress or to the State Department and tells the committee or officials concerned that it would be a national disaster for them to remove or reduce the tariff on British sweaters. He now sells his sweaters for $50 each, but English manufacturers could sell their sweaters of the same quality for $25. A duty of $5, therefore, is needed to keep him in business. He is not thinking of himself, of course, but of the thousand men and women he employs, and of the people to whom their spending in turn gives employment. Throw them out of work, and you create unemployment and a fall in purchasing power, which would spread in ever-widening circles.

   (Henry Hazlitt, *Economics in One Lesson,* 1946)

4. Who says Disney is bad for kids? Sexist role models? Racism? That's crazy! I watched Disney when I was a kid and I turned out alright.

5. Hayward CA: A jury began deliberating last week in the Murder case against three young men charged with beating and strangling a teenager after discovering she was biologically male. Attorneys for two of the defendants argued that the killing of 17-year-old Gwen Araujo—who was born male but passed as a woman—was manslaughter, not murder, because the men acted out of panic and shock over Araujo's sexual deception. But prosecutor Chris Lamiero rejected that theory as he made his final argument to jurors. "The provocation did not flow from [Gwen] Araujo. The provocation flowed from within them," Lamiero said. As jurors deliberate the case, community advocates are anxiously waiting. "It is huge," said Shannon Minter, legal director of the National Center for Lesbian Rights. "We are all on pins and needles waiting to see what the jury does and it will be devastating if they don't respect Gwen's humanity and see through the offensive and irrational arguments the defense attorneys have made."

   (*New York Blade,* June 11, 2004)

Another element of inductive argument is that whereas the conclusion of a deductive argument merely rearranges the given premises to uncover knowledge implied within them, *the conclusion of an inductive argument is an inference: it is a leap from the given premises to new knowledge.* Being able to make such an inference, with confidence, is very valuable. Those incapable of inductive reasoning have to obtain particular and direct evidence before accepting a conclusion. Such a person asks "How do I know that jumping off a cliff will kill me unless I try it?" The rest of us, however, can look at a large and representative sample of other people who have jumped off cliffs and generalize about what will probably happen if we do it. Or we can collect facts about gravity, the cliff's height, force of impact, and the nature of the human body, and from those causal factors infer a probable effect. (Note: because children are generally incapable of inductive reasoning, it's good to keep them away from cliff edges.)

This chapter will focus on the first kind of inductive argument, generalization, as well as two related forms of argument, argument by analogy and argument by application of a general principle. Chapter 8 will focus on the second kind of inductive argument, causal reasoning.

7.2 Generalization

When we generalize, we make a general claim about something based on specific evidence about that something. We often think of **generalization** as a bad thing, and indeed it is when it's based on an insufficient or unrepresentative sample (see Sections 7.2.2 and 7.2.3); stereotyping is usually an example of this kind of unjustified generalization.

But generalization can also be a good thing. It helps us survive. (The cliff, remember?) We generalize a thousand times a day: the sun rose yesterday and the day before and the day before that, so it'll probably rise tomorrow. The chocolate bars I've eaten so far have been very good, so any chocolate bar I eat henceforth will probably be very good. It hurt when I let the match burn down to my fingers, so I probably shouldn't walk into that burning building. And on and on. We generalize from the particular to the general, from the few to the many, from one time to another time, from one place to another place, and so on.

Note that generalizations usually mean simply "in general"; they allow for exceptions. In fact, those that are universal statements (claims about "all" or "none," "always" or "never") are often overgeneralizations (an error, see Section 7.2.1); all it takes to disprove such an overgeneralization is one counterexample. For example, suppose someone was foolish enough to observe a thousand white swans and, on that basis, conclude "All swans are white"—all it would take to disprove that claim, that generalization, is a single black swan.

However, in the face of a counterexample, one need not toss out the generalization altogether. Consider revising the generalization—changing the qualifier from "all" or "none" to "most" or "some," from "always" or "never" to "often" or "sometimes," and so on. To reconsider the preceding example, having found that black swan, one might conclude instead "Most swans are white."

287

7.2a Practice imagining counterexamples

For each of the following generalizations, what claim would constitute a counter-example that would disprove (or weaken) the generalization?

1. As price increases, demand decreases because people will become less able to afford the product.

2. Marriage for homosexuals should not be permitted because they can't have children.

3. Women can't be good soldiers because of their physical size.

4. Abortion is wrong because it is wrong to kill.

5. We are quite justified in banning songs like Ice-T's "Cop Killer"—so many black rap artists glorify killing.

6. There's never been a war between democratic countries.

7. There are no rights without responsibilities.

8. The purpose of business is to make profit.

9. Poverty leads to crime

10. Entrepreneurs should be allowed to keep the millions they make—that's the payoff for taking risks.

There are two important elements of a generalization: *quantities* and *qualities*. For example, when we argue that the sun has risen every day to date, so it will probably rise every day henceforth, we are generalizing from the total number of days up to that point to the total number of days from that point. Because of this numerical, or quantitative, element, generalization is sometimes referred to as induction by enumeration. However, we're also assuming that the days henceforth will be *like* the previous days; we're assuming a similarity, a qualitative similarity, between the previous days and the future days (for if tomorrow is *not* going to be like yesterday in relevant ways, maybe we *can't* conclude that the sun will rise).

Good generalizations are usually based on surveys or experiments (recall our thorough consideration of surveys and experiments, Section 6.4.2): people survey or study a certain number of particulars (people, trees, stars, or whatever) and then, based on what they've observed, make a general claim about all or most of those particulars (all or most people, trees, stars, or whatever). The studied group of particulars is called the **sample**; the total group about which the generalization is made is called the **population**, or sometimes the **target population**.

With regard to the first element—quantities—it's critically important that there are *enough* particulars in the sample group; that is, the sample group should constitute a certain proportion of the whole group. If the sample is too small, you'd have no basis on which to generalize (see Section 7.2.2 regarding the "insufficient sample" error). The larger the sample, proportionally speaking, the stronger the argument (up to a point—see Section 7.2.2).

With regard to the second element—qualities—it's critically important that the particulars in the sample group are *representative* of the particulars in the whole group; that is, they should have the same relevant qualities. Otherwise, you'd have no basis on which to generalize (see Section 7.2.3 regarding the "nonrepresentative sample" error). The greater the relevant similarities and the fewer the relevant dissimilarities, the stronger the argument. Also note that not only should the sample group have the same qualities as the target population, but it should have them in the same proportion. For example, if half of the population to which you're going to generalize is female, then half of your sample group should be female.

There are different ways to obtain a sample group, some of which result in more representative samples than others. A **self-selected sample** is one that includes only people who voluntarily come forward to be part of the sample; that is, they are the only ones who mailed back the questionnaire, for example, or who responded to the advertisement for interview subjects. This kind of sample is unlikely to be representative because often it will include only the more vocal or opinionated among us. Any sample that pays its participants also risks being unrepresentative because it will include only those who have the time and need the money. A **simple random sample** is one in which people are selected at random; for example, one might select every third person from a list or every tenth person who walks by. In this case, everyone has an equal chance of being included. A simple random sample is generally more representative than a self-selected sample. And if the random sample is large enough, it might be sufficiently representative, but perhaps only by luck. So a **stratified random sample** is even better: in this kind of sample, important categories are identified and a random sample of representative size within each category is taken. For example, if 25 percent of your population-as-a-whole is under-15 years of age, and age is important, then if your entire sample will consist of 1,000 people, you make sure that 250 are randomly selected from the under-15 segment. Of course, it's not always clear at the outset which categories are important, but when it is, a stratified random sample is the best choice.

7.2b Practice recognizing generalizations

Which of the following arguments are inductive arguments leading to a generalization? For those that are, identify the quantities and qualities involved.

1. The most recent poll indicates that 77 percent of those surveyed believe that nuclear power plants are unsafe. So I guess the world *isn't* ready for nuclear power after all.

2. According to our survey, most people do not read a lot: only 267 of 3,000 people reported reading more than one book per week.

3. Well, we asked our employees—all 31 of them, actually—and 27 wanted to go on a flextime program. In fact, 20 of them agreed to work 40 hours per week instead of the current 37.5 if it meant they could work those hours according to a schedule they themselves set. So there you have it: almost 90 percent of our employees want flextime.

4. Only the rich pay taxes! The top 50% pay 96.54% of all income taxes; the top 1% pay more than a third, 34.27%.
   (From http://www.rushlimbaugh.com/home/today.guest.html)

5. Based on a survey of 1,000 people aged 30 to 50 in the United States and another 1,000, also aged 30 to 50, in Europe, we can say that middle-aged Americans are incredibly out of shape compared to their European counterparts.

6. Every year I ask my students to fill out a questionnaire in addition to the standard course survey, and though they all complain during the year, at the end, they all say yeah, they could've worked harder. I tell you most students don't deserve the As we're giving out!

7. Given that a lot of men don't really want their girlfriends or wives to be smarter than them or to make more money than them, yeah, I'd say we're still living in a patriarchal society.

8. Every Republican I know believes in individual responsibility, so yes, I'd say that's a fundamental Republican principle.

9. Every morning there's some delay with the subway. I am so sick and tired of just waiting, wasting my time, and of being late! The system really needs an overhaul of some kind—I don't know whether the problem is old equipment, bad maintenance, slow drivers, or poor scheduling, but something's got to be done!

10. In a recent study, we found that daycares staffed by only women seemed to have more stereotyped girls and boys; for example, the girls would play with dolls and the boys would play with guns. However, in daycares staffed with women *and* men, the children seemed less stereotyped; little boys would play with stuffed toys, for example. Whether the staffing is a cause or an effect, that is whether the male staff somehow encourage the boys to be less macho or whether male staff are attracted by daycares with a less polarized clientele, is hard to say. But what we can say is that in general, daycares with male staff have less genderized children than daycares with

mixed staffing, so if we want to reduce sexism, we should hire more male daycare workers.

7.2c More practice with generalizations

1. Describe a survey from which you can make a generalization. Be specific about your method (indicating who, where, when, and how you'd survey— as well as the actual questions you'd ask) and your results (make something up), then clearly state your conclusion (the generalization based on your survey results).

2. Describe an experiment from which you can make a generalization. Be specific about your procedure (indicating exactly what, how, when, and where you'd do to what or who) and your results (make something up), then clearly state your conclusion (the generalization based on the results of your experiment).

7.2.1 Overgeneralization (an error)

Although sometimes we undergeneralize (we conclude more narrowly than we need to), almost all errors of generalization are errors of **overgeneralization** (we conclude more broadly than we should). The overgeneralization can involve three elements: *scope*, in which we conclude that "some" implies "many" or "all," or that "few" implies "none"; *frequency*, in which we conclude that "sometimes" implies "often" or "always," or that "seldom" implies "never"; or *certainty*, in which we conclude that "possibly" implies "probably." Basically, the error involves going beyond the evidence.

That said, when we are reasonably certain that our single case is typical of all such cases, we can safely generalize from one to many. For example, we don't have to eat a thousand olives in order to determine that we don't like olives. One will do. (Or maybe two if we want to be sure the first one we had wasn't odd in some way.)

Here's an example of an overgeneralization:

Everyone gets more conservative as they grow older.

Well, not *everyone*. Consider "The Raging Grannies" (http://www.geocities.com/raginggrannies), one of whom once said "Y'know, we started out aging gracefully but it just got too damn boring!" This is an overgeneralization with respect to scope.

We may make this error because universal claims sound so authoritative: "Tests are ineffective measures of ability" sounds so much more authoritative than "This test didn't measure ability very well." Or perhaps our overgeneralization is just the result of laziness: it's too difficult or too time-consuming to obtain the required evidence, data from a sufficiently large and representative sample, so we end up generalizing from an insufficient or unrepresentative sample, which means we end up overgeneralizing.

Here's another example of an overgeneralization:

I am sure that every time people go to the mall, they get suckered into buying something they don't need.

Assuming there's at least one person who at least one time hasn't been suckered into buying something he or she didn't need, this is an overgeneralization with respect to scope and frequency. Also, given that this is a matter about which absolute certainty is highly unlikely, the "I am sure" makes it an overgeneralization with respect to certainty.

7.2.1a Practice recognizing an overgeneralization

In which of the following is the conclusion an overgeneralization? Where applicable, indicate what would be an acceptable generalization.

1. I read the other day that 90 percent of medical research and development funding goes towards diseases that cause 10 percent of the harm. So all those drug studies and medical experiments—they're completely useless!

2. You never ever support me! No matter what I say or do, you always criticize!!

3. This is the breakdown by sex of the 2004 SAT scores: the average score for females was 504 on the verbal section and 501 on the math section, whereas the average score for males was 512 on the verbal and 537 on the math. And that's out of 1.42 million students. So it's pretty clear that sex accounts for a significant proportion of the difference in scores. The SAT scores certainly support the widely-held opinion that men are better at math than women! Employers and graduate schools are wise to keep this in mind.

4. I swear to tell the truth, the whole truth and nothing but the truth.

5. In the end, virtually all the solutions involve making drivers pay. More realistic fuel prices would make a difference: a gallon of [fuel] costs around $2.50 in California, compared with $5.90 in Britain. There are some subsidies for greener fuels, but there is no enthusiasm for a carbon tax, even though [fuel] taxes produce in real terms about one third of the revenue per vehicle mile that they did in 1970.
    ("America's Great Headache," *The Economist*, no author, June 4, 2005)

7.2.1b More practice with overgeneralizations

Write three arguments that overgeneralize.

7.2.2 Insufficient sample (an error)

As its name reveals, the error of an **insufficient sample** indicates a failure to meet the criterion of sufficiency: the sample is of insufficient size—it's too small to justify your conclusion.

So when is a sample large enough? That depends on the population you're generalizing to. Consequently, the sample size should be thought of as a proportion rather than as an absolute number. The sufficiency of your sample size also depends on your conclusion: a sample consisting of 50 percent of the population you're generalizing about will bear the weight of a broader and more certain conclusion than a sample consisting of 10 percent of the population will. At least, that's true up to a certain point: once your target population is over 25,000, the same margin of error can be achieved with very small increases in sample size (assuming you're using random sampling methods). For example, to achieve a margin of error of 4 percent with a target population of 100,000, you need a sample of 597 people; to achieve the same margin of error with a target population of 1,000,000, a population 10 times as large, you need a sample of 600 people—only three more people, not 10 times as many. (There are statistical charts that researchers refer to in order to figure this out. And, as mentioned in the previous chapter, a sample of 1,200 is generally considered sufficient by social scientists.) Certainly, however, a sample of one—one's personal experience—is insufficient!

Here's an example of an insufficient sample:

> I've just subscribed to one of those DVD-by-mail rental companies and I've received three DVDs to date. All three have had problems playing. Three out of three! I'm going to cancel my subscription.

At first glance, this argument may seem to involve a sufficient sample: after, all three out of three is 100 percent. But the relevant proportion is three out of however many DVDs the company has, which makes the sample considerably less than 100 percent. So it is indeed an insufficient sample on which to base the implied conclusion that all, or even most, of the DVDs that will be coming from that rental company will have playback problems.

7.2.2a Practice recognizing an insufficient sample

Which of the following arguments are based on an insufficient sample? Where applicable, indicate what would be a sufficient sample.

1. Eventually you will have to ask: who is doing the art that's getting censored? Mapplethorpe was gay, Serrano is Hispanic, Scott Tyler is black. The San Diego billboard group is multicultural, promoting a black cause. While this

censorship crisis may be a surprise to many, any multicultural, gay or feminist artist can give you a litany of examples.

(Steven Durland, "Censorship, Multiculturalism, and Symbols," *High Performance*, Fall 1989)

2. *Sue*: If you're having trouble with your knee, you should try this cream! It really works! I tried physio and everything, but the pain just kept coming back. Then I tried this cream, and no pain since!

Dan: She's right! I've got a bad back from a football injury. I use the same thing. It's great!

3. I've asked 500 of the students here and most of them say that credit card companies should not give someone a credit card unless they have paid in full whatever they owe on all previous credit cards, so I'm concluding that that's probably the opinion of most students at this university.

4. In separate aviaries littered with twigs and pocked with holes and crevices, ornithologists [Ben Kenward and his colleagues at the University of Oxford] hand-raised two New Caledonian crow chicks, each in isolation. The young birds spontaneously began to use the twigs to reach into the holes and crevices, and, at the tender ages of sixty-three and seventy-nine days, respectively, they got hold of their first tasty morsels. (Two other chicks, raised together and tutored in the art of twig probing by the investigators, first retrieved food from crevices on days sixty-eight and seventy-two.) On day ninety-nine, one of the isolated birds even shaped its own tool by tearing up a proffered leaf and probing for food with the remaining rib.

If two random New Caledonian crows can, by themselves, acquire expertise in twig usage—and if having companions and regular tutelage doesn't speed up the learning process—it seems safe to assume that most members of the species are naturals with an organic version of the bar that bears their name. The scientists conclude that the crow's brain is well wired for both tool use and toolmaking.

Stephen Reebs, "Crow Bar," *Natural History*, 2005

5. Talking about the characters in Michael Crichton's novel *State of Fear*, reviewer Gregory Mone says "At one point, Sanjong shows Evans a graph revealing a 116-year temperature decline in Punta Arenas, Chile. 'There's your global warming,' he says with irony."

(*Popular Science*, May 2005)

7.2.2b More practice with insufficient samples

Write three arguments based on an insufficient sample.

7.2.3 Unrepresentative sample (an error)

The error of an **unrepresentative sample** indicates a failure to meet the criterion of relevance: an unrepresentative sample is one which does *not* have the relevant features of the population generalized to. For example, when we're talking about people, we need to consider features such as sex, age, class, skin color, health, culture, residence (north/south/east/west, urban/rural, and so on), time period, and so on. So, for example, the proportion of west coast residents in a sample should be the same as the proportion of west coast residents in the target population. We might even have to consider handedness (right- or left-handed)— it really depends on the study: what's relevant?

So how representative is representative enough? As with sample size, that depends on the certainty of your conclusion. The more certain you want to be, the more representative your sample should be. And again, personal experience is generally not representative enough!

Noteworthy examples of unrepresentative samples abound in the medical profession. Many studies have been done using only men as subjects, and since disease often develops in women differently, and therefore generates different symptoms, generalizations based on such studies should have been limited to men—but they weren't; consequently, heart disease, for example, is often undetected in women. Clinical trials are often limited to ill people, and on that basis alone, such trials may be unrepresentative. In addition, the drop-out rate in clinical trials is high because of unpleasant side-effects, and that makes the sample even more unrepresentative: the drop-outs won't be included in the final tallies of results, so you end up with only those who *didn't* experience unpleasant side-effects, so your conclusion that the drug in question has no side-effects will be unjustified. The results of animal studies may or may not be applicable to humans; it depends on what was studied and which animals were used. For example, Vioxx, which is safe and even beneficial to the heart in animals, causes heart attacks and strokes in people.

Photographic evidence is usually induction with an unrepresentative sample. A candidate's campaign photographs show him and his loving wife walking on the beach with their children. They show him late at night reading important books and thinking deeply about the problems of the day. The pictures you see are chosen from dozens taken by professional photographers and media people who arranged settings, chose clothes, and told the candidate how to stand and what to do.

Daniel McDonald and Larry W. Burton, *The Language of Argument*, 1999

7.2.3a Practice recognizing an unrepresentative sample

Which of the following arguments are based on an unrepresentative sample? Where applicable, indicate what would be a representative sample.

1. Based on a study of 500 boys, researchers conclude that violence on television makes children more violent than they would otherwise be.

2. Based on a telephone survey conducted between the hours of 9:00 am and 5:00 pm, Monday to Friday, using residential phone numbers, researchers conclude that most people think the current income tax rates are fair.

3. Researchers plan to study the deposition of fat in rats in order to draw conclusions about humans and the effect of high-fat diets.

295

4. A study conducted simultaneously in California and New York, involving a stratified random sample of people in both states ensuring that age, sex, and class were proportionately represented, led to the conclusion that the American people do not feel superior to European people.

5. I'm a psychiatrist with a large number of teenagers and all of them are troubled. So don't tell me teenagers aren't troubled!

7.2.3b More practice with unrepresentative samples

Write three arguments based on an unrepresentative sample.

7.3 Analogy

An **argument by analogy** involves reasoning from one situation to an analogous, or similar, situation; a conclusion is reached about something on the basis of it being similar to something else. The form of an argument by analogy is, roughly, this: A has/is x, and so B applies; C also has/is x, so B should also apply. For example, an orange is round, and it rolls; this ball is also round, so it should also roll.

The strength of an argument by analogy depends on whether there are sufficient *relevant similarities* and *no relevant dissimilarities*. The more relevant similarities there are, and the fewer relevant dissimilarities, the stronger the argument. For example, roundness is relevant to rolling; since both the orange and the ball are round, they are similar in that relevant feature. Are there any other relevant features? If so, are the orange and ball similar or dissimilar in those regards? The orange is orange, and let's say the ball is red, but color is irrelevant to rolling, so that dissimilarity is okay. But perhaps smoothness of surface is also relevant to rolling, and suppose that the orange is smooth but the ball is rough (perhaps it has a spiked surface). That dissimilarity in relevant feature would make the argument by analogy less strong.

Consider this example, another argument by analogy:

Let me ask you to imagine this. You wake up in the morning and find yourself back to back in bed with an unconscious violinist. A famous unconscious violinist. He has been found to have a fatal kidney ailment, and the Society of Music Lovers has canvassed all the available medical records and found that you alone have the right blood type to help. They have therefore kidnapped you, and last night the violinist's circulatory system was plugged into yours, so that your kidneys can be used to extract poisons from his blood as well as your own. The director of the hospital now tells you, "Look, we're sorry the Society of Music Lovers did this to you—we would never have permitted it if we had known. But still, they did it, and the violinist now is plugged into you. To unplug you would be to kill him. But never mind, it's only for nine months.

By then he will have recovered from his ailment, and can safely be unplugged from you." Is it morally incumbent on you to accede to this situation?

(Judith Jarvis Thomson, "A Defense of Abortion,"
Philosophy & Public Affairs, Fall 1971)

Thomson proposes this thought experiment to make an argument by analogy about the ethics of abortion. Specifically, she is putting to the test the argument that abortion is wrong because the fetus' right to life overrides the pregnant person's right to decide what happens in and to her body. If we answer Thomson's question with a "no," then, by analogy, we are saying there is something wrong with that argument. (Abortion may be morally wrong on other grounds, but not that one.) So we need to determine whether or not the situation she describes is analogous to pregnancy. What features are relevant, and are they the same in the case of the violinist as in the case of a pregnant woman? There are several relevant features: (1) If you unplug the violinist, he will die; if you have an abortion, the fetus will die; (2) Staying plugged will mean your own life is significantly changed, but not in danger; being pregnant usually means the same thing; (3) The state of affairs in both cases will last nine months; (4) The violinist was attached without consent; this would be analogous to pregnancies resulting from failed contraception and rape. If these are the only relevant features, since they are similar, we have a strong argument by analogy. Thus, if we say it's morally okay for the person not to stay plugged to the violinist, we are also saying it is morally okay for a person to have an abortion.

Since an argument by analogy moves from one specific case to another specific case, it is not an argument of generalization (which, you'll recall, moves from a number of specific cases to the general case). However, the strength of both generalizations and analogies depends on the extent of relevant similarities between the initial case or cases and the case about which a conclusion is being drawn.

However, if you think about it, you'll see that an argument by analogy often *depends* on a generalization (Section 7.2) or a general principle (Section 7.4). The argument about the orange and the ball, for example, depends on the missing premise that "All round things roll"—which is a general principle (perhaps based on enumeration, in which case it's a generalization, or perhaps based on other evidence, in which case it's not a generalization). The complete argument would be something like this:

[All round things roll.]
This orange is round.
Therefore, this orange rolls.
This ball is round.
Therefore, this ball should also roll.

If not for that opening premise—that all round things roll—on what basis could you possibly reason from the round orange rolling to the expectation that the round ball would roll? It's the general principle that all round things roll that establishes the relevance of the feature of roundness, and thus enables us to examine the argument for relevant similarities. If it weren't for the case expressed by the principle that all round things roll, we might as justifiably make an argument that since both the orange and the ball are two inches in diameter and the orange rolls, the ball should also roll.

That said, one might wonder why one should even bother with the analogy. Why not just make the argument thus:

> All round things roll.
> ~~This orange is round.~~
> ~~Therefore, this orange rolls.~~
> This ball is round.
> Therefore, this ball should also roll.

Excellent question. Why use the analogy? Isn't it superfluous? Isn't it just an example of the more important principle? Perhaps often it is. Or perhaps it's a substitution for the real argument, made because the real argument isn't understood. Perhaps the underlying principle—that all round things roll, for example—is not recognized as *being* the underlying principle. Or not fully understood—how many of us really understand the physics of shape and motion such that we can assess the acceptability of the premise "All round things roll"? Certainly, however, the real argument is preferable.

An important subset of argument by analogy is the *appeal to precedent*, usually made in the legal context. The form of an appeal to precedent is, roughly, this: since such-and-such a decision was made in a previous case A, the same decision should be made in this case B, because this case B is similar, in all the relevant ways, to that case A. If one's overriding goal is consistency, then the possibility that the argument was incorrectly drawn in the previous case is unimportant; we did whatever in that case, so we should do the same thing in this similar case, case closed. However, if one's overriding goal is justice, then such a possibility is very important. Maybe the first judge sentenced a petty thief to life imprisonment, reasoning that all crime warrants life imprisonment, petty thievery is a crime, so petty thievery warrants life imprisonment. The general principle used in the precedent-setting argument ("All crime warrants life imprisonment") may not be acceptable. In that case, the argument that appeals to that precedent, and thus depends on that unacceptable general principle, is not acceptable.

7.3a Practice identifying arguments by analogy

Which of the following are arguments by analogy? For those that are, identify relevant similarities and dissimilarities.

1. Having an organ transplant is like cannibalism. And cannibalism is wrong. So organ transplants are wrong.

2. Do you realize three out of four Americans now believe in angels? . . . What about goblins? Doesn't anybody believe in goblins?
    (George Carlin, *Napalm & Silly Putty*, 2001)

3. *Pernecsky*: I can't believe my pay was reduced because I was doing personal stuff on company time!
    Santoz: Well, it's like stealing supplies from the storeroom—shouldn't you have to pay for that?

4. It is obviously not justifiable for me to kill another person because it is in my self-interest to do so . . . So why has national self-interest sometimes been flagged up as a reason to go to war?
    (Julian Baggini, *Making Sense: Philosophy behind the Headlines*, 2002)

5. Here in the West, poverty means a bad life. But poverty in the Third World means death.
    (Fareed Zakaria, "The Education of Paul Wolfowitz," *Newsweek*, March 28, 2005)

6. Veterans rightly have legislation to make it easier for them to get a job or an education, but what about all those women who stayed at home and worked in munitions factories and raised those soldiers' children—don't they deserve a similar break?

7. As long as we have capital punishment for people who kill other people, we should apply the same principle to corporations: corporations whose activities kill people, immediately or in the long-term, directly or indirectly (through destroying water and the natural resources needed to produce food) should also be put to death—their corporate existence should be ended, their assets taken and sold at public auction.
    (Inspired by comments of Eliot Spitzer, Attorney General, New York State)

8. Most dogs I've met are friendly unless they have a specific reason not to be, so I think it's safe to say you can approach almost any dog without fear.

9. Anyone who has ever struggled to fix a paper jam in a copier knows that most machines aren't very adaptable. When machines break, they don't release a host of component parts to heal themselves. They remain broken until someone calls tech support. Likewise, with the exception of the virtual machines of software, most technology isn't capable of adaptive self-assembly.
    (Steven Johnson, "Self-Assembling Robots," *Discover*, April 2005)

10. What do you want in a female companion? What is the first thing that attracts you? Her ability to cook and keep house, or the way she looks? It's not politically correct, GM hates it when I draw that analogy. But it's absolutely correct. The initial pull comes from the exterior performance.

    (General Motors Vice Chair Bob Lutz, likening women to an automobile's exterior design at a product seminar in September 2004, according to *Ms. Magazine,* Winter 2004/2005)

7.3b More practice with arguments by analogy

Write your own argument by analogy.

7.3.1 Weak or false analogy (an error)

Recall that an argument by analogy—that is, saying something like "This is/should be the case in X, Y is like X, so it is/should be the case in Y"—is generally a legitimate form of argument *if* the two things being compared are *sufficiently similar* in the *relevant aspects* (relevant to the claim, that is). A **weak analogy** is one in which few of the relevant features are similar; in such a case, your conclusion follows only weakly from your premises (and should therefore be accepted with minimal confidence). A **false analogy** is one in which none of the relevant features are similar, or worse, they're *dis*similar in the relevant aspects; in such a case, you've made a faulty comparison and the argument should be rejected.

So you can be mistaken about one of two things (or both): *you can be mistaken about whether the relevant aspects are indeed sufficiently similar,* and/or *you can be mistaken about what the relevant aspects are.* Actually, recalling the appeal to precedent, there's one more thing you can be mistaken about: whether, in the first place, "This is/should be the case in X."

We often make this error because of a sort of lazy assumption: we assume that if two things are similar in some ways, they're similar in other, relevant, ways.

A noteworthy example of a weak analogy is "Paley's Watch," an argument made to support the existence of God on the basis of intelligent design:

In crossing a heath, suppose I pitched my foot against a stone, and were asked how the stone came to be there; I might possibly answer that for anything I knew to the contrary, it had lain there forever; nor would it perhaps be very easy to show the absurdity of this answer. But suppose I had found a watch upon the ground, and it should be inquired how the watch happened to be in that place . . . The watch must have had a maker because its several parts are framed and put together for a purpose [that being to tell time].

(William Paley, *Natural Theology, or Evidences of the Existence and Attributes of the Deity Collected from the Appearances of Nature,* 1802)

Paley goes on to reason that since the natural world shows not only as much, but more, design toward a purpose, it too must have had a maker. This argument from design for the existence of a creator god is actually, then, an argument by analogy: the watch is to the watchmaker as the natural world is to the creator god.

Is the analogy a strong one? First, *is* the natural world as "framed and put together" as a watch? One can point to several instances that suggest not. For example, the sun's light could be distributed in a more even fashion: parts of the world receive far too much and other parts receive far too little. To focus on Paley's example, the human eye, one need only point out that it's useless unless there's light and even then, it has quite a limited range. Second, *do* the parts of the natural world work together "for some purpose"? One might respond that the purpose of much of the natural world, ourselves included, is not as evident as the purpose of the watch. Furthermore, even if the parts of the natural world *do* fit together, achieving some purpose, is a maker the only explanation possible? Perhaps the parts fit together because those that didn't fit together (didn't adapt to their environment) didn't survive.

Here's an example of an argument by analogy in which the speaker is mistaken about which aspects are relevant:

> *Caks*: I'm going to ask for an extension on the assignment. I'd like until next Monday to hand it in.
>
> *Raudolz*: Yeah, wouldn't we all?
>
> *Caks*: Yeah, but I've been in the hospital for the last three weeks, unable to do any academic work. And since we just got the assignment last week, there was no way I could have done it beforehand, though, actually, even if I had known about it at the beginning of the course, I wouldn't have done it that far in advance . . . after all, I didn't know I'd be in the hospital, let alone for three weeks.
>
> *Raudolz*: Look, everyone else is required to hand in their assignment by Friday. So you should be too. You're a student in this course just like the rest of us.

While Caks' status as a student in the course is relevant, Raudolz seems to be ignoring another relevant aspect: having a reasonable time period in which to complete the assignment. The other students had that, but Caks did not (due to the unforeseen hospitalization); due to this relevant *dis*similarity, Raudolz' analogy between Caks and the other students is weak, and his or her conclusion (that an extension is unwarranted) unjustified.

7.3.1a *Practice recognizing weak or false analogies*

Which of the following arguments contain a weak or false analogy? Where applicable, indicate what would be a more acceptable analogy.

1. Just as a football player does not become great without pain, so too with a pianist. I'll bet every great football player has at one time or another torn muscles, ligaments, or tendons; many have broken something; surely all have come away from practice bruised. So you want to be great? You want to be a concert pianist one day, a virtuoso? Then I want to see you hurt! I want to see you bleed, I want to see sprained or crushed fingers!

2. Did you see Arlen Specter's justification for subsidizing stem cell research on human embryos? The senator from Pennsylvania noted that "there are some 400,000 of these frozen embryos, which were created for in-vitro fertilization, which are going to be thrown away. . . ." So why not put them to good use?

   Listening to the senator brought back the reasoning that German doctors once used to justify their experiments on concentration camp inmates. They were going to die anyway; why just throw them away?
   (Paul Greenberg, "Stem Cell Rhetoric," *am New York,* June 23, 2005)

3. We should license parents. After all, we already license pilots, scuba divers, plumbers, electricians, teachers, veterinarians, cab drivers, soil testers, and television repair people . . . Are our TVs and toilets more important to us than our children?
   (Based on Roger McIntire, "Parenthood Training or Mandatory Birth Control: Take Your Choice," *Psychology Today,* October 1973)

4. Politics is like football. That's why the briefcase that contains the secret codes that launch our nuclear weapons? The one that follows our President everywhere, day and night? It's called the "football." Politics is all about strategy, defense, offense, feints. It's us against them. And of course the only object of the game is winning. Really, nothing else matters. That's why, as your President, I will be as tough, as aggressive, as I can be.

5. [This scenario is intended to be analogous to the development of nuclear power. The Routleys are suggesting that since the scenario described is unjustified, so too is the development of nuclear power.] A long distance country train has just pulled out. The train, which is crowded, carries both passengers and freight. At an early stop in the journey, someone consigns as freight, to a far distant destination, a package which contains a highly toxic and explosive gas. This is packed in a very thin container which, as the consigner is aware, may well not contain the gas for the full distance for which it is consigned, and certainly will not do so if the train should strike any real trouble, for example, if the train should be derailed or involved in a collision, or if some passenger should interfere inadvertently or deliberately with the freight, perhaps trying to steal some of it. All of these sorts of things have happened on some previous journeys. If the container should break, the resulting disaster would probably kill at least some of the people on the train

in adjacent carriages, while others could be maimed or poisoned or sooner or later incur serious diseases. Most of us would roundly condemn such an action. What might the consigner of the parcel say to try to justify it?

(Richard and Val Routley (also known as Richard Sylvan and Val Plumwood), "Nuclear Power—Some Ethical and Social Dimensions," in Tom Regan and Donald Van De Veer, eds., *And Justice for All: New Introductory Essays in Ethics and Public Policy*, 1982)

7.3.1b More practice with weak or false analogies

Write three arguments based on a weak or false analogy.

7.4 General principle

An **argument by application of a general principle** involves reasoning from a general principle to a particular instance of that general principle. The form of this kind of argument is, roughly, this: all A are subject to X; B is an A; so B is subject to X. For those of you who worked through the categorical logic supplement, you'll recognize this argument as a valid categorical syllogism. Often, however, instead of being a strict universal claim ("All A are subject to X"), the general principle involved is something more like "Most A are subject to X" or "In general, A are subject to X" or "Each A is probably subject to X."

Despite the clear relation to deductive argument, we're discussing this kind of argument here, in a chapter dealing with inductive argument, for two reasons. First, in a way, this kind of argument is a reverse generalization: it moves from the general to the particular rather than from the particular to the general. Second, as in the case of arguments by analogy, it is critical that relevant qualities or features be present.

Here's an example of an argument involving the application of a general principle:

Emergency vehicles always have the right of way. They trump traffic lights, stop signs, and general rules of the road. So if an ambulance is coming toward you at an intersection, you should pull over immediately (if it's safe) or at least stop where you are (again, if it's safe), even if the signal is green.

The argument, in standard form, is this:

1. Emergency vehicles have the right of way.
2. An ambulance is an emergency vehicle.

Therefore, you should stop to give way to an ambulance at an intersection even though you have the green light.

303

The general principle is expressed in the first premise: emergency vehicles have the right of way. That principle is then applied to the particular instance of an ambulance coming toward you at an intersection, in order to reach the conclusion that you should pull over or stop rather than proceed through the intersection.

The strength of an argument by application of a general principle depends on two things: the acceptability of the general principle and the extent to which the particular instance *is* an instance of that general principle. So with reference to the preceding example, one evaluates the argument by, first, evaluating the general principle: should emergency vehicles have the right of way? Then, one evaluates the extent to which the particular instance is an instance of that general principle: is an ambulance an emergency vehicle, and is your ceasing to proceed through the intersection giving the emergency vehicle the right of way?

7.4a Practice identifying arguments by application of a general principle

Which of the following arguments involve the application of a general principle? For those that do, identify the general principle and the particular instance to which it is being applied.

1. *Rogail*: Of course the government is justified in forcing a blood transfusion for a child whose parents have refused permission. Hell, they should take the kid away from such parents. After all, they're looking out for the best interests of the child!

   Santana: Yeah, but the parents will argue that that's exactly what *they're* doing! It's just that their conception of the interests of the child go beyond life here on Earth. If the child has a transfusion, their child will be denied the possibility of eternal life. If that's not looking out for their interests, I don't know what is!

2. *Doleske*: It's not just what ads say that bothers me—it's what they don't say. Don't you remember that awful Nestlé infant formula thing? Mothers in developing countries mixed it with polluted water since that's all they had, and since they couldn't afford very much of the formula, they diluted it, so a lot of babies died of malnutrition and disease.

   Barlow: There's no way they can blame that on Nestlé! The formula itself was okay. Nestlé can't be held responsible for polluted water! Or for their decision to dilute it! Besides, caveat emptor! Let the buyer beware!

3. *Huerjo*: If you have a choice between letting several people die and killing just one in order that those several will live, I do think the one should be killed. It would be nice, of course, if that one person gave consent, but even if not . . . I know it sounds wrong, but trust me, it's really the most moral course of action.

Jortas: So what's stopping you? Walk in to the nearest hospital and donate your body. You'll save several lives, what with your heart, lungs, liver, kidney . . .

4. *Ruffo*: You are responsible for your own behavior.
   Bok: Yeah, which is why whenever my supervisor tells me he's responsible for what I do, I tell him to shove it.

5. Studies show that most people who become sick, with a cold, or the flu, or even with AIDS, are more concerned about their being sick than about the possibility of passing it on to others. We are indeed a self-centered society.

6. My body, my choice, you say? Okay, then, I most certainly have a say in whether or not you have an abortion! That's my sperm in there!

7. *Bouraoui*: Police and juries often consider those who beat to death homosexual men to be acting in justified self-defense. Their actions are an understandably panicked response to an unwelcome sexual overture.
   Chevalier: So, women can now just go ahead and kill any man who makes an unwelcome sexual advance toward them? Great!

8. I really get pissed off with all those celebrities who shove their way through reporters and put their hands in front of the cameras. I mean, the public has a right to know!

9. We don't know what will happen if we go ahead with genetic engineering, and it might be horrible, so we shouldn't go there. Look at Oppenheimer and all those so-called brilliant scientists who invented the atom bomb: they were so blinded by the science, by a problem that is so "technically sweet," isn't that the phrase they used? They didn't consider the morality! Only *after* they developed and exploded the thing did they think, oh dear, maybe we shouldn't have done that.

10. People who don't contribute to the office birthday fund shouldn't expect a birthday present. It's that simple. We keep a list of people's birthdays, and we keep a list of contributions, which are collected once a month, so we know who's who.

7.4b More practice with arguments by application of a general principle

Write your own argument involving the application of a general principle.

7.4.1 Misapplied general principle (an error)

This error, a **misapplied general principle**, involves applying a general principle to a particular instance in which the principle doesn't apply. Perhaps the most common misapplication is applying the principle too broadly. The general principle or rule is not applicable because of the absence or presence of certain critical qualities which disqualify or make the particular instance an exception to the rule.

Here's an example of a misapplied general principle:

> Well, I think it's stupid, but I can see why your TA suggested you go see someone. Didn't you see the latest campus newspaper? The new Director of Student Services has apparently managed to have this directive passed in Senate: Any student who seems to be experiencing distress should be referred to Student Services for counseling. And you *were* upset about your grade.

Presumably, the Director meant distress a little more serious than being upset about a grade; if so, then the general principle has been applied too broadly.

We tend to make this mistake when we don't carefully consider or understand either the principle we're applying or the instance we're applying it to.

7.4.1a *Practice recognizing misapplied general principles*

Which of the following arguments contain a misapplied general principle? Where applicable, re-craft the argument so it is error-free.

1. Emergency vehicles have the right of way, so if a car is coming at you at an intersection, and it's speeding and it's out of control, you should pull over, get out of its way!

2. From each according to his or her ability, to each according to his or her need. That's why we're justified in taxing those with high incomes more than those with low incomes, and then using that money to provide social programs for the latter.

3. The death penalty is awful to carry out and awful to watch, so we should abolish it.

4. Merely challenging any one of your precious opinions disturbs your peace—are you going to arrest everyone who dares to disagree with you?

5. It says right here in the course info: "Students are not allowed to obtain any assistance for any assignments; doing so will be considered cheating and a grade of zero will be given." If I can't get help from a tutor with my homework, I won't be able to pass!

7.4.1b More practice with misapplied general principles

Write three arguments based on a misapplied general principle. Where applicable, rewrite your arguments so they're error-free.

7.4.1c Practice recognizing errors of generalization, analogy, and application of a general principle

Which of the following arguments involve one or more of the following errors? Where applicable, re-craft the argument so it is error-free.

- overgeneralization
- insufficient sample
- unrepresentative sample
- weak or false analogy
- misapplied general principle.

1. I called the local vet to inquire about the risk of spaying adult cats and dogs (as opposed to spaying them at six months of age, the traditionally recommended age) and was told she'd performed five adult cat and dog spays that month and there had been no complications with any of them. I concluded that there was no risk involved in spaying adult cats and dogs.

2. We traveled to every single national dance competition and interviewed a random sample of the competitors at each one (we simply chose every fifth name on the registration lists). We can say with a reasonable degree of confidence that most advanced competitive dancers believe dance is "far more difficult" than other physical activities (including the most popular ten sports).

3. I have never yet seen her play her best in a play-off; in practice, yes, and in games throughout the season, yes. But in a play-off? No. She will undoubtedly never be her best when it really counts.

4. So, if abortion is seriously wrong because it kills a potential person, then the use of a contraceptive is equally seriously wrong. In using a spermicide, one commits mass murder! Indeed, even abstinence is wrong, insofar as it prevents the development of a new human being.

   (Bonnie Steinbock, *Life Before Birth: The Moral and Legal Status of Embryos and Fetuses*, 1992)

5. Students left a pile of surveys about library hours at the library's check-out counter beside a box for completed surveys. After one week, they emptied the box, tallied the results, and concluded that most students were happy with the library's current hours.

6. 80 percent of our subscribers responded to our survey, and 70 percent of that 80 percent said they were happy with the magazine just as it is. So I can say with absolute certainty that most of our subscribing readers are happy indeed with our magazine.

7. When medical resources are limited, one should attend first to those in the most critical condition. McDuff's injuries are the most serious, so I'll treat him first.

8. The township council says that residents must submit a plan and obtain the approval of a building inspector prior to undertaking any home improvements. That's a ridiculous lot of trouble just to repaint the house!

9. Consider a language you don't understand. In my case, I do not understand Chinese. To me Chinese writing looks like so many meaningless squiggles. Now suppose I am placed in a room containing baskets full of Chinese symbols. Suppose also that I am given a rule book in English for matching Chinese symbols with other Chinese symbols. The rules identify the symbols entirely by their shapes and do not require that I understand any of them. The rules might say such things as, "Take a squiggle-squiggle sign from basket number one and put it next to a squoggle-squoggle sign from basket number two."

   Imagine that people outside the room who understand Chinese hand in small bunches of symbols and that in response I manipulate the symbols according to the rule book and hand back more small bunches of symbols. Now, the rule book is the "computer program." The people who wrote it are "programmers," and I am the "computer." The baskets full of symbols are the "data base," the small bunches that are handed in to me are "questions" and the bunches I then hand out are "answers."

   Now suppose that the rule book is written in such a way that my "answers" to the "questions" are indistinguishable from those of a native Chinese speaker. For example, the people outside might hand me some symbols that unknown to me mean, "What's your favorite color?" and I might after going through the rules give back symbols that, also unknown to me, mean, "My favorite is blue, but I also like green a lot." I satisfy the Turing test for understanding Chinese. All the same, I am totally ignorant of Chinese. And there is no way I could come to understand Chinese in the system as described, since there is no way that I can learn the meanings of any of the symbols. Like a computer, I manipulate symbols, but I attach no meaning to the symbols.

   . . . if I do not understand Chinese solely on the basis of running a computer program for understanding Chinese, then neither does any other digital computer solely on that basis . . . A program merely manipulates symbols, whereas a brain attaches meaning to them.

   (John R. Searle, "Is the Brain's Mind a Computer Program?" *Scientific American*, 262.1, 1990)

10. "Suppose that there be a machine, the structure of which produces thinking, feeling, and perceiving; imagine this machine enlarged but preserving the same proportions, so that you could enter it as if it were a mill. This being supposed, you might visit its inside; but what would you observe there? Nothing but parts which push and move each other, and never anything that could explain perception." Therefore, Leibniz concludes, the mind is more than the brain; thinking, feeling, and perceiving cannot be explained by mechanism, by mere parts and movements of parts.

(Gottfried Wilhelm von Leibniz, *Monadology,* 1714, trans. Paul Schrecher and Anne Martin Schrecher, 1965)

Review of terms

Define the following terms:

- sufficiency

- generalization

- sample

- target population

- self-selected sample

- simple random sample

- stratified random sample

- argument by analogy

- argument by application of a general principle

- overgeneralization

- insufficient sample

- unrepresentative sample

- weak analogy

- false analogy

- misapplied general principle.

Thinking critically about what you see

Think critically about each of the following. Consider, especially, the role of generalizations, analogies, and general principles.

1.

No gang colors allowed

No gang colors allowed

No gang colors allowed

2.

Bipedal robot created by Shadow Robot Company, London. Image copyright: Siobhan Hapaska. Courtesy of Kerlin Gallery.

Thinking critically about what you hear

Listen to the audio clip under the Student Resources tab on the companion website at www.routledge.com/textbooks/tittle. Any response?

Thinking critically about what you read

Think critically about each of the following, paying special attention to sufficiency, whether the argument involves a generalization, an analogy, or a general principle.

You may want to consult the template to be sure you're applying all of the skills you've acquired to this point.

1. Changizi and Shimojo studied more than a hundred writing systems, and what

Template for critical analysis

1. What's the point (claim/opinion/conclusion)?

   ■ Look for subconclusions as well.

2. What are the reasons/what is the evidence?

   ■ Articulate all unstated premises.
   ■ Articulate connections.

3. What exactly is meant by . . .?

   ■ Define terms.
   ■ Clarify all imprecise language.
   ■ Eliminate or replace "loaded" language and other manipulations.

4. Assess the reasoning/evidence:

   ■ If deductive, check for truth/acceptability and validity.
   ■ If inductive, check for truth/acceptability, relevance, and sufficiency.

5. How could the argument be strengthened?

   ■ Provide additional reasons/evidence.
   ■ Anticipate objections—are there adequate responses?

6. How could the argument be weakened?

   ■ Consider and assess counterexamples, counterevidence, and counter-arguments.
   ■ Should the argument be modified or rejected because of the counter-arguments?

7. If you suspend judgment (rather than accepting or rejecting the argument), identify further information required.

emerged was a consistent economy of expression. Each character, on average, is made up of three strokes, no matter how many characters occur in the writing system. Such economy might be explained by earlier findings that people can store roughly three objects at a time in visual short-term memory.

(T.J. Kelleher, "Kindred Strokes for Different Folks," *Natural History*, April 2005)

2. Everything Christians possess of time, money, and resources is given to them by God as a stewardship for which they will give an account before a holy God. Many entertainment providers including, but not limited to, the Disney Company are increasingly promoting immoral ideologies such as homosexuality, infidelity, and adultery, which are biblically reprehensible and abhorrent to God and His plan for the world that He loves. We realize that we cannot do everything to stop the moral decline in our nation, but we must do what lies before us when it is right through a proper use of our influence, energies, and prayers, particularly when it affects our nation's children. Therefore . . . every southern Baptist should refrain from patronizing the Disney Company and any of its related entities.

(Based on resolution presented at Southern Baptist Convention, as printed in Daniel McDonald and Larry W. Burton, *The Language of Argument*, 9th edn., 1999)

3. So, um, why is it *exactly* that I should be afraid of black people?

I look around at the world I live in—and, folks, I hate to tell tales out of school, but it's not the African-Americans who have made this planet such a pitiful, scary place to inhabit. . . .

No, my friends, it's *always* the white guy. Let's go to the tote board:

- Who gave us the black plague? A white guy.
- Who invented PBC, PVC, PBB, and a host of chemicals that are killing us? White guys.
- Who has started every war America has been in? White men.
- Who is responsible for the programming on FOX? White men.
- Who invented the punch card ballot? A white man.
- Whose idea was it to pollute the world with the internal combustion engine? Whitey, that's who.
- The Holocaust? That guy *really* gave white people a bad name (that's why we prefer to call him a Nazi and his little helpers Germans).
- The genocide of Native Americans? White man.
- Slavery? Whitey!
- So far in 2001, American companies have laid off over 700,000 people. Who ordered the layoffs? White CEOs.
- Who keeps bumping me off the Internet? Some friggin' white guy, and if I find him, he's a dead white guy.

You name the problem, the disease, the human suffering, or the abject misery visited upon millions, and I'll bet you ten bucks I can put a white face on it faster than you can name the members of 'N Sync.

And yet when I turn on the news each night, what do I see again and again? *Black* men alleged to be killing, raping, mugging, stabbing, gangbanging, looting, rioting, selling drugs, pimping, ho-ing, having too many babies, dropping babies from tenement windows, fatherless, motherless, Godless, penniless. "The suspect is described as a black male . . . the suspect is described as a black male . . . THE SUSPECT IS DESCRIBED AS A BLACK MALE. . . ."

(Michael Moore, *Stupid White Men*, 2001)

4. Before He created the world He foresaw all the pain and misery that it would contain; He is therefore responsible for all of it . . . If I were going to beget a child knowing that the child was going to be a homicidal maniac, I should be responsible for his crimes.

(Bertrand Russell, *Why I Am Not a Christian*, 1957)

5. The question of what entails "economic activity" revolves around the question of value. It is said that obvious exclusions from such activity are goods and services on which no one could put a market price because their values are spiritual, psychological, social, or political. It is then argued that women's role as socializers, as articulators of class and gender ideology, and as (too often the easy) collaborators in reproducing the conditions of their own subordination, has no value. Yet non-profit organizations such as churches and clubs are included as productive services in the national accounts; so are therapists and voluntary agencies where the cost of production is met by members and benefactors. Agents of social reproduction—teachers, crime prevention officers, health workers—are included, as are political campaigners, and government administrative services on the grounds that the services have an economic price in terms of the cost of labor, capital, and materials to produce them. An infant born through the new "test-tube" technology or womb implant, or a child raised in an institution, is considered "products." Those who bring the fetus to term in the laboratory, or who care for the child in the orphanage or juvenile facility are seen as workers. They are economically active. But a mother, daily engaged unpaid in these activities, is "just a housewife."

(Marilyn Waring, *If Women Counted: A New Feminist Economics*, 1988)

6. Men consume pornography because they find that entering its fantasy world is enjoyable, not because it is sexually arousing to perpetuate discredited theories about the nature of women. Similarly, the massive consumption of romance novels by women is motivated by the enjoyment of contemplating a fantasy world in which everlasting loves are more plentiful than they happen to be; these novels hardly depict men as they are, yet they are not defamatory. The key here is that to engage in pretense is not to disseminate lies. Pornography is understood better by analogy with playing cops and robbers, than by analogy with a piece of journalism.

(Alan Soble, "Pornography: Defamation and the Endorsement of Degradation," *Social Theory and Practice*, Spring 1985)

7. [This scenario is presented by Hardin as a metaphor for the framework within which we must work out solutions to the problems of overpopulation and hunger: each lifeboat is a rich nation full of comparatively rich people, and in the ocean swim the poor of the world, having fallen out of their more crowded lifeboats.] Here we sit, say 50 people in a lifeboat. To be generous, let us assume our boat has a capacity of 10 more, making 60. . . .

The 50 of us in the lifeboat see 100 others swimming in the water outside, asking for admission to the boat, or for handouts. How shall we respond to their calls? There are several possibilities.

One. We may be tempted to try to live by the Christian ideal of being "our brother's keeper," or by the Marxian ideal (Marx 1875) of "from each according to his abilities, to each according to his needs." Since the needs of all are the same, we take all the needy into our boat, making a total of 150 in a boat with a capacity of 60. The boat is swamped, and everyone drowns. Complete justice, complete catastrophe.

Two. Since the boat has an unused excess capacity of 10, we admit just 10 more to it. This has the disadvantage of getting rid of the safety factor [a new plant disease or a bad change in the weather may decimate our population if we don't preserve some excess capacity as a safety factor], for which action we will sooner or later pay dearly. Moreover, *which* 10 do we let in? 'First come, first served?' The best 10? The neediest 10? How do we *discriminate*? And what do we say to the 90 who are excluded?

Three. Admit no more to the boat and preserve the small safety factor. Survival of the people in the lifeboat is then possible (though we shall have to be on our guard against boarding parties).

(Garrett Hardin, "Living on a Lifeboat," *BioScience*, October 1974)

8. The "bad blood" theory of crime has held appeal for both the public and experts alike. What could be more logical than "like father, like son," or "like mother, like daughter"? Criminal traits *must* be genetic since so many criminals have relatives who are also criminals, according to this thinking. The biological origins of crime were sometimes attributed to flawed genes, physiological body deficiencies, or other inherited defects. It was frequently argued that particular ethnic groups and/or races had a "predominance" of such criminogenic traits.

(Richard C. Monk, *Taking Sides: Clashing Views on
Controversial Issues in Crime and Criminology*, 1989)

9. [L]et us consider this pair of cases:

In the first, Smith stands to gain a large inheritance if anything should happen to his six-year-old cousin. One evening while the child is taking his bath, Smith sneaks into the bathroom and drowns the child, and then arranges things so that it will look like an accident.

In the second, Jones also stands to gain if anything should happen to his six-year-old cousin. Like Smith, Jones sneaks in planning to drown the child in his bath.

315

However, just as he enters the bathroom Jones sees the child slip and hit his head, and fall face down in the water. Jones is delighted; he stands by, ready to push the child's head back under if it is necessary, but it is not necessary. With only a little thrashing about, the child drowns all by himself, "accidentally," as Jones watches and does nothing.

Now Smith killed the child, whereas Jones "merely" let the child die. That is the only difference between them. Did either man behave better, from a moral point of view? If the difference between killing and letting die were in itself a morally important matter, one should say that Jones's behavior was less reprehensible than Smith's. But does one really want to say that? I think not. In the first place, both men acted from the same motive, personal gain, and both had exactly the same end in view when they acted. It may be inferred from Smith's conduct that he is a bad man, although the judgment may be withdrawn or modified if certain further facts are learned about him—for example, that he is mentally deranged. But would not the very same thing be inferred about Jones from his conduct? And would not the same further considerations also be relevant to any modification of this judgment? Moreover, suppose Jones pleaded, in his own defense, "After all, I didn't do anything except just stand there and watch the child drown. I didn't kill him; I only let him die." Again, if letting die were in itself less bad than killing, this defense should have at least some weight. But it does not. Such a "defense" can only be regarded as a grotesque perversion of moral reasoning. Morally speaking, it is no defense at all.

(James Rachels, "Active and Passive Euthanasia,"
New England Journal of Medicine, January 9, 1975)

10. I have said that the difference between animals like deer—or pigs and chickens, for that matter—whom we ought not to think of "harvesting," and crops like corn, which we may harvest, is that the animals are capable of feeling pleasure and pain, while the plants are not. At this point someone is bound to ask: "How do we know that plants do not suffer?"

This objection may arise from a genuine concern for plants; but more often those raising it do not seriously contemplate extending consideration to plants if it should be shown that they suffer; instead they hope to show that if we were to act on the principle I have advocated we would have to stop eating plants as well as animals, and so would starve to death. The conclusion they draw is that if it is impossible to live without violating the principle of equal consideration, we need not bother about it at all, but may go on as we have always done, eating plants and animals.

The objection is weak in both fact and logic. There is no reliable evidence that plants are capable of feeling pleasure or pain. Some years ago a popular book, *The Secret Life of Plants*, claimed that plants have all sorts of remarkable abilities, including the ability to read people's minds. The most striking experiments cited in the book were not carried out at serious research institutions, and attempts by researchers in major universities to repeat the experiments have failed to obtain any positive results. The book's claims have now been completely discredited (*Natural History* 83.3, p. 18).

In the first chapter of this book I gave three distinct grounds for believing that nonhuman animals can feel pain: behavior, the nature of their nervous systems, and the evolutionary usefulness of pain. None of these gives us any reason to believe that plants feel pain. In the absence of scientifically credible experimental findings, there is no observable behavior that suggests pain; nothing resembling a central nervous system has been found in plants; and it is difficult to imagine why species that are incapable of moving away from a source of pain or using the perception of pain to avoid death in any other way should have evolved the capacity to feel pain. Therefore the belief that plants feel pain appears to be quite unjustified.

So much for the factual basis of this objection. Now let us consider its logic. Assume that, improbable as it seems, researchers do turn up evidence suggesting that plants feel pain. It would still not follow that we may as well eat what we have always eaten. If we must inflict pain or starve, we would then have to choose the lesser evil. Presumably it would still be true that plants suffer less than animals, and therefore it would still be better to eat plants than to eat animals. Indeed this conclusion would follow even if plants were as sensitive as animals, since the inefficiency of meat production means that those who eat meat are responsible for the indirect destruction of at least ten times as many plants as are vegetarians! At this point, I admit, the argument becomes farcical, and I have pursued it this far only to show that those who raise this objection but fail to follow out its implications are really just looking for an excuse to go on eating meat.

(Peter Singer, *Animal Liberation*, 1975)

Thinking critically about what you write

Construct an argument outline more complex than any you've done so far and write it into two or three clear and coherent paragraphs. Make sure you articulate all your assumptions. And be careful to articulate every step.

Then construct a counterargument and write it up, also in two or three clear and coherent paragraphs. This might involve the presentation of counterevidence and/or counterexamples.

Join the two—change or add an introductory paragraph, add a paragraph linking the two, and write some sort of concluding paragraph. Your concluding paragraph should indicate whether you think your original argument stands—as is or in a modified form (if the latter, indicate how you would revise your argument). All told, you should have a paper of about 1,000 words.

© ScienceCartoonsPlus.com

"I THINK YOU SHOULD BE MORE EXPLICIT HERE IN STEP TWO."

Thinking critically when you discuss

Okay, ready to try a group of five people? This is about the maximum number of participants I'd recommend for an informal, but fruitful, discussion. Anything more than five and people usually resort to formal rules of proceeding as in debates or meetings, which, paradoxically, tend to stifle rather than foster genuine discussion.*

I can very easily imagine a state legislator screaming at a student "Who the hell sent you here?!" after committing five fallacies in three minutes and being called on each one. This would no doubt occur just as they are discussing funding for our university . . .

A professor reviewing this text at an early stage

---

*Speaking of which, it would be interesting, and valuable, to use your newly developed critical skills in such contexts. Why not attend a political debate, an ethics committee meeting at a local hospital, a council meeting of some governmental sort, a committee meeting at your university, a board meeting of some company, and so on. And just do what you've been doing when you have these discussions: listen very carefully to what's said, think about it, then respond.

No doubt people, especially those in power, will be, um, disconcerted to be told by a student that what they've just said is a non sequitur or a red herring, or that all they've done for the past half hour is make claim after claim with not one bit of evidence or line of reasoning to support any of it—but hey, *someone* has to tell them!

If you do decide to do this, and if you identify yourself as a student participating in some sort of course assignment, keep in mind that, like it or not, you are sort of an ambassador for the course, the value of critical thinking, your professor, and your university, so, a word about diplomacy: people often resent other people correcting them, especially when the person correcting them is younger than them or less experienced, and when you point out a weakness in someone's argument, or even the absence of an argument, you'll be correcting them. So think ahead and figure out how you want to introduce your commentary. "Ya bunch of coneheads" is not advisable.

Proceed in a very orderly fashion this time: someone start the discussion with a argument, then each person take a turn responding to that argument. Then loosen up a bit and deal with responses to the responses . . .

Suggestion: Remember not to respond to the conclusion, whether with agreement or disagreement or with evaluation. *Respond to the premises*—they, and only they, will indicate whether or not you should accept the conclusion. (If you just respond to the conclusion, you're ignoring the argument; you're responding as if the person merely asserted a claim *without any supporting line of reasoning*.)

Reasoning test questions

1. *Astronomer*: Astronomical observatories in many areas have become useless because light from nearby cities obscures the stars. Many people argue that since streetlights are needed for safety, such interference from lights is inevitable. Here in Sandsville, however, the local observatory's view remains relatively clear, since the city has restricted unnecessary lighting and installed special street lamps that direct all their light downward. It is therefore possible to have both well-lighted streets and relatively dark skies.

    The astronomer's argument proceeds by:

    (A) appealing to a scientific authority to challenge a widely held belief
    (B) questioning the accuracy of evidence given in support of the opposing position
    (C) proposing an alternative scientific explanation for a natural phenomenon
    (D) making a distinction between terms
    (E) offering a counterexample to a general claim

    (The Official LSAT Prep Test XXII, Section 2, #11)

2. The authors of a recent article examined warnings of an impending wave of extinctions of animal species within the next 100 years. These authors say that no evidence exists to support the idea that the rate of extinction of animal species is now accelerating.

    They are wrong, however. Consider only the data on fishes: 40 species and subspecies of North American fishes have vanished in the twentieth century, 13 between 1900 and 1950, and 27 since 1950.

    The answer to which one of the following questions would contribute most to an evaluation of the argument?

    (A) Were the fish species and subspecies that became extinct unrepresentative of animal species in general with regard to their pattern of extinction?
    (B) How numerous were the populations in 1950 of the species and subspecies of North American fishes that have become extinct since 1950?

319

(C) Did any of the species or subspecies of North American fishes that became extinct in the twentieth century originate in regions outside of North America?

(D) What proportion of North American fish species and subspecies whose populations were endangered in 1950 are now thriving?

(E) Were any of the species or subspecies of North American fishes that became extinct in the twentieth century commercially important?

(The Official LSAT Prep Test XXIV, Section 2, #16)

3. Advertisement: Anyone who thinks moisturizers are not important for beautiful skin should consider what happens to the earth, the skin of the world, in times of drought.

Without regular infusions of moisture, the ground becomes lined and cracked and its lush loveliness fades away. Thus your skin, too, should be protected from the ravages caused by lack of moisture; give it the protection provided by regular infusions of Dewyfresh, the drought-defying moisturizer.

The Dewyfresh advertisement exhibits which one of the following errors of reasoning?

(A) It treats something that is necessary for bringing about a state of affairs as something that is sufficient to bring about that state of affairs.

(B) It treats the fact that two things regularly occur together as proof that there is a single thing that is the cause of them both.

(C) It overlooks the fact that changing what people think is the case does not necessarily change what is the case.

(D) It relies on the ambiguity of the term "infusion," which can designate either a process or the product of that process.

(E) It relies on an analogy between two things that are insufficiently alike in the respects in which they would have to be alike for the conclusion to be supported.

(The Official LSAT Prep Test XXIV, Section 3, #2)

4. Currently, the city of Grimchester is liable for any injury incurred because of a city sidewalk in need of repair or maintenance. However, Grimchester's sidewalks are so extensive that it is impossible to hire enough employees to locate and eliminate every potential danger in its sidewalks. Governments should be liable for injuries incurred on public property only if they knew about the danger beforehand and negligently failed to eliminate it.

Which one of the following describes an injury for which the city of Grimchester is now liable, but should not be according to the principle cited above?

(A) A person is injured after tripping on a badly uneven city sidewalk, and the city administration had been repeatedly informed of the need to repair the sidewalk for several years.

(B) A person is injured after tripping over a shopping bag that someone had left lying in the middle of the sidewalk.

(C) A person is injured after stepping in a large hole in a city sidewalk, and the city administration had first learned of the need to repair that sidewalk minutes before.

(D) A person who is heavily intoxicated is injured after falling on a perfectly even city sidewalk with no visible defects.

(E) A person riding a bicycle on a city sidewalk is injured after swerving to avoid a pedestrian who had walked in front of the bicycle without looking.

(The Official LSAT Prep Test XXII, Section 4, #4)

5. *Consumer advocate:* One advertisement that is deceptive, and thus morally wrong, states that "gram for gram, the refined sugar used in our chocolate pies is no more fattening than the sugars found in fruit and vegetables." This is like trying to persuade someone that chocolate pies are not fattening by saying that, calorie for calorie, they are no more fattening than celery. True, but it would take a whole shopping cart full of celery to equal a chocolate pie's worth of calories.
Advertiser: This advertisement cannot be called deceptive. It is, after all, true.

Which one of the following principles, if established, would do most to support the consumer advocate's position against the advertiser's response?

(A) It is morally wrong to seek to persuade by use of deceptive statements.

(B) A true statement should be regarded as deceptive only if the person making the statement believes it to be false, and thus intends the people reading or hearing it to acquire a false belief.

(C) To make statements that impart only a small proportion of the information in one's possession should not necessarily be regarded as deceptive.

(D) It is morally wrong to make a true statement in a manner that will deceive hearers or readers of the statement into believing that it is false.

(E) A true statement should be regarded as deceptive if it is made with the expectation that people hearing or reading the statement will draw a false conclusion from it.

(The Official LSAT Prep Test XXI, Section 2, #16)

chapter 8

inductive argument: causal reasoning

Template for critical analysis of arguments

1. What's the point (claim/opinion/conclusion)?

   ■ Look for subconclusions as well.

2. What are the reasons/what is the evidence?

   ■ Articulate all unstated premises.
   ■ Articulate connections.

3. What exactly is meant by . . .?

   ■ Define terms.
   ■ Clarify all imprecise language.
   ■ Eliminate or replace "loaded" language and other manipulations.

4. **Assess the reasoning/evidence:**

   ■ If deductive, check for truth/acceptability and validity.
   ■ **If inductive, check for** truth/acceptability, relevance, and **sufficiency.**

5. How could the argument be strengthened?

   ■ Provide additional reasons/evidence.
   ■ Anticipate objections—are there adequate responses?

6. How could the argument be weakened?

   ■ Consider and assess counterexamples, counterevidence, and counter-arguments.
   ■ Should the argument be modified or rejected because of the counter-arguments?

7. If you suspend judgment (rather than accepting or rejecting the argument), identify further information required.

8.1 Causation

Causal reasoning involves determining which of several possible explanations is the best account for a given phenomenon or occurrence. The issue can involve causation of a natural sciences kind (for example, biological, chemical, or physical causation) or causation of a social sciences kind (for example, social or psychological causation). Causation of the first kind is easier to establish because, at least in theory, all is measurable; it may be incredibly complicated, intricate, and far-reaching, but even so, we can measure the elements involved (the presence of a certain chemical, for example). Because it involves whole human beings, the second kind of causation is more difficult to establish. Perhaps as we learn more about the brain and our genetic code, we may find, as behaviorists have said all along, that we are as transparent as our component elements and as easy to measure. In the meantime, we have to contend with messy but intriguing notions such as free will, agency, and the like.

Establishing cause is important for several reasons. First, it enables us to establish *explanations*, which will be dealt with in the next section (Section 8.2). Second, it enables us to make *predictions*, and thus assess various *plans and policies* about all sorts of things. If our causal explanations are correct, our predictions will become true or our plans and policies will achieve their goals. We'll consider predictions, plans, and policies in the subsequent section (8.3). Establishing cause can also enable us to *control* whatever it is we're talking about, and thus bring about desired ends, possibly through plans and policies, but also more certainly through direct action. Lastly, establishing cause enables us to correctly and thus fairly assign *responsibility*, which is important in all sorts of ways.

What complicates causal reasoning, as mentioned in Chapter 6 (Section 6.1.2), is that we never actually see something cause something else. We see one thing happen, and then we see another thing happen. Sometimes. Sometimes the other thing happens a second later, sometimes a day later, sometimes a millennium later. But we never actually observe (with our own senses or with instruments) the one thing *cause* the other. Consequently, we can never actually *prove* that one thing causes another; the best we can do is *infer* that the one thing causes the other.

Hume's constant conjunction

Suppose a person . . . endowed with the strongest faculties of reason and reflection [were] to be brought on a sudden into this world; he would, indeed, immediately observe a continual succession of objects, and one event following another; but he would not be able to discover anything farther. He would not, at first, by any reasoning, be able to reach the idea of cause and effect; since the particular powers, by which all natural operations are performed, never appear to the senses; nor is it reasonable to conclude, merely because one event, in one instance, precedes another, that therefore the one is the cause, the other the effect. Their conjunction may be arbitrary and casual. There may be no reason to infer the existence of one from the appearance of the other. And in a word, such a person, without more experience, could never employ his conjecture or reasoning concerning any matter of fact, or be assured of anything beyond what was immediately present to his memory and senses.

Suppose, again, that he has acquired more experience, and has lived so long in the world as to have observed familiar objects or events to be constantly conjoined together; what is the consequence of this experience? He immediately infers the existence of one object from the appearance of the other. Yet he has not, by all his experience, acquired any idea or knowledge of the secret power by which the one object produces the other; nor is it, by any process of reasoning [that] he is engaged to draw this inference. But still he finds himself determined to draw it: And though he should be convinced that his understanding has no part in the operation, he would nevertheless continue in the same course of thinking. There is some other principle which determines him to form such a conclusion.

This principle is *custom* or *habit* . . . [A]fter the constant conjunction of two objects—heat and flame, for instance, weight and solidity—we are determined by custom alone to expect the one from the appearance of the other . . . All inferences from experience, therefore, are effects of custom, not of reasoning.

(David Hume, *An Enquiry Concerning Human Understanding*, Section V, Part I, 1748)

As with all inductive arguments, a strong causal argument is one in which the premises are true or acceptable, relevant, and sufficient. And again, the degree of acceptability, relevance, and sufficiency affects the degree of strength. Often, additional information may increase our certainty about the conclusion; by all means, when that's the case, identify and obtain the required additional information!

8.1.1 Correlation and causation

Perhaps one of the most important distinctions to be made is that between correlation and causation. Although causal claims are usually based on correlation, the two concepts are quite different. **Correlation** refers simply to association: when things are correlated, they are merely associated, perhaps occurring at the same time or in the same space. Correlations can be positive, in which case one thing increases when another thing increases, or they can also be negative, in which case one thing increases when another thing decreases. The important thing to understand is that a correlation could be merely a coincidence. Or it could be due to some causal process. Of course, if the correlation is regular—if it is always the case that the things occur together or if they occur together more often than chance would predict—then the likelihood of a causal relationship increases.

And a causal relationship, or **causation**, implies a very special association, a way in which one thing is the reason or explanation for the other (see section 8.2). The important thing to understand is that *correlation does not imply causation*. "Whenever X occurs, Y occurs" is not the same as "X causes Y"; "linked to" is not the same as "caused by." To repeat, just because things happen together, it doesn't mean they're causally connected. People started getting AIDS at about the same time they started driving SUVs. Shall we conclude that SUVs cause AIDS? Of course not.

8.1.1a *Practice distinguishing between correlation and causation*

Which of the following statements describe correlation and which describe causation?

1. Most motor vehicle accidents occur when one is driving within a fifty-mile radius of home.

2. Christopher Pittman shot his grandparents then set their house on fire, after taking the antidepressant Zoloft for just three weeks, and Donald Schell killed his wife, daughter, granddaughter, and himself three hours after taking his first two tablets of the antidepressant Paxil.

   (Based on Rob Waters, "Prosecuting for Pharma,"
   Mother Jones, November/December 2004)

3. Ryanair, a low-cost airline based in Dublin, posted a 19% rise in net profit to €268.9m ($338m) for the year ending March 31st. The carrier said its decision not to follow the trend of imposing fuel surcharges on its fares led to an increase in passengers.

   ("Business," *The Economist*, June 4, 2005)

Timing has a lot to do with the outcome of a raindance.

Anon.

327

4. Since 2001, when the No Child Left Behind Act tied federal school funding to performance on annual tests for students in grades three through eight, critics have charged that the law encourages schools to boost their test scores artificially. A new study of one potential score-padding maneuver—suspending probable low scorers to prevent them from taking the test—provides grist for this argument. Researchers examined more than 40,000 disciplinary cases in Florida schools from the 1996–1997 school year (when Florida instituted its own mandatory testing) to the 1999–2000 school year. They found that when two students were suspended for involvement in the same incident, the student with the higher test score tended to have a shorter suspension. This isn't in itself surprising: high achievers are often cut some slack. But the gap was significantly wider during the period when the tests were administered, and it was wider only between students in grades being tested that year.

(David N. Figlio, "No Smart Bully Left Behind," summary of "Testing, Crime and Punishment," National Bureau of Economic Research, *The Atlantic Monthly*, July/August 2005)

5. Areas with strongest anti-gun laws have highest rates of crime, so allowing people to have guns will result in low crime rates.

8.1.2 Cause, time, and space

Another important notion to understand is the temporal and spatial relation between cause and effect. While a cause necessarily precedes its effect, it need not be immediately preceding. *An effect may occur long after its cause.* Some effects take lifetimes, even millions of years, to develop from their causes.

Also, an effect need not occur where its cause occurred. *An effect may occur far from its cause.* So just because an effect is not evident here and now, that doesn't mean the cause in question isn't in fact a cause. For example, the use of DDT in the 1940s in the United States caused serious reproductive problems in polar bears in the far North in the 1990s—a clear case of the effect being distant, in both time and space, from its cause.

8.1.3 Direct and indirect causes

Causation often operates in a chain fashion, with one thing causing another, which causes another, and so on. The cause closest to the final effect is called the **direct cause** or proximate cause. The other causes are called **indirect causes** or remote causes. We often identify the direct cause simply because it is most immediate in time and space. However, it's important to also consider the possibility of indirect or remote causes.

328

For example, consider this:

Snags [dead standing trees] provide habitat and food for a variety of insects, which in turn support birds, such as woodpeckers that feed on them. Snags may also be important as perches and nesting sites for large birds, such as eagles.

(J.P. Kimmins, Forest Ecology, 3rd edn., 2004)

The causal chains established by the speaker are as follows:

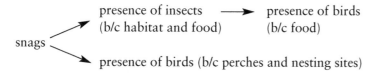

So, snags are both a direct and indirect cause of the presence of birds, and the presence of insects is a direct cause of the presence of birds.

8.1.3a Practice distinguishing between direct causes and indirect causes

Identify the causes described in each of the following as direct or indirect.

1. Darker-skinned blacks generally have higher blood pressure than lighter-skinned blacks. One might conclude, therefore, that skin color is a direct determinant of blood pressure. However, . . . darker skin color in the United States is associated with less access to scarce and valued resources of the society, which causes greater stress, which increases blood pressure.

   (Based on Troy Duster, "Race and Reification
in Science," Science, February 18, 2005)

2. If we used wood products to insulate our houses, that would reduce the use of oil for heating, which of course would reduce polluting emissions.

3. It's not because you're a man that you're getting paid more than me. It's because you're more experienced and have more seniority. And that's only because you weren't the one to take a few years off to be the primary parent of your child.

4. If we allow euthanasia for those who are senile, that will lead to euthanasia for anyone who is cognitively deficient, whether old or not. And then that will lead to euthanasia for people who are physically deficient in some way. And no doubt that will lead to euthanasia for those who are financially deficient!

329

5. A 1991 review of the published research on the relationship between religious commitment and suicide rates conducted by my colleagues and I found that religious commitment produced lower rates of suicide in nearly every published study located. In fact, Stephen Stack, now of Wayne State University, showed that non-church attenders were four times more likely to kill themselves than were frequent attenders and that church attendance predicted suicide rates more effectively than any other factor including unemployment.

    (David B. Larson, "Have Faith: Religion Can
    Heal Mental Ills," *Insight*, March 6, 1995)

8.1.4 Necessary and sufficient causes

A third principle to understand is the difference between necessary and sufficient causes. Basically, it's the same as the difference between necessary and sufficient conditions (see Section 5.3.2). A **necessary cause** is a condition that *must* be present for the effect-in-question to occur. A **sufficient cause** is a condition which *alone* results in the effect-in-question.

For example, suppose your physician says that in order to overcome a certain illness, you need lots of rest. Getting lots of rest is thus a necessary cause: it is necessary that you get lots of rest in order to achieve the effect of getting better. But rest is probably insufficient: perhaps you also need to take certain medication in order to get better. So getting lots of rest is not a sufficient cause for the effect of getting better.

When you assume that a necessary cause is a sufficient cause, you have failed to consider additional causes (see Section 8.4). Keep in mind that *an effect may have more than one cause*. These contributing causes may be quite *independent* of each other (each being a direct cause) or they may *interact* with each other (one or more being an indirect cause). Also, the cause and its effect may interact with each other to create a sort of feedback loop.

8.1.4a *Practice distinguishing between necessary and sufficient causes*

Identify the causes described in each of the following as necessary and/or sufficient.

1. In order to get a job, you have to have the right qualifications. But luck is also required.

2. All you need to succeed in business is immaturity—a two-year-old's capacity for exclusive self-interest along with his absolute willingness to throw a tantrum if he doesn't get those interests met.

3. In order for snow to form, it must be cold enough and there must be a sufficient amount of water vapor in the air.

4. The animal must feel threatened in order for the flight or fight response to be triggered.

5. In order for cohesion to develop, one of two things must happen: the members of the group must have a common goal or they must share similar histories.

8.1.5 Mill's methods

If we can't see or even measure causation, how do we establish a causal relationship? Well, there are ways. They don't lead to certainty, but they do provide a high degree of probability. John Stuart Mill, a nineteenth-century philosopher, established a few methods, the underlying principles of which are still pretty much in use.

The *method of agreement* involves looking for the element that is in common in each case, the element that is always present when X happens. If you're just observing, look for something that's there whenever the effect occurs. If you're experimenting, keep the suspected cause present while you change other things; if the effect keeps occurring, you have probably correctly identified its cause. For example, suppose you suspect that your running shoes are causing your tendonitis to flare up. You might change your running route (perhaps to one with fewer hills), or your speed, or your distance, or the amount of stretching you do before and after you run, or the kinds of stretching exercises you do before and after you run—but don't change your shoes. If, in every single case, you experience tendonitis, it's probably your shoes—that's the only thing that stayed the same. (At the very least, you can eliminate route, speed, distance, and stretching as possible causes.)

Note, however, that I said "probably." That's because, one, the cause may be something you haven't yet considered and eliminated, such as humidity (maybe it was always humid when you ran). Two, maybe a combination of factors causes the tendonitis; perhaps it *is* the shoes, but only when it's humid, so both elements together cause your tendonitis.

The *method of difference* involves looking for the element that makes a difference. If you're observing, try to figure out what was different in the case in which the effect occurs compared to the case in which it doesn't. If you're experimenting, take the suspected element out of the picture and see what happens, keeping the rest of the picture the same; if the effect doesn't happen, then, again, you've probably correctly identified the cause. So, to use the same example, keep everything the same—run the very same route, at the same speed, doing the very same stretching exercises before and after—but first time, use the suspected shoes, and second time, use a different pair of shoes. If you experience tendonitis the first time but not the second, it's probably the shoes—they were the only thing that changed.

But again, one must be careful not to assume that the shoes are the *sole* cause. It could be that the shoes in combination with running hills causes tendonitis (after all, when you wore the shoes in question, you *also* ran hills).

These two methods are often used together. When you note that some element X is present in all cases exhibiting Y and absent in all cases without Y, and you conclude that X is probably causing Y, then you are using both methods. Noting that X is present in all cases of Y is noting what's in common—that's using the method of agreement. Noting that X is absent in all cases without Y is noting what's different—that's using the method of difference.

The use of a control group in an experiment is a case of using both the method of agreement and the method of difference. The experimental group has the suspected cause; for example, if stress is thought to cause depression, people in the experimental group are exposed to stress. The control group doesn't have the suspected cause; to use the same example, people in the control group are not subjected to stress. *Within* each group, the method of agreement is used: the people themselves are different, and they probably eat different foods and engage in different levels of physical activity, but they all are subjected to stress—that's kept the same. *Between* the two groups, the method of difference is at work: the two groups are basically the same (they each contain similarly diverse people), but one is subjected to stress, and the other is not—that's the difference.

The *method of concomitant variation* involves looking for the element that when changed (rather than eliminated as in the method of difference), changes the effect. If you're observing, notice what changes and whether the effect changes along with it; if it does, that's your cause. If you're experimenting and there's an element you can't eliminate altogether in order to employ the method of difference, try to modify it; if changing the suspected cause changes the effect, then there is likely a causal connection. For example, suppose you suspect that it's not your shoes, but your speed that causes the tendonitis. Well, you can't eliminate that factor, you can't take speed out of the picture altogether (or else you wouldn't be running). But you can change your speed. So increase your speed on one run, decrease it on another, and see if the tendonitis changes along with the changes in speed. If it does, you've identified speed as a probable cause.

Note that the observed change in the example just given involved a positive correlation: an increase in speed results, let's say, in an increase in tendonitis. However, a negative correlation may also indicate causation: for example perhaps an increase in stretching results in a decrease in tendonitis.

Also, note that this method doesn't enable us to determine whether the cause we identify is necessary or sufficient. As with the previous two methods, there may be other contributory causes we haven't identified.

The *method of residues* involves a process of elimination whereby one looks for the element which is left over when we have attributed several causes to several effects but one: the remaining effect is caused by the leftover element. Suppose I know from all my years of running that lack of stretching causes overall soreness, increased speed causes increased fatigue, and new shoes cause blisters. And suppose after a run on a new route with hills, I'm sore, tired, blistered, *and* my tendon hurts. I eliminate stretching, speed, and shoes because I have already attributed those elements as causes of other effects; the leftover element is the hilly route, so that must be the cause of the leftover effect: the tendon pain.

8.1.5a Practice identifying Mill's methods

Which of Mill's methods is being used in the following?

1. But all such theories founder on a striking fact: the nearly invisible relationship between unemployment and crime rates. Charting homicide since 1900 reveals two peaks. The first is in 1933. This represents the crest of a wave that began in 1905, continued through the prosperous '20s and then began to *decline* in 1934 as the Great Depression was deepening. Between 1933 and 1940, the murder rate dropped nearly 40%. Property crimes reveal a similar pattern.

    Between 1940 and 1960 the homicide rate remained relatively stable. In the early '60s, a sharp increase began that peaked in 1974, when the murder rate was more than double that of the late 1950s, and far higher than it had been in the depths of the Depression. Between 1963 and 1973 homicides in New York City tripled. Again, property and most other forms of crime followed a similar pattern.

    The cause of this remarkable increase in crime certainly was not unemployment—which was, by contemporary standards, enviably low. In 1961, the unemployment rate was 6.6% and the crime rate was 1.9 per 1,000. By 1969, unemployment had dropped to 3.4% while the crime rate nearly doubled to 3.7 per 1,000. The incidence of robbery nearly tripled. Interestingly, the recession of 1980 to 1982 was accompanied by a small but clearly discernible drop in crime. As the economy revived, so did the crime rate.

    (David Rubinstein, "Don't Blame Crime on Joblessness," *The Wall Street Journal*, November 9, 1992)

2. You and your partner have had arguments before, but you've always been able to reconcile the next day. This time, it's been a few days and things are still not resolved. You replay the argument and your reconciliation attempts over and over in your head trying to figure it out—what was different this time?

3. Anuradha Patel, a pediatric anesthesiologist, tested whether playing with a Game Boy before surgery reduces anxiety. Some children had only their parents to help them cope with their anxiety. Others, also accompanied by their parents, were given an anti-anxiety drug called Midazolam. And a third

group, also accompanied by parents, was given a Game Boy about 30 minutes before anesthesia.

> (Based on "Between the Lines," editorial, *U.S.1*, June 1, 2005)

4. For all the worries over global warming, there's one quick, though impractical, way to turn down the heat: ground all the jets. That's one conclusion to be drawn from a new NASA study linking the world's rising temperatures to the proliferation of wispy cirrus clouds that can form as a result of trails of condensation left by airliners. A team headed by Patrick Minnis, a senior scientist at NASA's Langley Research Center in Hampton, Va., analyzed 25 years of cirrus-cloud counts and 20 years of temperature records and found that cloud cover increased most where jet traffic was heaviest, including flight corridors over the Atlantic and Pacific Oceans.

   . . .

   The only way to prove the point [that contrails should be included in climate-change scenarios because they lead to increased cloud formation which leads to increased temperatures] is to keep the jets on the tarmac and see what happens.

   > (Jeffrey Kluger, "Why High-Flying Planes
   > Make Us Less Cool," *Time*, May 17, 2004)

5. Some days your car starts and some days it doesn't. You start paying attention and note that every time it doesn't start, it's below freezing. You conclude that it's the cold that's causing your car not to start.

8.1.5b Practice using Mill's methods to establish cause

Describe how you would use Mill's methods to establish cause in each of the following cases.

1. You think that perhaps your marks could be higher if you spent more time reading the course material.

2. You want to figure out why your child has started fussing at bedtime and not sleeping through the night.

3. Some teenagers shoot their classmates and some don't. How can we account for that?

4. They recovered because someone prayed for them.

5. In a study commissioned by Hewlett-Packard, researchers found that extensive use of email and text messaging can temporarily drop your IQ-test performance

by as much as ten points—more of a dip than occurs after losing a night's sleep or smoking pot. It's linked to a new condition dubbed 'infomania,' wherein people become addicted to email, instant messaging and text messages.

(*Reader's Digest*, November 2005)

8.2 Explanations

As implied in the previous section, *an explanation is an accounting for a given phenomenon or occurrence.* Typically, explanations involve causation, an accounting of how one thing is the reason for another. However, in the context of critical thinking and argument, we're concerned only with explanations that are in contention. We're not concerned, therefore, with explanations about how to do something (how to tie one's shoes, for instance) or explanations about why someone did something (assuming there's no room for disagreement). The explanations we're interested in are the ones for which arguments need to be made.

8.2.1 Alternative explanations

Given that an explanation is still in contention, there will be several possibilities—several competing, or sometimes complementary, explanations. The best explanation may be one we aren't even aware of. The more knowledge you have and the more imaginative you are, the better you'll be at coming up with alternative explanations, especially ones that are worth looking into.

Consider "Clever Hans," the famous horse who apparently could spell, read, and do math; he would respond correctly to all sorts of questions by thumping his foot a number of times. Well, it turns out he wasn't spelling, reading, or doing math at all. There was an alternative explanation: he was perceiving subtle cues of his handler, who would sigh with relief or joy when the correct number of thumps was reached, and Hans would stop at that point. (No less clever for that, perhaps!) How was this alternative explanation established as the better one? Well, the greater the distance between Hans and his questioners, the worse his performance was. Also, if whoever was asking the questions didn't know the answers (and so didn't unintentionally provide the right answer to Clever Hans by some subtle gesture), then Clever Hans didn't do so well.

© John Callahan

8.2.1a Practice forming alternative explanations

List as many possible explanations for each of the following as you can think of, no matter how implausible.

1. As soon as telephones were installed in an area that previously had no telephones, the crime rate doubled.

2. Public schools in the wealthiest neighborhoods win state team championships at more than twice the rate of poor school districts.

    (*Mother Jones*, November/December 2004)

3. About twenty years ago, Japan had a population of 115 million, of which 10,000 were lawyers. At the same time, the U.S. had more than double Japan's population, but over forty times as many lawyers.

4. Compared with kids who were never hit, white non-Hispanic toddlers who were spanked five times a week were four times as likely to have behavioral problems later [measured by having "trouble at school"]. No significant link was found between spanking and later misbehavior in black and Hispanic children.

    (Sora Song, *Time*, May 17, 2004)

5. Back in the eighteenth century, church towers were more often struck by lightning than the gambling houses next to them.

8.2.2 Good explanations

Okay, now that we've come up with a bunch of possible explanations, how do we determine which is the best explanation? Partly, the answer to that question is "by eliminating all the less adequate ones." But we still need to know on what basis do we eliminate those alternative explanations—how do we determine they're the less adequate ones? We'll consider four features of a good explanation; in order to decide which of several possible explanations is the best explanation, you'll need to consider each of these features.

- *A good explanation is one that accounts for all of the relevant facts*. Note that there are three tasks implied in that one statement: deciding what facts are relevant, obtaining all the relevant facts, and then figuring out which explanation accounts for all of those relevant facts. If you mess up with any of those, chances are the explanation you determine to be the best isn't. Relevance is something we've already covered (Chapter 4), but basically, knowing what's relevant to what comes down to, well, knowledge. So it becomes a bit of a circle: if you don't understand what's going on (and you don't—that's exactly what you're trying to figure out), how can you know what's relevant and what's not? But if you don't know what's relevant and what's not, how can you figure out which is the best explanation for what's going on? Welcome to the fascinating world of scientific investigation!

  As for the second task, obtaining all the relevant facts, well, that's just a lot of work. Not much else can be said about that. Whether you do the work first-hand or whether you collect the information from those who've done the first-hand work, it's still a lot of work.

  As for the third task, there's where your critical thinking skills will come into play the most: you simply have to work through each possibility, follow the logical connections between the proposed cause and the probable effects, figure out and consider the implications of each proposal . . . and see what makes the most coherent picture out of all the pieces you have. On this measure, whichever explanation accounts for the most, whichever explanation leaves the least bits unaccounted for, that's the best one. Consider these two competing explanations:

  1 The Grand Canyon started eroding about 5 million years ago, as a result of the Colorado River, and the now-exposed layers reveal a 1.75 billion year span of the Earth's history.
  2 The Grand Canyon was carved during Noah's Flood, a few thousand years ago, when the sediment was still soft.

The second explanation doesn't account for how the soft sediment remained upright to form walls instead of slumping down into a pile of mush; nor does it account for why the canyon's river channels aren't as wide and as deep as is the case when channels are carved by floods instead of by rivers. The first explanation does not have these problems. Therefore (assuming no other problems—a big assumption), the first one is the better explanation of the two.

Here's another example. One theory about how planets formed is the core accretion theory. Basically, according to this theory, gas and dust, which was a byproduct of the formation of the sun, swirls around, and as it does so, clumps of matter hit each other, and as they collide, they stick together. Eventually, these clumps become large enough to form a rocky core, which eventually grows into a planet, like Mercury, Venus, and Earth. Further from the sun, however, ice condenses, and when the cores get large enough, their gravitational force starts pulling in gas, and you end up with a giant gas planet, such as our Jupiter.

However, this theory doesn't explain 51 Pegasi: it's a gas giant like Jupiter, but it's quite close to its "Sun"—in fact, it orbits around its "Sun" even more closely than Mercury orbits our sun. So that doesn't fit the picture. Also, by the time a gas giant forms by accretion, its gas would have dissipated.

So astrophysicists came up with a revised theory, called the gravitational instability theory. According to this theory, if gas discs around stars are massive enough and cold enough, small-scale gravitational instabilities in the disc will occur. These instabilities could cause parts of the disc to condense into regions of higher density which then contract and collapse to form giant planets. So, according to the instability theory, giant planets need not be far from their "Sun" in order to become giant planets.

So the second theory is better than the first, because it explains more—notably, planets like 51 Pegasi. (However, the second theory has other problems . . . so another theory is that the large gas planets formed far away from their star but then moved closer over time. This may seem frustrating, but scientists are constantly on the lookout for problems with current models, so that they can be more realistic when compared to observation.)

8.2.2a Practice comparing explanations on the basis of the scope of their explanatory power

Each of the following presents several facts and then two or more competing explanations. In each case, determine which explanation accounts for most of the relevant facts. (That's right: some of the facts presented aren't relevant! Identify and eliminate those first.)

1. A ship that continues to sail west will end up where it started. Most nights, when we look at the moon, we see part of it as a curved shadow as if a round

object were between it and the sun. When we look at an object traveling away from us, we see the bottom of it disappear before the top.

(A) The earth is flat.
(B) The earth is round.

2. Your professor hasn't shown up for class. Instead, there's a note on the door, not in her handwriting, saying she is at the hospital. Until now, she has never been absent. She drives a car. Her partner is very pregnant. She is a cautious no-risk sort of person. The university is in a rural area, and while traffic is light, it is high-speed highway traffic.

(A) Her partner has gone into labor.
(B) She has been in a car accident.

3. The continents of South America and Africa look like they fit together like a jigsaw puzzle. Shorelines are continuously undergoing modification by erosion and deposition. Identical animal fossils have been found on South America and Africa. Some animals can swim long distances. Identical plant fossils of a fern with large seeds that could not be blown very far have been found on South America and Africa. There is no now sunken remnant of a huge land bridge connecting South America and Africa. The Appalachian mountain belt in North America connects with mountain belts of similar age and structure that start in the British Isles and Scandinavia if one imagines the land masses joined together.

(A) The present-day continents were at one time joined together into one or two big chunks that have since broken apart and drifted.
(B) The shapes of South America and Africa indicate cosmic yin-yangness; they are complementary, in balance.

4. Researchers studying foraging behavior observed an adult baboon named Mel digging in the ground, trying to extract a nutritious plant bulb. A young baboon named Paul approached Mel and looked around. There were no other baboons within sight. Suddenly he let out a yell, and within seconds his mother came running, chasing the startled Mel over a small cliff. Paul then took the bulb for himself.

(A) Paul engaged in deceptive behavior (misleading his mother into thinking he was being attacked, in order to get the bulb Mel had extracted).
(B) Paul was simply repeating earlier behavior that had led to getting food (something like "Scream, Mom comes, and I get fed").

(Based on James Shreeve, "Machiavellian Monkeys," *Discover*, June 1991)

339

5. Although their numbers have since risen, musk-oxen had virtually disappeared from Banks Island in the High Arctic by 1917. The first Europeans to spend time on the island's shores were the crew members of the HMS *Investigator*, which stopped there for two years in 1852. Written records kept by the *Investigator*'s crew indicate that while they found many musk-ox bones, they shot only seven of the animals. The Copper Inuit later found the abandoned *Investigator* and made numerous trips to the ship to salvage its wood, metal, and so on. Scientists have since documented catastrophic declines of musk-oxen on the Queen Elizabeth Islands, also in the High Arctic, due to climatic conditions that left most of the islands' food resources buried under crusts of thick ice and snow, inaccessible to the musk-oxen. Wolves, which prey on musk-oxen, were not eradicated from Banks Island until 1955.

(A) The Copper Inuit pushed the musk-oxen to the brink of extinction by killing hundreds of the animals while en route to the *Investigator*.

(B) Most of the musk-oxen on Banks Island starved to death.

(Based on Ed Struzik, "And Then There Were 84,000," *International Wildlife*, January/February 2000)

- *A good explanation doesn't invoke more puzzles than it solves.* One could respond, with respect to the Grand Canyon example described above, that God, being omnipotent, made it so the sediment didn't slump, and he just made the channels that way, we don't need to know why. But that just creates more puzzles: who is this God? How do you know he exists? How do you know he did what you say he did? Why did he do what you say he did? And so on.

A common rule, called "Occam's Razor," says that the explanation with the least assumptions is the best. That's probably a good rule to follow, but beware of preferring an explanation just because it's the simplest one: remember that *all* of the facts must be accounted for. Also, just because an explanation is complicated, that's no reason to reject it; some things are simply complicated!

8.2.2b Practice comparing explanations on the basis of their creating-puzzles-ness

Which one of each of the following sets of explanations creates more puzzles than it solves? Articulate the things it implies that need explanation.

1. A ship that continues to sail west will end up where it started. Most nights, when we look at the moon, we see part of it as a curved shadow as if a round object were between it and the sun. When we look at an object traveling away from us, we see the bottom of it disappear before the top.

(A) The earth is flat.
(B) The earth is round.

Suppose you're an engineer charged with explaining why a bridge collapsed and someone remarks, "I know why it collapsed. It collapsed because an incomprehensible being zapped it with an incomprehensible force." Because you are interested in exploring all possibilities, you inquire, "Can you tell me any more about this being or force?" "No," he replies. "Do you have any tangible evidence that this occurred?" you ask. "No," he admits. At this point you would do well to thank him for his help and show him to the door.

Theodore Schick, Jr. and Lewis Vaughn, *How to Think about Weird Things: Critical Thinking for a New Age*, 2007

2. Someone is unexpectedly in your third storey apartment.

   (A) The person found the key hidden under the mat and unlocked your door.
   (B) The person levitated to the third storey, then dematerialized enough to pass through the screened balcony door.

3. I took a mental empowerment course wherein participants were taught certain techniques that enabled them to diagnose strangers and then, by visualizing white light shining upon them, heal them. At the end of the course, each new student was paired with a guide, who walked us through the newly learned technique; when we were at the appropriate mental level, our guide read the name, age, sex, and symptoms of someone from a file. We were then to proceed and determine what ailment the person was suffering from. I "saw" that the person I was told of had fused vertebrae; no wonder he felt stiff and had trouble walking! Imagine my surprise when, after I had "surfaced," I saw written in the person's file exactly that: "fused vertebrae"!

   (A) I had successfully mastered the mental empowerment technique.
   (B) My guide had written "fused vertebrae" into the file after I had said it, while my eyes were still closed (before I had surfaced).

4. Taffi is limping one day. The previous day we went on a long walk through the winter woods, and she spent most of her time off the path chasing rabbits.

   (A) Taffi is limping because she hurt her leg while chasing rabbits.
   (B) Taffi is limping because something bit her and her leg is infected.

5. There was a tsunami in the India Ocean in 2004, causing an estimated 283,000 deaths.

   (A) The tsunami occurred as a punishment by Allah because humans have been ignoring his laws.
   (B) The tsunami occurred as a result of an undersea earthquake.

• As suggested in the preceding section, *a good explanation will enable you to make predictions.* In fact, that's a good test of explanations. For example, suppose you want to know why your cat scratches the upholstery. You collect as much information about the matter as you can, perhaps guessing as to what's relevant and what's not (could be anything from its emotional health to its biochemistry to its genes . . .?), and you finally decide that the best explanation is that your cat scratches the furniture because its claws are too long. So you can make a prediction: once you cut your cat's claws, it will stop scratching at the furniture. If your prediction turns out to be correct, that

There are two brothers in Dubai, Arab Emirates. They sent an e-mail saying, "We want the million dollars." [Randi's foundation offers one million dollars for evidence of paranormal powers.] I said, "Okay, why?" "Well, because the two of us make the sun rise every morning."

Well, I thought about that. I wonder how we could design a test? So I said, wait, wait, this may be just a joke. Well, whether it is or not, I'll treat it as if it's serious. So I wrote back to them and I said, "Which one of you makes it rise?" "Um, we don't know. We both work on it and the sun rises every morning, you can see that." I said, "Yes, the evidence is 100 percent in your favor." Then I said, "I have an experiment. One of you shoot the other one. Then if the sun rises the next morning, it wasn't him. Must be you. Well, then, what you do is you shoot yourself, and if the sun rises the next morning, you lose. But if the sun doesn't rise the next morning, I'll pay you." I don't think we've heard back from them.

James Randi, "Fakers and Innocents," Committee for the Scientific Investigation of Claims of the Paranormal, at: http://www.csicop.org/si/2005-07/randi.html

increases the likelihood that your explanation is correct. Note that it doesn't *prove* it—it just *supports* it. We usually can't know which is the *correct* explanation; we have to settle for which is the *best* explanation. (Recall the discussion in Section 6.1 about the difficulty of proving things and the relative ease of disproving them.)

And note that if an explanation enables prediction, *it will be testable.* There should be something you can do, some specific information you can obtain, that could eliminate the explanation (falsify the hypothesis). For example, you could test your explanation by cutting your cat's claws and observing whether or not it subsequently scratched the furniture. Not being testable doesn't mean a hypothesis is wrong; it just means we can't establish that it's right.

8.2.2c *Practice determining whether an explanation is testable (and can enable prediction)*

Which of the following explanations are testable? For each, explain what test you could carry out—what prediction you could make, the truth of which would support the explanation.

1. People can walk over hot coals without burning their feet. Three explanations have been put forth: (a) such people have been trained to put "mind over matter"; (b) such people have supernatural powers; (c) wood coal has a low specific heat (like lava rock, unlike a frying pan), so anyone can walk over hot coals without burning their feet.
    (Thanks to James Randi's *Encyclopedia of Claims, Frauds, and Hoaxes of the Occult and Supernatural*, at: www.randi.org)

2. It is better to be bullied for the first time as a young child than as an adolescent.
    (*Harper's Magazine*, January 2005)

3. The flood during the time of Noah covered the entire earth.

4. Fossils have been placed in rocks by the devil to mislead people. Or God created them when he created Earth and placed them where they've been found as a sort of picture of things to come. Either that or they're discards—the animals God created and didn't like.
    (Explanations proposed some time between 1500 and 1700)

5. Psychics can help police find victims, perpetrators, evidence, and so on.

- Lastly, *a good explanation doesn't contradict established knowledge.* The iffy thing here is "established knowledge" because sometimes established knowledge is incorrect, and it takes a contradicting explanation to make that clear. The important thing to keep in mind is that when you have contradictory claims, they can't both be true. So if your explanation contradicts some already established claim, either your explanation or that other claim is incorrect.

8.2.2d Practice determining whether an explanation contradicts established knowledge

Which of the following explanations contradict established knowledge? Specify what knowledge is contradicted.

1. Murder rates increased in the 1960s and the first half of the 1970s; then they held steady for a while, and in 1981 and 1982 they declined steadily. Therefore, it would seem that Americans were more violent for a while and then became less violent.

2. Many people think the pyramids were built as tombs for pharaohs.

3. America's system of education ranges from the superb to the awful. Its universities, especially at the graduate level, are the best in the world, gaining some 60% of all Nobel prizes awarded since the second world war. Its public-school system, however, is often marked by poor teaching, dilapidated buildings and violence (although the rate of violent incidents is falling, more than 5% of schoolchildren played truant last year to avoid violence at school) (*The Economist*, October 9, 2004).

    So either those who win Nobel prizes are foreign students, students who have not come up through American public schools to its universities, or what happens at public school has no bearing on what happens at a university (once they're at a university, students can easily make up missing ground).

4. She left Halifax on Monday and arrived in Vancouver on Friday. I know she hates flying, and that's pretty unlikely for a road trip, especially since she was traveling alone. She must have taken the train.

5. A child in Chile or Malaysia is less likely to die before one year of age than a black-skinned baby born in certain areas of the United States. This is most likely because there is so much more crime in the U.S. than in Malaysia.

8.2.2e Practice identifying best explanations

Consider each of the following sets of explanations for the described phenomenon, and decide which is the best explanation. Articulate your reasons.

Be sure to consider each of the four criteria for a good explanation covered in this section:

- It accounts for all of the relevant facts.
- It doesn't create more puzzles than it solves.
- It's testable, enabling you to make predictions.
- It doesn't contradict established knowledge.

1. Eating out, once an occasional luxury, has become a way of life.

   (A) The standard of living has increased.
   (B) Eating out has become inexpensive due to fast food chains.

2. Adverse reactions to vaccinations have risen in the last couple of decades.

   (A) Vaccinations have become stronger in the last couple of decades.
   (B) Vaccinations have become more contaminated in the last couple of decades.
   (C) Children are less resilient than they were before.
   (D) Doctors are required now to report all reactions—something they were not previously required to do.

3. Clogged arteries are more prevalent in old people than in young people.

   (A) Age causes clogged arteries.
   (B) Poor muscle tone causes clogged arteries.
   (C) A life-long diet rich in meats and other high cholesterol foods causes clogged arteries.

4. Men by far commit more crimes than women.

   (A) Crime is related to testosterone.
   (B) Crime is related to the Y chromosome.
   (C) Women are simply better people than men.
   (D) Women are less risk-taking than men, possibly because they feel more responsible for their children.
   (E) Men simply have more opportunity than women to commit crime.

5. Artists have tended to paint portraits in profile, more often painting the left side of the face than the right side. This left-side bias has been more prevalent in portraits of women than men. The left-side bias was very prevalent in the fifteenth century, but has decreased over time; paintings done in the twentieth century show no left- or right-side bias.

   (A) Right-handed artists find it easier to draw portraits when the model looks to the right.

(B) Right-handed mothers are likely to hold their babies in their left arms; consequently babies imprint the left side of their mothers' faces; this imprinting influences artists, who are then more likely to depict the left side of women's faces in portraits.

(C) The right hemisphere of the brain mediates emotions, which are expressed more vividly in the left side of the face; artists are inclined to depict women as emotional, perhaps less so now than in previous centuries.

(Based on Anjan Chatterjee, "Portrait Profiles and the Notion of Agency," *Empirical Studies of the Arts*, 20.1, 2002)

8.3 Predictions, plans, and policies

Mention was made in the previous section about the role of prediction as a test for causal explanations. However, there is a whole category of arguments in which prediction is the main point, rather than a test for the main point. That is, one argues for a prediction, based on causal reasoning: we predict X will happen tomorrow not just because it's happened yesterday and the day before (a generalization based on quantity), but also because the conditions will be the same tomorrow as they were yesterday and the day before (a generalization based on quality)—*and those conditions are what cause* X (there's the causal reasoning part).

Arguments advocating a certain plan or policy involve prediction: we predict this plan or policy will have such-and-such a result; that's why we should implement it. Usually these predictions are based on social causation rather than physical causation (both broadly defined). Plans or policies may apply to the public sphere (for example, one might argue about whether the government should fund national healthcare or whether it should pass a law making marijuana use illegal), or they may be quite personal (for example, one might make an argument about whether or not one should go to college). Typically, such arguments present as premises advantages and disadvantages or pros and cons of implementing the plan or policy.

Here's an example:

> The government should fund national healthcare because it's in the best interests of the nation—both its economic and defensive interests—that its citizenry be in good health.

Note that the speaker advocates a certain policy—the government should fund national healthcare—and presents two advantages of such a policy: a citizenry in good health is in the nation's best economic interests and a citizenry in good health is in the nation's best defensive interests.

Here's another example:

I should not go to college because if I do, I'll be expected to spend a lot of time learning and I don't really enjoy learning. Plus, I'll have to spend a lot of time in a formal institution and that's not exactly the kind of life I want.

In this case, a plan is put forward: the plan not to go to college. And in support of the plan, two disadvantages of its opposite, going to college, are given: going to college involves learning and, worse, doing so in a formal institution.

But there is, I think, a better way of presenting and then assessing such arguments. We could articulate the desired goal of the plan or policy, and then articulate the causal process that would lead from the current position to that goal (this might include generalization). To the extent the plan or policy in question proposes or includes such a process, the achievement of that goal is likely.

Here are the same two examples presented in this manner:

1. A citizenry in good health will be able to defend the nation.
2. A citizenry in good health will be economically productive.
3. A government-funded national healthcare plan will increase the health of the citizenry.
Therefore, the government should fund a national healthcare plan.

1. I don't enjoy learning.
2. I don't enjoy formal institutions.
3. Going to college involves both learning and formal institutions.
Therefore, I shouldn't go to college.

When the argument is laid out this way, one can evaluate each premise, for truth or acceptability, relevance, and sufficiency, and thus evaluate the concluding plan or policy.

8.3a Practice identifying arguments that advocate a plan or policy

Which of the following are arguments for a plan or policy intended to achieve a certain goal? Articulate the desired goal and the causal processes believed to lead to that goal.

1. Given the increasing sales of alcoholic beverages with less alcohol content than regular alcoholic beverages, and given the increasing disapproval of alcoholism, we should expand our line of low-alcohol beverages.

2. Cloning should be allowed because a lot of people would like to have a clone so that it may lead the life that was meant to be theirs. Typically, these are

people who have suffered some terrible physical or mental handicap and feel robbed of the opportunities they should have had in life. Some see this life as a sacrifice so that the life of their clone may be enriched.

(Simon Smith at: http://www.humancloning.org/allthe.php)

3. Pornography spreads a distorted view of women's nature that supports sexist attitudes and reinforces women's oppression and exploitation.

(Helen Longino, Pornography, Oppression, and Freedom: A Closer Look," in Laura Lederer, ed., *Take Back the Night: Women on Pornography*, 1980)

4. "When I started as a financial advisor 20 years ago, there were almost no couples in this situation," says Bob Mecca, a certified financial advisor in Mt. Prospect, IL, a suburb of Chicago. "Now 40 percent of the couples who come through my door have a wife who earns more than her husband."

The simplest explanation for this change is a practical one: Women today are better educated and better prepared for the workforce than ever. "The number of women getting high school, college, and advanced degrees is higher now than at any other point in history," says Randi Minetor, author of *Breadwinner Wives and the Men They Marry*. In fact, women today are *more* educated than men. In 1998, there were 125,000 more college-educated women than men, according to the Center for the Study of Opportunity in Higher Education.

(Kimberly Goad, "Big-Earning Wives," *Redbook*, March 2005)

5. Some 10,000 loudspeakers, all blaring at once: is this an ad man's fantasy or the latest pop concert gimmick? No, the idea was cooked up by Egypt's Ministry of Religious Affairs. It plans to hook all the mosques in Cairo to a city-wide wireless network, so that five times a day they can amplify the Muslim call to prayer in a single voice, in the same instant . . .

The plan is needed to uphold Islam's "civilized face." The religious affairs ministry says it is barraged with complaints about the poor timing, excessive loudness and harsh voices of many *muezzins*. The religious revival that has swept Egypt in the past two decades has packed the country with more mosques than it needs. It is common to find two or more houses of worship on one city block, competing to be noticed.

(*The Economist*, October 2, 2004)

8.3b *Practice imagining an appropriate plan or policy*

For each of the following, consider the given facts (eliminate those that are irrelevant), and the stated goal, then come up with a plan or policy that is likely to achieve that goal.

1. The township needs someone to plow its roads in winter. It placed an advertisement in the local newspaper, offering pay equivalent to that of similar positions in neighboring townships, but no one applied for the position. If someone had applied, they would have been interviewed by a committee of three people. However, a few calls from interested people suggest the problem is that the position is seasonal, providing income for only six months of the year.

2. Your adult son has come back home to live. He says he can't find a good-paying job, and it's expensive to rent an apartment. Unfortunately, he also expects the kind of looking after he received when he was twelve. Neither you nor your spouse is particularly happy with his return—you rather liked having the house to yourselves again, and you figure your job as parents is pretty much done. You live in a medium-sized city.

3. It takes a long time to trust someone with your life. Generally, people have sex with each other long before that point is reached. Yet in the age of AIDS, having sex with someone is trusting them with your life.

4. People are required by law to pay taxes. Taxes are generally, but not exclusively, based on one's level of income. The government is responsible for paying for many things that the public needs and wants. Many people object to many of the things that tax money is used to purchase.

5. Political campaigns are funded mostly by the rich. This seems inevitable because they cost so much—there are formidable legal and accounting expenses, not to mention advertising and touring expenses; most of us can't afford to give thousands of dollars, let alone hundreds of thousands, to a candidate for his or her campaign. So when a candidate gets elected, he or she feels obligated to pay back his or her supporters with legislation in their favor. Thus, government fails to serve the public interest, the interests of the not-rich.

8.3c *Practice assessing whether a plan or policy will work*

For each of the following, assess whether or not the plan or policy will achieve the stated goals, given the information provided. If you require additional information, indicate what information is required and why.

1. Much of the on-site violence at School X is between members of different gangs. Students often wear gang colors to school. In order to reduce gang-related violence at school, the principal proposes a mandatory school uniform of non-gang colors.

2. I read the other day that coffee consumption is connected with heart disease. I'm planning to decrease my coffee consumption!

3. Police in one district of Mexico City are learning by the book. They have to. If they don't read at least one tome a month, they won't get promoted. Mexican cops have a reputation for being corrupt and incompetent, and the folk promoting the strategy believe higher literacy levels will improve standards, making for better officers and better people. Mexican writers will be giving conferences especially tailored to the cops. Will this mandatory book-of-the-month club be enforced? You betcha: Officers will be regularly tested. Perhaps it's time to consider investing in the Spanish version of Coles Notes.
   (*Reader's Digest*, November 2005)

4. HIV infection is more prevalent among homeless individuals than among the non-homeless. So, in order to lower HIV infection incidence, we should provide low-cost housing and low-skilled jobs.

5. Based on current demographics—the number of people, their ages, their sex, etc.—we can predict that we'll need 100 new physicians to serve our region in the next decade, so that's what we're going to budget for.

8.4 Errors in causal reasoning

Causal reasoning often involves errors of insufficient evidence—insufficient to rule out alternative explanations. Also, most errors in causal reasoning reveal a lack of understanding of the complexity of causation; they're essentially errors of simplification. The following are common specific errors of causal reasoning.

8.4.1 Mistaking correlation for causation

This is perhaps the most basic and most general error in causal reasoning. Just because two (or more) things occur more or less together in time and/or space, it doesn't mean that causation is involved. More specifically, just because A and B occur together, it doesn't mean A causes B. The association could be mere coincidence. Or perhaps B causes A, in which case you've reversed cause and effect (see Section 8.4.5). Or perhaps C causes both A and B, in which case you've failed to consider a common cause (see Section 8.4.3).

Here's an example of this particular error:

> The more religious the country, the more violence there is in that country. That proves that religion incites violence.

The speaker has assumed that a correlation between religion and violence indicates a causal connection between the two—specifically that religion leads to violence. It could be the other way around: perhaps violence leads to religion (people may cope with the relentless pain and suffering, and injustice, of violence by believing in a pain-free and just afterlife). Or perhaps there is some third element that causes both religion and violence.

We make this error probably because we're overly influenced by the proximity in time and space between the cause and the effect.

8.4.1a Practice recognizing when correlation is mistaken for causation

In which of the following arguments is correlation mistaken for causation? Where applicable, re-craft the argument so it is error-free.

1. The mind is able to heal because when I was sick, I kept thinking positive thoughts, imagining myself better, and I did, in fact, recover!

2. Wherever I see grass, I see dirt. The grass must cause dirt to form.

3. The child's arm started to hurt right after a bee stung her. And of course bee venom can cause pain, as well as swelling, and sometimes even more serious reactions. So that's probably why her arm hurts—a bee stung her.

4. There is an increase in men beating up their wives on Superbowl weekend. See? Watching sports incites violence!

5. There have been more than fifty studies of the relationship between social class and rates of schizophrenia. Almost without exception, these studies have shown that schizophrenia occurs most frequently at the lowest social class levels of urban society.

> (Melvin L. Kohn, "The Interaction of Social Class and Other Factors in the Etiology of Schizophrenia," *American Journal of Psychiatry*, February 1976)

8.4.1b More practice with correlation and causation

Write three arguments that mistake correlation for causation. Then rewrite them in such a way as to avoid that error.

8.4.2 Post hoc ergo propter hoc

This is one of the few errors of reasoning that has, for some reason, retained its Latin name (albeit shortened to "post hoc"): "post hoc ergo propter hoc" means "after this therefore because of this." So the error involves assuming that just because B came *after* A, it was *caused by* A; conversely, it involves assuming that because A happened *before* B, A was the *cause* of B. (So, you'll notice that this error is a sort of subset of mistaking correlation for causation.)

Here's an example of the post hoc fallacy:

> Since the Arctic peregrine falcon population recovered once it was put on the Endangered Species list, we can conclude that the birds were able to replenish their numbers because people stopped shooting them!

The speaker has assumed that since B (recovery) came after A (the cessation of hunting), B was caused by A. In fact, scientists have established that their recovery is actually due to the ban on pesticides like DDT, which happened before the Endangered Species Act.

This fallacy may be a case of mistaking a necessary condition for a sufficient condition: after all, an effect must necessarily come after its cause. But that's not *all* that's involved. Before any given B, there are a million things that happened; so if you think that happening before is sufficient to establish causation, then you have to say that every one of those million things caused B.

Perhaps more to the point, we make this error because we obtain a lot of knowledge by experience, and one of the principles we use is temporal contiguity (see Hume's "Constant Conjunction" in Section 8.1). The toddler touches a hot stove, PAIN! Henceforth, fortunately, it associates stoves with pain and keeps its distance. And it does so because the pain occurred immediately after touching the stove—after this therefore because of this.

A noteworthy and common post hoc error is the claim that prayers are answered. Certainly it is often the case that one prays for something, and then that something happens. But how often are alternative explanations investigated— a million other things happened before that something, and any one of them could have caused it to happen.

8.4.2a Practice recognizing the post hoc error

In which of the following arguments is the post hoc error made? Where applicable, re-craft the argument so it is error-free.

1. If we allow people to sell their organs, we will end up with a murder epidemic—people will go on killing sprees, hoping to sell their victims' organs.

2. As Halley's comet approached the earth, the price of ice-cream cones in Boston rose regularly. So of course the increase in the price of ice-cream cones in Boston was due to Halley's comet!

    (Thanks to Stephen J. Gould)

3. Last January, we implemented random after-lunch breathalyzer tests for middle management personnel; since then reports of excessively long lunches

If lung cancer developed shortly after having a cigarette, people would quickly learn to avoid cigarettes.

James Alcock, "Things that Go Bump," *Humanist in Canada*, Autumn 2003

(And if the ozone layer popped a hole, preferably with cool audiovisual effects, ten minutes after we started manufacturing CFCs . . .)

and afternoon aggressiveness toward subordinates have decreased. It seems to have worked quite well, and I say we include upper management starting next month.

4. Civarro claims that since she has been hired, sales have doubled; she therefore asks for a raise.

5. The argument that nuclear weapons have prevented global conventional wars is open to serious question. Two of the five deadliest wars in U.S. history [took place during the Cold War]. The fact that there [was] no major war in Europe is a result of the cleancut division into two blocs, neither with any real reason to start a war.

(Lincoln Wolfenstein, "End Nuclear Addiction,"
The Bulletin of the Atomic Scientists, May 1991)

8.4.2b More practice with the post hoc error

Write three arguments that involve a post hoc error. Where applicable, rewrite your three arguments so they're error-free.

8.4.3 Failing to consider a common cause

As already suggested, when A and B occur together, it could be coincidental. Or it could be that A caused B, or it could be that B caused A. There is a third possibility: it could be that some one thing, let's call it C, caused both A and B— there could be a common cause for A and B (in which case they are not cause and effect at all, but two effects).

Consider the following argument:

I'm feeling very tired lately. That must be why I've been so irritable—it's almost as if my personality is changing.

The speaker is suggesting that A (feeling tired) is causing B (increased irritability). That may well be, but it could be that C (a brain tumor) is causing both the fatigue and irritability.

Why do we fail to consider a common cause? Partly because of the "this then that" attraction: I note two elements, one after the other, so one must cause the other. But there is probably another reason for this lapse of reasoning: involving a third element that causes the two observed elements is more complicated. And we are such simple creatures.

8.4.3a Practice recognizing a failure to consider a common cause

For each of the following, think of a plausible common cause for the presumed cause and effect.

1. Most heart attack victims are obese, so obesity must cause heart disease.

2. Since there are more churches in big cities, as well as a higher overall consumption of alcohol, it must be that churches somehow encourage drinking.

3. The numbers of predator fish A are declining, probably because its prey, fish B, have declined.

4. The child speaks so quickly; that's why he's stuttering.

5. Because many drug addicts tried marijuana before trying other drugs such as crack, cocaine, heroin, and so on, it's likely that marijuana use causes addiction to hard drugs.

8.4.3b More practice with common causes

Write three arguments that fail to consider a common cause, indicating what that common cause might be.

8.4.4 Failing to consider additional causes

This error is a case of mistaking a partial cause for a complete cause. In other words, we may be right in establishing that A causes B, but it may be that C is *also* required to cause B. So, to use language we're now familiar with, A may be a necessary cause, but it may not be a sufficient cause; there may be other causes required that, together with A, cause B.

Consider this argument:

> My running times always get worse come winter, and they get progressively worse as the winter proceeds. I figure that it's because muscles don't work as well when it's cold, and of course it gets colder as the winter proceeds.

That's probably true (though as warm-blooded creatures, isn't muscle temperature regulated internally? by stretching, for example?), but it's probably not the whole story. I tend to eat more during the winter so I gain weight, which, of course, makes my running times worse. And I wear a lot more clothing when I run in the winter—so that's even more weight, as well as more bulkiness. And if it's just snowed and the plow hasn't gone by yet, it's like running on sand; if the road is hard packed snow or ice, even with my spikes on, I'm running more carefully, and therefore more slowly.

As with some of the previous errors, we probably make this mistake because we don't fully understand the complexity of the causal processes involved. But even if we don't understand how additional elements may be causal, we should at least consider the possibility that there may be additional elements in play.

8.4.4a Practice recognizing a failure to consider additional causes

For each of the following, list as many plausible additional causes as you can think of.

1. The art of this period doesn't have a lot of blue, you'll notice. We believe it's because blue was a very rare, difficult to get or make, pigment.

2. Our accounting is a mess this month! All because of that new computerized system we're using!

3. There has been a decrease in the number of marriages, and certainly we can point to the effect of unemployment among men aged 18 to 25: surely it leads them to think twice about marriage and family.

4. Lung cancer is on the decrease! Must be all those improved treatments we keep hearing about!

5. In the late 1990s, beetles imported to Lake Victoria, which borders Kenya, Tanzania and Uganda, were credited with clearing water hyacinth, an introduced plant that was choking both the lake and the economies of surrounding countries.
    ("El Niño Helped Beetles Beat Invader," *New Scientist*, June 4, 2005)

8.4.4b More practice with additional causes

Write three arguments that fail to consider additional causes, indicating what those additional causes might be.

8.4.5 Reversing cause and effect

This error is simply a case of getting it wrong: assuming or concluding that A causes B, when in fact B causes A. You might think this seldom happens, but not so: we often mistake the effect for the cause or the cause for the effect.

For example, we often hear arguments along these lines:

If we simply got rid of all the guns and bombs and what have you, we'd get rid of all the violence.

Such arguments suggest that weapons cause violence. But Hans Morgenthau suggests the opposite causal relation: "Men do not fight because they have arms. They have arms because they . . . fight." (Which one is correct?)

Sometimes this error is a matter of being mistaken about which came first. Other times it's just a matter of being mistaken!

8.4.5a Practice recognizing a reversal of cause and effect

In which of the following arguments is it plausible that cause and effect are reversed?

1. Researchers have noticed a correlation between high self-esteem and high academic achievement. So teachers at many schools have started focusing more on their students' self-esteem than, perhaps, on their academic work. They tried very hard, and in very many ways, to make their students feel good about themselves. And eventually they did. Students began to feel very confident about their abilities. But their academic performance did not improve.

2. It's quite clear to me that your headache is due to your excessive drinking.

3. Their employees are always getting wage increases. And they do such good work. We should get wage increases too. Maybe then our work would improve as well.

4. *Gunthera:* Haven't you noticed that every time you have a so-called "out of body" experience, you're either very stressed or very tired?
    Milocz: Well, yeah, it's very stressful and tiring to *have* an out-of-body experience!

5. Champion athletes have endurance and self-control. This proves that sport builds character.

8.4.5b More practice with reversing cause and effect

Write three arguments that reverse cause and effect. Then rewrite your three arguments so they're error-free.

Sir: Martin Kelly ("Fishy business in Loch Ness", 28 March) reports Dr. Ian Winfield as saying that the fish stocks in Loch Ness are not big enough to feed a monster, therefore a monster does not exist. He confuses cause and effect.

It is perfectly obvious to me that the reason why the fish stocks are low is because the monster keeps eating them.

Peter Stanton, Letters to the Editor, *The Independent*, March 31, 1995

355

8.4.6 Failing to consider a reciprocal causal relation

The previous error indicates that *instead* of A causing B, it may be that B causes A. This error indicates that *in addition to* A causing B, B may cause A. That is, perhaps the causal relationship is not reversed, but reciprocal; perhaps A causes B *and* B causes A. This sort of two-way causation is often called a "feedback loop"—one thing causes another thing which in turn increases or exacerbates the first thing, causing it to cause more of the second thing, causing the second thing to cause more of the first thing . . . you get the idea.

For example, many plants grow tall in order to obtain a lot of sunlight. But it's also the case that plants that obtain a lot of sunlight grow tall. See the causal loop in the relationship between growing tall and getting sunlight?

Again, a deficiency in understanding may lead us to mistake a reciprocal causal relation for a one-way causal relation. But it is a deficiency of imagination that prevents us from even considering it!

8.4.6a Practice recognizing a failure to consider a reciprocal causal relation

In which of the following arguments is there plausibly a reciprocal causal relation?

1. People who are intelligent think a lot.

2. I'm too tired to exercise!

3. Viruses are the leading cause of "computer frustration." Though 'frustration' might be putting it mildly: not only do viruses result in work slowdowns and even stoppage, they also result in lost data—and given the widespread use of computers in hospitals, each of these has, at some point, meant that someone died. Literally.

4. We should get rid of all these discrimination programs, the affirmative action hiring policies and the security racial profiling policies. Such policies just cause prejudice.

5. Well, it serves him right! No wonder he never gets any of the jobs he interviews for! He's so pessimistic and unenthusiastic before he even walks through the door!

8.4.6b More practice with reciprocal causal relations

Write three arguments that fail to consider a reciprocal causal relation. Then rewrite your arguments so the possibility is considered.

8.4.7 Slippery slope

If A leads to B which leads to C which leads to D, and D is undesirable, and on that basis we conclude that we shouldn't do A, then we have a legitimate chain argument—if indeed A does lead to B, B leads to C, and C leads to D. If, however, one or more connections between the links in the chain are untenable (suppose, for example, B doesn't really lead to C) and we still conclude that because D is undesirable, we shouldn't do A, we've committed the slippery slope error: we've presented as inevitable an outcome that is, in fact, not inevitable; we've presented as a slippery slope a path that, in fact, has spots at which we can stop.

There are perhaps two reasons for why we might be mistaken about, for example, B leading to C. First, we can simply be wrong about the causal connection; we may think B causes C, but it doesn't. Second, we may have assumed that the argument that connects A to B also connects B to C, perhaps because A, B, and C are similar in some way. However, what justifies the first step may *not* necessarily justify all the other steps; if the next step is different in relevant ways from the first step, taking the next step would require a different argument. In this case, committing ourselves to the first step, accepting its argument, doesn't necessarily mean we have committed ourselves to the next step or the next. If a line can be drawn between one step and another, the slide down the slope isn't inevitable; the slope isn't as slippery as one thinks—there are places along the slope at which one can get a grip and stop the progression.

Here's an example of a slippery slope argument:

> If we implement the parent licensing program you advocate and require people to demonstrate a certain level of maturity and knowledge before they are allowed to become parents, next we'll require them to have a certain level of income, and eventually, we'll require them to have a certain sexual orientation or a certain skin color. What you're advocating is very dangerous and I, for one, do not want to go down that road. No to parent licensing!

One can argue that a certain level of maturity and knowledge is relevant to being a good parent, so making those aspects a prerequisite is justified. Having a certain level of income is also relevant to being a good parent (one needs to be able to provide adequate food, shelter, and so on). But how are sexual orientation and skin color relevant to being a good parent? In order to make those aspects a prerequisite, one would have to come up with a different argument. So accepting the first part (and the second part) does not commit us to accepting the last part; it is not, as the speaker implies, a slippery slope from making maturity and knowledge a prerequisite to making sexual orientation and skin color prerequisites. Therefore, the argument as presented provides no reason to reject the first part.

That said, it is a fact of human nature that accepting one thing may make it easier to accept another similar thing (whether or not it's logically implied by accepting the first thing). So, to refer to the preceding example, requiring people to have a certain level of maturity and knowledge before they're allowed to become a parent may indeed ease the way to requiring them to be of a certain sexual orientation or skin color, and perhaps we should therefore be wary of endorsing the idea of parent licensing. So while logically, the slope is not slippery (one can draw a clear and defensible line between one step and the next), psychologically or socially, it may be (for alas, we are not always logical creatures).

It is often a fear of slippery slopes that leads us to make absolute claims: if we say "always" then we never have to decide "when"—we never have to deal with the complicated ifs ands or buts that can guide us in drawing a line part way down the slope. For example, if we say killing is always wrong, we don't have to do the hard work of figuring out the difference between unjustified and justified abortion, unjustified and justified euthanasia, unjustified and justified capital punishment, unjustified and justified war, and so on.

It makes sense, then, to suggest that we make this mistake when our understanding isn't quite up to the task, when we don't see our mistake in thinking B causes C or we don't see that the argument connecting A to B isn't the same as that which would connect B to C.

8.4.7a Practice recognizing a slippery slope

In which of the following arguments is there a slippery slope? Where applicable, re-craft the argument so it is error-free.

1. If I allow the student who's in the hospital because of a car accident to take the final exam at a later date, then I have to allow the one who's home in bed from mono to take it later, and then the one who's home in bed with a migraine will want to take the exam later, and then of course I'll have to allow any student who has a headache or a cold or what have you to take it later. So, no. My policy is that if you don't show up at the scheduled time to take the final exam, you're simply out of luck. I'm sorry, but that's life.

2. First we gave several days off at Christmas, then we agreed to sick days, then we were talked into a day off if someone got married. Pretty soon they're going to want "Earth Day" declared a holiday, then they'll ask for a holiday in memory of Louis Riel, and eventually they'll ask for a day off to celebrate their bird's birthday! I tell you we should have stopped with Christmas!

3. Implementing a flex-time program which allows employees to choose their working hours (within limits) will make them feel more like the adults they are than like children who are not allowed to make any decisions of their own. As a result, they will act more like adults, being more responsible on the job, making better decisions. They will become more productive. They

will like their jobs more. As a result, they will call in sick less often and be late less often.

4. If we let the Communists take over Nicaragua or El Salvador, pretty soon they will be in other countries like Guatemala and Honduras. Soon all of Central America will be Communist. Then the Communists will take over Mexico, and we'll be looking at Russian troops and missiles from El Paso.

(Ex-President Ronald Reagan's argument
for war in Nicaragua and El Salvador)

5. Truthfully, I have no problem with genetic engineering to prevent a newborn from having, for example, Tay-Sachs—it's excruciatingly painful and we'd be cruel to intentionally bring such a life into existence when we could do otherwise. I don't even think preventing something like blindness with genetic engineering is a problem. But then you're going to have parents wanting to jiggle the genes to give their kid a few more IQ points, or a little less shyness. And I'm just not sure that's where we want to go.

8.4.7b More practice with slippery slopes

Write three arguments that involve a slippery slope. Then rewrite your arguments so a clear, defensible chain argument is made.

8.4.7c Practice recognizing errors in causal reasoning

Which of the following arguments involve one or more of the following errors in causal reasoning?

- mistaking correlation for causation
- post hoc ergo propter hoc
- failing to consider a common cause
- failing to consider additional causes
- reversing cause and effect
- failing to consider a reciprocal causal relation
- an erroneous appeal to a slippery slope.

Where applicable, re-craft the argument so it is error-free.

1. Lately I've noticed that whenever I'm tired, my eyes itch. I don't know why being tired should make my eyes itch, do you?

2. Suppose we do say that groups that have been discriminated against in the past are entitled to some sort of compensation. How much is enough? This much? No, this much then? *This* much?

3. You know what makes me laugh? All those vanity license plates—if I couldn't spell, I wouldn't advertise that fact on my license plate!

4. All this increase in hurricanes, tornadoes, tsunamis, and so on? Started happening 'bout the same time people started using cell phones in a big way. I tell you, cell phones are EVIL! Every last one of them should be pulverized!

5. Assisted suicide is a form of killing, so if we make it legal, we'll be on a slippery slope to making all sorts of homicide legal.

6. Our clinical studies revealed that people who took our antidepressant drugs became less depressed, proving its effectiveness at combating depression.

7. The more TV people watch, the shallower they become.

8. You shouldn't use such long cords where a short cord will do—think of all that extra electricity you're using and paying for!

9. According to Adam Smith (*The Wealth of Nations*, 1776), each individual, pursuing his or her own selfish interests in a competitive market, will be led by an invisible hand to promote an end which was no part of his intention. So even though they're pursuing their own personal gain, they will serve the common good because, for example, they will have to keep their prices down and their quality up if they are to compete with others.

10. People with high self-esteem were judged by others to be more attractive than people with low self-esteem. This shows that being attractive causes high self-esteem.

Review of terms

Define the following terms:

- correlation

- causation

- direct cause

- indirect cause

- necessary cause

- sufficient cause

- Mill's method of agreement

- Mill's method of difference

- Mill's method of concomitant variation

- Mill's method of residues

- mistaking correlation for causation

- post hoc ergo propter hoc

- failing to consider a common cause

- failing to consider additional causes

- reversing cause and effect

- failing to consider a reciprocal causal relation

- slippery slope.

Thinking critically about what you see

Think critically about each of the following. Consider, especially but not exclusively, the role of causation.

1.

© Getty Images

2.

© Getty Images

Thinking critically about what you hear

Listen to the audio clip under the Student Resources tab on the companion website at www.routledge.com/textbooks/tittle. Any response?

Thinking critically about what you read

Think critically about each of the following, paying special attention to sufficiency, especially when the argument involves causation (as explanation or as the basis of a plan or policy). You may want to consult the template—no wait, it's not here! Guess why.

1. People born soon after World War II were much more likely to move out of their parents' class than those born in later decades. Perhaps the kids were more motivated for success than their parents. Or perhaps the kids started that much lower than their parents and so had more room to move up than they did. Yet another possible explanation is that due to post-war economic boom and the depleted population that resulted because of war, there were far more job opportunities for those born after the war.

2. Most internet activists are liberals, but most of the actual content of newsgroups, chatrooms, and so on, is conservative. What can explain this apparent paradox? There is a small but very vocal group of conservative users.

3. "The USA is the only developed market where Formula 1 doesn't play a role like every-where else in the world," he explains. "So, we said, there must be a reason. It cannot be because of Formula 1, and it cannot be because of the U.S. series, which are strong, so we came to the conclusion that it's because there is no U.S. Formula 1 team."

   (As reported by John Zimmerman, "Riding the Red Bull," *Road & Track*, February 2005)

4. Men typically refuse to ask questions because they perceive such a stance as neediness, and that puts them "one down" in the competition that is life. Also, real men know everything. And anything they don't know isn't very important. Or it could be that the men who don't ask questions simply don't know what questions to ask—they don't know what they don't know. Or maybe it's just that it's more fun to figure it out for yourself.

5. Older people are even more likely to react strongly against any further acceleration of change. There is a solid mathematical basis for the observation that age often correlates with conservatism: time passes more swiftly for the old.

   When a fifty-year-old father tells his fifteen-year-old son that he will have to wait two years before he can have a car of his own, that interval of 730 days represents a mere 4 percent of the father's lifetime to date. It represents over 13 percent of the boy's lifetime. It is hardly strange that to the boy the delay seems three or four times longer than to the father. Similarly, two hours in the life of a four-year-old may be the felt equivalent of twelve hours in the life of her twenty-four-year-old mother. Asking the child to wait two hours for a piece of candy may be the equivalent of asking the mother to wait fourteen hours for a cup of coffee.

There may be a biological basis as well, for such differences in subjective response to time. "With advancing age," writes psychologist John Cohen of the University of Manchester, "the calendar years seem progressively to shrink. In retrospect every year seems shorter than the year just completed, possibly as a result of the gradual slowing down of metabolic processes." In relation to the slowdown of their own biological rhythms, the world would appear to be moving faster to older people, even if it were not.

(Alvin Toffler, *Future Shock*, 1970)

6. I've just read that fetal alcohol syndrome means that the child is actually unable to see the consequences of its actions; it can't reason from cause to effect because certain centers in its brain were destroyed by the alcohol put into its system when it was developing. Can you imagine what a life you would have if you couldn't connect cause and effect? Even as little as one drink a week will do it! I think we should have a policy such that any person who gives their child alcohol, whether before birth or after, should take full responsibility for everything their child does. So if it burns down a house because it didn't see the connection between lighting a match and the house burning down, the parent should have to pay for the house. And serve the time. And if the kid, as an adult, spends its money on movies and beer, not foreseeing that it wouldn't have enough for rent, the mother should pay its rent (not the state, not us). And so on.

7. To be a state is also, in practice, to fight wars, and the bigger and more powerful the state, the more frequent its wars. The belief that lies at the root of all deterrence theory, either nuclear or conventional—that great military strength is the surest guarantee that a country will be left in peace—is demonstrably false and is indeed the exact reverse of the truth.

During the entire period of modern European history from 1480 to 1940, it has been calculated that there were about twenty-six hundred important battles. The only country that was a leading military power during the whole of that period, France, participated in 47 percent of those battles, and Germany (Prussia), Russia, and Britain all fought in between 22 percent and 25 percent of them. By contrast Spain, which ceased to be a major military power at the beginning of the nineteenth century, soon afterward dropped out of Europe's wars almost entirely and can only offer an attendance record of 12 percent over the whole period, and the Netherlands and Sweden (great powers only for brief periods) were present at only 8 percent and 4 percent of Europe's battles respectively [Quincy Wright, *A Study of War*, 1964].

By any other yardstick—the amount of time a given European country has spent at war, the number of wars it has participated in, the proportion of its population that has been killed in war over the years—the result is the same. There is a steep and consistent gradient of suffering, in which the most powerful nations fight most often and lose most heavily in lives and wealth. Nor are these facts unique to Europe. For example, the United States, which has been a great power on the make since soon after its independence, has seen only 25 years of its entire history (now over two centuries) in which its army or navy has not been involved in active operations somewhere during some part of the year, while Sweden, which long ago abandoned its great-power ambitions, has not used its armed forces in a war for 170 years.

(Gwynne Dyer, *War*, 1985)

8. The ACLU's got to take a lot of blame for [the terrorist attack on the World Trade Center, September 11, 2001] . . . But, throwing God out successfully with the help of the federal court system, throwing God out of the public square, out of the schools. The abortionists have got to bear some burden for this because God will not be mocked. And when we destroy 40 million little innocent babies, we make God mad. I really believe that the pagans, and the abortionists, and the feminists, and the gays and the lesbians who are actively trying to make that an alternative lifestyle, the ACLU, People for the American Way—all of them who have tried to secularize America— I point the finger in their face and say "you helped this happen."

(Jerry Falwell at: http://www.rotten.com/library/
bio/religion/televangelists/jerry-falwell/)

9. In a series of four experiments, we examined the relationship between male dominance and female preference in Japanese quail, *Coturnix japonica*. Female quail that had watched an aggressive interaction between a pair of males preferred the loser of an encounter to its winner. This superficially perverse female preference for losers may be explained by the strong correlation between the success of a male in aggressive interactions with other males and the frequency with which he engages in courtship behaviors that appear potentially injurious to females. By choosing to affiliate with less dominant male quail, female quail may lose direct and indirect benefits that would accrue from pairing with a dominant male. However, they also avoid the cost of interacting with potentially harmful, more aggressive males.

(Abstract of Alexander G. Ophir and Bennett G. Galef, Jr.,
"Female Japanese Quail that 'Eavesdrop' on Fighting Males
Prefer Losers to Winners," *Animal Behaviour*, 66, 2003)

10. This is the end of the text! Now, go out into the world and find your own bit(s)—and think critically about whatever you read!

Thinking critically about what you write

Okay, here's the culmination of this component of the course: write a 2,000-word thesis essay. That is, advocate some claim (your thesis), supporting your position with as full an argument as possible, presented in a clear, coherent essay.

It might help to diagram your argument before you start writing it up in complete sentences and paragraphs. Think very carefully: double-check the relevance of your premises (evidence, lines of reasoning). Be sure of the truth of your premises (yes, this will involve research and citations). Make sure your premises are sufficient, given your conclusion. (The stronger your conclusion, the stronger must be your support.)

Don't forget to consider counterevidence, counterexamples, and counterarguments, and deal with them, showing that they don't weaken your argument. (If they do, and you end up modifying your argument, rewrite your paper.) (Until you can't think of any more weakening counterarguments—that is, until you've got as strong an argument as you can make.)

When you start writing, be very careful with your language. You may find your definitions aren't as precise as you thought they were, not as precise as you need them to be. Pause and make them so before continuing.

Ta-dah!

Thinking critically when you discuss

All right, last step in the process: groups of five, free form discussion (that's "free form"—not "free for all"). It'll be complicated (messy), but it'll be real. Keep in mind everything we've covered so far. And see if you can sound like an intelligent bunch of people discussing something and reaching some sort of clarity. (Instead of like the worst TV or radio talk show you've ever seen or heard.)

Suggestion: Don't forget the possibility of enriching the given argument, either by adding detail or example, or with additional lines of reasoning.

Reasoning test questions

1. A group of unusual meteorites was found in Shergotty, India. Their structure indicates that they originated on one of the geologically active planets, Mercury, Venus, or Mars. Because of Mercury's proximity to the Sun, any material dislodged from that planet's surface would have been captured by the Sun, rather than falling to Earth as meteorites. Nor could Venus be the source of the meteorites, because its gravity would have prevented dislodged material from escaping into space. The meteorites, therefore, probably fell to Earth after being dislodged from Mars, perhaps as the result of a collision with a large object.

The argument derives its conclusion by

(A) offering a counterexample to a theory
(B) eliminating competing alternative explanations
(C) contrasting present circumstances with past circumstances
(D) questioning an assumption
(E) abstracting a general principle from specific data

(The Official LSAT Prep Test XXIV, Section 2, #3)

2. Most small children are flat-footed. This failure of the foot to assume its natural arch, if it persists past early childhood, can sometimes result in discomfort and even pain later in life. Traditionally, flat-footedness in children has been treated by having the children wear special shoes that give extra support to the foot, in order to foster the development of the arch.

    Which one of the following, if true, most calls into question the efficacy of the traditional treatment described above?

    (A) Many small children who have normal feet wear the same special shoes as those worn by flat-footed children.
    (B) Studies of flat-footed adults show that flat feet are subject to fewer stress fractures than are feet with unusually high arches.
    (C) Although most children's flat-footedness is corrected by the time the children reach puberty, some people remain flat-footed for life.
    (D) Flat-footed children who do not wear the special shoes are as likely to develop natural arches as are flat-footed children who wear the special shoes.
    (E) Some children who are not flat-footed have hip and lower leg bones that are rotated excessively either inward or outward.

(The Official LSAT Prep Test XXII, Section 2, #4)

3. Fact 1: Television advertising is becoming less effective: the proportion of brand names promoted on television that viewers of the advertising can recall is slowly decreasing.

    Fact 2: Television viewers recall commercials aired first or last in a cluster of consecutive commercials far better than they recall commercials aired somewhere in the middle.

    Fact 2 would be most likely to contribute to an explanation of fact 1 if which of the following were also true?

    (A) The average television viewer currently recalls fewer than half the brand names promoted in commercials he or she saw.
    (B) The total time allotted to the average cluster of consecutive television commercials is decreasing.

367

(C) The average number of hours per day that people spend watching television is decreasing.

(D) The average number of clusters of consecutive commercials per hour of television is increasing.

(E) The average number of television commercials in a cluster of consecutive commercials is increasing.

(GMAT® mini test #3)

4. Essayist: The existence of a moral order in the universe—i.e., an order in which bad is always eventually punished and good rewarded—depends upon human souls being immortal. In some cultures this moral order is regarded as the result of a karma that controls how one is reincarnated, in others it results from the actions of a supreme being who metes out justice to people after their death. But however a moral order is represented, if human souls are immortal, then it follows that the bad will be punished.

Which one of the following most accurately describes a flaw in the essayist's reasoning?

(A) From the assertion that something is necessary to a moral order, the argument concludes that that thing is sufficient for an element of the moral order to be realized.

(B) The argument takes mere beliefs to be established facts.

(C) From the claim that the immortality of human souls implies that there is a moral order in the universe, the argument concludes that there being a moral order in the universe implies that human souls are immortal.

(D) The argument treats two fundamentally different conceptions of a moral order as essentially the same.

(E) The argument's conclusion is presupposed in the definition it gives of a moral order.

(The Official LSAT Prep Test XXIV, Section 2, #23)

5. Write your own reasoning test question, with explanation.

appendix 1

extended arguments for analysis

1. The new know-nothingism: five myths about immigration

DAVID COLE

(*The Nation*, October 17, 1994, reprinted with permission of *The Nation*, excerpt)

[L]et's look at five current myths that distort public debate and government policy relating to immigrants.

- *America is being overrun with immigrants*. In one sense, of course, this is true, but in that sense it has been true since Christopher Columbus arrived. Except for the real Native Americans, we are a nation of immigrants.

  It is not true, however, that the first-generation immigrant share of our population is growing. As of 1990, foreign-born people made up only 8 percent of the population, as compared with a figure of about 15 percent from 1870 to 1920. Between 70 and 80 percent of those who immigrate every year are refugees or immediate relatives of U.S. citizens.

  Much of the anti-immigrant fervor is directed against the undocumented, but they make up only 13 percent of all immigrants residing in the United States, and only 1 percent of the American population. Contrary to popular belief, most such aliens do not cross the border illegally but enter legally and remain after their student or visitor visa expires. Thus, building a wall at the border, no matter how high, will not solve the problem.

- *Immigrants take jobs from U.S. citizens*. There is virtually no evidence to support this view, probably the most widespread misunderstanding about immigrants. As documented by a 1994 A.C.L.U. Immigrants' Rights Project report, numerous studies have found that immigrants actually *create* more jobs than they fill. The jobs immigrants take are of course easier to see, but immigrants are often highly productive, run their own businesses and employ both immigrants and citizens. One study found that Mexican immigration to Los Angeles County between 1970 and 1980 was responsible for 78,000 new jobs. Governor Mario Cuomo reports that immigrants own more than 40,000 companies in New York, which provide thousands of jobs and $3.5 billion to the state's economy every year.

- *Immigrants are a drain on society's resources*. This claim fuels many of the recent efforts to cut off government benefits to immigrants. However, most studies have found that immigrants are a net benefit to the economy because, as a 1994 Urban Institute report concludes, "immigrants generate significantly more in taxes paid than they cost in services received." The Council of Economic Advisers similarly found in 1986 that "immigrants have a favorable effect on the overall standard of living."

Anti-immigrant advocates often cite studies purportedly showing the contrary, but these generally focus only on taxes and services at the local or state level. What they fail to explain is that because most taxes go to the federal government, such studies would also show a net loss when applied to U.S. citizens. At most, such figures suggest that some redistribution of federal and state monies may be appropriate; they say nothing unique about the costs of immigrants.

Some subgroups of immigrants plainly impose a net cost in the short run, principally those who have most recently arrived and have not yet "made it." California, for example, bears substantial costs for its disproportionately large undocumented population, largely because it has on average the poorest and least educated immigrants. But that has been true of every wave of immigrants that has ever reached our shores; it was as true of the Irish in the 1850s, for example, as it is of Salvadorans today. From a long-term perspective, the economic advantages of immigration are undeniable.

Some have suggested that we might save money and diminish incentives to immigrate illegally if we denied undocumented aliens public services. In fact, undocumented immigrants are already ineligible for most social programs, with the exception of education for schoolchildren, which is constitutionally required, and benefits directly related to health and safety, such as emergency medical care and nutritional assistance to poor women, infants and children. To deny such basic care to people in need, apart from being inhumanly callous, would probably cost us more in the long run by exacerbating health problems that we would eventually have to address.

Aliens refuse to assimilate and are depriving us of our cultural and political unity. This claim has been made about every new group of immigrants to arrive on U.S. shores. Supreme Court Justice Stephen Field wrote in 1884 that the Chinese "have remained among us as a separate people, retaining their original peculiarities of dress, manners, habits, and modes of living, which are as marked as their complexion and language." Five years later, he upheld the racially based exclusion of Chinese immigrants. Similar claims have been made over different periods of our history about Catholics, Jews, Italians, Eastern Europeans and Latin Americans.

In most instances, such claims are simply not true; "American culture" has been created, defined and revised by persons who for the most part are descended from immigrants once seen as anti-assimilationist. Descendants of the Irish Catholics, for example, a group once decried as separatist and alien, have become Presidents, senators and representatives (and all of these in one family, in the case of the Kennedys). Our society exerts tremendous pressure to conform, and cultural separatism rarely survives a generation. But more important, even if this claim were true, is this a legitimate rationale for limiting immigration in a society built on the values of pluralism and tolerance?

■ *Noncitizen immigrants are not entitled to constitutional rights.* Our government has long declined to treat immigrants as full human beings, and nowhere is that more clear than in the realm of constitutional rights. Although the Constitution literally extends the fundamental protections in the Bill of Rights to all people, limiting to citizens only the right to vote and run for federal office, the federal government acts as if this were not the case.

In 1893 the executive branch successfully defended a statute that required Chinese laborers to establish their prior residence here by the testimony of "at least one credible white witness." The Supreme Court ruled that this law was constitutional because it was reasonable for Congress to presume that nonwhite witnesses could not be trusted.

The federal government is not much more enlightened today. In a pending case I'm handling in the Court of Appeals for the Ninth Circuit, the Clinton Administration has argued that permanent resident aliens lawfully living here should be extended no more First Amendment rights than aliens applying for first-time admission from abroad—that is, none. Under this view, students at a public university who are citizens may express themselves freely, but students who are not citizens can be deported for saying exactly what their classmates are constitutionally entitled to say.

Growing up, I was always taught that we will be judged by how we treat others. If we are collectively judged by how we have treated immigrants—those who appear today to be "other" but will in a generation be "us"—we are not in very good shape.

2. Rap and hip-hop's negative impact on society

JOSHUA SMITH

(*Issues*, October 2007, at: http://socyberty.com/issues/
rap-and-hip-hops-negative-impact-on-society; excerpt)

Secular rap as a whole has a negative impact on society, particularly on our youth, through its explicit content. It sends a powerful message of hate and violence that is devouring the minds of our youth, playing a major role in such problems as rape, racism, teen pregnancy, suicide, homicide and even gang violence.

Throughout the years rap, particularly secular rap, has had a huge impact on our society. Not only are millions of CDs produced every year but popular rap songs receive heavy rotation on multiple hip hop radio stations. It seems that society—or rather, today's youth—is engulfed in the hip hop culture.

According to Patrice B. Jones, the author of an article written in 2005 on secular rap, the affects [sic] of secular rap on society and our youth could be detrimental. He states that African Americans are "portrayed unfairly and unattractively" by secular rap. Secular rap is simply harmful and is polluting society.

Secular rap music portrays African Americans in a negative light through its lyrics. Many secular rap lyrics consist of horrid tales of violence, such as black on black violence, alcohol abuse, and drug related crimes. Secular rap basically adds on to an already existing stereotype that all black males are violent and dangerous.

This in turn makes life even harder for young African Americans because now they are looked upon as being a "potential threat" to a person's life, or should I say, a person's well-being. This only increases the amount of racism against African Americans and rightfully so because people believe what they hear and may begin to develop a fear of those spoken of in rap lyrics.

Though there is obvious damage being done, these rap artist [sic] refuse to put themselves in the shoes of a young black male who is trying to succeed in a "White Man's World." The way some of the rap songs portray African Americans puts them in an even deeper hole because they have to prove that they are different from the roughhousing gang bangers depicted in secular rap.

As secular rap has progressed and evolved, it has begun to lean more and more towards sexually explicit lyrics which in turn has damaged the image of women. Unlike the "old days" or the so called "early stages" of secular rap, today's rap music portrays women in a negative light through sexually inappropriate remarks.

Popular rap artist [sic] such as E-40, 50 Cent, Ludacris, and Young Buck are well-known for their sexual lyrics. The popular song "Money Maker" by Ludacris not only destroys the image of women, but it also encourages them to prostitute themselves: "Shake, shake, shake your money maker / Like you were shakin' it for some paper."

Critics of my position really seem to not see the whole picture; they do not fully understand how women are being dehumanized by these lyrics and in turn are now being looked upon as sexual objects by our youth. In my opinion this not only puts women in a losing situation (same as African Americans who have to prove they are different from the stereotype) but it also puts many women in danger of sexual crimes, such as rape.

What a person listens to can have a dramatic impact on the emotions and actions of that person. Being a male, I fully understand the influence that sexually related lyrics have on a person. It causes their minds to wander and to think inappropriate things about women. Soon they began to view women not as humans who have feeling, but as sex objects which they must have.

Along with its controversial lyrics on sex and races, secular rap also promotes gang violence and at times even glorifies it. Many of today's popular rap artists, such as Snoop Dogg (Crip), The Game (Blood) and Lil Scrappy (Blood), promote their life of crime through their music. A good example of the promotion of gang violence would be a song released in 2002 by Tupac Shakur (2Pac) entitled

"Ghetto Star." Though I myself am a fan of 2Pac because of some of the good things he stood for, he was also very gang related.

The first verse of the song basically demonstrates how violent secular rap is nowadays: "I hit the weed / And hope to god I can fly high / Witness my enemies / Die when I ride by / They shouldn't have tried me / Send they bodies to their parents up north / With they faces they wrists and they nuts cut off."

Secular rap is not only sending a message of violence to our youth and society as a whole, but it is also glorifying these acts of violence ("Ghetto Star"). This, in turn, leads directly to an immense problem our world is facing today. People die daily in the streets of New York, Compton, Long Beach, Houston and just about every other urban city across the United States.

According to areaconnect.com, in LA and NY alone a little more than 1000 people were murdered in 2005. The crime rates continue to rise almost every year, and you have to wonder if secular rap is influencing this in any way.

One of the most disturbing aspects of secular rap is its violent words directed towards cops and other authority figures. Rappers today continuously attack police officers verbally, even using profanity to describe them. Back in the early days of rap, N.W.A made the phrase "F*** the police" famous and it just has continued to grow even more violent.

According to raplyricssearch.com, in a song by Kool G, he describes a train robbery in which he shoots and kills four cops; and in a song made by Makaveli (aka, 2Pac) entitled "Open Fire," he goes into great detail about an event (made up) in which he escapes from the cops, leaving multiple officers dead. These words of hate directed towards cops are poisonous to society because of the affects [sic] they have on the youth. Today's generation is strongly influenced by the hip-hop culture, made evident through the millions of CDs produced every year, so the views of these rappers can easily influence their listeners to see things in the same light. This is one of the reasons why the youth today are so out of control.

They lack respect for any real authority figure and most secular rap simply reinforces this thinking. Without question the impact of secular rap has led to many slain cops. According to axt.com, the controversial song "Cop Killer" by Ice-T has been "implicated in at least two shootings." One of the deadliest ones happened in 1992.

According to axt.com, "While on patrol in July 1992, two Las Vegas police officers were ambushed and shot by four juvenile delinquents who boasted that Ice-T's 'Cop Killer' gave them a sense of duty and purpose, to get even with 'a f—king pig.' The juveniles continued to sing its lyrics when apprehended."

Secular rap's promotion of cop killings is a very disturbing problem that should in no way be overlooked. Secular hasn't always been so bad, but throughout time it seems to have strayed from the path. Back in the 1980s, hip hop/rap was born. Artists such as Run DMC, LL Cool J, Sugarhill Gang, and GangStarr all were very popular. They were, as many would call, the pioneers of rap.

Unlike today's music, vulgar language was rarely used; instead, they spoke about more social issues and changes that could be made to make society better. Even rappers of the early 1990s, such as 2Pac, were making positive impacts on society through their lyrics. 2Pac touched many people's lives through songs such as "Keep Ya Head Up," "Trapped," and "Hold on be Strong," encouraging the black community (as well as everyone else) to continue to fight and to be strong even when tragedy occurs.

Hip hop didn't always used to be negative and vulgar, no; it started off as a good thing, a positive thing. As a result, crimes were somewhat down and society seemed to be growing. Then came rappers such as N.W.A and Ice-T, who promoted the use of violence when confronted by policemen and gang violence. Also with this came many other rappers such as Biggie and Nas. Violence grew as the 2Pac vs. Biggie feud emerged, which led to both of them being murdered. To show how negative an effect these two feuding rappers had on society during this time period, you need not look any further then their deaths.

After 2Pac of Deathrow records (ties with the Bloods) was apparently killed by a Crip, the following week gang violence between the Bloods and the Crips in Compton, California was intense. Several people were slain in retaliation, which ultimately led to the death of Biggie. Their feud had a negative impact on society, proving that we are indeed affected by what we listen to.

Today, the music has gotten even worse and this seems to be one of the reasons society, in general, is failing. What if the positive tactics of the early days of rap were used in today's music? Would it change things? There is no doubt that it would send a more positive message to the youth, which in turn would change the way we as a society think . . .

3. In defense of negative campaigning

WILLIAM G. MAYER

(Reprinted by permission from *Political Science Quarterly*, 111 (Fall 1996): 437–455, excerpt)

When televised presidential debates were first held in 1960, many commentators deplored them for their shallow, insubstantial nature. But when scholars write about those debates today, they almost invariably comment about how much better the Kennedy–Nixon encounters seem than any of the more recent presidential debates. Students to whom I have shown excerpts from these debates usually have the same reaction. Compared to the Great Confrontations of [today], the 1960 debates seem more civil, more intelligent, more substantive. Especially noticeable is what is missing from the 1960 debates: the antsiness, the evasions, the meaningless memorized one-liners designed only to be featured on the postdebate newscasts, the boos and applause from the studio audience.

. . .

This nascent reform movement has a number of specific targets and criticism, but one of the most widely mentioned is negative campaigning. Whenever commentators compile a catalogue of the most heinous sins in current American politics, negative campaigning and attack advertising usually wind up near the top of the list . . .

. . .

To many observers, the problem is sufficiently serious to require laws and regulations that would discourage or penalize negative campaigning . . . One frequently made proposal . . . would require any candidate who uses radio or television commercials to attack another candidate to deliver the attack in person. Another suggestion is to allow television and radio stations to charge higher rates for negative commercials than for positive ones. Some critics have even argued that the United States should follow the example of Venezuela and bar candidates entirely from referring to their opponents by name or by picture in their ads.

. . .

There is little doubt that contemporary American election campaigns do fall short of the standards commended in our civics books. But in the laudable desire to improve our campaigns, surprisingly little attention has been paid to the easy, almost reflexive assumption that negative campaigning is bad campaigning: negative speeches and advertising are always morally wrong and damaging to our political system. In part, perhaps, the problem is one of semantics. Negative campaigning certainly sounds bad: it's so, well, you know, negative. But if we move beyond the label, what really is so bad about negative campaigning?

The purpose of this article, as its title indicates, is to challenge the accepted wisdom about negative campaigning. Negative campaigning, in my view, is a necessary and legitimate part of any election; and our politics—and the growing movement to reform our election campaigns—will be a good deal better off when we finally start to acknowledge it.

The value of negative campaigning

What exactly is negative campaigning? Most people who use the term seem to have in mind a definition such as the following: Negative campaigning is campaigning that attacks or is critical of an opposing candidate. Where positive campaigning dwells on the candidate's own strengths and merits, and talks about the beneficial politics he would adopt if elected, negative campaigning focuses on the weaknesses and faults of the opposition: the mistakes they have made, the flaws in their character or performance, the bad policies they would pursue. And the more one focuses on the reality and consequences of such practices, the more clear I think it becomes that negative campaigning is not the plain and unmitigated evil that it is frequently portrayed to be. To the contrary, negative campaigning provides voters with a lot of valuable information that they definitely need to have when deciding how to cast their ballots.

To begin with, any serious substantive discussion of what a candidate intends to do after the election can only be conducted by talking about the flaws and shortcomings of current policies. If a candidate is arguing for a major change in government policy, his first responsibility is to show that current policies are in some way deficient. If the economy is already growing rapidly with low rates of inflation, if the "environmental crisis" has been greatly exaggerated, if present policies have largely eliminated the possibility that nuclear arms will actually be used, then everything the candidates are proposing in these areas is useless, even dangerous. The need for such proposals becomes clear only when a candidate puts them in the context of present problems—only, that is to say, when a candidate "goes negative." . . .

But the information and analysis embodied in negative campaigning are also valuable on their own terms, for they tell us something extremely relevant about the choices we are about to make. We need to find out about the candidates' strengths, it is true, but we also need to learn about their weaknesses: the abilities and virtues they don't have; the mistakes they have made; the problems they haven't dealt with; the issues they would prefer not to talk about; the bad or unrealistic policies they have proposed. If one candidate performed poorly in his last major public office, if another has no clear or viable plan for dealing with the economy, if a third is dishonest, the voters really do need to be informed about such matters. I need hardly add that no candidate is likely to provide a full and frank discussion of his own shortcomings. Such issues will only get a proper hearing if an opponent is allowed to talk about them by engaging in negative campaigning.

Finally, negative campaigning is valuable if for no other reason than its capacity to keep the candidates a bit more honest than they would be otherwise. One doesn't have to have a lot of respect for the truth and intelligence of current campaign practices in order to conclude that things would be a lot worse without negative campaigning. If candidates always knew that their opponents would never say anything critical about them, campaigns would quickly turn into a procession of lies, exaggerations, and unrealistic promises. Candidates could misstate their previous records, present glowing accounts of their abilities, make promises they knew they couldn't keep—all with the smug assurance that no one would challenge their assertions. Every campaign speech could begin with the words, "I think I can say without fear of contradiction . . ."

. . .

I have frequently encountered [this] surprising reaction: . . . "Nobody criticizes *all* negative campaigning. When people criticize negative campaigning they're not worried about attacks that are true and deal with significant issues. What they're upset about is that so much of this attack advertising is misleading or nasty or about made-up issues that have no real relevance to governing. *That's* what the furor's all about."

To this argument, I would make two responses. First, I would urge anyone who thinks I am overstating the case to read through a substantial part of the writing that has built up recently around the question of negative campaigning. What you will find is that the vast majority of this work . . . does, indeed, indict all campaign activities that are aimed at criticizing one's opponents, regardless of the particular issues they deal with, without even investigating whether the attacks are true or not . . . [M]ost writing on the topic criticizes *all* negative campaigning, without any attempt to draw distinctions about its truth, relevance, or civility . . .

. . .

To defend negative campaigning, of course, is not to deny that positive campaigning is also important . . .

4. Television and violent crime

BRANDON S. CENTERWALL

(*The Public Interest*, no. 111, Spring 1993, pp. 56–71, excerpt. Reprinted with permission of National Affairs, at: www.nationalaffairs.com)

From 1945 to 1974, the white homicide rate in the United States increased 93 percent. In Canada, the homicide rate increased 92 percent. In South Africa, where television was banned, the white homicide rate declined by 7 percent.

Could there be some explanation other than television for the fact that violence increased dramatically in the U.S. and Canada while dropping in South Africa? I examined an array of alternative explanations. None is satisfactory:

■ Economic growth. Between 1946 and 1974, all three countries experienced substantial economic growth. Per capita income increased by 75 percent in the United States. 124 percent in Canada, and 86 percent in South Africa. Thus differences in economic growth cannot account for the different homicide trends in the three countries.

■ Civil unrest. One might suspect that anti-war or civil-rights activity was responsible for the doubling of the homicide rate in the United States during this period. But the experience of Canada shows that this was not the case, since Canadians suffered a doubling of the homicide rate without similar civil unrest.

Other possible explanations include changes in age distribution, urbanization, alcohol consumption, capital punishment, and the availability of firearms. As discussed in *Public Communication and Behavior* (1989), none provides a viable explanation for the observed homicide trends.

In the United States and Canada, there was a lag of ten to fifteen years between the introduction of television and a doubling of the homicide rate. In South Africa, there was a similar lag. Since television exerts its behavior-modifying effects primarily on children, while homicide is primarily an adult activity, this lag represents the time needed for the "television generation" to come of age.

The relationship between television and the homicide rate holds *within* the United States as well. Different regions of the U.S., for example, acquired television at different times. As we would expect, while all regions saw increases in their homicide rates, the regions that acquired television first were also the first to see higher homicide rates.

Similarly, urban areas acquired television before rural areas. As we would expect, urban areas saw increased homicide rates several years before the occurrence of a parallel increase in rural areas.

The introduction of television also helps explain the different rates of homicide growth for whites and minorities. White households in the U.S. began acquiring television sets in large numbers approximately five years before minority households. Significantly, the white homicide rate began increasing in 1958, four years before a parallel increase in the minority homicide rate.

Of course, there are many factors other than television that influence the amount of violent crime. Every violent act is the result of a variety of forces coming together—poverty, crime, alcohol and drug abuse, stress—of which childhood TV exposure is just one. Nevertheless, the evidence indicates that if, hypothetically, television technology had never been developed, there would today be 10,000 fewer homicides each year in the United States, 70,000 fewer rapes, and 700,000 fewer injurious assaults. Violent crime would be half what it is.

5. A crime by any other name

JEFFREY H. REIMAN AND PAUL LEIGHTON

(Jeffrey H. Reiman and Paul Leighton, *The Rich Get Richer and the Poor Get Prison*, © 2010 Pearson Education, Inc. Reproduced by permission of Pearson Education, Inc.)

If it takes you an hour to read this chapter, by the time you reach the last page, two of your fellow citizens will have been murdered. *During that same time, at least 4 Americans will die as a result of unhealthy or unsafe conditions in the workplace!* Although these work-related deaths could have been prevented, they are not called murders. Why not? Doesn't a crime by any other name still cause misery and suffering? What's in a name?

The fact is that the label "crime" is not used in American to name all or the worst of the actions that cause misery and suffering to Americans. It is primarily reserved for the dangerous actions of the poor.

In the March 14, 1976 edition of the *Washington Star*, a front-page article appeared with the headline: "Mine Is Closed 26 Deaths Late." The article read in part:

> Why, the relatives [of the 26 dead miners] ask, did the mine ventilation fail and allow pockets of methane gas to build up in a shaft 2,300 feet below the surface? . . .
>
> [I]nvestigators of the Senate Labor and Welfare Committee . . . found that there have been 1,250 safety violations at the 13-year-old mine since 1970. Fifty-seven of those violations were serious enough for federal inspectors to order the mine closed and 21 of those were in cases where federal inspectors felt there was imminent danger to the lives of the miners working there.
>
> (*The Washington Star*, March 14, 1976, pp. A1, A9)

Next to the continuation of this story was another, headlined: "Mass Murder Claims Six in Pennsylvania" (Ibid. p. A9). It described the shooting death of a husband and wife, their three children, and a friend in a Philadelphia suburb. This was murder, maybe even mass murder. My only question is, why wasn't the death of the miners also murder?

Why do 26 dead miners amount to a "disaster" and 6 dead suburbanites a "mass murder"? Murder suggests a murderer, while "disaster" suggests the work of impersonal forces. But if over 1000 safety violations had been found in the mine—three the day before the first explosion—was no one responsible for failing to eliminate the hazards? Was no one responsible for preventing the hazards? And if someone could have prevented the hazards and did not, does that person not bear responsibility of the deaths of 26 men? Is he less evil because he did not want them to die although he chose to leave them in jeopardy? Is he not a murderer, perhaps even a mass murderer? . . .

It is important to identify this model of the Typical Crime because it functions like a set of blinders. It keeps us from calling a mine disaster a mass murder even if 26 men are killed, even if someone is responsible for the unsafe conditions in which they worked and died. In fact, I argue that this particular piece of mental furniture so blocks our view that it keeps us from using the criminal justice system to protect ourselves from the greatest threats to our persons and possessions.

What keeps a mine disaster from being a mass murder in our eyes is the fact that it is not one-on-one harm. What is important here is not the numbers but the *intent to harm someone*. An attack by a gang on one or more persons or an attack by one individual on several fits the model of one-on-one harm. That is, for each person harmed there is at least one individual who wanted to harm that person. Once he selects his victim, the rapist, the mugger, the murderer, all want this person they have selected to suffer. A mine executive, on the other hand, does not want his employees to be harmed. He would truly prefer that there be no accident, no injured or dead miners. What he does want is something legitimate.

It is what he has been hired to get: maximum profits at minimum costs. If he cuts corners to save a buck, he is just doing his job. If 26 men die because he cut corners on safety, we may think him crude or callous but not a killer. He is, at most, responsible for an *indirect harm*, not a one-on-one harm. For this, he may even be criminally indictable for violating safety regulations—but not for murder. The 26 men are dead as an unwanted consequence of his (perhaps overzealous or undercautious) pursuit of a legitimate goal. And so, unlike the Typical Criminal, he has not committed the Typical Crime. Or so we generally believe. As a result, 26 men are dead who might be alive if cutting corners of the kind that leads to loss of life, whether suffering is specifically intended or not, were treated as murder.

6. Does society have the right to force pregnant drug addicts to abort their fetuses?

GEORGE SCHEDLER

(*Social Theory & Practice*, 17.3 (Fall 1991), excerpt. Reprinted with permission of *Social Theory & Practice* and the author)

My argument in brief is that, first, society has a duty to insure that infants are born free of avoidable defects, and, second, that those defects caused by chemical abuse of the pregnant mother are easily avoidable. Third, it follows that society can prevent pregnant addicts from giving birth. The paper is divided into three parts containing the argument for each of these propositions in turn.

1. Society has a duty to insure that infants are born free of avoidable defects

There are three arguments for this proposition: one, based on the rights of the fetus as a future infant; another, based on the rights of future persons; and a third, based on the economic and human costs of drug abuse during pregnancy. The first two arguments are rights-based, while the third is utilitarian. Although the first and second arguments have in common an appeal to our duties to future persons, they differ insofar as the first focuses on our duties to presently existing creatures that will become persons, while the second focuses on the precautions we must generally take to avoid unnecessary suffering for future persons.

A. The Right of the Fetus as a Future Infant. This argument is based on the general principle that all creatures—even those who are not persons now—

have a right to be free of the injurious (but avoidable) effects other people knowingly inflict as a result of their socially harmful activities. Prenatal injury to infants is special because the injurious effect occurs before the infant begins to exist but while a potential infant exists. This should not be troublesome, however, because we deal here not with the rights of all fetuses, but only with those that will become infants. Perhaps the argument will be more plausible if we begin with the less controversial right of a child to be compensated for prenatal injury. . . .

B. The Rights of Future Infants Generally. My second argument discusses the burdens that can legitimately be imposed on presently existing people, so people who come into existence later can be spared some suffering. Instead of focusing on a presently existing creature that will later develop into a person, it concentrates on the precautions we must take to prevent suffering in the future. It has much in common with arguments for preservation of the environment . . .

C. The Economic and Human Costs. Even a libertarian of a Millian stripe for whom there must be a clear adverse effect on society generally to justify interference in the private lives of citizens would be forced to admit that pregnant women should be prohibited from using drugs and that those who refused to do so should be forced to undergo abortions. Besides the utilitarian argument, there is an argument from fairness that we will consider. Both arguments must take into account the economic costs and the enormous suffering avoided by forcing pregnant drug addicts to undergo abortions (when they refuse to refrain from drug use).

Clearly, the economic cost of caring for children with fetal alcohol syndrome and for "crack babies" is huge. Equally clearly, the perpetrators of the afflictions, the mothers, are in no position to pay these costs. Instead, insurance companies or private or public hospitals and public schools will absorb these costs and pass them on in the form of taxes or higher insurance premiums. Thus, the general public, qua taxpayers and insured persons, must involuntarily pay the price for the drug abuse of others.

Insofar as the public must ultimately pay the bill, it seems only fair that society be allowed to minimize the total cost in reasonable ways. Surely, one such reasonable demand is that pregnant women who do not intend to abort their fetuses be prohibited from abusing drugs. The more difficult question is whether pregnant women can be forced to undergo abortions if they do not refrain from drug use. However, the human suffering avoided should make a convincing case at least for utilitarians.

By forcing a pregnant drug addict to undergo an abortion, all the suffering that the resulting infant must undergo is avoided. Less important but significant is that those who would have cared for the infant would be occupied with less depressing work, and teachers would be free to devote themselves to other students with fewer learning and behavioral difficulties. Also, any relatives of the child would not experience the unhappiness of knowing one of their relatives is a "crack baby" or a child with fetal alcohol syndrome (FAS).

Although it may seem cruel to force a woman to undergo an abortion or drug treatment, the suffering a woman undergoes in either case pales in comparison with the suffering of the infant and of others working with or related to it. This is especially so for those infants who do not receive the proper care and education as they grow older. In the case in which a woman is forced to undergo a successful drug treatment program, the increased happiness of a life free from drugs must be put in the balance. If the state must force a woman to undergo an abortion, the pain of the abortion is not that great. The larger utilitarian concern—at least for someone like Mill—is that the state may have interfered wrongly. But this is not likely, given how high the probability of fetal injury is and how obvious drug addiction is.

It might be objected that this argument ignores what is really controversial about forced abortions. What is at issue, it might be said, is not the physical pain or the health risks the procedure entails but the psychological trauma of being deprived of one's future child. It is arguably worse than a spontaneous miscarriage, because, unlike the latter which is due to happenstance, the loss is brought about by a decision on society's part.

However much significance the trauma may have on a visceral level, it does not figure importantly on a moral level, because my argument is that a woman's rights do not include the right to give birth to infants under these circumstances. So the trauma involved can only have significance at a utilitarian level. But for "crack" addicts, whose lives are filled with degradation, interspersed with brief periods of pleasure, an involuntary abortion would be an experience of lesser moment. To be sure, for a woman who had been striving unsuccessfully to give birth, coerced abortion would be devastating, but pregnant addicts like this would be rare indeed. The overall utilitarian calculation, then, would favor coerced abortion.

Given all the pain and expense unhindered drug abuse by pregnant women imposes on infants, on those connected with them, and on society generally, on the one hand, and on the other, the relatively small cost of abortion and drug treatment and the greater happiness either would generate in the long run, there is a good argument from fairness here: it is simply unfair to the infant, those connected with it, and to society in general not to prevent such infants from being born. Even the parties in Rawls's original position would prefer a society that restricts women's reproductive freedom as I have suggested. That is, if one considers the worst-off position in either scenario, it is easy to reach the conclusion that it is better to be a drug addict forced to undergo an abortion than to be a "crack baby" or an infant with FAS. This certainly provides some basis for the conclusion that it is fairer to force pregnant drug addicts to abort than not to place any restrictions on them.

2. Those defects caused by chemical abuse of the pregnant mother are easily avoidable

There are two ways a woman contemplating pregnancy can continue to abuse drugs without violating the rights of any infant to whom she might give birth: she can cease using drugs or she can abort the fetus . . .

3. Therefore, society can justifiably prevent pregnant addicts from giving birth

Society has the right in principle to take reasonable steps to insure that infants are not born with afflictions that result from drug abuse during pregnancy.

7. Condoms: the new diploma

RUSH LIMBAUGH

The logic and motivation behind this country's mad dash to distribute free condoms in our public schools is ridiculous and misguided. Worse, the message conveyed by mass condom distribution is a disservice and borders on being lethal. Condom distribution sanctions, even encourages, sexual activity, which in teen years tends to be promiscuous and relegates to secondary status the most important lesson to be taught: abstinence. An analysis of the entire condom distribution logic also provides a glimpse into just what is wrong with public education today.

First things first. Advocates of condom distribution say that kids are going to have sex, that try as we might we can't stop them. Therefore they need protection. Hence, condoms. Well, hold on a minute. Just whose notion is it that "kids are going to do it anyway, you can't stop them"? Why limit the application of that brilliant logic to sexual activity? Let's just admit that kids are going to do drugs and distribute safe, untainted drugs every morning in homeroom. Kids are going to smoke, too, we can't stop them, so let's provide packs of low-tar cigarettes to the students for their after-sex smoke. Kids are going to get guns and shoot them, you can't stop them, so let's make sure that teachers have bulletproof vests. I mean, come on! If we are really concerned about safe sex, why stop at condoms? Let's convert study halls to Safe Sex Centers where students can go to actually have sex on nice double beds with clean sheets under the watchful and approving eye of the school nurse, who will be on hand to demonstrate, along with the principal, just how to use a condom. Or even better: If kids are going to have sex, let's put disease-free hookers in these Safe Sex Centers. Hey, if safe sex is the objective, why compromise our standards?

There is something else very disturbing about all this. Let's say that Johnny and Susie are on a date in Johnny's family sedan. Johnny pulls in to his town's designated Teen Parking Location hoping to score a little affection from Susie. They move to the backseat and it isn't long before Johnny, on the verge of bliss, whips out his trusty high school-distributed condom and urges Susie not to resist him. She is hesitant, being a nice girl and all, and says she doesn't think the time is right.

"Hey, everything is okay. Nothing will go wrong. Heck, the *school gave me this condom*, they know what they're doing. You'll be fine," coos the artful and suave Johnny.

Aside from what is obviously wrong here, there is something you probably haven't thought of which to me is profound. Not that long ago, school policy, including that on many college campuses, was designed to protect the girls from the natural and instinctive aggressive pursuit of young men. Chaperones, for example, were around to make sure the girls were not in any jeopardy. So much for that thinking now. The schools may just as well endorse and promote these backseat affairs. The lads are going to do it anyway.

Well, here's what's wrong. There have always been consequences to having sex. Always. Now, however, some of these consequences are severe: debilitating venereal diseases and AIDS. You can now die from having sex. It is that simple. If you look, the vast majority of adults in America have made adjustments in their sexual behavior in order to protect themselves from some of the dire consequences floating around out there. For the most part, the sexual revolution of the sixties is over, a miserable failure. Free love and rampant one-night stands are tougher to come by because people are aware of the risks. In short, we have modified our behavior. Now, would someone tell me what is so difficult about sharing this knowledge and experience with kids? The same stakes are involved. Isn't that our responsibility, for crying out loud, to teach them what's best for them? If we adults aren't responding to these new dangers by having condom-protected sex anytime, anywhere, why should such folly be taught to our kids?

Let me try the Magic Johnson example for you who remain unconvinced. Imagine that you are in the Los Angeles Lakers locker room after a game and you and Magic are getting ready to go hit the town. Outside the locker room are a bunch of young women, as there always are, and as Magic had freely admitted there always were, and that you know that the woman Magic is going to pick up and take back to the hotel has AIDS. You approach Magic and say, "Hey, Magic! Hold on! That girl you're going to take back to the hotel with you has AIDS. Here, don't worry about it. Take these condoms, you'll be fine."

Do you think Magic would have sex with that woman? Ask yourself: Would you knowingly have sex with *anyone* who has AIDS with only a condom to

385

protect you from getting the disease? It doesn't take Einstein to answer that question. So, why do you think it's okay to send lads out into the world to do just that? Who is to know who carries the HIV virus, and on the chance your kid runs into someone who does have it, are you confident that a condom will provide all the protection he or she needs?

Doesn't it make sense to be honest with lads and tell them the best thing they can do to avoid AIDS or any of the other undesirable consequences is to abstain from sexual intercourse? It is the best way—in fact, it is the only surefire way—to guard against sexual transmission of AIDS, pregnancy, and venereal diseases. What's so terrible about saying so?

Yet, there are those who steadfastly oppose the teaching of abstinence, and I think they should be removed from any position of authority where educating children is concerned. In New York, the City Board of Education *narrowly won* (4-3) the passage of a resolution requiring the inclusion of teaching abstinence in the AIDS education program in the spring of 1992. No one was trying to eliminate anything from the program, such as condom distribution or anal sex education (which does occur in New York public school sex education classes). All they wanted was that abstinence also be taught. Yet, the Schools Chancellor, Joseph Fernandez, vigorously fought the idea, saying it would do great damage to their existing program! Well, just how is that? The fact is that abstinence works every time it is tried. As this book went to press, the New York Civil Liberties Union was considering filing a lawsuit to stop this dangerous new addition to the curriculum. Now what in the name of God is going on here? This is tantamount to opposing a drug education program which instructs students not to use drugs because it would not be useful.

The Jacksonville, Florida, school board also decided that abstinence should be the centerpiece of their sexual education curriculum, and the liberals there were also outraged about this. What is so wrong with this? Whose agenda is being denied by teaching abstinence and just what is that agenda?

Jacksonville teachers are telling seventh-graders that "the only safe sex is no sex at all." Sex education classes provide some information about birth control and sexually transmitted diseases, but these areas are not the primary focus of the classes. Nancy Corwin, a member of the school board, admits the paradox when she says that the schools send a nonsensical message when they teach kids not to have sex but then give them condoms.

Instead of this twaddle, the Jacksonville school board has decided to teach real safe sex, which is abstinence. However, six families, along with Planned Parenthood and the ACLU, are suing the schools over this program. This bunch of curious citizens says that teaching abstinence puts the children at a greater risk of catching AIDS or other sexually transmitted diseases. Greater risk? !£#$£@! How can that be? What kind of contaminated thinking is this? The suit alleges that the schools are providing a "fear-based program that gives children incomplete, inaccurate, biased, and sectarian information." You want more? Try this:

Linda Lanier of Planned Parenthood says, "It's not right to try to trick our students." Trick the students? #£&@£!? If anyone is trying to trick students, it's Planned Parenthood and this band of hedonists who try to tell kids that a condom will protect them from any consequences of sex.

Folks, here you have perhaps the best example of the culture war being waged in our country today. To say that "teaching abstinence is a trick" is absurd. Is Ms. Lanier having sex every night of the week? What adjustments has she made in her sex life because of AIDS? Does she think that a little sheath of latex will be enough to protect her?

This is terribly wrong. The Jacksonville public school system is attempting to teach right from wrong, as opposed to teaching that sex does not have any consequences, which I believe is the selfish agenda these people hold dear. I have stated elsewhere in this book, and I state it again here, that there are many people who wish to go through life guilt-free and engage in behavior they know to be wrong and morally vacant. In order to assuage their guilt they attempt to construct and impose policies which not only allow them to engage in their chosen activities but encourage others to do so as well. There is, after all, strength in numbers.

Promiscuous and self-gratifying, of-the-moment sex is but one of these chosen lifestyles. Abortions on demand and condom distribution are but two of the policies and programs which, as far as these people are concerned, ensure there are no consequences. As one disgusted member of the Jacksonville school board said, "Every yahoo out there has a social program that they want to run through the school system. We are here for academic reasons and we cannot cure the social evils of the world."

The worst of all of this is the lie that condoms really protect against AIDS. The condom failure rate can be as high as 20 percent. Would you get on a plane —or put your children on a plane—if one in five passengers would be killed on the flight? Well, the statistic holds for condoms, folks.

Ah, but there is even more lunacy haunting the sacred halls of academe. According to the *Los Angeles Times*, administrators in the Los Angeles public schools have regretfully acknowledged that the sex education courses undertaken in the early 1970s "might" have a correlation to the rising teen pregnancy rates in their schools which can be traced to the same years. They have devised an enlightened and marvelous new approach to modernize and correct the sex education curriculum. It is called Outercourse. I am not making this up. Outercourse is, in essence, instruction in creative methods of masturbation.

"Hi, class, and welcome to Outercourse 101. I am your instructor, Mr. Reubens, from Florida, and I want to remind you that this is a hands-on course." We will know the graduates of Outercourse 101 in about forty years. They will be the people walking around with seeing-eye dogs.

8. It's OK to vote for Obama because he's black

GARY KAMIYA

(Salon.com, February 2008. This article first appeared in Salon.com, at http://www.salon.com. An online version remains in the Salon Archives. Reprinted with permission)

I admit it: I'm voting for Barack Obama because he's black. Yes, I'm voting for him because he's qualified, intelligent, charismatic and competent—and because unlike Hillary Clinton, he opposed the Iraq war from the beginning. But if he weren't black, and Hillary had opposed the war, I'd probably vote for her because of her greater experience. In any case, it's a moot point, because if Obama weren't black, he would not be the Democratic front-runner.

I believe that most of Obama's supporters are voting for him for the same reason. Like me, they're drawn to his idealism, his youthful energy, his progressive politics. But it's his blackness that seals the deal.

And that's OK. In fact, it's wonderful.

There's a lot of resistance to this idea, and a lot of discomfort about even expressing it. In online discussions, many whites vehemently deny that Obama's race played any role at all in their decision to support him. They insist that his color doesn't matter, that they decided to support him simply because he's the best candidate.

This reaction is understandable. It feels more racially enlightened. To baldly proclaim that you support Obama because he's black seems to diminish his real qualities and achievements—his stellar academic career, his work in the urban trenches, his liberal voting record, his ability to inspire. Foregrounding Obama's ethnic heritage implies that you're unhealthily obsessed with race, and make artificial decisions based on it. It can be seen as patronizing, as a merely sentimental, pie-in-the-sky gesture.

Unable to directly challenge Democratic voters' race-driven enthusiasm for Obama because that would make her look racially insensitive, Clinton's attacks on Obama as a false messiah covertly echo this theme. "Now I could stand up here and say, 'Let's get everybody together, let's get unified, the sky will open, the light will come down, celestial choirs will be singing,'" she said sarcastically one Sunday in Rhode Island. "'And everyone will know we should do the right thing, and the world will be perfect.'"

Neocon pundit Bill Kristol, whose unerringly wrong track record on Iraq earned him a spot on the New York Times' Op-Ed page, joined Clinton in bashing Obama as a bogus messiah (also without mentioning race). In his Monday column, Kristol wrote, "[T]he effectual truth of what Obama is saying is that he is the one we've been waiting for."

Some critics who directly acknowledge the racial nature of Obama's appeal have argued that the wave of white support for Obama bespeaks not a genuine desire to bridge the racial divide but a bad-faith attempt to escape into some post-racial never-never land. David Ehrenstein, who is black, wrote a widely discussed column last year in the L.A. Times in which he argued that Obama's appeal derives from his role as the "Magic Negro," a benign, unthreatening figure who suddenly shows up to offer racial absolution to mildly guilty whites. "The less real he seems, the more desirable he becomes," Ehrenstein writes. "If he were real, white America couldn't project all its fantasies of curative black benevolence on him."

Some conservatives, not surprisingly, have blasted the racial component of Obama's white support, seeing it as a kind of affirmative action for undeserving minorities. A post on the right-wing site Townhall.com excoriated Democrats for treating the campaign like an affirmative action program, handing a "completely unqualified" candidate the nomination "because he's part of a minority."

All of these criticisms, whether they acknowledge it or not, are based on the fact that Obama's blackness is his indispensable asset. Without it, he would not have a snowball's chance in hell of being elected president.

Let me be absolutely clear: This does not mean he's not qualified. He is—and if he weren't, he wouldn't have a chance to be elected either. I support Obama for a lot of reasons that have nothing to do with his race. I want to take a chance on a younger candidate who is less entrenched with special interests. I've had enough of the Bush/Clinton dynasties. And, above all, I support him because he was opposed to the Iraq war, and will turn decisively away from the disastrous militarism and ideological extremism of the Bush years.

But if Obama were a white junior senator from Illinois with the same impressive personal and professional qualities—the same intelligence, empathy, speaking skills, legislative tenure and life story—there'd be no way he'd have the name recognition to mount a major campaign in the first place. And if he did manage to run, it's unlikely he would have inspired such a passionate and widespread following.

Obama's charisma, which is his unique political strength, is real, but it cannot be separated from the fact that he's black. When Obama speaks of change and hope and healing divisions, his words carry an electric charge because of who he is: He *embodies his own message,* the very definition of charisma. As a black man offering reconciliation, he is making a deeply personal connection with whites, not merely a rhetorical one.

So white enthusiasm for Obama is driven by his race. But there's nothing wrong with that fact. Those who criticize it are simultaneously too idealistic and too cynical: They assume that it's possible to simply ignore Obama's race, while also imputing unsavory motivations to those who are inspired by it. The truth is that whites' race-driven enthusiasm for Obama is an almost unreservedly positive thing—both because electing a black president is a good thing in its own right, and because of what that enthusiasm says about race relations in America today.

Yes, there can be a touch of bathos and self-congratulation in white Obama-mania. But so what? Great historical shifts are often accompanied by such feelings. Besides, sincerity and sentimentality are not mutually exclusive. Barack is no Magic Negro. The truth is, the more white voters find out about Obama, the more they like him. His story and personality resonate with whites. Obama has been able to bridge the gap between white America and black America because figuratively and literally, he's both black and white. Because of his personality, he's the perfect racial go-between: His nonthreatening demeanor allows him to connect with whites, while the fact that he's black—and proudly and avowedly so—makes that connection feel racially redemptive.

As for the right-wing dismissal of Obama as an unqualified recipient of a national affirmative action program, that argument is absurd because Obama *is* qualified. If he is indeed the beneficiary of a kind of affirmative action, it is one that he earned, and that is given freely—it isn't mandated or coerced. White Americans have been waiting for a chance to bridge the racial divide, to affirm a universalist ethos. Obama has tapped into that need, and it turned out to be a gusher.

It's true that voting for Obama is in some ways a symbolic gesture, one that won't instantly solve America's race problems. But it will help. Symbolism is powerful. The racial politics that started at the symbolic plane can and will trickle down to real people. Having a black president would give the country a deeper comfort level in talking about racial issues. It would help Americans of all races break out of the sterile guilt/victim dialogue, or the fear of falling into it, that too often inhibits real communication. It could radically change our entire racial landscape, in ways we can't even predict.

And an Obama presidency would have far more than symbolic impact on America's race problems. Who doubts that Obama, a staunch liberal and former Chicago community organizer, will move aggressively and creatively to address the critical problems of black poverty and violence? And that when he appeals to black responsibility and self-empowerment, his words will have a million times more impact than when they come from a white Republican?

Many dismiss the Obama phenomenon as a mere "cult of personality." It is in some ways a cult, but not one of personality—it's a cult of racial healing, of racial transcendence. For many whites, voting for Obama is a kind of appeal to one's better self, and the better self of the country. It is, in a way, a promise. It could even be seen as a kind of prayer.

Of course, Obama-mania can be accompanied by lightheadedness, irrational euphoria and giddiness. The post-racial sky will not open. There are limits to charismatic politics. And there will no doubt be an Obama hangover if he is elected.

Barack Obama is not a savior. But there's every reason to believe that if elected he will be a good president—and maybe a great one. And every day that

Obama is in office, even the bad ones, we'll be able to tell ourselves: We elected a black man president of this country. That thought, with all that it says about where we came from as a nation and where we hope to be going, will be a light that no one can put out.

9. The argument for an obligation to assist

PETER SINGER

(From *Practical Ethics* by Peter Singer, Cambridge University Press, 1979, pp. 229–232. Reprinted with the permission of CUP)

The path from the library at my university to the Humanities lecture theatre passes a shallow ornamental pond. Suppose that on my way to give a lecture I notice that a small child has fallen in and is in danger of drowning. Would anyone deny that I ought to wade in and pull the child out? This will mean getting my clothes muddy, and either canceling my lecture or delaying it until I can find something dry to change into; but compared with the avoidable death of a child this is insignificant.

A plausible principle that would support the judgment that I ought to pull the child out is this: if it is in our power to prevent something very bad happening, without thereby sacrificing anything of comparable moral significance, we ought to do it. This principle seems uncontroversial . . .

Nevertheless the uncontroversial appearance of the principle that we ought to prevent what is bad when we can do so without sacrificing anything of comparable moral significance is deceptive. If it were taken seriously and acted upon, our lives and our world would be fundamentally changed. For the principle applies, not just to rare situations in which one can save a child from a pond, but to the everyday situation in which we can assist those living in absolute poverty. In saying this I assume that absolute poverty, with its hunger and malnutrition, lack of shelter, illiteracy, disease, high infant mortality and low life expectancy, is a bad thing. And I assume that it is within the power of the affluent to reduce absolute poverty, without 'sacrificing anything of comparable moral significance'. If these two assumptions and the principle we have been discussing are correct, we have an obligation to help those in absolute poverty which is not less strong than our obligation to rescue a drowning child from a pond. Not to help would be wrong, whether or not it is intrinsically equivalent to killing. Helping is not, as conventionally thought, a charitable act which it is praiseworthy to do, but not wrong to omit; it is something that everyone ought to do.

This is the argument for an obligation to assist. Set out more formally, it would look like this.

1. If we can prevent something bad without sacrificing anything of comparable significance, we ought to do it.
2. Absolute poverty is bad.
3. There is some absolute poverty we can prevent without sacrificing anything of comparable moral significance.

Therefore, we ought to prevent some absolute poverty.

The first premise is the substantive moral premise on which the argument rests, and I have tried to show that it can be accepted by people who hold a variety of ethical positions.

The second premise is unlikely to be challenged. Absolute poverty is, as McNamara put it, 'beneath any reasonable definition of human decency' and it would be hard to find a plausible ethical view which did not regard it as a bad thing.

The third premise is more controversial, even though it is cautiously framed. It claims only that some absolute poverty can be prevented without the sacrifice of anything of comparable moral significance. It thus avoids the objection that any aid I can give is just 'drops in the ocean' for the point is not whether my personal contribution will make any noticeable impression on world poverty as a whole (of course it won't) but whether it will prevent some poverty. This is all the argument needs to sustain its conclusion, since the second premise says that any absolute poverty is bad, and not merely the total amount of absolute poverty. If without sacrificing anything of comparable moral significance we can provide just one family with the means to raise itself out of absolute poverty, the third premise is vindicated.

I have left the notion of moral significance unexamined in order to show that the argument does not depend on any specific values or ethical principles. I think the third premise is true for most people living in industrialized nations, on any defensible view of what is morally significant. Our affluence means that we have income we can dispose of without giving up the basic necessities of life, and we can use this income to reduce absolute poverty. Just how much we will think ourselves obliged to give up will depend on what we consider to be of comparable moral significance to the poverty we could prevent: colour television, stylish clothes, expensive dinners, a sophisticated stereo system, overseas holidays, a (second?) car, a larger house, private schools for our children . . .

Objections to the argument

Taking care of our own

Anyone who has worked to increase overseas aid will have come across the argument that we should look after those near us, our families and then the poor in our own country, before we think about poverty in distant places.

No doubt we do instinctively prefer to help those who are close to us. Few could stand by and watch a child drown; many can ignore a famine in Africa. But the question is not what we usually do, but what we ought to do, and it is difficult to see any sound moral justification for the view that distance, or community membership, makes a crucial difference to our obligations.

Consider, for instance, racial affinities. Should whites help poor whites before helping poor blacks? Most of us would reject such a suggestion out of hand ... people's need for food has nothing to do with their race, and if blacks need food more than whites, it would be a violation of the principle of equal consideration to give preference to whites.

The same point applies to citizenship or nationhood. Every affluent nation has some relatively poor citizens, but absolute poverty is limited largely to the poor nations. Those living on the streets of Calcutta, or in a drought-stricken region of the Sahel, are experiencing poverty unknown in the West. Under these circumstances it would be wrong to decide that only those fortunate enough to be citizens of our own community will share our abundance.

We feel obligations of kinship more strongly than those of citizenship. Which parents could give away their last bowl of rice if their own children were starving? To do so would seem unnatural, contrary to our nature as biologically evolved beings—although whether it would be wrong is another question altogether. In any case, we are not faced with that situation, but with one in which our own children are well-fed, well-clothed, well-educated, and would now like new bikes, a stereo set, or their own car. In these circumstances any special obligations we might have to our children have been fulfilled, and the needs of strangers make a stronger claim upon us . . .

Property rights

Do people have a right to private property, a right which contradicts the view that they are under an obligation to give some of their wealth away to those in absolute poverty? According to some theories of rights (for instance, Robert Nozick's) provided one has acquired one's property without the use of unjust means like force and fraud, one may be entitled to enormous wealth while others starve. This individualistic conception of rights is in contrast to other views, like the early Christian doctrine to be found in the works of Thomas Aquinas, which holds that since property exists for the satisfaction of human needs, 'whatever a man has in superabundance is owed, of natural right, to the poor for their sustenance'. A socialist would also, of course, see wealth as belonging to the community rather than the individual, while utilitarians, whether socialist or not, would be prepared to override property rights to prevent great evils.

Does the argument for an obligation to assist others therefore presuppose one of these other theories of property rights, and not an individualistic theory like Nozick's? Not necessarily. A theory of property rights can insist on our *right* to retain wealth without pronouncing on whether the rich *ought* to give to the poor. Nozick, for example, rejects the use of compulsory means like taxation to redistribute income, but suggests that we can achieve the ends we deem morally desirable by voluntary means. So Nozick would reject the claim that rich people have an 'obligation' to give to the poor, in so far as this implies that the poor have a right to our aid, but might accept that giving is something we ought to do and failing to give, though within one's rights, is wrong—for rights is not all there is to ethics.

The argument for an obligation to assist can survive, with only minor modifications, even if we accept an individualistic theory of property rights. In any case, however, I do not think we should accept such a theory. It leaves too much to chance to be an acceptable ethical view. For instance, those whose forefathers happened to inhabit some sandy wastes around the Persian Gulf are now fabulously wealthy, because oil lay under those sands; while those whose forefathers settled on better land south of the Sahara live in absolute poverty, because of drought and bad harvests. Can this distribution be acceptable from an impartial point of view? If we imagine ourselves about to begin life as a citizen of either Kuwait or Chad—but we do not know which—would we accept the principle that citizens of Kuwait are under no obligation to assist people living in Chad?

Population and the ethics of triage

Perhaps the most serious objection to the argument that we have an obligation to assist is that since the major cause of absolute poverty is overpopulation, helping those now in poverty will only ensure that yet more people are born to live in poverty in the future.

In its most extreme form, this objection is taken to show that we should adopt a policy of 'triage'. The term comes from medical policies adopted in wartime. With too few doctors to cope with all the casualties, the wounded were divided into three categories: those who would probably survive without medical assistance, those who might survive if they received assistance, but otherwise probably would not, and those who even with medical assistance probably would not survive. Only those in the middle category were given medical assistance. The idea, of course, was to use limited medical resources as effectively as possible. For those in the first category, medical treatment was not strictly necessary; for those in the third category, it was likely to be useless. It has been suggested that we should apply the same policies to countries, according to their prospects of becoming self-sustaining. We would not aid countries which even without our help will soon be able to feed their populations. We would not aid countries which, even with our help, will not be able to limit their population to a level they can feed. We would aid those countries where our help might make the difference between success and failure in bringing food and population into balance . . .

In support of this view Garrett Hardin has offered a metaphor: we in the rich nations are like the occupants of a crowded lifeboat adrift in a sea full of drowning people. If we try to save the drowning by bringing them aboard our boat will be overloaded and we shall all drown. Since it is better that some survive than none, we should leave the others to drown. In the world today, according to Hardin, 'lifeboat ethics' apply. The rich should leave the poor to starve, for otherwise the poor will drag the rich down with them . . .

Putting aside the controversial issue of the extent to which food production might one day be increased, it is true, as we have already seen, that the world now produces enough to feed its inhabitants—the amount lost by being fed to animals itself being enough to meet existing grain shortages. Nevertheless population growth cannot be ignored. Bangladesh could, with land reform and using better techniques, feed its present population of 80 million; but by the year 2000, according to World Bank estimates, its population will be 146 million. The enormous effort that will have to go into feeding an extra 66 million people, all added to the population within a quarter of a century, means that Bangladesh must develop at full speed to stay where she is. Other low income countries are in similar situations. By the end of the century, Ethiopia's population is expected to rise from 29 to 54 million; Somalia's from 3 to 7 million, India's from 620 to 958 million, Zaire's from 25 to 47 million. What will happen then? Population cannot grow indefinitely. It will be checked by a decline in birth rates or a rise in death rates. Those who advocate triage are proposing that we allow the population growth of some countries to be checked by a rise in death rates—that is, by increased malnutrition, and related diseases; by widespread famines; by increased infant mortality; and by epidemics of infectious diseases.

The consequences of triage on this scale are so horrible that we are inclined to reject it without further argument. How could we sit by our television sets, watching millions starve while we do nothing? Would not that . . . be the end of all notions of human equality and respect for human life? Don't people have a right to our assistance, irrespective of the consequences?

Anyone whose initial reaction to triage was not one of repugnance would be an unpleasant sort of person. Yet initial reactions based on strong feelings are not always reliable guides . . .

The question is: how probable is this forecast that continued assistance now will lead to greater disasters in the future? Forecasts of population growth are notoriously fallible, and theories about the factors which affect it remain speculative. One theory, at least as plausible as any other, is that countries pass through a 'demographic transition' as their standard of living rises. When people are very poor and have no access to modern medicine their fertility is high, but population is kept in check by high death rates. The introduction of sanitation, modern medical techniques and other improvements reduces the death rate, but initially has little effect on the birth rate. Then population grows rapidly. Most poor countries are now in this phase. If standards of living continue to rise, however, couples begin to realize that to have the same number of children surviving to maturity as in the past, they do not need to give birth to as many children as their parents did. The need for children to provide economic support in old age diminishes. Improved education and the emancipation and employment of women also reduce the birthrate, and so population growth begins to level off. Most rich nations have reached this stage, and their populations are growing only very slowly.

If this theory is right, there is an alternative to the disasters accepted as inevitable by supporters of triage. We can assist poor countries to raise the living standards of the poorest members of their population. We can encourage the governments of these countries to enact land reform measures, improve education, and liberate women from a purely child-bearing role. We can also help other countries to make contraception and sterilization widely available. There is a fair chance that these measures will hasten the onset of the demographic transition and bring population growth down to a manageable level. Success cannot be guaranteed; but the evidence that improved economic security and education reduce population growth is strong enough to make triage ethically unacceptable. We cannot allow millions to die from starvation and disease when there is a reasonable probability that population can be brought under control without such horrors.

Population growth is therefore not a reason against giving overseas aid, although it should make us think about the kind of aid to give. Instead of food handouts, it may be better to give aid that hastens the demographic transition. This may mean agricultural assistance for the rural poor, or assistance with education, or the provision of contraceptive services. Whatever kind of aid proves most effective in specific circumstances, the obligation to assist is not reduced.

10. All the reasons to clone human beings

SIMON SMITH

(http://www.humancloning.org/allthe.php. Reprinted with permission)

Medical breakthroughs—Human cloning technology is expected to result in several miraculous medical breakthroughs. We may be able to cure cancer if cloning leads to a better understanding of cell differentiation. Theories exist about how cloning may lead to a cure for heart attacks, a revolution in cosmetic surgery, organs for organ transplantation, and predictions abound about how cloning technology will save thousands of lives. You can read about many of the expected medical benefits in the essay "The Benefits of Human Cloning."

Medical tragedies—Many people have suffered accidental medical tragedies during their lifetimes. Read about a girl who needs a kidney, a burn victim, a girl

396

born with cosmetic deformities, a man who needs a liver, a woman who is infertile because of cancer, and a father who lost his only son. All these people favor cloning and want the science to proceed.

To cure infertility—Infertile people are discriminated against. Men are made to feel like they are not "real men." Women are made to feel as if they are useless barren vessels. Worse, being infertile is often not considered a "real medical problem" and insurance companies and governments are not sympathetic. The current options for infertile couples are painful, expensive, and heart-breaking. Cloning has the potential to change the world for infertile couples almost overnight.

To fund research—People whose lives have been destroyed or have not been able to reproduce in this lifetime due to tragedy could arrange to have their DNA continued and fund research at the same time. For example: A boy graduates from high school at age 18. He goes to a pool party to celebrate. He confuses the deep end and shallow end and dives head first into the pool, breaking his neck and becoming a quadriplegic. At age 19 he has his first urinary tract infection because of an indwelling urinary catheter and continues to suffer from them the rest of his life. At age 20 he comes down with herpes zoster of the trigeminal nerve. He suffers chronic unbearable pain. At age 21 he inherits a 10 million dollar trust fund. He never marries or has children. At age 40 after hearing about Dolly being a clone, he changes his will and has his DNA stored for future human cloning. His future mother will be awarded one million dollars to have him and raise him. His DNA clone will inherit a trust fund. He leaves five million to spinal cord research. He dies feeling that although he was robbed of normal life, his twin/clone will lead a better life.

Bad parents—Did your parents destroy your life? Were they alcoholic, child-beating molesters? Did you never have a chance? Interestingly, human cloning allows you the opportunity to participate in choosing the parents for your clone.

A child's right to be better than its parents—It's been suggested that parents have a duty to see that their children have better lives than they do. This may mean making our children live longer, helping them to be resistant to cancer, heart disease, any familial diseases, and all the other problems that can be cured using what we learn from human cloning technology.

To take a step towards immortality—Human cloning essentially means taking a human being's DNA and reversing its age back to zero. Dr. Richard Seed, one of cloning's leading proponents, hopes that cloning will help us understand how to reverse DNA back to age 20 or whatever age we want to be. Cloning would be a step towards a fountain of youth.

To make a future couple financially secure—With human cloning you could give a couple in the future both a child from your DNA and the financial assets from your lifetime to start out financially secure instead of struggling as most couples do now.

Because you believe in freedom—Freedom sometimes means having tolerance for others and their beliefs. In America, some people believe in gun control and some don't. Some people believe in one religion and others in another. In a free society we know that we must tolerate some views that we don't agree with so that we all may be free. For this reason human cloning should be allowed.

To be a better parent—Human cloning can improve the parent-child relationship. Raising a clone would be like having a child with an instruction manual. You would have a head start on the needs and talents of your child. We are not saying that a clone would be a carbon copy with no individuality. Our talents and desires are genetic, developmental, and environmental. We would have a head start on understanding the genetic component of a cloned child.

Endangered species could be saved—Through the research leading up to human cloning we will perfect the technology to clone animals, and thus we could forever preserve endangered species, including human beings.

Animals and plants could be cloned for medical purposes—Through the research leading up to human cloning, we should discover how to clone animals and plants to produce life-saving medications.

You want your clone to lead the life that was meant to be yours—The Human Cloning Foundation has been surprised by the number of people that write to say that they would like to have a clone so that it may lead the life that was meant to be theirs. Typically, these are people who have suffered some terrible physical or mental handicap and feel robbed of the opportunities they should have had in life. Some see this life as a sacrifice so that the life of their clone may be enriched.

To have a better sense of identity—If we had some information about ourselves, perhaps we could sooner or better discovery who we are. A clone would have access to a tremendous amount of information about his or her parent that could greatly help in understanding one's psyche and physical attributes. All of this information could provide a better sense of identity.

Because so many people want cloning—Please read the dozens of essays by people from all over the world in support of human cloning and published by the Human Cloning Foundation.

Religious freedom—At least two religions, the Raelian Religion and the Summum Religion, believe in cloning as one of their tenets.

Because of the special relationship that twins have—Twins often have very special relationships. While many people go through their lives never having a special relationship with another person, there are stories of twins in which they are so close they are perhaps psychically connected. More than one person has written the Human Cloning Foundation (including a twin that feels close to her identical twin) that since a clone is virtually the equivalent of an identical twin, they suspect a very special relationship would exist between a clone and its DNA parent. Some twins describe their twin relationship as more wonderful and meaningful than any other relationship in their lives.

Economics—Countries that fail to research human cloning will suffer economically. The industrial revolution and Internet revolutions enriched the United

States of America. Biotechnology will lead the next economic revolution. Those countries that jump in first will reap the rewards. Those who fail to begin research right away will fall behind. As an example: Japan failed to jump on the Internet bandwagon and is now playing catch-up. Japan has banned human cloning and will probably suffer by falling behind during the biotech revolution. One day in the not too far distant future, Japan may realize its mistake.

Gay couples—From one of our readers: "Gay couples go through so much . . . not to mention all the controversy . . . when they decide that they are ready for a baby. People question their right to bring a child that technically isn't related to them into a lifestyle that falls below societies views of normal . . . human cloning could allow two gay men to take 23 chromosomes from each male and put them into a single egg to truly have a baby of their own. Also two gay women could use this technology to conceive a child of their own using their individual 23 chromosomes." (To our knowledge the type of reproduction described here has not yet been done, but someday it will probably be possible.)

A cure for baldness—From one of our readers: "But how about the possibility of using cloning technology to get more hair on a balding scalp. For example cloning can be used to get more hair from a few sample hair follicles or grafts from the patient's head and then grow them . . . later transplant the grafts where it is needed. This will eliminate the need to do an incision in back of the scalp for donor hair and will literally give the patient MORE hair."

Because the sick will demand it—Those resisting human cloning research will probably find themselves shouted down by the sick and the maimed who desperately need such research. Human cloning technology promises to cure many or all incurable diseases and the moral weight of the dying and infirm will undoubtedly sway the politicians more than the arguments of the healthy, who often remain ignorant of the potential of human cloning, because they have never been motivated by suffering to look desperately for a cure.

Hope—On the Charlie Rose television show on February 14th, 2001, three anti-cloners debated against one reporter. The anti-cloners made the case for stem cell research while alleging that cloning itself would not result in any major scientific breakthroughs. It is likely that the anti-cloners are quite wrong. Learning the process of reprogramming, differentiation, and dedifferentiation is likely to result in just as many medical miracles as stem cell research. The two lines of research go hand in hand and should complement each other. The three anti-cloners came across as people who would destroy hope. They kept alleging that things were impossible. They reminded me of the same types of people who proclaimed that cloning was impossible years ago. Furthermore, they seemed happy and willing to take away the hope of infertile couples and others with severe diseases that human cloning technology might one day lessen their suffering or save their lives. The anti-cloners also seemed to feel that they had the ability to predict the timing and course of science advancement, which history has shown to be folly.

Living on through a later-born twin—Some childless people feel that by being cloned by their later-born twin would help them or their DNA to live on in the same sense that people who have children live on.

11.   Why people watch reality TV

STEVEN WEISS AND JAMES WILTZ

(*Media Psychology*, 6, 2004, pp. 373–375, excerpt. Reprinted by permission of the publisher, Taylor and Francis Journals)

. . .

Because this was the first study to evaluate Reiss motivational profiles of a television audience, its significance may be the suggestion of a new method of potentially productive research in the fields of mass culture and communications. Prior to this study, efforts to describe audiences in terms of personality traits were mostly unsuccessful. Personality tests have a powerful tendency to yield the norms every time groups of 100-plus people are tested; consequently, they often do not show profiles for audiences of television shows. The Reiss Profile is a new kind of personality instrument, however, based on motivational constructs rather than on traditional personality constructs. The results of this study showed a statistically significant, motivational profile for people who view reality television. This encourages future research aimed at developing motivational profiles of other groups identified by their interest in particular shows or aspects of culture.

The results of our study on reality television supported the theoretical perspective that Reiss's 16 basic desires and values are associated with viewing and enjoying reality television shows. The results showed that status is the main motivational force that drives interest in reality television. The more status-oriented people are, the more likely they are to view reality television and report pleasure and enjoyment. . . . people who are motivated by status have an above-average need to feel self-important. Reality television may gratify this psychological need in two ways. One possibility is that viewers feel they are more important (have higher status) than the ordinary people portrayed on reality television shows. The idea that these are "real" people gives psychological significance to the viewers' perceptions of superiority—it may not matter much if the storyline is realistic, so long as the characters are ordinary people. Further, the message of reality television—that millions of people are interested in watching real life experiences of ordinary people—implies that ordinary people are important. Ordinary people can watch the shows, see people like themselves, and fantasize that they could gain celebrity status by being on television.

Reality television viewers are more motivated by vengeance than are nonviewers. The desire for vengeance is closely associated with enjoyment of competition (Reiss, 2000a)—in prior psychometric research, the people who said they value and enjoy getting even with others also tended to say they value and enjoy competition. Further, people who avoid conflict, anger, and competition may avoid viewing reality television shows because these shows often portray competition and interpersonal conflict.

Because reality television is widely watched, it is often a topic of discussion at the office. It is not surprising, therefore, that sociable people are significantly more likely than nonsociable people to watch reality television, although the differences are small.

The finding that viewing reality TV shows is negatively associated with the extent to which a person embraces morality (honor) is not surprising because much reality television shows champion expedience over ethics. These differences, although statistically significant, were small.

Small, significant effects also were obtained for the value of order. This finding suggests that people who dislike rules may react negatively to the many rules that must be followed by the participants of reality television shows. The finding concerning romance suggests that the sexual aspects of some shows attract viewers but not very many because the effect is small in magnitude.

Some have questioned the intellectualism of reality television viewers, and others have questioned the physical laziness of people who like to watch television. No support was found for either of these hypotheses. Both viewers and non-viewers were equally motivated by curiosity, and the same was shown for the motive of physical exercise.

Although reality television viewing is generally about status, specific shows may appeal to different psychological needs. *Temptation Island*, for example, portrays infidelity, which may appeal to people who value expedience (low honor) more than morality. *Survivor*, in contrast, has more of a competitive theme, perhaps appealing to people who value vengeance.

The results of this study should be interpreted cautiously. Many different shows are classified as "reality television," so that current or future shows may have an appeal different from the shows evaluated here. Although the results of this study were not affected by gender, future studies may show gender preferences in how viewing habits are connected with basic desires. Gender effects probably occur but perhaps at magnitudes too small to be identified by the methods used in this study.

The results of this study are consistent with those reported by Nabi et al. (2003) regarding the psychological appeal of reality-based television. Nabi et al. showed that curiosity (including need for cognition) was not a significant motive for watching reality television; the results of this study also showed no correlation between curiosity and viewing of reality television. Nabi et al. also showed that voyeurism ("getting a peek") does not motivate viewing reality television. Because Reiss and Havercamp (1998) and Reiss (2000a) implied that voyeurism is motivating only as a means to 1 of more than 16 basic goals, we did not study voyeurism. (It is not a fundamental or intrinsically desired motive.) Nabi et al.

reported a small correlation between the "unscripted nature" of reality shows and impulsivity. In our work, impulsivity is not a universal or fundamental motive (it is a personality trait), but flexibility falls under low or weak desire for order. We found a small correlation between order and viewing. Although the shows may be "unscripted," rules are salient features of these shows, so that arguably any expected association with order should be positive, not negative as Nabi et al. assumed.

In conclusion, these results supported the general hypothesis that cultural events such as reality television shows arouse specific combinations of 16 intrinsic feelings or joys. The appeal of reality events is influenced by the degree of match between (a) the pattern of intensities of 16 intrinsic joys the show arouses and (b) the individual's valuations of the 16 basic joys (called a Reiss Desire Profile). Future researchers can study the relevance of this model for a much wider range of television shows and cultural events. It is unlikely to work every time, of course, but it may produce reliable empirical results much more frequently than was the case with alternative methods.

12. "If a tree falls . . ."—letters by John Palmer and Eugene Tan, and "The economics of extinction"

KENT A. PEACOCK

(University of Western Ontario *Gazette*, 1992/
*Living with the Earth: An Introduction to Environmental
Philosophy* by Kent A. Peacock, ed., 1996)

Letter to the editor from John Palmer

We can continue to log our brains out, and we probably won't run out of wood for another 50 years. But we will run out, because current management is not sustainable.

The above quotation from a touchy-feely tree-hugger is pure and simple hogwash. Why? Because the writer has an incomplete understanding of economics.

Will we run out of timber for logging? Not likely. As current supplies are harvested, the decline in supply will cause prices to rise. Furthermore, as population and wealth increase, so will the demand for timber, also putting upward pressure on prices.

But these higher prices provide important signals. They encourage people who would like to earn some profits to plant more trees. And they encourage potential buyers to look for substitutes for timber and to cut down on their use of lumber.

We will not run out of timber, because, despite the warnings of naive tree-huggers, prices will rise, eliciting responses that promote conservation and more production.

If the tree-huggers really believe we will run out of timber, they should buy up lots of land and plant lots of trees. And they and their progeny will be rich beyond their wildest dreams, if their predictions of doom and gloom are correct.

But if they *do* plant more trees now, there will be more trees in the future, and their predictions will be wrong. And even if the doomsayers don't plant the trees, some people will; the anticipation of future profits will keep us from running out of timber.

There is a heavy shadow of doubt clouding this rosy picture, though. It comes from the spectre of government intervention in the timber market in two ways.

First, as the government gets involved in tree-planting and the leasing of timber lands, the incentive for lumber companies to practice conservation is diminished. "Why conserve," they reasonably ask themselves, "if the government is going to undercut our actions with their own programs?"

Second, government intervention designed to keep prices low will further deter private conservation efforts. "Why plant more trees," people will reasonably ask, "if we can't sell them for a price high enough to cover all our costs?"

And so the more the government tries to keep future prices down, the more it deters private conservation efforts.

Will we run out of timber? Only if we implement really stupid government policies that discourage private conservation.

Letter to the editor from Eugene Tan

On March 13, an article by John Palmer, a professor of economics, appeared in *The Gazette*. He accused environmentalists ("tree-huggers") of having an incomplete understanding of economics and of naivety. He pleaded for unencumbered markets to control forestry practices. Palmer's article affirmed that corporate North America is leading us down the path towards environmental degradation. The road to hell is paved with sickening rationalizations.

The Greek roots of economy and ecology are inextricably linked. Economy, from *oikonomic*, means the management of the household, whereas ecology, from the root *oikos* plus *logos*, means household.

But Palmer suggests that the free market will provide all that we need when it becomes profitable.

Palmer maintains that an incomplete understanding of economics has led to the naive view that trees are becoming endangered. The market will provide all that we need. Scientific reality maintains:

- The widespread destruction of trees for timber or farmland has contributed to global warming;
- Logging practices practically ensure soil destruction, harming future growth;
- Planting trees for short-term economic gain is an asinine proposition because trees take substantial time to grow;
- So much is wasted that demand-side economics just makes sense;
- One of the leading causes of animal species extinction is loss of habitat.

Has simple economics accounted for these factors or are they the "externalities" evoked by many economists when a model goes wrong? The presence of externalities means that economists don't understand all factors involved. I fail to see how Dr. Palmer's "complete" understanding of economics would preserve vital resources.

Palmer's article is guilty of the heinous crime of which he accuses environmentalists. Economists simply have an incomplete understanding of ecology and cannot begin to account for the infinite number of variables and nuances in an ecosystem. Physician, heal thyself.

The economics of extinction

Kent A. Peacock

Professor John Palmer condemns "treehuggers" for failing to understand economics. Don't worry about running out of trees, he tells us, market forces will guarantee that timber producers will do the right thing and make sure that there are lots of trees for the future. The only thing, he says, that could cause us to run out of timber would be government intervention in environmental management, since that would remove the incentive for private conservation.

I wish I could agree with this rosy picture of the magic of market economics; life would be so much simpler. But the relationships between market forces and ecological necessities are far more complex and problematic than Palmer is apparently aware. Of course there is an incentive to conserve a resource, or renew it if one knows how; that is elementary. However, the free-market boosters forget that all too often there are also enormous short-term *disincentives* to conservation and renewal. Sometimes it is highly economically advantageous to wipe out a resource rather than conserve it. This dismal process is known as the *economics of extinction*, and it is worthwhile, although unpleasant, to remind ourselves how it works.

As a resource (say timber, whales, cod, rhino horns) becomes more and more scarce, its market value approaches infinity. Market value often has little to do with the actual value of the resource for human welfare; we do need timber, but no one has any real need for pulverized rhino horns. Nevertheless, they command such a fabulous price on certain markets that poachers will risk death to hunt down the few remaining rhinos. No incentive to conserve can override the immediate gain to be made from cashing in the resource. Furthermore, any measure which could increase the supply (say, establishing a rhino ranch) would tend to lower its market value; the more effective the renewal method, the more it would tend to cancel out the scarcity value of the resource. Add to all this the fact that measures to renew and conserve a resource can be economically risky and have costs, often large, which may not be recoverable in the short term at all. Hence, when a resource is scarce there are positive *disincentives* to renew it. The scarcer the resource, the more it is in demand, and the harder it is to renew, the more these disincentives tend to operate. If nothing but pure market forces govern, the result (and this has happened time and again in history) is very often the extinction or commercial exhaustion of the resource, not its preservation.

Another practice that contributes to extinction is *discounting the future* when carrying out an economic cost-benefit analysis. This means that we often apply a discount to the value of a resource that we will not be able to profit from right away; the longer we will have to wait to use it, the more we discount it. This is just an academic way of saying that we often grab all of something for ourselves now, and let the future take care of itself. Sometimes people have even deliberately destroyed remaining stocks of a resource so that no one else can profit from it; butterfly collectors used to burn out the hillsides that were home to rare species so that they would have the only remaining specimens to sell (see Rolston 1989). The grab-it-all-now factor is especially likely to operate if the resource is very expensive or impossible to renew, if there is a very high immediate demand for it, or if its renewal is so slow that the money invested in the harvesting technology cannot be recovered if one waits for the resource to renew itself. (The latter is the case for whales; see Dobra 1978.)

Nothing I have said here should be news to anyone familiar with economics or the long and tragic history of resource depletion. Let's talk about forestry, for instance, since Palmer brought the subject up; the eroded, desiccated area of the world now known as Lebanon is a very good example of what can happen if the needs of commerce are allowed to determine the fate of a resource. (To be sure, commercial exploitation is not the only reason for the deforestation of the Levant—but it was one of the major reasons.) Three thousand years ago, Lebanon had at least two million acres in timber, the famous cedars of Lebanon. (See the selection in *Living with the Earth* by Carter and Dale, Chapter 4.) In fact, the topography, climate, and tree types were remarkably similar to those of British Columbia today. For several centuries, while the trees held out, forestry was the basis for the thriving Phoenician commercial empire. Eventually, though, the ecology collapsed, and with it the prosperity of the society it supported. Billions of tons of topsoil washed into the sea and the forests disappeared completely except for a few guarded sacred groves. The country today has only the remotest resemblance to its lush and fertile condition in Biblical times.

And this is just a typical example; there is very little historical evidence to support the faith that market forces by themselves can guarantee adequate renewal and conservation of resources, and much evidence against it. What almost always seems to happen is that the immediate demand for a resource outweighs the perceived advantage to be gained by long-term measures. Many societies in the past have desperately attempted to reforest, to replenish topsoil or conserve stocks of fish or game; only a few have succeeded, because the short-term pressure to exploit the resource was always too great.

Still speaking of forestry, Palmer also shows no sensitivity to the really tough biological and technical problems posed by reforestation. In fact, it is very unclear that we really know how to replace the forests that we are harvesting so rapaciously. Foresters would have us believe that they are competent to replace them with "managed" forests as good as or better than those that they clear-cut away. This, like the belief in the power of the "invisible hand" itself, is mostly an article of faith; there is insufficient evidence that present methods work, and some evidence that they do not (in the sense that they may lead to a long-term but inevitable decline in the vitality of the ecology). I am certainly not saying that sustainable harvesting of forest products is impossible, but I am saying that we have not yet found a completely reliable method, especially if we insist on continuing to be able to harvest at the rate and scale that we now find necessary.

The biggest problem we face right now is just the problem that Aldo Leopold identified many years ago: there is very little correspondence between the market value of a "resource" such as a plant or animal species and its real value to the health and functioning of the ecology. We must figure out how to devise an economic system that reflects ecological reality, or our hi-tech culture will go the way of all the other failed cultures whose ruins lie weathering in the deserts they created.

Invited response from John Palmer

On a recent trip to Alberta, I was subjected to a lengthy lecture from a retired gentleman about all the trains passing his house, carrying lumber from British Columbia to the east. He was quite concerned about all the trees being cut down in British Columbia. I suggested that if his concerns have merit, he could do his grandchildren a great service by buying up a bunch of land and planting trees on it—he'd be able to leave them an extremely valuable resource.

The point of this story, and of my original brief editorial, is simply this: people respond to incentives. When people expect prices to rise in the future, some will respond by trying to make sure they have more to sell then, when prices are higher. The second point of the editorial was that government programs which keep timber prices low will inhibit both the incentives (prices) and the response (private reforestation), thus creating more future deforestation than we would have with an unfettered market.

The key to having the market work effectively is that there be well-defined and well-enforced property rights. Only if people can rely on being able to capture future gains will they make decisions to conserve now and plant more for the future. We don't have persistent shortages of wheat, eggs, or cattle for this very reason: people know they can reap what they have sown. We do have persistent shortages, however, of things for which property rights cannot be well-defined or well-enforced, such as whales, even though whales, like cattle, are replenishable resources.

The difference in sustainability between whales and cows is not the fault of the market economy. Non-market economies have the same problems of over-exploitation of resources. Rather, the difference between whales and cows is that property rights to cows are relatively easily defined and enforced. Property rights to whales aren't, and so whales have been seriously over-hunted to the brink of extinction.

The same thing can happen to our forests. We have myriad government programs that continue to erode property rights and the expectations that people will be able to reap what they have sown. For example, stumpage fees on government lands are set so low that in many instances private reforestation doesn't pay.

Note that nowhere have I discussed other values of having forests. The only point I wished to make initially was that we won't run out of wood (see the initial quotation on which I based the original editorial) if market forces are allowed to work. I was very disappointed that those commenting on my original piece chose to ignore this simple point and raise other issues I did not have the space to address in that editorial. I do, however, discuss the concepts of externalities and other market failures at length in my book, *The Economic Way of Thinking* (Paul Heyne and John Palmer, Prentice Hall, 1999).

13. House of Representatives debate on the "Personal Responsibility in Food Consumption Act"

(Hearing before the Subcommittee on Commercial and Administrative Law of the Committee on the Judiciary, House of Representatives, 108th Congress, June 2003, excerpt; http://commdocs.house.gov/committees/ judiciary/hju87814.000/hju87814_0.HTM)

The Honorable Chris Cannon (Representative in Congress from the State of Utah, and Chairman, Subcommittee on Commercial and Administrative Law)

Recently the food industry has been targeted by a variety of legal claims alleging it should pay monetary damages and be subject to equitable remedies based on legal theories holding it liable for overconsumption of its legal products by others. Our hearing today will explore the threat the food industry faces from frivolous litigation, the threat to personal responsibility posed by the proliferation of such litigation, and the need for H.R. 339, the "Personal Responsibility in Food Consumption Act." . . .

The frivolous litigation we have seen already against the so-called fast food industry if allowed to proliferate will lead by their false logic to lawsuits against the food industry generally. According to the *Journal of the American Medical Association*, even the portion sizes of foods cooked at home have grown substantially in the last two decades. As one commentator has written, quote, one should understand who is at risk, who big food really is. It is not just McDonald's, KFC, Burger King and Wendy's, it is every food company in the country. If McDonald's is liable for selling high caloric meals, then so are local pizzerias and grocery stores, unquote.

Some say these lawsuits will soon reach your own backyard barbecue unless Congress acts. It is clear that obesity is a problem. Equally clear, however, is that obesity is caused by a combination of too much consumption and too little exercise. Recent findings drawn from Government databases and presented at the Scientific Conference of the Foundation of American Societies for Experimental Biology showed that over the past 20 years teenagers have on average increased their caloric intake by 1 percent. During that same period of time, the percentage of teenagers who said they engaged in some sort of physical activity for 30 minutes a day dropped 13 percent. Not surprisingly, teenage obesity over that 20-year period increased by 10 percent, indicating that it is not just junk food that is making teenagers fat, but rather their lack of activity.

Public schools could offer more physical education classes of course, but according to John Banzhaf, one of the witnesses who will be here with us today, school boards will be the next targets of obesity-related lawsuits because they allow vending machines in schools. These lawsuits will take money away from the schools just when they need more physical education programs and transfer that money to personal injury attorneys.

And since inactivity is the leading cause of childhood obesity, who might be sued after school boards? Television manufacturers and those who produce popular television shows? Manufacturers of comfortable couches?

Besides threatening to erode values of personal responsibility, the legal campaign against the food industry threatens the separation of powers. Nationally coordinated lawsuits seek to accomplish through litigation that which cannot be achieved by legislation and the democratic process . . .

The House recently passed H.R. 1036, the "Protection of Lawful Commerce in Arms Act," by a large bipartisan vote. That bill bars frivolous lawsuits against the firearms industry for the misuse of its legal products by others. H.R. 339, which similarly seeks to bar frivolous lawsuits against the food industry for the overconsumption of its legal products by others, may also be an appropriate congressional response to a growing legal assault on the concept of personal responsibility . . .

Banzhaf (Professor, George Washington University Law School)

Mr. Chairman and Members of the Committee, in 2001 the U.S. Surgeon General issued a report showing that the United States was suffering from an epidemic of obesity which annually killed 300,000 people and cost us over 100 billion a year. Since that time, Congress has done virtually nothing of consequence to deal with this problem, just as for many years it did nothing of consequence to address the problem of smoking.

However, since I first proposed that legal action could be a powerful weapon against obesity and as I suggested and then helped prove that it could be a powerful weapon against the public health problem of smoking, three fat lawsuits have been won, two are poised to be won, one is going to be heard in court later this month. More importantly, numerous articles and reports have noted that the very threat of these lawsuits have already prompted many food companies to take steps likely to reduce obesity. Yet some Members not content to shrink Congress' responsibility to do something meaningful about America's second most preventable health problem, now support an industry-sponsored bailout and protection bill to end what seems to be one of the few effective tools against the problem . . .

This bill is premised on two faulty assumptions. The first is that the problem of obesity is caused solely by lack of personal responsibility. But virtually everyone agrees that obesity and obesity-related diseases occurred suddenly within the past 15 to 20 years. There is no evidence that there has been a sudden corresponding drop in personal and parental responsibility.

The second faulty assumption is that contrary to virtually every serious study, the fast food industry, with its ubiquitous advertising, misleading advertising, failure to identify ingredients, as most foods do, or to provide any kinds of warnings that this is such an insignificant cost of our current problem of obesity, contrary to every report, that they should be given unprecedented immunity from all liability. And let me emphasize we are not seeking to hold them liable for all the liability, only their fair share, as we did with tobacco.

409

Now neither proposition can be seriously advanced, much less proven. And the public, according to recent surveys, is about willing to hold them liable. There is liability now. Juries are about to hold them liable as they are in tobacco suits.

In this bill, prematurely, Congress assumes that it can predetermine that in no set of facts involving obesity litigation should any company be held liable even for its fair share of those costs. This is presumptuous as well as preposterous. It departs also from the 200-year-old tradition in which courts initially decide product liability cases and then the legislature steps in only if the results seem to be clearly contrary to the public interest. This is especially egregious here because the bill unnecessarily and unreasonably interferes with the rights of the sovereign States to have their courts decide these product liability issues at least initially. And it seems to affect matters which have no relationship to interstate commerce and, as the Supreme Court has recently reminded us, therefore may be beyond Congress' ability to legislate.

For all of these reasons, I respectfully suggest that it is very premature for Congress at this time when not a single judgment has been held, not a single trial has been held, for you suddenly to step in and say on the one hand the suits are frivolous, on the other hand the danger is so imminent that Congress has to adopt unprecedented legislation to grant immunity, something Congress wisely refused to do with the tobacco industry . . .

Schwartz (Shook, Hardy & Bacon law firm)

Very recently, the American Law Institute, which is the fountain head for restating the law of torts, and this is tort law, restated the law after a 30-year-period of time. And the people who are involved in that are judges and lawyers and plaintiff's lawyers, purportedly the best in the Nation, and they look at the case law, they look at American case law. And what they decided was food manufacturers and food sellers can be liable in three instances.

If they have something in food, there is a pebble in a can of tuna fish or there is a needle in food you ate in a restaurant, the company is liable. And if you fail to warn about something that people may not know about, such as an allergen of coloring, you are liable. And if you violate regulations that are there to protect people, you are liable . . .

Watt (Representative in Congress from the State of North Carolina, and Ranking Member, Subcommittee on Commercial and Administrative Law)

Mr. Schwartz and Mr. Banzhaf, first of all, is this just about tort law? Mr. Schwartz talked about a restatement of torts, which I think I fully understand and first good lesson I have had since I was in law school about the restatement of torts. So I needed that reminder, but it came back to me quickly. But is this only about the tort standards or are there things in this prospective litigation that deal with things other than torts, such as trade practices and false advertising and some of the claims that were being made in the tobacco context?

Declared Statement of Neal D. Barnard (President, Physicians Committee for Responsible Medicine)

The Personal Responsibility in Food Consumption Act is strongly anti-consumer, anti-health, and anti-safety.

First, the bill is needless. While its stated purpose is "to prevent frivolous lawsuits against the manufacturers, distributors, or sellers of food or non-alcoholic beverage products," this goal is readily achieved without legislation. Using currently available legal remedies, frivolous lawsuits can be and generally are dismissed before significant costs are incurred.

Second, because the bill not only prevents frivolous lawsuits, but also meritorious ones, the bill runs strongly contrary to consumers' interests and effectively robs them of their day in court.

It would have shielded the Jack in the Box chain, where E. coli food poisoning killed four people and sickened hundreds more in the Pacific Northwest in 1992, from any legal responsibility. As it is currently written, the bill requires plaintiffs to prove the production of tainted or otherwise unsafe food violated federal regulations. But federal regulations are extremely weak and actually permit the sale of the foods containing microbial contamination. Had this proposed legislation been in force at the time of the Jack in the Box tragedy, parents who had lost their children in that episode would have had no legal recourse.

Manufacturers who introduce new additives, such as sweeteners, coloring agents, or preservatives that later prove to be toxic will be totally shielded from all responsibility for their actions. While manufacturers must have their additives approved initially, it is clear that significant toxic effects are sometimes seen only after approval. To suggest that lawsuits in relation to the damage they may have caused are necessarily frivolous is an insult to consumers. The merit of these issues deserves to be weighed by the courts.

Aspartame, which is marketed as NutraSweet, is the subject of an ongoing debate as to its safety. While this debate continues, consumers have a right to have legitimate grievances weighed in a court of law at the appropriate time. To give manufactures immunity from litigation is to remove much of their responsibility for marketing safe products.

Some manufacturers are now spiking beverages with ever-larger amounts of caffeine and other chemicals and marketing them to children. It is unclear where the food-additive industry is headed, and it is inappropriate to shield manufacturers from all consumer actions, should they overstep the bounds of safety.

Some industries deliberately target consumers who are vulnerable to food addictions. At a dairy industry conference on December 5, 2000, Dick Cooper, the Vice President of Cheese Marketing for Dairy Management, Inc., described the demographics that allowed them to spot a group he referred to as "cheese cravers," and laid out plans to go after them. "What do we want our marketing program to do?" he asked, in a set of slides released under the Freedom of Information Act. "Trigger the cheese craving," was his reply. And industry has done exactly that, deliberately attempting to trigger addictive patterns of food consumption with marketing programs through fast-food chains. Cooper's presentation concluded with a cartoon of a playground slide with a large spider web woven to trap children as they reached the bottom. The caption had one spider saying to another, "If we pull this off, we'll eat like kings."

The dairy industry is well aware of biochemical characteristics of food products that may contribute to their addictive qualities—characteristics that are essentially unknown to the lay public. Over the past 20 years, dairy industry journals have carried scientific analyses showing that opiate compounds are released from casein, the dairy protein that is particularly concentrated in cheese products. One of these casomorphins, as they are called, has about one-tenth the opiate power of morphine. Simultaneously, research studies using opiate-blocking drugs have shown that opiate effects do indeed influence consumption of certain foods—not only cheese, but also chocolate, sugar, and meat—the very foods that doctors would like us to trim from our diets but that we end up quite literally hooked on.

At best, the bill is dangerously premature. Questions regarding the role of the food industry in our nation's obesity epidemic are just now being brought to light. Rather than immediately absolve the entire industry of all potential liability, we should learn more about what has happened to contribute to this crisis.

In summary, the food industry is right to object to frivolous lawsuits. But legal remedies already exist to eliminate such suits at early stages. To seek to avoid frivolous lawsuits by banning all litigation regardless of its merit is to deprive consumers of fundamental rights.

Declared Statement of Richard Berman (Executive Director, Center for Consumer Freedom)

The written testimony submitted by Neal D. Barnard on June 19, 2003 is hopelessly biased and should be wholly disregarded by Congress.

Barnard is an acknowledged career animal-rights movement leader, not a nutritionist. He is a psychiatrist by training, and he does not currently practice medicine.

His organization, the misnamed "Physicians Committee for Responsible Medicine" (PCRM) has long-standing ties to the well-known animal rights group PETA (People for the Ethical Treatment of Animals). Barnard is PETA's "medical advisor," and he holds one of only three seats on the board of PETA's foundation.

In addition, PETA has used this foundation (originally called the Foundation to Support Animal Protection, recently d/b/a/ "The PETA Foundation") to funnel nearly $1 million to PCRM. The foundation also maintains PCRM's financial accounting.

The noted animal-rights watchdog publication *Animal People News* calls PETA and PCRM "a single fundraising unit," and has accused them of attempting to "evade public recognition of their relationship."

Barnard is scheduled to deliver a speech on June 29, titled "Reaching the Mainstream," to the "Animal Rights 2003" convention in Northern Virginia. The arguments in his June 19 written testimony regarding the supposedly "addictive" qualities of dairy foods are typical of Barnard's methods of bringing destructive animal rights messages to the mainstream public.

Barnard has also collaborated with some of the animal rights movement's most violent criminals. In 2001 he co-signed a series of letters (example attached) with one Kevin Kjonaas, a former "spokesperson" for the FBI-designated "domestic terrorist" Animal Liberation Front.

Kjonaas now manages the U.S. campaign of an animal rights group known as SHAC ("Stop Huntingdon Animal Cruelty"). SHAC's criminal activists have made countless death threats against employees of companies they don't like. They have beaten people with baseball bats, detonated car bombs, and relentlessly stalked Americans and their families for the "sin" of rejecting the animal rights philosophy.

Setting the animal-rights issue aside, Neal Barnard's organization (PCRM) has been censured by the American Medical Association. In the past, the AMA has called PCRM's recommendations "irresponsible" and "dangerous to the health and welfare of Americans." At present, the AMA has two policy statements in force specifically condemning PCRM for its willful misrepresentation of medical science.

Barnard is currently on a book tour, encouraging unsuspecting Americans to buy his latest title (called *Breaking the Food Seduction*), in which he claims

413

that meat and dairy foods are as addictive as heroin. He (literally) calls cheese "morphine on a cracker."

He is adding to his notoriety through a direct connection to the latest frivolous lawsuit filed against a restaurant chain (*Pelman et al v. McDonald's*). Barnard is cited four times in *Pelman*'s latest pleading as an "expert"; he has also filed two separate affidavits in that case. I fear that Barnard is using the recent flurry of fast-food litigation (and last week's timely hearing on H.R. 399) as a vehicle to draw even more attention to himself and to his skillfully hidden animal-rights agenda.

Purveyors of such irresponsible and baseless claims should be identified as hucksters and dismissed from the public arena. When social activists put on the sheep's clothing of the medical profession, it can become difficult to know who's credible. I am hopeful that Congress will recognize Neal D. Barnard as a publicity-seeking animal rights zealot—not an honest broker on the issue of restaurant litigation—and wholly dismiss his testimony.

14. Who is Peter Singer and why should you care about him?

DANIEL G. JENNINGS

(http://www.mofed.org/Who%20is%20Peter%20Singer.htm)

Who is Peter Singer and why should you care about him? *Simple, Peter Singer may be the most dangerous man in the world today.* Singer could be the most dangerous man in the world, because he is the stupid and misguided fool leading a vicious and mindless assault on human rights and the idea of freedom itself.

The vast majority of you, don't know who Singer is and there is no reason you should know. Singer is a philosopher, a professor at a university in Melbourne, Australia, who is currently a visiting lecturer at Princeton. He also wrote the article on ethics in the current *Encyclopedia Britannica*.

Singer, judging by his writings, is also a complete idiot, but a large portion of the world's intellectuals are hailing him as a genius and an expert on ethics and philosophy. Therein lies the danger, Singer is promoting a set of ideas that if applied to the real world will lead to complete and total disaster.

Singer could be the most dangerous man in the world, because he is the blind man leading the rest of the blind straight over the edge of a cliff. This wouldn't be so bad, except that these blind people want to take the rest of us along with them on their journey over the cliff.

Singer's ludicrous ideas include that of "animal liberation." In his most important work to date (*Animal Liberation*), Singer advanced the moronic argument that animals are entitled to the same rights as human beings.

414

Singer has claimed that the raising of animals for food is the moral equivalent of slavery or the Nazi Holocaust. He has termed the owning and exploitation of animals by human beings "enslavement," and even coined a stupid term "specieism" to describe the belief that human beings are superior to animals. Singer claims that mistreating animals is the equivalent of racism. Singer claims that human beings are not superior to animals and that human beings have no moral right to use animals as food, draft animals, pets or subjects in medical experiments.

Singer has compared factory farms raising chickens, pigs and cattle to concentration camps and even called pigs intelligent. This has led to violence against fur farms, researchers conducting medical experiments designed to save human lives, farmers, butcher shops, ranchers, etc. It has led to efforts to ban circuses because they involve tricks conducted by animals.

Singer is the father of the animal rights movement, animal rights activists have conducted terrorist acts against farmers, scientists, fur farmers and others. *These idiots have set off bombs, shot at hunters, set buildings on fire, and mailed razor blades to people who disagree with their sick beliefs.*

To make matters worse, Animal rights ideas are being enacted into law. Cities such as Seattle have banned circuses and rodeos because they're cruel to animals. Congress has considered bans on animal testing. The trapping of animals has been banned or restricted even though it might be necessary to public safety and the environment.

Singer's argument about animal rights makes a mockery of the idea of human rights. Human beings are superior to animals, they do think and do many things that animals can't. They write constitutions, create literature, invent machines, come up with scientific theories, tell jokes, create art, create music, write societies [sic], organize societies and do much more.

No animal can do these things. Nor can any animal demand its rights, human beings can and do. *Even the most ignorant kindergarten student can see Singer's argument is garbage.* Yet it is now accepted as the cutting edge of ethics and philosophy by intellectuals throughout the world. If this wasn't bad enough, Singer has made other idiotic pronouncements. He has said that some animals have had a greater right to exist than many human beings and in a work called *Practical Ethics* claimed that *retarded, deformed and ill babies should be put to death because they are a burden on the human race.*

This is the same argument adopted and promoted by the Nazis and put into practice by them. Historians estimate that a Nazi program of Euthanasia or mercy killing directed at the retarded, mentally ill and disabled killed around 200,000 people. It was based on many of the same arguments Singer makes.

Singer also promotes the utterly moronic idea that people who have committed the crime of being born or living in advanced nations have a moral duty to donate much of their income to poor and starving people in "underdeveloped nations." In other words Singer believes people are committing a crime because they are living well because they happen to live in a country whose government has adopted sensible and effective economic policies. This makes about as much sense as branding people criminals because their parents or grandparents went to a Synagogue instead of a church. Yet, the man hailed as a great philosopher finds it desirable.

Singer claims that the people of America, Europe, Japan and other developed nations are responsible for poverty and starvation in the so-called Third World. This is not true. The poverty in those nations was caused by the bad economic policies adopted by those nations' leadership or by the colonial exploitation of those nations by other nations.

For example the much publicized starvation in Ethiopia was caused by that nation's now deposed and Soviet-supported Communist dictatorship.

The widespread poverty in India was caused largely by the now discredited socialist policies of the Congress Party which adopted the ideas of British socialists and deliberately suppressed capitalism in that nation.

Recent food shortages in Cuba are solely the result of Fidel Castro's arrogant dictatorship.

Singer's argument that people in prosperous nations should donate much of their income to famine and poverty relief for poor nations is stupid. The poverty and hunger in those nations are not the fault of people in prosperous nations, it is almost solely the result of the policies adopted by those nations' governments. Poorer nations that have adopted sensible economic policies and political regimes have prospered and advanced. The sad truth is that policies in which money is transferred to poorer nations by richer nations, actually hurts [sic] poorer nations.

If third world governments can rely on the gravy train from Washington they have no incentive to reform. If a third world dictator can rely on aid shipments from Uncle Sam he has no incentive to adopt a sensible economic policy or reforms that could lead to progress and prosperity. The dictator can squander his resources on yachts and Rolls Royces while handing out U.S. grain to the mob. The dictator can also sell the grain, then use the proceeds to pay mercenaries to keep himself in power and buy weapons for those mercenaries. Worse, much of this aid finds its way straight back to the pockets of the politicians in the first world in the form of bribes and campaign contributions. Since this money is usually placed in overseas bank accounts politicians have little fear that the press will find out about it and report it. This aid is also a form of corporate welfare, much of the food is purchased from agribusiness which Singer supposedly opposes. Agribusiness makes big bucks, politicians make big bucks and the poor in the third world are still stuck in poverty.

Singer's ideas, if applied, would make the gap between rich and poor nations worse. Poor nations would have no incentive to adopt reforms that would better their people's lot, while the hardworking people of richer nations would see much of their money poured down a sinkhole from which it would never return. Worse, the leaders of the third world have piles of cash to squander upon yachts, Rolls Royces, mansions and the gambling tables at Monte Carlo.

Singer himself claims to donate much of his income to "relief organizations" that purport to help the poor in less developed nations. There is no evidence whatsoever that any of these organizations have bettered the condition of any poor person in any less developed nation. There is much evidence, however, that many relief organization officials draw huge salaries and live the good life on the non-taxable donations they receive. Many of which, are taken from poor, elderly and working class people who are barely able to support themselves. Many, if not most, of the people in charge of the relief organizations are con artists ripping off the poor and elderly. *Most of the money donated to these organizations goes into the bank accounts of the executives who run them* not the poor children in the third world.

Since Singer's beliefs are nonsense and easily dispelled by common sense, the average man and woman out there working for a living might ask: why should I care about Peter Singer? Because people are listening to him, the worst kind of people. Arrogant, overfed and stupid intellectuals. People who have no experience of the real world, people who have never worked for a living or had to worry about where the next paycheck is coming from. People who have never known want or oppression.

Yet, these people who are making many of the decisions in our society. Many educated people believe that Singer is a great man even though he has never done anything constructive in his life. Never created anything or made a worthwhile contribution. Singer is an ignorant fool. There is nothing great about him, yet he is honored and admired and his thinking is used as a guideline to the future of our society. That in itself should be frightening. Still, many people out there ask why should I care about this crackpot university professor named Peter Singer? *Sure his ideas are stupid but no SANE person will listen to them.*

Well, what if in the year 1880, somebody had asked a 19th-century Russian businessman why should you worry about some crackpot German intellectual living in London named Karl Marx? Marx after all had labeled private property evil. The Russian businessman would have said, "I don't give a damn about this Marx guy. He's a nut nobody in their right mind will listen to him." Within forty years, thugs claiming to be putting Marx's ideas into practice, were forcing Russians to give all of their land and property to the Bolshevik regime. Within fifty years Russians who owned too much property were being murdered by Marxists.

Or what if in the year 1880 somebody had told some rich German or Austrian Jew that within fifty years your children and grandchildren will be murdered because you tolerated anti-Semitic cranks within your midst. In the late 19th century anti-Semitism became respectable in Germany; an anti-Semitic crank was even allowed to serve as the personal chaplain to Germany's Emperor, Kaiser William II. Within fifty years, an anti-Semitic crank, Adolph Hitler, was absolute leader of Germany and having Jews murdered because of those crackpot ideas.

If forty years from now, cattle ranchers find themselves being burned at the stake by Animal Rights activists or middle-class Americans have their homes seized and auctioned off to pay for the King of Zimbabwe's new private space shuttle, they'll have only themselves to blame for tolerating Peter Singer in their midst. I'm not saying that Peter Singer doesn't have a right to hold and promote his idiotic ideas. He does. I'll defend Singer's right to hold his opinions and voice them to the death. I'm saying that no sane society would allow somebody like Singer who attacks its basic ideas to serve in an important position at a distinguished institution of higher learning.

In a sane society, Peter Singer would be manning the cash register at Waldenbooks and spreading his ideas on the Internet in his spare time. What I'm saying is this, it's time that everybody who donates money to an institution of higher learning find out what kind of courses are taught there and what individuals are tolerated there. I have no problem with Singer's books in Princeton's library, the university allowing him to give a guest lecture there, or his ideas being studied in a class there, as one possible alternative. What I hate is a great American University endorsing and promoting a man who proudly repudiates everything America stands for and promotes ideas that threaten the livelihood and the very life of the average man. That is exactly what Peter Singer is doing. *Singer has a right to promote his ideas, but we have a right not to give money to those who promote Singer's ideas.*

If every rich American who disagreed with Singer and his moronic beliefs called the President of Princeton tomorrow and said they wouldn't donate any money to the university until Singer was gone, within a few hours, security guards would escort Singer off the campus and tell him never to come back.

The vast majority of the intellectual elite who hold ideas similar to Singer's would quickly change their minds, and Singer would be only of interest to philosophers and students of philosophy. If that happened, I wouldn't be at all surprised that within a few weeks or months Singer himself would publish articles retracting all of his beliefs and begin giving lectures and writing books refuting everything he had said before. It has often happened before in human history when pressure was applied to self-proclaimed men of ideas, especially soft ones who've never had to work for a living. Unfortunately, I doubt that's going to happen anytime soon.

Singer will go right on spreading his crackpot ideas until he dies or society collapses around him because some morons listened to him and tried to put those ideas into practice. *Those who are paying no attention to Peter Singer and his ilk today, may end up being very sorry in the future.*

15. Twitter nation has arrived

ALEXANDER ZAITCHIK

(Alternet.org, February 2009, at:
http://www.alternet.org/media/127623?page=entire)

Welcome to Twitter Nation. What was once an easily avoided subculture of needy and annoying online souls is now a growing part of the social and media landscapes, with Twittering tentacles reaching into the operations of major newspapers, networks, corporations and political campaigns.

Suddenly, our skies are dark with brightly colored cartoon birds. As in a nightmare, they are everywhere.

This has all happened very fast. It was less than three years ago that Twitter hatched as a harmless Web 2.0 curio modeled on Facebook's status-update feature. Twitter offered people a forum devoted exclusively to short blog entries known as "tweets," most of which answer the company's tagline question, "What are you doing now?"

By mid-2008, the San Francisco-based site was garnering feature coverage in national magazines and batting away $500 million buyout offers. With nearly six million users and counting, it is now on a Plague-like pace to obliterate last year's growth clip of 900 percent. Twitter is growing so fast that 2009 may come to be known not as the year America swore in its first black president or nationalized the banks, but the year America learned to think and communicate in 140 characters or fewer.

Over the last several months, the bird has flown the coop and begun flitting madly through the wider culture. For some, the breakout came with the site's role during the Mumbai terror attacks in November. For others, it was the Dalai Lama's decision to start Twittering. Some might point to Twitter feeds featured on cable news, or the dozens of Fortune 500 companies now Twittering their way to better sales and mitigated PR disasters. But there's no debating that a tipping point has been reached. Use of the site is now mainstream standard practice for everyone from national politicians to editors at highbrow publications like *Harper's*. Sites are popping up that discuss music and economics using the Twitter formula and size. Not a week passes without another creepily overeager *New York Times* trends piece about the site. Earlier this month, a Twitter style guide was released, and the first national Twitter awards ceremony, known as the Shorties, was convened in New York. Hosted by Twitter's own Walter Cronkite, CNN's Rick Sanchez, the awards ceremony featured acceptance speeches limited to 140 characters.

Can it be long before the entire country is tweeting away in the din of a giant turd-covered silicon aviary? And how scared should we be?

There is evolutionary logic to the building Twitter surge. The progression has been steady from blogs to RSS feeds to Facebook. But Twitter brings us within sight of an apotheosis of those aspects of American culture that have become all too familiar in recent years: look-at-me adolescent neediness, constant-contact media addiction, birdlike attention-span compression and vapidity to the point of depravity. When 140 characters is the ascendant standard size for communication and debate, what comes next? Seventy characters? Twenty? The disappearance of words altogether, replaced by smiley-face and cranky-crab emoticons?

I am a veteran Twitter hater—a "twater" in the cutesy Twitter mode. People like me have shadowed the site since it was still crying blind in the nest. As early as 2007, tech blogger Robert Scoble called Twitter hate "the new black." The first wave of Twitter hatred tended to be visceral and knee-jerk, a reaction to the site's unique ability to make everyone using it sound annoying and pathetic.

How can you not hate a site that encourages people to post, "At the park—I love squirrels!" and "F@*K! I forgot to tivo Lost last night." How can you not want to slap these people with a mackerel? It's no coincidence that the second-most Twitter-happy people on Earth are the Japanese, the undisputed champions of self-infantilization. Twitter provides the closest thing most people will ever get to their very own paparazzi or reality show, a trail of imagined eyes on their every move, thought and taste.

The old Twitter hatred now feels quaint. Before, the site and its users were simply annoying. Now there is serious talk about "Twitter Journalism" and "Twitter Criticism." What was once just a colorful special-needs classroom on the Internet is starting to look like a steel spike aimed at the heart of what remains of our ability to construct and process grammatical sentences and complete thoughts.

Twitter's defenders roll their eyes at such criticisms. People have been saying this about the Internet for years, they say. You're just a grumpy old snob, they say. (It's true that at 34 I am old by social-networking standards, three years older than the average Twitter user. But nothing reveals age more than being terrified of being thought old, a fear that is obviously driving so much uncritical Twitter coverage.)

What's more, say Twitter's defenders, haters like me focus on the banality and chirpiness of tweets because we are ignorant of the wonderful personal and social benefits of regular Twitter use. The company's founders go so far as to call it the ultimate civilizational feel-good experience. "It is about the triumph of the human spirit," Twitter CEO Biz Stone recently told *New York* magazine.

Chief among the Twampions of the Human Spirit is the tech journalist and blogger Clive Thompson, who has been on self-appointed Twitter guard duty since 2007. In the first conceptual defense of microblogging ever penned, Thompson concedes in *Wired* that tweets are often grating and vapid. But, he argues, over the course of hundreds and thousands of individually insufferable tweets, eventually an "ambient awareness" is achieved that creates greater empathy toward, and understanding between, groups of people. Within the patterns of minutia about office life and television habits, argues Thompson, dwells an online cosmic consciousness:

> *Twitter and other constant-contact media give a group of people a sense of itself, making possible weird, fascinating feats of coordination. Twitter is almost the inverse of narcissism. It's practically collectivist—you're creating a shared understanding larger than yourself.*

And what do these "weird, fascinating feats" of Twitter-enabled coordination look like? In awe of the power of the "practically collectivist" Twitter, Thompson relays the story of the time he met a friend for lunch. Even before sitting down, he already knew from reading her Twitter feed that this friend "was nervous about last week's big presentation, got stuck in a rare spring snowstorm, and [was] addicted to salt bagels."

But salt bagels are just the beginning for the mighty Twitter Overmind, ever a work in progress. Just last week, Thompson contributed to Twitter's national epic psychosocial genome project by tweeting: "I'm extremely sad that I can't find Liz Phair's 'Rocket Boy' to blip on blip.fm." Frowny faces all around, Clive.

Thompson builds upon his edifice of bullshit in a September 2008 cover story for the *New York Times* magazine. With the need to fill up several magazine pages, Thompson gushes that Twitter not only melds a group of individuals into a near "telepathic" unit of kinship, it is the ultimate Socratic app:

> *The act of stopping several times a day to observe what you're feeling or thinking can become, after weeks and weeks, a sort of philosophical act. It's like the Greek dictum to 'know thyself,' or the therapeutic concept of mindfulness. Having an audience can make the self-reflection even more acute.*

Again, Thompson instructs us to put up with thousands of idiotic and maddening tweets in order to "get" the full beauty and bounty of the site. Only after we burn swaths of our lives reading mindless tweets will the Twitter oracle reveal the wisdom it reserves for dedicated supplicants. Thompson doesn't explain why having an audience makes self-reflection "even more acute," whatever that means. Nor does he betray any concern that 140 characters might be enough space to state a tiny fact about a Liz Phair song, but not enough to reflect or meditate on it by any meaningful definition of the words.

But taking people like Thompson seriously isn't necessary when the proof is right there on Twitter.com. What does the praxis of "acute self-reflection" look like in the Twitter Age?

It looks like this: "someone has coffee and it smells gooood. must resist." (Twitter name: dorisnight), and "hey, i still have the # for twitter on my cell phone. whatever. im bored" (Twitter name: DomGatto). "Bladder has been treated. Best part of that appointment? I've lost 12 pounds total since I started dieting." (Twitter name: Blueinsideout)

The most maddening defense of Twitter is that it constitutes some form of art. Boosters like to claim that compressing communication into 140 characters results in a kind of computer-age poetry. "[Twitter users are] trying to describe their activities in a way that is interesting to others: the status update as a literary form," writes Thompson in his *NYT* piece. Howard Lindzon, founder of StockTwits, recently told the *Financial Times* that the format "is an art form."

So is speaking through burps. Again, any attempt to defend Tweets as some kind of new American haiku runs up against the reality of site. Here's that great 21st century New York Twitter version of the haiku poet Basho, known as "aliglia": "OMG, I want brownies! When are we having dinner again? :)"

It may not be true that only morons are drawn to Twitter, but everyone on Twitter sounds like a moron.

It could be that the best Twitter has to offer—delicious prose, supernovas of self- and communal knowledge—are visible only near the top of the Twitter hierarchy (defined in Twitterville as those with the most followers). Let's check out the Twitter feed of CNN's Rick Sanchez, a legend in the Twitter community for incorporating the site into his cable news program.

Here's Sanchez Twittering to his viewers last week: "anybody got anything real good out there, btw.. thanks for tip on dentist kid.. wow that funny!"

Some say the glorious potential of Twitter will be fully realized in bite-sized Twitter citizen journalism. My AlterNet colleague Rory O'Conner has studied the evolving impact of social-network media on the news business and concluded that sites like Twitter are "not only supplementing but supplanting" traditional news. As others have done, O'Conner notes that the first photo of U.S. Airways flight 1549 in the Hudson was posted not on the *New York Times* site, but on TwitPic.

"When it comes to breaking news—from heroism on the Hudson to terror in Mumbai to calamity in California—Twitter leads the pack these days," writes O'Conner. "Twitter has become a go-to source of news you can use when and where you want and need it—often when and where the legacy media cannot yet or no longer supplies it."

It's true that Twitter has been used to get information out during crises. But so what? Does that make it journalism? When people started calling in stories to their editors by phone, did we start talking about "AT&T journalism?" And imagine if telephones only allowed you to speak for 8 seconds before cutting you off. Whatever events Twitter may allow us to report a few minutes faster, it is still limiting that reportage to a space that can't even hold an Associated Press wire blurb about a minor bomb blast in Sri Lanka.

When the *Los Angeles Times* ran a Twitter feed about local wildfires on its home page, it was an informational service to its readers that was distinct from and complementary to its coverage. It was not, let us hope, "the future of journalism." Efforts to use Twitter as a vehicle for first-person reportage with voice—*Slate* tried to cover the Olympics this way, Talking Points Memo lamely tweeted the inaugural parties—have been laughably bad and quickly aborted.

The problem with Twitter Journalism is the same as with communication. Twitter can provide stick-figure snapshots, nothing more. Worse, the constant posting and following of these snapshots takes up lots of precious time, sucking up and fracturing the dwindling number of solid blocks of minutes that remain after checking e-mail, Facebook, Myspace, and other now-routine diversions.

But Twitter is unique and more dangerous because of the rolling, inherently content-less and bite-sized nature of the tweets. It reflects and feeds an autistic culture unable to focus on anything but the tiny feed box in front of it, and even that only when medicated. Programs like Tweetdeck (currently in public beta) are working to perfect a permanent desktop scroll and filter—an intravenous Twitter drip.

It takes a feat of dark imagination to look at Twitter and see art, the future of journalism or a gigantic shared-consciousness project. The thing Twitter reminds me of most is Mike Judge's under-appreciated 2006 satiric masterpiece, *Idiocracy*. The story revolves around an Army private, played by Luke Wilson, who wakes up in the year 2506. This future America is defined by its stupidity: nobody can read, write or think for more than a few seconds at a time. There is a prolonged national drought because a popular power-drink called Brawndo ("It's got electrolytes!") is being used to water the crops.

On his first day exploring this idiotic future, Wilson wanders into a movie theater, where a new film is playing, titled *Ass*. The movie consists entirely of a stationary shot of a man's ass, which farts at irregular intervals. The audience is laughing hysterically. In Judge's dystopia, *Ass* wins eight Oscars, including Best Screenplay. *Idiocracy* ends with Wilson as president giving a rousing State of the Union speech:

> *There was once a time in this country a long time ago, when people wrote books and movies in which you cared whose ass it was—and why it was farting. And I believe that day can come again.*

When future generations are watching movies in which it's not clear whose ass is farting, or why, we'll look back at Twitter as a milestone. But we won't be using the word "fart." We'll call them "tweets."

And then we'll giggle like the Japanese schoolgirls we've become.

423

16. Put on your bras, shave your armpits and quit your bitching

MADDOX

(http://www.thebestpageintheuniverse.net/c.cgi?u=feminazi)

Why do so many women insist on carrying out this war against men? Absolute gender equality isn't going to happen; we have gender equality now. Even if in a million years, men and women somehow made this unrealistic ideal happen, there will always be a sexual distinction between men and women causing some sort of inequality (if only on the level of basic physical needs). Or should I say women and men, as not to imply a male superiority? Why the hell should people go out of their way to be politically correct and use this "he/she" nonsense so a few chicks with language complexes won't be offended? Oops, I said "chicks". Damn.

Why the hell do women get offended when they're called *chicks*? I don't see how that word can be remotely offensive in anyway. But, some women think it's derogatory and belittling. Some women are so petty, that they resent any male implication in the English language. Who cares? What if guys suddenly felt like bitching and wanted to eradicate all the derogatory male phrases from the language? *Buster, Pal, Buddy, Stud, Hunk*. Oooh, don't call me a buster, I'll be offended.

Who's to say what's offensive anyway? Just because a few feminist extremists think that something's offensive, does the whole *society* have to change their way of doing things? I don't want *Mother* Nature being called Mother Nature anymore, but rather Father Nature. I don't want ships to be referred to as female anymore, but rather male. The phrase "she's a good ship" offends me. I don't want liberty to be a lady. Why does it have to be lady liberty? Why do people say "she's beautiful" when referring to cars? Why not he? Who cares? It's just the way things have always been. It's not meant to be offensive, so why doesn't the offended party pull their head out of their ass, and stop bitching about it.

Why there will never be absolute gender equality is because of the inherent contradictions between equality and liberty. For example, if a guy wanted to say a joke about women at work, or hung pornography in the work place, it would make the women work in an environment that may seem hostile to them. If someone at work frequently referred to women as *chicks*, and a woman was offended by it, the woman would then be working in a hostile environment. If a woman wants to be treated equally in the work place, then she shouldn't be offended at what guys usually talk about. I think it's unreasonable for all women to be content with whatever people do at work, and for guys to go out of their way to change their lifestyles to conform to what's politically correct. It's impossible to live your life without being offended at something. Violence, foul language, pornography, sex, religion, whatever it is, you're bound to be offended by it sooner or later. So rather than bitching about it, just deal with it and move on. Men aren't out to get women; we're not the bad guys.

424

Why would anyone do anything that's degrading to themselves? Would you strip down in front of a crowd of people? Probably not. But would you do it if they were paying you $250 per hour? Or if they paid you $1000 per hour? Maybe then. It doesn't seem so degrading when there's a huge incentive for you to do it. So why do some feminist extremists think pornography is degrading to women? Obviously the women in pornography don't think it's degrading, otherwise they wouldn't do it. Their dignity has a price, and they were willing to sell it. They don't represent all women in general, but only the few who chose to go into that business, just as women who choose not to go into pornography don't represent the women who do. So the phrase "pornography is degrading to women" doesn't make sense.

What's the point of not shaving your armpits and not wearing your bras? If you like yourself better with hairy armpits, then by all means don't shave. But if you're not shaving to make some stupid point, you're a fool. Nobody cares. You won't be a social outcast if you don't shave your armpits. Same thing goes for not wearing a bra. If you'd rather not wear a bra, then don't. If you want to walk around in public without your shirt on, then by all means do it. I'm sure most guys wouldn't mind. If you want that kind of attention, then walk around naked. It won't help your image with men that already think of women as little more than sex objects. What straight man wouldn't like to see a nude woman? I think women, nude or not, are attractive, as do most guys. I'd consider someone looking at me in admiration more of a compliment than anything else. Some feminists go ballistic when a guy looks at her breasts. Why? Not wearing a bra just draws more attention to a woman's breasts. While women shouldn't have to worry about some pervert always staring at them, it's bound to happen. Wait, I've got an idea. If you don't like guys staring at your breasts, WEAR A BRA. It's hard not to notice a girl when she has a pair of daggers poking out of her chest. I referred to nipples as daggers. Oops. There I go again, offending you crazy feminists. While most guys don't practice self-discipline and don't respect women enough not to stare at their breasts, a woman shouldn't go ape shit when she catches a guy looking at her. Most women try to accentuate parts of their body that men find attractive anyway. Is this so bad? Who doesn't like to feel attractive? While it can be overdone, it's really been blown out of proportion by feminist extremists.

Feminism is in a lot of ways like fascism. Your average fascist will disregard any scientific argument unless the conclusion supports his existing belief. The ideology comes first and the fascist looks for anything to back it up, no matter how trivial, unreliable or discredited. Much like today's feminists and their ideology. Fascists attempt to rationalize their beliefs and portray them as truth by twisting the facts. A fascist might, for example, cast blame for unemployment and work discontent on immigrants "stealing" their jobs. Feminists similarly cast blame for women's lower average pay onto another party (men). Both feminists and fascists are quick to cast blame on someone else for anything that goes wrong in their lives. Most feminists seem to conform to feminist stereotypes. I can usually pick out a feminist in a crowd of women. She'll usually have short hair, regular pants, a regular shirt, and an unbathed (*sic*) look; she'll look very much like a stereotypical guy. I think why a feminist might appear like this is to make a statement that "if men can do it and be accepted, then women should be able to". How bold, to go around and look like a stereotypical guy as opposed to a stereotypical girl. Who cares? Either way, you're an ass for thinking anybody cares about the statement you're making. If you're trying to prove a point to the average guy that's only concerned with women as sex objects, you're wasting your time. A guy that's concerned with women as sex objects is going to be concerned with women as sex objects regardless of how you look. Not every woman will share feminist ideals, so a possible argument that "if all women did it, then guys would have to respect us" isn't very realistic. If you really want to make a point, surgically remove your breasts. Or is that going too far? Feminism serves as nothing more than a wedge to further separate the sexes, segregating men and women into cultures that wouldn't otherwise exist.

I'm pretty damn sick of hearing feminists bitch about men being paid more than women. If 100 male chemical engineers that worked for Fortune 500 companies were compared to 100 female chemical engineers that worked for Fortune 500 companies, their pay would probably be the same, if not very close. If it were not, then sexual discrimination would probably be a good candidate as to why it's not. The reason why women get paid less than men on average is because women and men simply prefer different occupations, and different lifestyles. If a woman decides to have a child, chances are that she would end up taking more time off from work to take care of her child than would a guy (if only for child labor alone). It's unfair, but usually the case. Women are usually more family oriented, and nurturing, while men are usually less sensitive and work oriented. All this is of course changing, but it's to be expected that women get paid less than men. If for example, pay for men in the armed forces was compared to pay for women in the armed forces, the men would probably swamp the women in pay comparison simply because of the military's past male domination and segregation policies. That does not necessarily imply the same segregation today.

I work at a telemarketing company. I'm a network operator. I've been with the company for almost 4 years (3 yrs, 9 months), and I get paid less than almost every woman in my facility, except for two. I get paid less than people with only a fraction of the experience I have. I'm living proof that not all women get paid less than men. Bottom line: feminazis, stop your bitching. It's nobody's fault but yours if you can't do as well as a man. Take responsibility for your own life.

appendix 2

errors of reasoning

Absence of reasoning

1. emotional display
2. appeal to intuition
3. appeal to instinct
4. appeal to faith

Weak reasoning

Relevance

1. appeal to tradition, past practice
2. appeal to custom, habit, common practice
3. appeal to emotion

Truth

1. questionable premise
2. suppressed evidence

Sufficiency

1. insufficient evidence
2. appeal to authority

Errors in reasoning

Errors of definition

1. excessive inclusion (too broad)
2. excessive exclusion (too narrow)
3. equivocation

Errors of form

1. appeal to ignorance
2. circular reasoning
3. affirming the consequent

4. denying the antecedent
5. broken chain
6. backwards chain
7. affirming a disjunct
8. denying a conjunct

Errors of relevance

1. appeal to ignorance
2. appeal to the person, ad hominem
   (a) to the person's character—simple positive or negative ad hominem
   (b) to the person's practices—tu quoque
   (c) to the person's interests—poisoning the well
3. genetic fallacy
4. appeal to inappropriate authority
5. appeal to moderation (or lack of)
   (a) appeal to moderation
   (b) appeal to extreme
6. appeal to popularity (or lack of)
   (a) appeal to the majority, bandwagon, authority of the many
   (b) appeal to the minority, authority of the elite
7. two wrongs
8. paper tiger, straw man
9. red herring
10. non sequitur
11. false analogy, faulty comparison
12. misapplied general principle
13. the is/ought fallacy
14. the arbitrary line fallacy

Errors of truth

1. appeal to ignorance
2. false premise
3. the either/or fallacy
4. fallacy of composition
5. fallacy of division
6. gambler's fallacy
7. false analogy
8. mistaking correlation for causation
9. reversing cause and effect
10. slippery slope

Errors of sufficiency

1. overgeneralization
2. insufficient sample
   (a) size
   (b) representation
3. weak analogy
4. post hoc ergo propter hoc
5. failing to consider a common cause
6. failing to consider additional causes
7. failing to consider a reciprocal causal relation
8. slippery slope

Errors of assumption (mistakenly assuming something to be true, relevant, or sufficient)

1. appeal to ignorance
2. appeal to emotion
3. appeal to tradition, past practice
4. appeal to custom, habit, common practice
5. appeal to moderation
6. appeal to popularity
7. two wrongs
8. the either/or fallacy
9. fallacy of division
10. fallacy of composition
11. insufficient sample
12. false analogy, faulty comparison
13. mistaking correlation for causation
14. post hoc propter hoc
15. failing to consider a common cause
16. failing to consider additional causes
17. reversing cause and effect
18. failing to consider a reciprocal causal relation
19. slippery slope
20. the is/ought fallacy
21. the arbitray line fallacy

Errors of causality

1. mistaking correlation for causation
2. post hoc ergo propter hoc
3. failing to consider a common cause
4. failing to consider additional causes
5. reversing cause and effect
6. failing to consider a reciprocal causal relation
7. slippery slope

Errors of response

1. appeal to ignorance
2. appeal to the person, ad hominem
3. genetic fallacy
4. two wrongs
5. paper tiger
6. red herring

Considering the source of the argument instead of the argument itself

1. appeal to the person
   (a) to the person's character (simple positive or negative ad hominem)
   (b) to the person's practices (tu quoque)
   (c) to the person's interests (poisoning the well)
2. genetic fallacy
3. appeal to authority

Appealing to an inappropriate standard

1. appeal to inappropriate authority
2. appeal to tradition or past practice
3. appeal to custom, habit, or common practice
4. appeal to moderation (or lack of)
   (a) appeal to moderation
   (b) appeal to the extreme
5. appeal to popularity (or lack of)
   (a) appeal to the majority, appeal to the authority of the many, bandwagon fallacy
   (b) appeal to the minority, appeal to the authority of the elite
6. two wrongs

431

Passing the buck instead of making the argument yourself

1. appeal to authority
2. appeal to tradition, past practice
3. appeal to custom, habit, common practice
4. appeal to moderation (or lack of)
   (a) appeal to moderation
   (b) appeal to extreme
5. appeal to popularity (or lack of)
   (a) appeal to the majority, bandwagon, authority of the many
   (b) appeal to the minority, authority of the elite
6. two wrongs
7. appeal to ignorance

Going off-topic

1. paper tiger
2. red herring
3. non sequitur
4. appeal to emotion

Glossary

absolute numbers—individual numbers such as one, two, three . . . (Section 6.4.2); see, for contrast, percentages

acceptability—a claim is acceptable to the degree it is plausible (possible and reasonable), conforms to other claims known to be true, and has implications that are acceptable (Section 6.1.2)

ad hominem—see appeal to the person (Section 4.2.1)

appeal to custom, habit, or common practice—an appeal to some custom, habit, or common practice to support a claim (Section 4.3.3)

appeal to emotion—the use of an emotional response to a claim as reason to accept or reject said claim (Section 4.4.4)

appeal to ignorance—this error occurs when one concludes that a claim is true because there is no evidence that it is false (Section 2.8)

appeal to inappropriate authority—an appeal to the judgment of someone who is neither relevantly qualified nor reliably accurate and unbiased (Section 4.3.1)

appeal to moderation (or lack of)—an appeal to the moderate or extreme nature of a position as support for that position (Section 4.3.4)

appeal to the person (ad hominem)—a response to the person making the argument (to the person's character, practices, or interests), rather than to the argument itself (Section 4.2.1)

appeal to popularity (or lack of)—an appeal to the popularity of a position as support for that position (appeal to the majority) or to the lack of popularity as support for that position (appeal to the minority) (Section 4.3.5)

appeal to tradition or past practice—an appeal to some tradition or past practice to support a claim (Section 4.3.2) argument—one or more premises leading to a conclusion (Section 2.1)

argument by analogy—an argument that involves reasoning from one situation to an analogous, or similar, situation: A has/is X, so B applies; C also has/is X, so B should also apply (Section 7.3)

argument by application of a general principle—an argument that involves reasoning from a general principle to a particular instance of that general principle: all A are subject to X; B is an A; so B is subject to X (Section 7.4)

burden of proof—the responsibility for providing proof for some claim (Section 2.7)

causation—an association such that one thing is the reason or explanation for the other (Section 8.1)

chain argument—an argument in which the conclusion of one argument becomes a premise of the next argument (and, possibly, so on) (Section 3.6)

circular argument—an invalid argument in which the same point serves as both premise and conclusion; an argument in which one assumes to be true what one is trying to prove to be true (Section 2.4)

coherence theory of truth—a theory of truth proposing that something is true if it fits with other things we hold to be true (Section 6.2.2)

conclusion—some statement of fact or opinion that is supported by one or more premises (Section 2.2)

correlation—mere association, in time or space, not necessarily evidence of causation (Section 8.1.1)

correspondence theory of truth—a theory of truth proposing that something is true if it accords with the way things are (Section 6.2.3)

counterargument—an argument whose conclusion in some way counters that of another argument (Section 2.5)

critical thinking—judicious thinking about what to believe and, therefore, what to do (1.1)

deductive argument—an argument in which the conclusion makes explicit what's already implicitly contained in the premises, and the conclusion follows necessarily from the premises (Section 2.10)

direct cause—the cause closest in time to the final effect (also called the proximate cause) (Section 8.1.3)

divergent structure—an argument in which one line of reasoning leads to two or more conclusions (Section 3.5)

either/or fallacy—the presentation of two options as if they're the only options when in fact they're not, and/or the presentation of two options as if one can't choose both or as if both can't be true when in fact one can or they can (Section 6.5.1)

empiricism—a theory of knowledge proposing that all of our ideas are obtained through experience (Section 6.3.1)

equivocation—an error of reasoning that occurs when one uses the same word to refer to different things (Section 5.3.4)

exclusiveness—definitions that are too narrow are too exclusive (they exclude more than you want) (Section 5.3.3)

fact—a statement about the world as it is (Section 2.9)

failing to consider additional causes—assuming that a partial or necessary cause is the complete or sufficient cause (Section 8.4.4)

failing to consider a common cause—failing to consider the possibility that some common thing, C, is causing both A and B (presumed to be in a causal relationship) (Section 8.4.3)

failing to consider a reciprocal causal relation—failing to consider that in addition to A causing B, B may be causing A (Section 8.4.6)

fallacy of composition—an assumption that what is true for individual parts is necessarily true of the whole formed by those parts (Section 6.5.2)

fallacy of division—an assumption that what is true of a whole is necessarily true of the individual parts that form that whole (Section 6.5.3)

false analogy—an analogy in which none of the relevant features are similar (or they're *dis*similar in the relevant aspects) (Section 7.3.1)

falsifiability—a claim is falsifiable if one can describe conditions under which one can show it to be false (Section 6.1.1)

gambler's fallacy—assuming that previous occurrences affect probability of current occurrences (Section 6.5.4)

generalization—a general claim about something based on specific evidence about that something; generalizations are usually based on quantities (also called induction by enumeration) or qualities (Section 7.2)

genetic fallacy—a response to the origin (genesis) of an argument, rather than to the argument itself (Section 4.2.2)

genus and species—"genus" refers to the larger group to which a thing belongs and "species" refers to the features that set this particular thing apart from others in that larger group; useful for defining terms (Section 5.3.1)

inclusiveness—definitions that are too broad are too inclusive (they include more than you want) (Section 5.3.3)

indirect cause—a cause removed in time from the direct cause of an effect (also called a remote cause) (Section 8.1.3)

inductive argument—an argument in which the conclusion goes beyond the information given in the premises, and the conclusion follows with some degree of probability from the premises (Section 2.10)

innate ideas—a theory of knowledge proposing that we are born with certain ideas (Section 6.3.1)

insufficient sample—a sample that is too small to justify the conclusion (Section 7.2.2)

level of confidence—an indication of the likelihood that the given results do in fact reflect reality (Section 6.4.2)

loaded language—language that is "loaded" with value judgments (Section 5.2.1)

margin of error—the largest plausible difference between the given results of a study and reality (Section 6.4.2)

mean—the number obtained by adding all the numbers and dividing by how many there are; often called "the average" (Section 6.4.2)

median—the number in the middle of a series (there are as many numbers above it as there are below it) (Section 6.4.2)

Mill's method of agreement—this method of determining cause involves looking for the element that is in common in each case, the element that is always present when X happens (Section 8.1.5)

Mill's method of concomitant variation—this method of determining cause involves looking for the element that when changed, changes the effect (Section 8.1.5)

Mill's method of difference—this method of determining cause involves looking for the element that makes a difference, the element that when taken out of the picture also seems to take out the effect (Section 8.1.5)

Mill's method of residues—this method of determining cause involves a process of elimination whereby one looks for the element which is left over when we have attributed several causes to several effects but one: the remaining effect is caused by the leftover element (Section 8.1.5)

misapplied general principle—an error of reasoning that occurs when one applies a general principle to a particular instance to which the principle doesn't apply because of the absence or presence of certain critical qualities which disqualify or make the particular instance an exception to the rule (Section 7.4.1)

mistaking correlation for causation—assuming that mere association in time and/or space implies causation (Section 8.4.1)

mode—the most often occurring number in a series (Section 6.4.2)

multiple-linked convergent structure—an argument in which two or more linked (dependent) lines of reasoning lead to one conclusion (Section 3.4)

multiple-separate convergent structure—an argument in which two or more separate (independent) lines of reasoning lead to one conclusion (Section 3.3)

multi-structured argument—an extended argument consisting of several subarguments of various structure (Section 3.6)

necessary cause—a condition that <u>must</u> be present for the effect-in-question to occur (Section 8.1.4)

necessary conditions—those conditions or attributes that are required (necessary) in order for something to fall within a definition (Section 5.3.2)

non sequitur—any statement that doesn't follow from whatever it was it was presumed to have followed from (Section 4.4.3)

opinion—a statement about the world as one thinks it is or should be or could be (Section 2.9)

overgeneralization—a generalization that goes beyond the evidence in terms of scope, frequency, or certainty (Section 7.2.1)

paper tiger—this error occurs when a person responds to an argument that is not the argument that was presented, but is, usually, a simpler version or a more extreme version of the original argument (Section 4.4.1)

percentages—how many per hundred (Section 6.4.2); see, for contrast, absolute numbers

post hoc ergo propter hoc—this error of reasoning occurs when one assumes that because B happens after A, B is caused by A (Section 8.4.2)

premise—evidence or reasons supporting a conclusion (Section 2.2)

proximate cause—see direct cause (Section 8.1.3)

rationalism—a theory of knowledge proposing that one can know things without experience, by use of one's reason alone (Section 6.3.1)

red herring—an irrelevant response usually intended as a distraction from the presented argument (Section 4.4.2)

relevance—the truth of the premise makes a difference to the merit of the claim it is supposed to support (Section 4.1)

remote cause—see indirect cause (Section 8.1.3)

reversing cause and effect—this error of reasoning occurs when one assumes or concludes that A causes B, when in fact B causes A (Section 8.4.5)

sample—the studied group of particulars from which a generalization is made (Section 7.2)

self-selected sample—a group that includes only people who voluntarily come forward to be part of the study (Section 7.2)

simple random sample—a group that includes only people selected at random (Section 7.2)

single convergent structure—an argument in which one premise leads to one conclusion (Section 3.2)

slippery slope—this error of reasoning involves presenting a chain argument in such a way as to suggest that the first step link in the chain makes the final outcome inevitable when, in fact, it does not (Section 8.4.7)

stratified random sample—a group that includes a random sample of representative size of each of the relevant categories (Section 7.2)

subjectivism—a theory of truth proposing that something is true if you believe it's true (Section 6.2.1)

sufficiency—the degree of support provided by the premises of an argument for its conclusion (also called adequacy); a premise or a series of premises is sufficient when their truth or acceptability and relevance make the conclusion more probable than alternative conclusions (Section 7.1)

sufficient cause—a condition which alone results in the effect-in-question (Section 8.1.4)

sufficient conditions—those conditions or attributes that if present are all that is required (sufficient) for something to fall within a definition (Section 5.3.2)

target population—the total group about which a generalization is made (Section 7.2)

truth—a claim is true if it accords with the facts (according to the correspondence theory) (Section 6.1.1)

"two wrongs" fallacy—the suggestion that a particular action is acceptable if others are doing the same thing (Section 4.3.6)

unrepresentative sample—a sample that does not have the relevant features of the target population (Section 7.2.3)

verifiability—a claim is verifiable if we can describe conditions under which we can show it to be true (Section 6.1.1)

weak analogy—an analogy in which few of the relevant features are similar (Section 7.3.1)

Index